Navigating the DMA: Application Across National Jurisdictions

Forewords by
Oreste Pollicino and Andreas Schwab

Epilogue by
Alberto Bacchiega

Editors
Gabriella Muscolo
Alessandro Massolo

Concurrences
Paris – New York – London

106 West 32nd Street, Suite 144 New York, NY, 10001, USA
www.concurrences.com
book@concurrences.com

First Printing, February 2025
978-1-954750-88-3 (Hardcover)
Library of Congress Control Number: 2025932841
Cover Design: Yves Buliard, www.yvesbuliard.fr
Book Design and Layout implementation: Nord Compo

Concurrences Books

Tributes

Harry First – A Global Vision for Competition Law, *S. Waller, A. Gavil, D. Bush (eds.), Forthcoming 2025*

James F. Rill – A Life in Antitrust, *J. Taladay, P. Lugard, J. Antonio (eds.), 2024*

Eleanor M. Fox – Antitrust Ambassador to the World, *2021*

Herbert Hovenkamp – The Dean of American Antitrust Law, *2021*

Frédéric Jenny – Standing Up for Convergence and Relevance in Antitrust, (Vol. I & II), *2019 & 2021*

Albert Foer – A Consumer Voice in the Antitrust Arena, *2020*

Richard Whish – Taking Competition Law Outside the Box, *2020*

Douglas H. Ginsburg – An Antitrust Professor on the Bench (Vol. I & II), *2018 & 2020*

Wang Xiaoye – The Pioneer of Competition Law in China, *A. Emch, W. Ng (eds.), 2019*

Ian S. Forrester – A Scot without Borders (Vol. I & II), *A. Komninos (eds.), 2015*

William E. Kovacic – An Antitrust Tribute (Vol. I & II), *2013 & 2014*

Practical Books

Compendium of International Cartels, *A. Capobianco, O. Schwartz (eds.), 2025*

Compendium of EU Competition Law, *C. Lemaire, 2024*

Artificial Intelligence and Competition Policy, *A. Abbott, T. Schrepel (eds.), 2024*

The 2023 U.S. Merger Guidelines: A Review, *S. Sullivan (ed.), 2024*

Competition Inspections in 25 Jurisdictions 2nd Edition – A Practitioner's Guide, *N. Jalabert-Doury (ed.), 2024*

EU Antitrust Enforcement – Law, Economics, History, Policy & Practice, *W. P. J. Wils, 2024*

The EU Foreign Subsidies Regulation, *A. Reindl, I. Van Damme, 2024*

Compendium of Antitrust Damages Actions – ICC – 2nd edition, *J.W.H. Denton AO, F. Brunet, S. Williams, C. Inthavisay (eds.), 2023*

Pharmaceutical Antitrust: An Analysis of US and EU Law, *M. Thill-Tayara, G. Gordon (eds.), 2023*

Innovation Paradox in Merger Control, *G. Gurkaynak, 2023*

Antitrust and the Digital Economy, *Y. Katsoulacos (ed.), 2023 (in collaboration with CRESSE)*

Judicial Review of Competition Cases, *D. Ginsburg, T. Eicke (eds.), 2023*

Competition Law Treatment of Joint Ventures, *B. Bleicher, N. Campbell, A. Hamilton, N. Hukkinen, A. Khan, A. Mordaunt (eds.), 2022 (in collaboration with the IBA)*

Information Exchange & Related Risks, *Z. Marosi, M. Soares (eds.), 2022 (in collaboration with the IBA)*

Rulemaking Authority of the US Federal Trade Commission, *D. Crane (ed.), 2022*

The International Competition Network at Twenty, *D. Anderson & P. Lugard (eds.), 2022*

Competition Case Law Digest – 5th Edition, *F. Jenny, N. Charbit (eds.), 2022*

Competition Inspections in 21 Jurisdictions – A Practitioner's Guide, *N. Jalabert-Doury (ed.), 2022*

Perspectives on Antitrust Compliance, *A. Riley, A. Stephan, A. Tubbs (eds.), 2022 (in collaboration with the ICC)*

Turkish Competition Law, *G. Gürkaynak, 2021*

Competition Law – Climate Change & Environmental Sustainability, *S. Holmes, D. Middelschulte, M. Snoep (eds.), 2021*

Merger Control in Latin America – A Jurisdictional Guide, *P. Burnier da Silveira, P. Sittenfeld (eds.), 2020*

Competition Inspections under EU Law – A Practitioner's Guide, *N. Jalabert-Doury, 2020*

Gun Jumping in Merger Control – A Jurisdictional Guide, *C. Hatton, Y. Comtois, A. Hamilton (eds.), 2019 (in collaboration with the IBA)*

Choice – A New Standard for Competition Analysis? *P. Nihoul (ed.), 2016*

PhD Theses

The Economics of Digital Markets – Essays in Theoretical and Empirical Industrial Organization, *E. Arnaud-Joufray, 2024*

Abuse of Platform Power, *F. Bostoen, 2023*

Reform of Chinese State-Owned Enterprises, *X. Bai, 2023*

Competition & Regulation in Network Industries – Essays in Industrial Organization, *J-M. Zogheib, 2021*

The Role of Media Pluralism in the Enforcement of EU Competition Law, *K. Bania, 2019*

Buyer Power, *I. Herrera Anchustegui, 2017*

General Interest

Why Competition? Voices from the Antitrust Community and Beyond, *D. Crane, D. Gerard, R. Tritell (eds.), 2024*

Competition Law Dictionary, *D. Healey, R. Whish, W. E. Kovacic, P. Trevisán (eds.), 2024*

The 5 Labours of Europe, *P.-E. Partsch, 2024*

Great Antitrust Enforcers, *W. E. Kovacic, 2023*

Competition – How to Speak Like an Expert, *E. Combe , 2023*

Women and Antitrust – Voices from the Field (Vol I & II), *E. Kurgonaite & K. Nordlander, 2020*

The views expressed in this book are those of the authors and not of the authorities and institutions of which they belong.

CONTRIBUTORS

Isabel Álvarez Fernández del Vallado
CNMC

Jasper van den Boom
Heinrich-Heine-University Düsseldorf

Friso Bostoen
Tilburg University

Bogdan Marius Chirițoiu
Romanian Competition Council

Cani Fernández Vicién
CNMC

Paul K. Gorecki
Trinity College Dublin

Alexander Iken
DG COMP

Mirta Kapural
Croatian Competition Agency

Šarūnas Keserauskas
Ellex

Dimitrios Kyriazis
Aristotle University of Thessaloniki

Irène Luc
French Court of Cassation

Alessandro Massolo
DG COMP

Giorgio Monti
Tilburg University

Gabriella Muscolo
Rucellai & Raffaelli

Michaela Nosa
Comenius University Bratislava

Michal Petr
Palacky University

Petar Petrov
University of Economics and Business (WU)

Nuno Pires Salpico
Sousa Ferro & Associados

Enrico Adriano Raffaelli
Rucellai & Raffaelli

Simon Reetz
DG COMP

Francisco Ripoll Vázquez
CNMC

Vlad Dan Roman
DG COMP

Sigurd Slot Jacobsen
Naviair

Miguel Sousa Ferro
Sousa Ferro & Associados

Jacques Steenbergen
KU Leuven

Elo Tamm
Cobalt

Katharina Voss
Swedish Government Secretariat

SUMMARY

ROMANIA

SLOVAKIA

SPAIN

SWEDEN

FOREWORD

ORESTE POLLICINO*
Bocconi University

The Digital Markets Act (DMA) represents a pivotal regulatory framework for the European Union, aiming to recalibrate the dynamics of digital markets in a way that ensures fairness and contestability. This book offers a comprehensive analysis of the DMA's implications, exploring its regulatory and competitional law dimensions. Building on Andreas Schwab's insight that the DMA is a dynamic and adaptive tool, this foreword adopts a complementary perspective, focusing on the constitutional and multi-level governance aspects of the relevant legislation.

At its core, the DMA introduces a centralized enforcement regime, granting the European Commission significant powers to designate gatekeepers and oversee compliance with *ex ante* obligations. This approach reflects a significant evolution in EU competition law. The book clearly highlights how the DMA's regulatory provisions, while rooted in principles of competition law, extend beyond traditional antitrust enforcement to address structural challenges in digital markets. There is potentially a growing tension between the centralized enforcement authority of the Commission and the role of National Competition Authorities (NCAs). It is clear that this tension should find its procedural way in a structured dialogue and not in a conflict.

From a constitutional perspective, this framework exemplifies the EU's asymmetrical integration model, balancing supranational authority with respect for Member States' autonomy. The DMA provides significant margins of maneuver for national jurisdictions, as detailed in Articles 1(5) and (6), allowing Member States to implement additional measures to address public interest objectives or enforce national competition laws. This dual approach ensures that the DMA respects the principle of subsidiarity, a cornerstone of EU constitutional law.

The DMA's designation of gatekeepers, based on quantitative thresholds, marks a departure from traditional competition law practices, such as defining market dominance. As underlined by the authors, this innovation raises important questions about proportionality and justification, particularly in its application to diverse economic and legal contexts across Member States. This regulatory approach is both a strength and a challenge, requiring careful calibration to avoid unintended consequences, such as over-regulation of smaller platforms or under-enforcement of emerging market dynamics.

Muscolo and Massolo also emphasize the need for harmonization between EU and national laws, a recurring theme in this volume. Their analysis of best practices in

* Professor of Constitutional Law and AI Regulation, Bocconi University, Founder of Oreste Pollicino *AI*dvisory, President of Centre of Digital Constitutionalism and Policy (DICOPO), Brussels

applying the DMA's collaborative mechanisms highlights how Member States can leverage their unique contexts to complement the regulation. For example, Italy's recent reforms on economic dependency in digital platforms illustrate how national legislation can address specific market challenges while aligning with EU-wide objectives.

The DMA does not exist in isolation. It is part of a broader ecosystem of EU digital policies, including the Digital Services Act (DSA), sector-specific rules on cybersecurity, and emerging frameworks for artificial intelligence. This book highlights the importance of coordination between these instruments to ensure consistency and effectiveness. For example, the High-Level Group established under the DMA plays a crucial role in addressing overlaps and fostering synergies between EU and national regulations.

As noted, the DMA complements, rather than replaces, Articles 101 and 102 TFEU, as well as national competition laws. The complementary nature of these frameworks is explored in several contributions, which examine how the DMA integrates with traditional competition tools to address new challenges in digital markets. The result is a layered regulatory approach that combines *ex ante* rules with *ex post* enforcement mechanisms, ensuring both flexibility and accountability. It should then be clear that the DMA redefines the traditional interplay between EU competition law and national regulatory frameworks. While the regulation provides clarity and uniformity across Member States, it simultaneously places NCAs in a supporting role, raising questions about the future of decentralized enforcement under Articles 101 and 102 TFEU.

Schwab's foreword rightly emphasizes the DMA's adaptability and its potential to drive innovation and competition. Another important point to consider is how the DMA will redefine the relationship between EU institutions, Member States, and private actors. Together, these perspectives provide a holistic view of the DMA as both a regulatory and constitutional milestone.

As the European Union continues to lead global efforts in digital regulation, the DMA stands as a model for balancing centralization and subsidiarity, harmonization and diversity, innovation and accountability. The DMA also sets a precedent for future regulatory frameworks in other sectors. By defining gatekeepers based on objective criteria, such as user thresholds and market impact, the regulation provides a model for addressing systemic risks in dynamic and fast-evolving markets. However, this approach also places a significant burden on the Commission, which must ensure that these criteria are applied consistently across diverse legal and economic contexts.

This volume offers invaluable insights into the regulatory conundrum described above, providing a roadmap for scholars, policymakers, and practitioners navigating this new landscape. The DMA is not just a set of rules but a de facto constitutional innovation that redefines the governance of digital markets in Europe, setting a benchmark for regulatory frameworks worldwide.

Another great merit of this volume in capturing the DMA's dual character is that it is simultaneously a robust EU-level regulatory tool and a framework that allows Member States to preserve national legislative prerogatives. Articles 1(5) and (6) of the DMA permit national rules pursuing legitimate public interest objectives, ensuring that local economic and social contexts are respected. Schwab rightly highlights this flexibility as essential for accommodating Europe's diverse digital ecosystems. From a constitutional viewpoint, this flexibility reflects the EU's commitment to subsidiarity, a principle that ensures regulatory intervention is proportional and sensitive to local needs.

This foreword, while introducing the contributions in this book, also invites further reflection on the DMA's broader significance for European constitutional law and digital market governance. The dialogue between centralization and national autonomy explored here will shape not only the DMA's legacy but also the future of EU governance in the digital age.

FOREWORD

ANDREAS SCHWAB*
European Parliament

The Digital Markets Act (DMA) has become a milestone in the digital landscape, shaping new rules and standards to promote fair competition and innovation.

The DMA has revolutionized the digital sector by introducing new rules and standards aimed at fostering fair competition and innovation, setting the stage for a pivotal moment in the governance of digital markets. As digital platforms become increasingly central to economic and social life, the DMA acts as a safeguard to ensure that big tech companies, known also as 'gatekeepers', behave in a manner that is fair and non-discriminatory. This *ex ante* regulatory approach is crucial in preventing abusive practices and promoting innovation, and consumer choice.

However, as the digital economy evolves, so too, must the regulatory frameworks that control it. The DMA is not just a static set of rules but a dynamic tool that can adapt to new challenges and opportunities in the digital sector. Adaptability is essential for addressing emerging issues such as algorithmic transparency, new generative AI tools, data privacy, and the ever-changing competitive dynamics among digital platforms.

The DMA's enforcement is also shaped by the degree of flexibility it allows national jurisdictions within the EU. While the DMA provides a unified regulatory approach and envisages the EU Commission as the sole enforcer, individual Member States retain a margin of maneuver to tailor its implementation to local contexts. This flexibility is essential for accommodating the diverse economic landscapes and digital market developments across Europe.

Indeed, national jurisdictions have to handle its implications and potential impact on their own digital economies. The aim of the book "Navigating the DMA: Application Across National Jurisdictions", edited by Gabriella Muscolo and Alessandro Massolo, is to explore the future application and leeway for national jurisdictions, with a particular focus on the actions taken by an EU Member State to facilitate integration and enhance synergies between EU and national legislation.

The European Union has been at the forefront of regulating the digital sector, aiming to create a cohesive and competitive digital market across its Member States. This regulatory landscape is characterized by a combination of EU-wide legislation and national legislative initiatives that seek to address the unique challenges posed by rapid digital transformation. The interplay between EU and national laws often leads to overlapping and sometimes conflicting regulatory frameworks, necessitating a harmonized approach to ensure consistency and effectiveness across the EU.

---

* Member of the European Parliament.

In response to these challenges, EU Member States have undertaken various actions to facilitate better integration and to enhance synergies between EU and national legislation. By fostering collaboration mechanisms, such as those delineated in Articles 1(5) and (6), 38(7), and 39 of the DMA, Member States aim to streamline the implementation of the DMA and coordinate efforts between asymmetric EU regulation and public and private enforcement by national competent authorities and national courts. Additionally, several legislative initiatives at the national level have been designed to ensure coherence with EU legislation, promoting a unified digital regulatory environment.

To this end, it is essential to delineate best practices in the application of the DMA's collaborative mechanisms and examine how these initiatives contribute to the broader goal of digital transformation with the overall goal of providing a comprehensive understanding of the evolving regulatory environment and its implications for digital markets across Europe. We also have to reflect on the DMA's role within the wider context of legislative initiatives, assessing the interactions between EU and national regulations, their impact on strategic areas such as digital platforms, public services, and emerging technologies and how EU Member States perceive the balance between EU-wide initiatives and national interests in fostering a robust digital economy.

In conclusion, the DMA and its enforcement represents a critical juncture in the digital landscape, requiring national jurisdictions to adapt and steer the complexities of the regulatory environment. The actions taken by EU Member States to facilitate integration and to enhance synergies between EU and national legislation are essential for ensuring a cohesive and competitive digital market across Europe. As the DMA continues to evolve, it is crucial to assess its role within the digital markets and evaluate its impact on those strategic areas to foster a robust digital economy that benefits all.

OVERVIEW

GABRIELLA MUSCOLO AND ALESSANDRO MASSOLO*

Rucellai & Raffaelli

DG COMP, European Commission

I. Introduction: General Views from an EU Member State

1. A New EU Tool Was Born: Opportunities and Potential Complications

1. The Digital Markets Act (DMA)[1] aims to make European digital markets more competitive and fairer.

2. It seeks to empower end users by expanding their choice of digital services, giving them more control over their data and digital footprint, simplifying their access to digital services, and ensuring unbiased search results.

3. For business users, the DMA strives to open closed ecosystems, ensure fair competition, enable access to valuable business data, improve interoperability, and guarantee fair rankings and sales terms.

4. While these goals are promising, it will take time to fully realise the benefits of this new EU regulation. Some positive effects will be visible in the short term, while others will emerge in the medium to long term. This is not only because some gatekeepers may not yet comply, but also because the European digital industry will need time to adapt and become financially and technologically equipped to fully leverage these positive changes.

5. Furthermore, as we will explore in the following sections, it is important to remember that the DMA is just one element of a broader landscape of EU and national legislative initiatives aimed at digital transformation. Consequently, coordination and cooperation will be essential to ensure the DMA's effective implementation.

2. Before and after the DMA: High-Level Impact Analysis on National Policies and Legislations

6. The DMA builds on previous European policy and legislative initiatives that have already made a significant impact on the digital transformation across the EU. As a result, several European countries had already been implementing the EU's digital agenda, contributing to the shaping of Europe's digital future. Many jurisdictions

* The Editors would like to thank Jacopo Maria Orsi, Francesco Ricchi and Irene Rizzelli for their research and editorial assistance.

[1] Regulation 2022/1925 of the European Parliament and of the Council of 14 September 2022 on contestable and fair markets in the digital sector and amending Directives 2019/1937 and 2020/1828 (Digital Markets Act or DMA) [2022] OJ L265/1.

were actively enforcing competition law in their national digital markets, and these cases served as an inspiration for the DMA.

7. Consequently, numerous EU Member States welcomed the adoption of the DMA and quickly began implementing legislative reforms to ensure cooperation and support for the European Commission's ('Commission') enforcement of the regulation.

8. In contrast, some countries have been slower to react to the new EU tool, primarily due to other enforcement priorities.

II. DMA as a Centralised – Not Too Centralised – EU Enforcement Tool: The National Approach for Coordination and Cooperation with National Public and Private Enforcement

9. The intention of the European legislator is thus to generate a specific system of rules that plays a complementary role to those of EU law and competition law, while at the same time generating cooperation and coordination between the Commission and the Member States capable of ensuring a consistent and effective application of the available legal instruments applied to gatekeepers under the DMA.

10. Therefore, even though enforcement powers are exclusively attributed to the Commission, mechanisms for cooperation and coordination between the Commission, the national competition authorities (NCAs) and the courts of the EU Member States are provided for.

1. Coordination with Competition Law and other National Rules

11. Article 1(5) and Recital (9) of the DMA do not preclude EU Member States from applying to gatekeepers 'other national rules which pursue other legitimate public interest objectives as set out in the Treaty on the Functioning of the European Union (TFEU) or which pursue overriding reasons of public interest as recognised by the case law of the Court of Justice of the European Union'.[2]

12. Furthermore, Article 1(6) clarifies that the DMA is without prejudice to the application of both Articles 101 and 102 TFEU and national competition laws prohibiting anti-competitive agreements, decisions by associations of undertakings, concerted practices and abuses of dominant positions, as well as other forms of unilateral conduct and Regulation 139/2004.

13. Indeed, according to Article 1(7), NCAs may not take decisions that would be contrary to a decision adopted by the Commission, and the Commission may consult NCAs on any matter relating to enforcement actions under the DMA.

---

[2] See, to that effect, Case C-384/93 *Alpine Investments BV* ECLI:EU:C:1995:126, para 44; Case C-36/02 *Omega Spielhallen- und Automatenaufstellungs-GmbH* ECLI:EU:C:2004:614, para 35; Case C-46-08 *Carmen Media Group* ECLI:EU:C:2010:505, para 55; Case C-108/09 *Ker-Optika bt* ECLI:EU:C:2010:725, paras 57–59; Case C-470/11 *SIA Garkalns* ECLI:EU:C:2012:505, paras 34 and 35; Joined Cases C-186/11 and C-209/11 *Stanleybet International and others* ECLI:EU:C:2013:33, paras 23–25; Case C-390/12 *Pfleger and Others* ECLI:EU:C:2014:281, paras 39 and 40; Case C-156/13 *Digibet and Albers* ECLI:EU:C:2014:1756, paras 21 and 22.

14. In this framework, in several Member States concurrent rules have already been adopted or are incoming, and enforcement cases have been decided or are pending, as highlighted below and examined in the national contributions.

2. Cooperation in the Implementation of the DMA

15. Following the line, Article 37 enshrines the principle of cooperation between the Commission and NCAs, which must work in close cooperation and coordination of their enforcement actions to ensure a coherent, effective and complementary application of the available legal instruments.

16. In this respect, the DMA mentions the European Competition Network (ECN) as an appropriate home for such cooperation and exchange of information, allowing, above all, to choose the most suitable instrument for the case at hand and to avoid unnecessary duplication of action.

17. It should also be pointed out that the Commission, in carrying out these activities, is assisted by the Advisory Committee on Digital Services, formed by members representing the Member States.

18. The committee – whose legal basis and functioning rules are to be found in Regulation 182/2011 (the so-called Comitology Regulation[3]), expressly recalled by the DMA provisions – is considered an independent advisory group of experts on digital services with an advisory role.

19. Based on the issue examined by the Commission, the Committee delivers an opinion that is communicated to the addressee together with the decision.

20. Based on the principle of cooperation, as for Article 38(6), the Commission may also ask NCAs to carry out market investigations on its behalf.

21. Furthermore, as for Article 38(7), NCAs will be able to actively participate in monitoring non-compliance with the DMA by initiating and conducting an investigation.

22. However, where the Commission opens a proceeding under this Regulation, it precludes the NCAs from conducting investigations, or where it is already underway, it closes them. In this case, the authorities report to the Commission the results of the investigation carried out so far.

23. The DMA high-level group will identify and assess potential interactions between the DMA and the sector-specific rules applied by NCAs belonging, among others, to the ECN and the European Regulatory Group of Audiovisual Media Regulators.

3. Coordination with Private Enforcement

24. As regards the coordination of the DMA application and private enforcement, a preliminary issue has been raised. On coordination of the DMA application and private enforcement, a preliminary issue has been opened by some scholars,

---

3 Regulation 182/2011 of the European Parliament and of the Council of 16 February 2011 laying down the rules and general principles concerning mechanisms for control by Member States of the Commission's exercise of implementing powers [2011] OJ L55/13. See, in particular, arts 4 and 5 of the Regulation, to which art 50 DMA makes express reference when establishing the committee procedure.

concerning the admissibility of private litigation following the Commission's decision implementing the DMA.

25. On the one hand, some scholars argue that a widespread system of private enforcement, resulting in clashes of decisions in different jurisdictions, would lead to a risk of fragmentation in DMA enforcement. Therefore, they believe it is more appropriate that national court intervention may at least be limited to follow-on actions and thus occur *ex post*, only after the Commission has adopted a decision finding infringement by the gatekeeper.[4]

26. On the other hand, three reasons have been raised as to why private enforcement should play a key role in DMA enforcement.[5] The first one is that the right to use the judicial remedies provided within an individual jurisdiction is a general principle of the European Union.[6] On this point, it should be noted that in the application of the DMA, the centralised competence in the hands of the Commission is not an obstacle to the recognition of the role of the national court. Indeed, Article 39 expressly provides for coordination between the Commission and national courts.

27. The second reason is related to the experience we have had in the field of competition law, where it has been observed that private enforcement has assumed a key role in ensuring the effectiveness of antitrust law and policies. As the European Court of Justice has reiterated on many occasions, both systems (public enforcement and private enforcement) have been found to be complementary in the prosecution of the public interest in effective and free competition in the market.[7]

28. The third reason relies on the possibility of enhancing the uniformity of case law in private litigation related to the DMA as well as to antitrust enforcement through the networking of European judges and their common training.[8]

29. Article 39 DMA contains directly applicable rules on cooperation with national courts: in particular, paragraph 1 expressly provides that 'national courts may ask the Commission to transmit to them information in its possession or its opinion on questions concerning the application of [the DMA]', and paragraph 3 that 'the Commission, acting on its own initiative, may submit written observations to national courts', and that, with the permission of the court in question, 'it may also make oral observations'.

---

4 See, in this regard, Assimakis P Komninos, 'The Digital Markets Act and Private Enforcement: Proposals for an Optimal System of Enforcement' in Nicolas Charbit and Sébastien Gachot (eds), *Eleanor M. Fox Liber Amicorum: Antitrust Ambassador to the World* (Concurrences 2021); Assimakis P Komninos, 'Private Enforcement of the DMA Rules before the National Courts' (*SSRN* 2024) <https://papers.ssrn.com/sol3/papers.cfm?abstract_id=4791499>; Giuseppe Colangelo, *The Digital Markets Act and EU Antitrust Enforcement: Double & Triple Jeopardy* (ICLE White Paper 2022-03-23, 2022).

5 See Magnus Strand, 'Private Enforcement Under the Digital Markets Act: Rights and Remedies Revisited' (2024) 7(2) Nordic Journal of European Law 120.

6 Case C-453/99 *Courage Ltd v Bernard Crehan and Bernard Crehan v Courage Ltd and Others* ECLI:EU:C:2001:465; Joined Cases C-295/04 and C-298/04 *Manfredi and others* ECLI:EU:C:2006:46.

7 *Courage* (n 6); Case C-360/09 *Pfleiderer AG v Bundeskartellamt* ECLI:EU:C:2011:389.

8 The Association of European Competition Law Judges, in collaboration with the European Commission's DG-COMP, has since 2003 played a crucial role in both directions.

30. Furthermore, paragraph 4 adds that '[f]or the purpose of the preparation of their observations only, the Commission may request the relevant national court to transmit or ensure the transmission... of any documents necessary for the assessment of the case'.

31. Therefore, the *amicus curiae* mechanism – already provided for in Article 15 of Regulation 1/2003, titled 'Cooperation with national courts'[9] – in its articulations, has also been extended by the European legislator to the DMA private litigation.

32. In addition, Article 39(5) of the DMA states that the courts cannot adopt decisions that run counter to the Commission's enforcement of the DMA itself.

33. Article 39(5) of the DMA is an important mechanism of coordination already envisaged by Regulation 1/2003 in Article 16, titled 'Uniform application of Community competition law'. Indeed, this article provides for the binding effect of the decision adopted by the Commission towards national courts and NCAs.[10]

34. Furthermore, Article 9 of Directive 2014/104/UE ('Directive' or 'Damages Directive')[11] provides that (i) a national competition authority's final infringement decision should have a 'binding effect' in follow-on proceedings before the courts in the Member State where the infringement has been ascertained and that (ii) before courts of other Member States, it should constitute at least *prima facie* evidence of such infringement.[12]

35. Unlike Article 16 of Regulation 1/2003, which refers to a Commission decision, even if this decision has not been already subject to judicial review, Article 9 of the Directive refers to an infringement decision irrefutably established by a final decision of an NCA or by a review court; it applies only when the administrative decision becomes *res judicata*, even if the '*res judicata* effect' stems from the fact that the decision has not been appealed.

---

9 Regulation 1/2003 of 16 December 2002 on the implementation of the rules on competition laid down in Articles 81 and 82 of the Treaty [2003] OJ L1/1, art 15 'Cooperation with national courts'.

10 This principle whereby national courts should avoid rulings that conflict with Commission decisions finds its origins in the *Delimitis* ruling (Case C-234/89 ECLI:EU:C:1991:91), in which the Court of Justice underlined that the Commission 'is responsible for the implementation and orientation of Community competition policy' (para 44) and that, in a system of parallel competences, in order not to breach the general principle of legal certainty, national courts must avoid issuing decisions that would conflict with a decision contemplated by the Commission.

11 Directive 2014/104/EU of the European Parliament and of the Council of 26 November 2014 on certain rules governing actions for damages under national law for infringements of the competition law provisions of the Member States and of the European Union (also known as 'Damages Directive') [2014] OJ L349/1.

12 Directive 2014/104/UE, art 9, 'Effect of national decisions', provides: '1. Member States shall ensure that an infringement of competition law found by a final decision of a national competition authority or by a review court is deemed to be irrefutably established for the purposes of an action for damages brought before their national courts under Article 101 or 102 TFEU or under national competition law. 2. Member States shall ensure that where a final decision referred to in paragraph 1 is taken in another Member State, that final decision may, in accordance with national law, be presented before their national courts as at least *prima facie* evidence that an infringement of competition law has occurred and, as appropriate, may be assessed along with any other evidence adduced by the parties. 3. This Article is without prejudice to the rights and obligations of national courts under Article 267 TFEU.'

36. That said, the scope of Articles 16 of Regulation 1/2003 and 9 of the Directive has been largely debated:[13] the primacy accorded to administrative proceedings over national courts' proceedings had no precedent in our legal system and even raised some criticisms of its incompatibility with constitutional law.

37. Therefore, the extension of the binding effects of a Commission decision in the DMA application is expected to be one of the main open issues in follow-on private litigation.

38. However, in our opinion, the aforementioned provisions, which are of a Euro-Union matrix, can only be interpreted with the criterion of conformity with European law. Indeed, they do not conflict with any fundamental principle of European constitutions, and there is no basis for invoking the theory of counter-limits elaborated in some jurisdictions, and for referrals to constitutional courts in this regard.

39. Rather, the Court of Justice remains competent to decide on the interpretation to be given to these norms: the diffuse control, relying on the pro-European interpretation of the specialised courts of first and second instance, and the recourse, if necessary, of the courts of last resort to the nomophylactic role of the European

---

13 The literature is very wide: see Gabriella Muscolo, 'Il nuovo assetto istituzionale del private antitrust enforcement in Italia e nell'Unione europea' in Gian Antonio Bennacchio and Michele Carpagnano (eds), *L'applicazione delle regole di Concorrenza in Italia e nell'Unione europea* (Editoriale Scientifica 2018); Ginevra Bruzzone and Aurora Saija, 'Private e public enforcement dopo il recepimento della direttiva. Più di un aggiustamento al margine?' ('Private and Public Enforcement in the Aftermath of the Transposition of the Damages Directive') (2017) (1) Mercato Concorrenza Regole 9; Paolo Comoglio, 'Note a una prima lettura del d.lgs. n. 3 del 2017. Novità processuali e parziali inadeguatezze in tema di danno antitrust' (2017) 71(3) Riv Tral lawim dir e proc civ 991; Roberto Chieppa, 'Il recepimento in Italia della Dir. 2014/104/UE e la prospettiva dell'AGCM' (2016) 24(4) Dir Ind 314; Renato Rordorf, 'Il ruolo del giudice e quello dell'Autorità nazionale della concorrenza e del mercato nel risarcimento del danno antitrust' (2014) (7) Società 784; Mario Siragusa, 'L'effetto delle decisioni delle autorità nazionali della concorrenza nei giudizi per il risarcimento del danno: la proposta della Commissione e il suo impatto nell'ordinamento italiano' (2014) (1) Concorrenza e Mercato 299; Aldo Frignani, 'La difesa disarmata nelle cause follow-on per danno antitrust. La Cassazione in guerra con se stessa' ('Lack of defence of the undertakings involved in antitrust follow on action. The "war" inside the Italian Supreme Court') (2013) (3) Mercato Concorrenza Regole 429; Andrea Giussani, 'Direttiva e principi del processo civile italiano' (2015) 24 AIDA 251; Rino Caiazzo, 'L'azione risarcitoria, l'onere della prova e gli strumenti processuali ai sensi del diritto italiano' in Lorenzo F Pace (ed), *Dizionario sistematico del Diritto della Concorrenza* (Jovene editore 2013); Roberto Pardolesi and others, 'Il Libro Bianco sul danno antitrust: l'anno che verrà' (2008) (2) Mercato Concorrenza Regole 229. In foreign literature, see: Francisco Marcos and Barry Rodger, 'Promotion and Harmonization of Antitrust Damages Claims by Directive EU/2014/104' in Barry Rodger, Miguel Sousa Ferro, and Francisco Marcos (eds), *The EU Antitrust Damages Directive: Transposition in the Member States* (OUP 2018); Wouter P J Wils, 'Private Enforcement of EU Antitrust Law and Its Relationship with Public Enforcement: Past, Present and Future' (2017) 40 (1) World Competition 3; Kathryn Wright, 'The Ambit of Judicial Competence After the EU Antitrust Damages Directive' (2016) 43(1) Legal Issues of Economic Integration 15; Alison Jones, 'Private Enforcement of EU Competition Law: A Comparison with, and Lessons from, the US, in Maria Bergström, Marios Iacovides and Magnus Strand (eds), *Harmonising EU Competition Litigation: The New Directive and Beyond* (Hart Publishing 2016); Renato Nazzini, 'The Effect of Decisions by Competition Authorities in the European Union' (2015) (2) Italian Antitrust Review 68; Sebastian Peyer, 'The Antitrust Damages Directive – much ado about nothing?' in Mel Marquis and Roberto Cisotta (eds), *Litigation and Arbitration in EU Competition Law* (Edward Elgar Publishing 2015); Michael J Frese, 'Harmonisation of Antitrust Damages Procedures in the EU and the Binding Effect of Administrative Decisions' (2015) 8(1) Review of European Administrative Law 27; Jacqueline Riffault-Silk, 'The Binding Effect of National Competition Authorities Decisions – Observations on Article 9 of the Commission Proposal of Directive on Antitrust Damages' (2014) (3) Concorrenza e Mercato 549.

Court of Justice is the only way to guarantee the effective and uniform application of the competition rules.[14]

40. In addition to the expressly provided mechanisms of cooperation between the Commission and national courts in DMA private enforcement, some issues remain open about the extension of forms of collaboration provided in the Damages Directive.

41. Some are especially relevant for access to the evidence phase: first, Article 6(7) of the Directive allows the claimant to present a reasoned request for access to the evidence referred to in points (a) or (b) of paragraph 6 concerning statements related to a leniency programme and settlement proposals, respectively. In such an assessment, national courts may request assistance from the competent NCA.[15]

42. Secondly, Article 6(11) establishes the right of NCAs to submit observations to the national court before which a disclosure order is sought, as a declination of the

---

14 In the context of the reference for a preliminary ruling, its mandatory nature for the courts of last instance, which finds its legal basis in the third paragraph of art 267 TFEU, is of central importance. See *Schipani and Others v Italy* App no 38369/09 (ECtHR, 21 July 2015) concerning non-referral to the Court of Justice by the court of last instance and the compatibility with the European Convention on Human Rights. See also Case C-561/19 *Consorzio Italian Management e Catania Multiservizi* ECLI:EU:C:2021:799, affirming important principles regarding the obligation to make a reference for a preliminary ruling under art 267 TFEU.

15 art 6, 'Disclosure of evidence included in the file of a competition authority', disposes: '1. Member States shall ensure that, for the purpose of actions for damages, where national courts order the disclosure of evidence included in the file of a competition authority, this Article applies in addition to Article 5. 2. This Article is without prejudice to the rules and practices on public access to documents under Regulation (EC) No 1049/2001. 3. This Article is without prejudice to the rules and practices under Union or national law on the protection of internal documents of competition authorities and of correspondence between competition authorities. 4. When assessing, in accordance with Article 5(3), the proportionality of an order to disclose information, national courts shall, in addition, consider the following: (a) whether the request has been formulated specifically with regard to the nature, subject matter or contents of documents submitted to a competition authority or held in the file thereof, rather than by a non-specific application concerning documents submitted to a competition authority; (b) whether the party requesting disclosure is doing so in relation to an action for damages before a national court; and (c) in relation to paragraphs 5 and 10, or upon request of a competition authority pursuant to paragraph 11, the need to safeguard the effectiveness of the public enforcement of competition law. 5. National courts may order the disclosure of the following categories of evidence only after a competition authority, by adopting a decision or otherwise, has closed its proceedings: (a) information that was prepared by a natural or legal person specifically for the proceedings of a competition authority; (b) information that the competition authority has drawn up and sent to the parties in the course of its proceedings; and (c) settlement submissions that have been withdrawn. 6. Member States shall ensure that, for the purpose of actions for damages, national courts cannot at any time order a party or a third party to disclose any of the following categories of evidence: (a) leniency statements; and (b) settlement submissions. 7. A claimant may present a reasoned request that a national court access the evidence referred to in point (a) or (b) of paragraph 6 for the sole purpose of ensuring that their contents correspond to the definitions in points (16) and (18) of Article 2. In that assessment, national courts may request assistance only from the competent competition authority. The authors of the evidence in question may also have the possibility to be heard. In no case shall the national court permit other parties or third parties access to that evidence. 8. If only parts of the evidence requested are covered by paragraph 6, the remaining parts thereof shall, depending on the category under which they fall, be released in accordance with the relevant paragraphs of this Article. 9. The disclosure of evidence in the file of a competition authority that does not fall into any of the categories listed in this Article may be ordered in actions for damages at any time, without prejudice to this Article. 10. Member States shall ensure that national courts request the disclosure from a competition authority of evidence included in its file only where no party or third party is reasonably able to provide that evidence. 11. To the extent that a competition authority is willing to state its views on the proportionality of disclosure requests, it may, acting on its own initiative, submit observations to the national court before which a disclosure order is sought.'

faculty to present observations as *amicus curiae* already provided by Article 15 of Regulation 1/2003 to which reference is made in Recital 30 of the Directive.[16]

43. Article 39 DMA does not provide for mechanisms of cooperation related to the collection of evidence; however, the analogies between the two private litigation, with particular reference to the asymmetric position of the parties, make it appropriate to extend the application at least of the second mentioned norm to actions for compensation of damages caused by the DMA infringement.

44. Furthermore, a very special *amicus curiae* intervention is set forth by Article 17 of the Directive: it provides that an NCA, upon request of a national court and subject to its discretion, assist that judge in the calculation of the harm, in the event that such assistance is appropriate.[17]

45. Although this declination of the *amicus curiae* intervention has not been specifically provided by Article 39, the already highlighted analogies make appropriate the application of this cooperation mechanism in DMA private litigation by the intervention of the Commission or the NCA enforcing the DMA, as *amicus curiae*.

III. The DMA as a Piece of a Wider Cosmos of EU and National Legislative Initiatives for Digital Transformation

1. Interactions (and Overlaps) between DMA and other EU Regulatory and Policy Initiatives (Adopted or Incoming) on National Digitalisation

46. The Digital Services Package, comprising the Digital Services Act (DSA) and DMA, was adopted through a remarkably swift legislative process of less than two years. However, while these new regulations are particularly innovative, they build upon other important legislative initiatives in the digital sector.

47. The DMA is part of a broader framework of EU legislative initiatives and is firmly rooted within it. For example, as noted by some of the authors of the national chapters in this book (hereafter referred to as 'the authors'), the DMA not only shares the same fairness objectives as the P2B Regulation[18], which imposes sub-

---

16 See note above.

17 art 17, 'Quantification of harm', provides: '1. Member States shall ensure that neither the burden nor the standard of proof required for the quantification of harm renders the exercise of the right to damages practically impossible or excessively difficult. Member States shall ensure that the national courts are empowered, in accordance with national procedures, to estimate the amount of harm if it is established that a claimant suffered harm but it is practically impossible or excessively difficult precisely to quantify the harm suffered on the basis of the evidence available. 2. It shall be presumed that cartel infringements cause harm. The infringer shall have the right to rebut that presumption. 3. Member States shall ensure that, in proceedings relating to an action for damages, a national competition authority may, upon request of a national court, assist that national court with respect to the determination of the quantum of damages where that national competition authority considers such assistance to be appropriate.'

18 Regulation 2019/1150 of the European Parliament and of the Council of 20 June 2019 on promoting fairness and transparency for business users of online intermediation services [2019] OJ L186/57.

stantive obligations, but also adopts similar definitions, such as those for online intermediation services and online search engines.

48. In the same vein, the DMA references other EU regulations, particularly the General Data Protection Regulation (GDPR)[19], when it comes to data obligations and obtaining consent from end users.

49. Thus, the DMA is seamlessly integrated into the broader digital policy narrative, which serves as both a precursor and a legal framework, particularly with respect to definitions. However, this complex legal structure, which includes multiple pieces of legislation and numerous cross-references, could lead to coordination challenges. As emphasised by several authors, effective coordination at the European level is crucial to ensure that enforcement activities are consistent and reflect the objectives of all relevant EU regulations.

50. In this context, the DMA high-level group plays a vital role by aligning the perspectives of various institutions and providing guidance on overarching matters. This coordination helps to prevent enforcement redundancies, resolves potential regulatory conflicts – whether real or perceived – and ensures legal certainty.

51. As highlighted by various authors, the complexity increases when considering national legislative initiatives on digitalisation. Each Member State is adopting new laws to support its digital transition, most of which align with EU policies and legislative initiatives such as the DMA, DSA, Data Act[20], Data Governance Act[21], AI Act[22], and Cybersecurity Act[23]. These national laws often confer new powers or involve multiple national institutions.

52. In this regard, some authors suggest the need for a 'digital governance model' that coordinates various clusters of national authorities and EU Directorate-Generals. This model would facilitate coordination between national authorities and the Commission in their respective EU networks and, where necessary, enable the exchange of relevant non-confidential information between national authorities across different EU networks, such as the ECN.

53. At present, several Member States have established 'interinstitutional steering committees' at the national level to support coordination. Examples include the Informal Platform for Digital Governance in Belgium, the National Coordination Network for Digital Services Regulation in France, the Digital Regulators Group

---

19 Regulation 2016/679 of the European Parliament and of the Council of 27 April 2016 on the protection of natural persons with regard to the processing of personal data and on the free movement of such data, and repealing Directive 95/46/EC [2016] OJ L119/1.

20 Regulation 2023/2854 of the European Parliament and of the Council of 13 December 2023 on harmonised rules on fair access to and use of data and amending Regulation 2017/2394 and Directive 2020/1828 [2023] OJ L.

21 Regulation 2022/868 of the European Parliament and of the Council of 30 May 2022 on European data governance and amending Regulation 2018/1724 [2022] OJ L152/1.

22 Regulation 2024/1689 of the European Parliament and of the Council of 13 June 2024 laying down harmonised rules on artificial intelligence and amending Regulations 300/2008, 167/2013, 168/2013, 2018/858, 2018/1139 and 2019/2144 and Directives 2014/90/EU, 2016/797 and 2020/1828 [2024] OJ L.

23 Regulation 2019/881 of the European Parliament and of the Council of 17 April 2019 on ENISA (the European Union Agency for Cybersecurity) and on information and communications technology cybersecurity certification and repealing Regulation 526/2013 [2019] OJ L151/15.

in Ireland, the Digital Regulation Cooperation Platform in the Netherlands, and similar initiatives planned in Slovakia. These committees, composed of various authorities, aim to ensure national coordination.

2. Possible Positive Integrations between DMA and National Initiatives for Digitalisation

54. As previously mentioned, Member States are adopting various national digitalisation initiatives across different sectors, into which the DMA should be integrated.

55. The DMA clearly states in Article 1(5) that Member States cannot impose additional obligations on gatekeepers for the purpose of ensuring fairness and contestability (see section II.1). Some authors have noted that this provision is complemented by other DMA articles. For instance, Article 8(1) ensures that compliance with the DMA does not exempt gatekeepers from adhering to other legislation, particularly in areas such as consumer protection, product safety, and accessibility requirements. Furthermore, Article 13(6) prohibits the use of 'dark patterns', which may also fall under other legislative areas, including consumer protection.

56. These authors observe that the combination of these DMA provisions creates a 'vacuum effect' that neutralises attempts by gatekeepers to game the system, ensuring the DMA and other national legislation are consistently applied.

57. From a governance perspective, it is noteworthy that the integration of the DMA into national systems, along with other European regulations, has broadened and strengthened the powers of national authorities in various countries. For example, the Danish Competition and Consumer Authority and the Irish Competition and Consumer Protection Commission have been designated as competent authorities for the enforcement of the DMA, the DSA, and the P2B Regulation. Similarly, the Lithuanian Competition Council, the Dutch Authority for Consumers and Markets, and the Romanian Competition Authority are responsible for the DMA and the P2B Regulation, while the Spanish National Markets and Competition Commission handles both the DMA and the DSA.

58. While we will not delve deeply into the topic of 'one-stop-shop' agencies, it is important to note that stronger regulators can lead to more efficient interinstitutional coordination, both nationally and at the European level, and may foster synergies in enforcement activities.

59. Moreover, many authors have discussed the integration of the DMA with national competition enforcement (i.e. Article 1(6) DMA), a topic previously addressed in section II.1. On the one hand, authors from Ireland, Estonia, and the Czech Republic have highlighted the importance of centralising the enforcement of the DMA and competition law in digital markets under the Commission or larger NCAs. Their reasoning includes factors such as limited resources and expertise, the lack of gatekeeper presence in local markets, and other enforcement priorities. On the other hand, authors from Italy, Germany, France, Spain, Denmark, Romania, and Sweden emphasise the continuing importance of national competition law enforcement, which not only contributed to the drafting of the DMA but will also help keep it future-proof, thanks to its flexibility.

60. In this context, some authors have emphasised the significance of Article 38(7), which is relevant for cases where it is unclear from the outset whether a gatekeeper is violating the DMA, competition law, or both.

61. Additionally, many authors stress the importance of cooperation between the Commission and NCAs. The ECN has proven to be an effective platform for collaboration, and initiatives such as memoranda of understanding for the formation of joint investigative teams on DMA-related issues are welcomed. The Commission has already signed such agreements with the Netherlands, Italy, Spain, Belgium, and Luxembourg. Another example is the joint market study conducted by NCAs from Poland, Latvia, and Lithuania, focusing on areas not covered by the DMA, financed by the EU and led by the Organisation for Economic Co-operation and Development (OECD).

62. Cooperation between the Commission and NCAs becomes even more critical for jurisdictions that have introduced new digital competition laws, such as Germany, Italy, France, Romania, Denmark, Sweden, and Greece. For instance, the Commission and the Bundeskartellamt closely collaborated on the German case against Alphabet concerning Google's data processing practices, reaching a positive outcome despite overlapping issues between Section 19a of the German Competition Act (GWB) and Article 5(2) DMA.

3. Grouping the Approaches

63. Most Member States have introduced national legislative initiatives to implement the DMA (see Appendix for further details). In the countries that proactively responded to the DMA from a legislative standpoint, NCAs have generally been designated as the sole competent authority for implementing the DMA.

64. As previously noted, several NCAs have also been assigned the responsibility of enforcing other EU regulations, such as the DSA and the P2B Regulation. In addition, many Member States have established interinstitutional steering committees to coordinate the activities of various national institutions involved in implementing both European and national regulations concerning the digital sector.

65. All Member States that have adopted, or plan to adopt, national initiatives for DMA implementation provide assistance to the Commission's investigations under the DMA (e.g. by supporting inspection activities).

66. Interestingly, not all NCAs have been granted the authority to conduct DMA investigations as outlined in Article 38(7). For example, the Irish NCA lacks sufficient resources and expertise in the digital sector, and the Czech Republic and Lithuanian NCAs are similarly not empowered to carry out such investigations.

67. Several jurisdictions have introduced new antitrust instruments targeting large online platforms, such as those in Germany, France, and Italy. Other countries, such as Romania and Italy, have been inspired by the UK's approach, enabling NCAs to conduct market investigations and impose remedies without the need to identify specific infringements.

68. Additionally, some jurisdictions, such as Italy, have revised their merger control regulations to capture smaller mergers, with a similar initiative being discussed in Sweden.

IV. Conclusion: A Recipe (e.g. Do's, Don'ts, Highlights, Governance, Open Questions) against Increasing Concerns about Techno-authoritarianism

69. Europe has responded to techno-authoritarianism[24] by creating what has been described as a 'worldwide factory for digital rules',[25] fostering a scenario of techno-democracy firmly grounded in the founding principles of the European Union.

70. The DMA is a key element of this Brussels package,[26] marking a milestone in the European digital agenda[27] and serving as a vital tool for digital sovereignty.

71. However, to make the regulation of big tech companies truly effective, two key issues remain open.

72. The first is the potential for a transatlantic alliance. Approximately 50% of the GAFAM (Google, Apple, Facebook, Amazon, and Microsoft) revenues come from the US market, while only 25% come from the European single market. Since the DMA has primarily targeted US companies thus far, establishing a new EU-US common agenda[28] and considering the role of the new US administration will be crucial for ensuring the DMA's success.

73. The second issue concerns the synergy between the DMA and national regulations, which is necessary for fostering fairer and more competitive markets and ensuring successful national digital transformations in each Member State. This is why we, the editors, believe it is important to gather national perspectives on such synergies.

74. After all, '[t]he notion that all we need to make the world a better place is "better regulation" is deeply embedded in our culture… Regulation, however, is not magic. Just because one wants a thing to be regulated, that does not make it capable of actually being regulated'.[29]

---

24 Yuval Noah Harari, *21 Lessons for the 21st Century* (Random 2018); Marta Dassù, 'L'Europa alla prova di Biden' *La Repubblica* (30 November 2020); see also the dedicated issue of *Formiche*, 'Tecnologia e democrazia. L'alleanza necessaria' (2020) 164 Formiche; Marcus Michaelsen and Kris Ruijgrok, 'Digital Authoritarianism' in Anne Wolf (ed), *The Oxford Handbook of Authoritarian Politics* (online edn, Oxford Academic 2024).

25 Carlo Alberto Carnevale Maffè, 'L'impero digitale colpisce ancora' (2020) 3 Italianieuropei.

26 Anu Bradford, *The Brussels Effect: How the European Union Rules the World* (Oxford Academic 2020) p 76. See also Anu Bradford, 'The European Union in a globalised world: the "Brussels effect"' (2021) (2) Revue européenne du droit 75.

27 European Commission, 'Shaping Europe's digital future' (Communication) COM/2020/67 final; European Commission, '2030 Digital Compass: the European way for the Digital Decade' (Communication) COM/2021/118 final.

28 European Commission, 'A new EU-US agenda for global change' (Joint Communication) JOIN (2020) 22 final. See Frances G Burwell, 'Looking ahead to the next chapter of US-EU digital collaboration' in James Batchik (ed), *Transatlantic Horizons: A collaborative US-EU policy agenda for 2025 and beyond* (Atlantic Council – Europe Center 2024) pp 14–17.

29 David Allen Green, 'The coming battle between social media and the state' *Financial Times* (11 January 2025).

The DMA and other Legislative Initiatives for the Digital Transformation: National Competition and other Competent Authorities

Belgium

JACQUES STEENBERGEN*

KU Leuven

Abstract

National competition authorities participate in the forms of cooperation between the Commission and national competition authorities provided for in the Digital Markets Act (DMA). They can develop in these contacts their views on the application and enforcement of the DMA, and also on the application and enforcement of national competition law on related issues. The different legislative initiatives for the digital transformation, such as the Digital Sevices Act, the Data Act, the Data Governance Act, the Artificial Intelligence Act and the Cybersecurity Act all involve various national authorities in their respective governance models. The 'digital governance model' can be described as a juxtaposition of clusters in which each relevant national authority can coordinate its positions with colleagues and the Commission in their respective networks, and may exchange non-confidential information with colleagues who are members of a different EU network.

---

* Emeritus Professor Dr Jacques Steenbergen, is the former president of the Belgian Competition Authority.

I. The DMA: General Views from the Perspective of a Competition Authority of a Member State

1. The Belgian Competition Authority (BCA) can participate as a competition authority of a Member State, whether or not at its own initiative, in the forms of cooperation between the Commission and national competition authorities provided for in the Digital Markets Act (DMA). The BCA is also the designated competent authority for Belgium.[1] It will therefore be able to participate in all of the many forms of cooperation provided for in the DMA. In these contacts and consultations, the BCA can develop its views on the application and enforcement of the DMA, and also on the application and enforcement of national competition law on related issues.

2. It may therefore be useful to list the DMA provisions relevant to the involvement of national authorities:

3. The DMA and the application of competition law:
   - Article 1(6): no impact on the application Articles 101 and 102 TFEU by the Commission or the national competition authorities. The latter is in particular relevant to competition authorities in smaller jurisdictions like Belgium because a comparatively higher percentage of agreements and behaviours is likely to affect trade between Member States, requiring them to assess their impact on competition by application of the Articles 101 and 102 TFEU.
   - Neither does the DMA affect private enforcement of EU or national competition law.[2]
   - Article 1(6)a: no impact on the application of national competition law equivalents of the Articles 101 and 102 TFEU, i.e. in Belgian law the Articles IV.1 and IV.2 of the Code of Economic Law (CEL).
   - Article 1(5) and 1(6)b: no impact on the application of other national rules prohibiting other types of unilateral conduct insofar as applied to non-gatekeepers, or imposing further obligations on gatekeepers provided these are not imposed for the purpose of ensuring contestable and fair markets (I assume as aimed at by the DMA). These provisions may apply in Belgium to the prohibition of abuse of economic dependency (Article IV.2/1 CEL), even though this is perhaps somewhat academic in respect of gatekeepers when holding a dominant position on the relevant market.[3] There can also be a discussion on the question whether the prohibition of economic dependency qualifies as a 'further obligation' in the meaning of Article 1(6)b DMA.

---

1 Code of Economic Law (CEL) art 7 of the Act of 28 March 2024, new art IV.16, §1/1. The DMA makes, as discussed hereafter, a distinction between national competent authorities (as designated by the Member States) and national competent authorities enforcing the rules referred to in DMA art 1(6), i.e. arts 101 and 102 TFEU. See above in this contribution in respect of the designation of the BCA as the Belgian national competent authority.

2 Regulation 2022/1925 of the European Parliament and of the Council of 14 September 2022 on contestable and fair markets in the digital sector and amending Directives 2019/1937 and 2020/1828 (Digital Markets Act or DMA) [2022] OJ L265/1, art 1(6) read together with DMA art 39.

3 The legislation on abuse of economic dependency is designed for cases in which the prohibition of abuse of a dominant position cannot apply. It is, however, not limited to cases in which there is no dominant position: presentations by Mrs A-M Witters (Market Court) and Mr K Stas (Crowell and Moring) to the VSME/AEDC in Brussels on 29 November 2023.

- And we may expect that the provisions of Articles 5 and 6 DMA will have an impact on the interpretation of the concept of abuse in the Articles 102 TFEU and 1V.2 CEL.

4. The national competition authorities (NCAs) of the Member States can give input to the Commission in respect of:
   - The review of the status of gatekeepers including the list of relevant core platform services provided for in Article 4 DMA. Even though there is no explicit provision, we may assume that a NCA can request a review in the meaning of Article 4(1) DMA, and the NCAs can give input in the framework of the regular review of the status of gatekeepers (Article 4(2) DMA read together with Article 38 DMA).
   - Suspension decisions (Article 9 DMA read together with Article 38 DMA).
   - Exemption decisions (Article 10 DMA read together with Article 38 DMA).
   - The updating of obligations for gatekeepers (Article 12 DMA read together with Article 38 DMA).
   - The obligation to inform about concentrations: Article 14(4) and (5) DMA explicitly provides that the Commission shall share information with the competent authorities of the Member States. This provision does not refer to the NCAs, but we may assume that references to the competent authorities of the Member States include the NCAs, and that the NCAs will in any case receive the information through the specific channels of the ECN pursuant to Article 38 DMA.

     It may be added that Belgian competition law has no equivalent of Article 21(1) of the Merger Regulation.[4] It can examine concentrations that do not meet the thresholds for merger control by application of the prohibition of abuse of a dominant position. The Brussels Court of Appeal decided in its judgement of 15 December 2006[5] that the provisions on merger control did not exclude the application of the prohibition of abuse of dominant provisions in Article IV.2 CEL to concentrations that did not need to be notified.[6]

     The BCA is therefore less likely to need a request to the Commission9 to examine a concentration pursuant to Article 22 of the Merger Regulation. And given its own jurisdiction, one can even question whether the BCA can ask for the application of Article 22.[7]

---

4 Regulation 139/2004 of 20 January 2004 on the control of concentrations between undertakings [2004] OJ L24/1.

5 In Case *Gabriella Rocco, Tijdschrift voor Belgische Mededinging*, 2007 (4) 39.

6 The Court of Appeal decided that a strategy to buy competitors is as such not sufficient evidence of a potential infringement of the arts IV.1 or IV.2 CEL (the equivalents of the arts 101 and 102 TFEU). In a later decision the Market Court (chamber of the Court of Appeal designated as the review court for BCA decisions), refusing to annul a refusal of interim measures by the BCA, followed the BCA in its judgement of 28 June 2017 in Case *Brouwerijen Alken-Maes v BCA*. The court decided that the application of art IV.2 CEL and 102 TFEU to concentrations required the finding of more specific negative consequences of the transaction than the mere realisation of the concentration (https://www.bma-abc.be/sites/default/files/content/download/files/20170628_hvbb_2016mr2_alkenmaes_abi.pdf)

7 The fact that the BCA may have jurisdiction, however, by analogy to the referral rules in merger control, should in my opinion not imply that the BCA may not support requests under art 22 by other national competition authorities.

The Market Court required the finding of more specific negative consequences of the transaction than the mere realisation of the concentration. In its *Towercast* judgement, the CJEU seemed to define a substantial impediment of competition justifying the application of Article 102 TFEU as ("*that is to say*")[8] a transaction that causes that only undertakings whose behaviour depends on the dominant undertaking would remain in the market. The CJEU is thus more specific and rather more demanding than the Market Court. Belgian law may therefore be considered to be stricter than Article 102 TFEU in the meaning of Article 3(2) of Regulation 1/2003 by having a somewhat wider scope of application. The real question is therefore not whether the BCA may apply Article 102 TFEU, but whether the BCA and the Market Court will continue the line of their existing case law or prefer in the interest of legal certainty to align future decisions more closely on the *Towercast* case: (i) in cases when Article 102 TFEU is applicable,[9] and (ii) in cases when Article 102 TFEU is not applicable because of a lack of impact on trade between Member States.

- The Commission may ask one or more national competent authorities to assist in a market investigation (Articles 16(5) and 38(6) DMA).
- Market investigations pursuant to Article 17 DMA (read together with Article 38 DMA).
- Market investigations into systematic non-compliance (Article 18 DMA read together with Article 38 DMA).
- Market investigations into new services and practices (Article 19 DMA read together with Article 38 DMA).
- I think we may assume that NCAs can suggest the adoption of interim measures (Article 24 DMA read together with Article 38 DMA).
- Commitment decisions (Article 25 DMA read together with Article 38 DMA).
- Article 27 DMA provides explicitly that information from third parties such as competitors or platform users can be given to a national competition authority[10] which shall have full discretion as regards the appropriate measures and with no obligation to act. If, however, the information indicates that there may be non-compliance with the DMA, the information must be transferred to the Commission.
- Article 36 DMA stipulates that information collected pursuant to the DMA may only be used for the purposes of the DMA. This provision applies to the national competent authorities and all who work for them. It must

---

8 Case C-449/21 *Towercast* ECLI:EU:C:2023:207, para 52.

9 In an interim measures decision in which the Competition College considered art 102 TFEU to be *prima facie* applicable, the College seems to have adopted the *Towercast* approach: Decision ABC-2023-RPR-17, 21 June 2023 in the *Proximus/EDPnet* case (BCA website), see Valérie Lefever, *The Belgian Competition Authority imposes interim measures on the incumbent telecoms operator following its acquisition of a failing rival following the jurisprudence of the EU Court of Justice in its Towercast ruling (Proximus/EDPnet)*, E-COMPETITIONS June 2023, art. No. 113147.

10 The text refers to a national competent authority enforcing the rules referred to in DMA art 1(6), i.e. the arts 101 and 102 TFEU.

be read together with Article 38(1) and (5) DMA in respect of national competition authorities.

- Article 38 DMA organises the relations between the Commission and the national competition authorities[11] when they enforce competition law:
- Article 38 (1) and (5) DMA provides for the exchange of information.
- Article 38(2) DMA requires the NCAs to inform the Commission when they intend to open an investigation under the national rules of competition on gatekeepers.
- Article 38(3) DMA requires the NCAs intending to impose obligations on a gatekeeper under the national rules of competition to submit their draft decision to the Commission in analogy with the rules applying to under Regulation 1/2003 in respect of the enforcement of the Articles 101 and 102 DMA.
- Article 38(7) DMA provides that, when enabled to do so under national law, a NCA can on its own initiative (and I assume also following a complaint) conduct an investigation in case of possible non-compliance with the Articles 5, 6 and 7 DMA after informing the Commission. In analogy with Regulation 1/2003, the NCA cannot continue its investigation after the opening of proceedings by the Commission pursuant to Article 20 DMA. As mentioned later, the Belgian Government intends to enable the BCA to make use of this provision.
- Article 40 DMA organises a High-level Group which may provide the Commission with advice and recommendations in particular in respect of interactions with sector-specific rules. The NCAs participate indirectly in this group via the ECN delegation.

5. Article 37 DMA requires close cooperation between the '*Commission and Member States*' under the heading '*Cooperation with national authorities*'. It stipulates that the Commission may consult the national authorities on any matter relating to the application of the DMA where appropriate. We may assume that the term 'national authorities' refers to all designated competent national authorities, including the NCAs. As the BCA has been designated as the only competent Belgian national authority, this provision technically also applies to the BCA, but it adds little if anything to the BCA's rights and obligations under Article 38 DMA as a member of the ECN.

6. It is less clear what the impact is of the reference to the Member States: does Article 37 DMA require a close cooperation with the States, i.e. their governments and not only the designated national competent authorities?

7. Article 41(1), (2) and (3) DMA provides that three or more Member States (Article 41(1) in respect of Article 17 DMA and 41(3)a in respect of Article 19 DMA), or one or more Member States (Article 41(2) in respect of Article 18 DMA) may request the Commission to open a market investigation. The Belgian legislator decided that such requests can be made on behalf of Belgium by the Prosecutor General of the BCA. Belgian authorities which are members of one of the networks

11 DMA art 1(6), i.e. the arts 101 and 102 TFEU.

referred to in Article 40(2) DMA and other relevant public bodies that wish the Commission to open an investigation can inform the Prosecutor General. He will seek the advice of the other relevant authorities before requesting the Commission to open a market investigation.[12]

8. Article 39 DMA organises the cooperation with the courts which may ask the Commission for information or its opinion. The Commission may, acting on its own initiative file an *amicus curiae* letter. The courts shall avoid giving judgements that run counter to decisions based on the DMA. It seems in view of Article 38 DMA, logical for the Commission to consult with the NCA in the relevant jurisdiction.

9. The DMA does not organise the interactions between the Commission as competition authority and the Commission as the enforcer of the DMA, except by providing in Article 1(6) DMA that the Commission continues to be empowered to enforce the rules of competition also in respect of the behaviour of gatekeepers.

10. We may conclude that the BCA can as a competition authority and as a designated competent authority of a Member State, make its views on the application and impact of the DMA known in different channels:

- Perhaps most important for NCAs, in the regular exchanges with the Commission and with other NCAs in the ECN framework. There they can discuss the interaction between the enforcement and development of the rules of competition and of the DMA, both with regard to Commission files and their own application and development of the EU and the national rules of competition.
- In the numerous opportunities to be heard directly as provided for in the DMA and listed in this chapter.
- By developing its own enforcement policy in respect of investigations of possible non-compliance by gatekeepers of the Articles 5, 6 and 7 DMA.
- By giving input to the ECN delegation in the High-level Group.
- And as the member for Belgium of the Digital Markets Advisory Committee set up by Article 50 DMA in the framework of the Committee procedure in the meaning of Regulation 182/2011. The president of the BCA or his representative can be accompanied by representatives of one or more authorities with experience in respect of the issues that are on the agenda. In case of a consultation referred to in Article 46 DMA, the president of the BCA invites a representative of the FOD/SPF Economie (ministry of economic affairs) to take part in the meeting of the Advisory Committee.[13]

11. It should also be recalled that Member States may prohibit other forms of unilateral conduct applied to non-gatekeepers and impose further obligations on gatekeepers as provided for in Article 1(6)b DMA. The possibility for the Member States to prohibit forms of unilateral conduct, other than those prohibited by Article 102 TFEU (and IV.2 CEL), makes it possible e.g. for Belgium to envisage

[12] Act of 28 March 2024 art 54, new art IV.100 CEL.
[13] Act of 28 March 2024 art 55, new art IV.101 CEL.

introducing in Book IV CEL a DMA-type legislation in case it is considered that platforms that do not have a 'DMA gatekeeper dimension' have a position and impact on the Belgian market comparable to that of gatekeepers on the larger EU market.

II. Actions Undertaken by the EU Member State to Facilitate the Integration and to Enhance Synergies between EU and National Legislations for the Digital Sector

1. In Respect of the DMA

A. *The BCA*

12. The Belgian Government enacted legislation:
    - Designating the BCA as the only national competent authority in the meaning of the relevant DMA provisions,[14]
    - Enabling the BCA pursuant to Article 38(7) DMA to conduct on its own initiative (and I assume also following a complaint), an investigation in case of possible non-compliance with Articles 5, 6 and 7 DMA after informing the Commission, and provided the Commission has not yet opened proceedings pursuant to Article 20 DMA.[15]
    - Empowering the Prosecutor General of the BCA to request a market investigation.[16]

13. Subject to private enforcement actions in Belgian courts and given the fact that the BCA is the independent Belgian competition authority in conformity with the ECN+ Directive,[17] the integration and synergies between 'Belgian' actions provided for in the DMA and Belgian competition law will primarily be organised in the existing framework of the ECN.

14. Integration and synergies can also be discussed in the various forms of cooperation between the Commission acting as DMA enforcer provided for in the DMA and listed in this chapter. They can in the future also be discussed in a cooperation framework as the Commission may develop to structure the cooperation with the national competent authorities of the Member States required by Articles 37 and 38 and other relevant provisions of the DMA. Competition authorities have, however, expressed a preference for a focus on the ECN. Designated as the only competent authority in the meaning of the DMA for Belgium, the relationship between cooperation with 'competent authorities' and the 'channelling' of discussions into the ECN, is of less relevance for the BCA, as well as for other Belgian authorities that will mainly be involved via the High-level Group.

---

14 Act of 28 March 2024 art 7, new art IV.16 CEL §1/1.

15 Act of 28 March 2024 arts 50–53, new art IV.96 CEL.

16 Act of 28 March 2024 art 54, new art IV.100 CEL.

17 Directive 2019/1 of the European Parliament and of the Council of 11 December 2018 to empower the competition authorities of the Member States to be more effective enforcers and to ensure the proper functioning of the internal market [2019] OJ L11/3, art 4.

B. *Other National Authorities*

15. With regard to the High-level Group for the Digital Market Act (Article 40 DMA), I assume that the European bodies and networks listed in Article 40(2) DMA will organise their contribution to the High-level Group in cooperation with the national regulators. The relevant Belgian regulators are the BIPT/IBPT (telecom regulator), the GBA/APD (data protection authority) and the media regulators of the Flemish, Francophone and Germanophone Communities. As there is no independent consumer protection authority, the FOD/SPF Economie is in charge of consumer protection and participates in the Consumer Protection Cooperation Network.

16. The institutional model is therefore one of a juxtaposition of clusters in which each relevant national authority can coordinate its positions with its colleagues and the Commission in their respective networks, which then meet in the High-level Group. Horizontal cooperation between clusters or members of different networks needs to respect the independence and confidentiality obligations of the relevant regulators.[18] Only the BCA as member of the ECN will be involved in actual case or regulation related decision making given the advisory role of the High-level Group.

2. Other Legislative Initiatives for the Digital Sector

A. *General Survey from a Belgian Perspective*

17. An informal platform for Digital Governance has been set up with federal authorities that are deemed relevant to the regulation of the digital sector(s): the BCA, the CCB (centre for cyber security), the FOD/SPF Economie (ministry of economic affairs), the Directorate General for Simplification and Digital Transformation of the FOD/SPF Policy and Support, the FSMA (financial markets authority), the GBA/APD (the data protection authority), and hosted by the IBPT/BIPT (telecom regulator) at the imitative of the Secretary of State for digitalisation after a designation in respect of the DMA had already been decided by the Minister for economic affairs.

18. The initial purpose was to prepare a proposal to the relevant Ministers for the designation of national competent authorities as required by the different EU legislative initiatives: the DMA, DSA, draft Data Act, draft Data Governance Act, draft Cybersecurity Act and the draft Artificial Intelligence Act.

19. The legislative initiatives referred to in this contribution are only a selection of the actions taken by the Commission in the framework of its digital strategy,[19] and the relevant Belgian legislation is not limited to laws and regulations that are considered directly relevant or related to the digital transformation. See e.g. Regulation 2019/1150 (the Platform to Business (P2B) Regulation), Directive 2011/83 on consumer rights and the relevant provisions of Book VI CEL on consumer protection and market practices.

---

18 See further below in this contribution.

19 European Commission, 'A Europe Fit for the Digital Age' <https://commission.europa.eu/strategy-and-policy/priorities-2019-2024/europe-fit-digital-age_en> accessed 1 July 2024.

20. The Minister of Economic Affairs has also commissioned a study on platform issues. This study is expected to be published in 2024.

21. The institutional provisions in the different legislative initiatives discussed in this contribution, and the Belgian distribution of competences in their respect, prior to the formal designation of national competent authorities, can be summarised as follows:

- For the DMA I refer to paras 1 and 8 of this contribution. Read together with the ECN+ Directive, the national competent authorities must be independent in respect of the tasks conferred to national competition authorities. They cooperate with the Commission and each other in the ECN.

  The government is expected to agree on legislation designating the BCA as the only Belgian national competent authority.
- The DSA requires the designation of Digital Services Coordinators. They must be impartial. Digital Service Coordinators shall act with complete independence and remain free from any external influence. They shall neither seek nor take instructions from any other public authority or private party. The Member States must ensure that they have all the necessary resources to carry out their tasks.[20]

  The DSA organises the cooperation between Digital Service Coordinators.[21] It establishes a European Board for Digital Services consisting of Digital Service Coordinators and chaired by the Commission. It is an advisory board set up in order to facilitate the application of the DSA and the coordination among the national authorities.[22]

  The DSA in Belgium primarily concerns competences of the BIPT/IBPT and the regional media regulators. There is said to be a political agreement on the designation of the BIPT/IBPT as the Digital Service Coordinator and national competent authority for federal matters, and of the regional media authorities for matters within their respective competences. This has not yet been formalised in draft legislation.
- The draft Data Act requires the Member States to designate the independent data protection authority in respect of personal data. A designated authority must have all the necessary resources to carry out their tasks and remain free from any external influence. They shall neither seek nor take instructions from any other public authority or private party.[23] The national competent authority responsible for the enforcement of the chapter on switching between data processing services must have experience in the field of data and electronic communication services.[24]

---

20 Regulation 2022/2065 of the European Parliament and of the Council of 19 October 2022 on a Single Market for Digital Services and amending Directive 2000/31 (Digital Services Act or DSA) [2022] OJ L277/1, art 50.

21 Regulation 2022/2065 art 57.

22 Regulation 2022/2065 arts 61–63.

23 Directive 2020/1828 of the European Parliament and of the Council of 25 November 2020 on representative actions for the protection of the collective interests of consumers and repealing Directive 2009/22 (Data Act) [2020] OJ L 409/1, art 31.

24 Directive 2020/1828 art 31(2)(c).

The draft Data Act requires cooperation between the national competent authorities in case more than one has been designated,[25] but it does not set up a coordinating body between designated authorities of the different Member States. It refers on the contrary to the competences of sectoral authorities.[26] It is not clear to me how the authorities dealing with non-personal data will relate to the European Data Protection Board set up by the GDPR Regulation as an independent body of the Union with some decision-making powers.[27]

The draft Data Act in Belgium primarily concerns competences of the GBA/APD and the BIPT/IBPT.

- The draft Data Governance Act provides that the competent authorities must be legally distinct and functionally independent from registered providers of data sharing services. It proposes incompatibilities for the top management of competent authorities.[28]

  The draft Data Governance Act provides for a European Data Innovation Board as an advisory body consisting of the national competent authorities and chaired by the Commission.[29]

  The draft Data Governance Act in Belgium is considered to be primarily concerned with competences of the FOD/SPF Economie, the Directorate General for Simplification and Digital Transformation of the FOD/SPF Policy and Support, but also with the GBA/APD, the BCA and the CCB.
- The draft Artificial Intelligence Act requires the Member States to designate a notifying authority that needs to be organised in such a way that decisions relating to the notification of conformity assessment bodies are taken by competent persons different from those who carried out the assessment of those bodies. The draft explicitly provides that Member States may designate a national accreditation body referred to in Regulation 765/2008 for market surveillance and the marketing of products. The Member States must ensure that they have all the necessary resources to carry out their tasks.[30]

  The draft Artificial Intelligence Act in Belgium is considered to be primarily concerned with competences of the FOD/SPF Economie, the FSMA, the BIPT/IBPT and the GBA/APD.
- The draft Cybersecurity Act differs from the other legislative initiatives because its 'hub' is not the Commission but the European Union Agency for Cybersecurity (ENISA). Its Board consists of representatives of the

---

25 Directive 2020/1828 art 31(4).

26 Directive 2020/1828 art 31(2)(b).

27 Regulation 2016/679 of the European Parliament and of the Council of 27 April 2016 on the protection of natural persons with regard to the processing of personal data and on the free movement of such data, and repealing Directive 95/46 (General Data Protection Regulation – GDPR), art 68.

28 Regulation 2022/868 of the European Parliament and of the Council of 30 May 2022 on European data governance and amending Regulation 2018/1724 (Data Governance Act) [2022] OJ L152/1, art 23.

29 Regulation 2022/868 arts 26–27.

30 Proposal for a Regulation of the European Parliament and of the Council Laying Down Harmonised Rules on Artificial Intelligence (Artificial Intelligence Act) and amending certain union legislative acts COM(2021) 206 final, arts 30 and 59.

Member States (no reference to national competent authorities) and the Commission.[31] For issues covered by a European cybersecurity scheme, national schemes can no longer be applicable and the relevant national certification authorities will be involved in the application of the European schemes. The draft explicitly requires that the activities of national certification authorities relating to the issuance of European cybersecurity certificates must be strictly separated from their supervisory activities under the Act. The Member States must ensure that they have all the necessary resources to carry out their tasks.[32]

There will be an ENISA Advisory Group consisting of experts representing relevant stakeholders, a Stakeholder Cybersecurity Certification Group also consisting of experts representing relevant stakeholders and a National Liaison Officers Network with representatives of the Member States.[33]

The draft Cybersecurity Act in Belgium is considered to be primarily concerned with competences of the CCB, the FOD/SPF Economie, the Central Bank, the FSMA and the GBA/APD.

22. Seen from the Belgian perspective, there is manifestly a need for an effective digital governance platform in Belgium where all the relevant authorities and bodies can meet. And given the significant differences between the various legislative initiatives, it seems at least as important that the platform provides for working parties of the federal and regional institutions and bodies that share competences in respect of a specific legislative initiative.

23. Given the EU and Belgian law provisions on the independence of the relevant institutions, it seems, at least in respect of DMA, DSA and Data Act issues and a participation of e.g. the BCA, the GBA/APD, the BIPT/IBPT or the FSMA, excluded that the platform or its working parties might develop into decision-making bodies. And this would also apply if one would attempt to bring boards or advisory bodies set up in respect of the different legislative initiatives together in a horizontal cooperation at the EU level.

24. The 'digital governance model' can therefore, as in respect of the DMA and subject to what follows concerning the specific role of competition authorities, be described as a juxtaposition of clusters in which each relevant national authority can coordinate its positions with colleagues and the Commission in their respective networks and may exchange non-confidential information with national colleagues who are members of a different EU network.

B. *The BCA and Other Legislative Initiatives*

25. The BCA, the GBA/APD, the BIPT/IBPT and the FSMA each have, subject to the jurisdiction of the courts, exclusive competences with regard to the enforcement of their respective legislations. The relations between the abovementioned

31 Proposal for a Regulation of the European Parliament and of the Council Amending Regulation 2019/881 as regards managed security services (Draft Cybersecurity Act) COM(2023) 208 final, art 14.

32 Draft Cybersecurity Act art 58.

33 Draft Cybersecurity Act arts 21–23.

regulations are in Belgium therefore determined by the relations between the competences of the relevant authorities.

26. Article 1(6) of the DMA explicitly provides that it has no impact on the applicability of the EU and national rules of competition. We may assume that this also applies to the other legislative initiatives concerning the digital transformation. It follows that, with the exception of the European Commission and the courts, and subject to the *ne-bis in idem* case law,[34] only the BCA can decide that an infringement in Belgium of one of the 'digital legislations' constitutes also an infringement of the rules of competition (Articles IV.1 or 2 CEL or Articles 101 or 102 TFEU).

27. But the BCA should in my opinion, at least in the absence of a sufficiently clear precedent from the competent regulator or the courts, refer the question whether there has been an infringement to the competent regulator. In the *BPost* case the CJEU ruled moreover that parallel proceedings in respect of the same facts of authorities enforcing legislations that pursue distinct objectives must be coordinated.

28. This leaves at least two questions. First, while in the case of parallel proceedings one knows who to coordinate with, it is in the absence of a clearly identified enforcing authority, less clear who to refer to, even in the case where several have been designated as competent national authorities. Clear, sufficiently precise designation decisions are therefore important for a correct balancing of the respective regulatory regimes.

29. And second, what degree of coordination is required in the absence of a cooperation agreement between the relevant authorities allowing for the exchange of confidential case related information? At present the BCA only has such cooperation agreements with the BIPT/IBPT (and with the energy regulator CREG). Discussions have started with the GBA/APD.

III. Conclusion: the DMA as a Piece of a Wider Cosmos of EU and National Legislative Initiatives for Digital Transformation?

30. The DMA is expected to be a laboratory for the development of both competition law and policy and of the cooperation between the Commission and national competition authorities in the enforcement of the EU rules of competition. This is most welcome as competition authorities search for a better balance between *ex post* and *ex ante* tools that helps them to give timely guidance to fast moving markets.

31. Given the impact of designated gatekeepers on the digital environment at national and EU level, the DMA is definitely an important component of the legislative toolkit for the governance of the digital transformation.

---

[34] Case C-117/20 *bpost SA v Autorite Belge de la Concurrence* ECLI:EU:C:2022:202, see Francis Donnat, *Ne bis in idem : La Cour de justice de l'Union européenne précise sa jurisprudence sur le principe ne bis in idem au regard de l'articulation entre réglementation sectorielle et droit de la concurrence et au regard de l'utilisation dans deux Etats membres des mêmes faits (Bpost) (Nordzucker)*, CONCURRENCES No. 2-2022, art. No. 106654.

32. The ‘digital governance model’ can be described as a juxtaposition of clusters in which each relevant national authority can coordinate its positions with colleagues and the Commission in their respective networks, and may exchange non-confidential information with colleagues who are members of a different EU network. Given the fact that we may assume that none of the legislative initiatives impact on the application of EU and national rules of competition (as is explicitly stipulated in Article 1(6) DMA), the DMA and its interaction with competition law is likely to be a laboratory for the complex interactions between regulatory clusters and with competition authorities. Competition authorities were already instrumental in the development of DMA prohibitions applicable to gatekeepers. These have been characterised (and sometimes criticised) as a codification of the case law on Article 102 TFEU. National competition authorities will continue to contribute to the enforcement of these prohibitions either directly or as members of the ECN, and by developing the relevant concepts when enforcing national rules in infringement cases or when imposing remedies.[35]

[35] See, on the earlier the interaction between competition law and sector regulations e.g. J Steenbergen, ‘*(Geliberaliseerde)openbare diensten en EU regelgeving*’ in H Cousy and others, *Liber Amicorum Walter van Gerven, Kluwer* (Deurne 2000) 427–448. And for an example of a decisions with remedies and reference to the GDPR: Decision BMA-2019-C/C-16, *Telenet/De Vijver* of 13 May 2019, see Simon Vande Walle, *Sole control: The Belgian Competition Authority clears a vertical merger in the audiovisual sector, subject to conditions (De Vijver Media / Telenet)*, Concurrences No. 3-2019, art. No. 91429, pp. 120–122.

No Particular Experience against Gatekeepers and an Increasing Focus on the Digital Sector

Bulgaria

PETAR PETROV*

University of Economics and Business (WU)

Abstract

Effective competition in digital markets is among the top priorities of the Bulgarian competition authority. Nonetheless, its current decisional practice does not focus on competition issues in the digital economy. Moreover, there are no specific provisions in the Bulgarian Competition Act on competition enforcement in digital markets. Over the past few years, the Bulgarian legislator has pursued the implementation into Bulgarian law of the recent EU initiatives in the digital sector.

---

* Petar Petrov is Teaching and Research Associate with the Competition and Digitalisation Work Group at the Vienna University of Economics and Business (WU) and a PhD candidate at the WU. His doctoral research focuses on the special responsibility of gatekeepers under EU competition law. Petar has clerked with the European Commission's Directorate-General for Competition, the Bulgarian Ministry of Finance and the Bulgarian Ministry for Foreign Affairs. He has worked in the fields of competition law with international law firms in Brussels, Luxembourg and Munich and is qualified to practice law in Belgium. He is a junior member of the Academic Society for Competition Law and the French Association for Competition Law (AFEC)

I. Introduction: General Views from Bulgaria

1. In Bulgarian law, antitrust infringements and national merger control are covered by the Law on Protection of Competition (*Закон за защита на конкуренцията* – LPC).[1] The latest amendment to the LPC entered into force in February 2021, transposing the ECN+ Directive of the European Parliament and of the Council of 11 December 2018, having for objective to empower the competition authorities of the Member States to be more effective enforcers and to ensure the proper functioning of the internal market.[2] The LPC in its latest version contains no particular provisions on competition law enforcement in digital markets nor any references to the Digital Markets Act (DMA).[3]

2. Effective competition in digital markets is among the top priorities of the Bulgarian competition authority, the Commission for Protection of Competition (CPC) in its 2024,[4] 2023[5] and 2022[6] priorities reports. Nonetheless, the decisional practice of the CPC seems not to focus on competition issues in the digital economy. For instance, the CPC has reviewed only one complaint against Microsoft for alleged abuse of dominant position under Article 102 TFEU and Section 21 LPC, ultimately dismissing the alleged unilateral conduct.[7] Furthermore, the CPC has not opened any inquiry for abuse of dominance or vertical restraints of competition by other high-tech giants, such as Apple, Amazon, Facebook, Google or TikTok. Nor has it opened an in-depth investigation into takeovers by any of these undertakings.

3. The Electronic Communications Act (*Закон за електронните съобщения* – ECA) lays down the regulatory framework for the sector of electronic communications.[8] The ECA includes various provisions on personal data protection, yet none related to competition law enforcement in the digital economy. Nor does it contain any references as to the application of the DMA by national jurisdictions, the CPC or other national regulatory bodies. Nonetheless, the recent amendments to the

---

1 Law on Protection of Competition, State Gazette No 102/2008 as amended up to 26 February 2021.

2 Directive 2019/1 of the European Parliament and of the Council of 11 December 2018 to empower the competition authorities of the Member States to be more effective enforcers and to ensure the proper functioning of the internal market [2019] OJ L11/3.

3 Regulation 2022/1925 of the European Parliament and of the Council of 14 September 2022 on contestable and fair markets in the digital sector and amending Directives 2019/1937 and 2020/1828 (Digital Markets Act or DMA) [2022] OJ L265/1.

4 Commission for Protection of Competition, Commission for Protection of Competition Priorities for 2024 in the Initiation of Proceedings under Chapters 9 and 12 of the Law on Protection of Competition, recital 2 <https://www.cpc.bg/media/about-kzk/annual-reports/KZK2024.pdf>accessed on 26 March 2024.

5 Commission for Protection of Competition, Commission for Protection of Competition Priorities for 2023 in the Initiation of Proceedings under Chapters 9 and 12 of the Law on Protection of Competition, recital 2;https://cpc.bg/media/about-kzk/annual-reports/%D0%9F%D1%80%D0%B8%D0%BE%D1%80%D0%B8%D1%82%D0%B5%D1%82%D0%B82023.docx > accessed on 24 February 2024.

6 Commission for Protection of Competition, Commission for Protection of Competition Priorities for 2022 in the Initiation of Proceedings under Chapters 9 and 12 of the Law on Protection of Competition, recital 2 <https://www.cpc.bg/media/about-kzk/annual-reports/%D0%9F%D1%80%D0%B8%D0%BE%D1%80%D0%B8%D1%82%D0%B5%D1%82%D0%B82023.docx> accessed on 24 February 2024.

7 Decision No 374-19 *Microsoft Ireland Operation Ltd and Microsoft Bulgaria EOOD*, March 2014.

8 Electronic Communications Act, State Gazette No 41/2007 as amended up to 6 October 2023.

ECA provide for compliance with the provisions and the objectives of the Digital Services Act (DSA).[9]

II. Actions Undertaken by Bulgaria to Facilitate the Integration and to Enhance Synergies between EU and National Legislation for the Digital Sector

4. The following section contains an overview of Bulgaria's competition policy regarding digital markets, the new framework on contracts for the supply of digital content and digital services, and the newest developments related to the enforcement of the DSA.

1. Competition Policy

5. Under Decision No 80/27.01.2022 the CPC adopted its annual priorities for the initiation of proceedings for breaches of antitrust rules and unfair trade practices.[10] In the area of antitrust enforcement, the CPC's activity focused on the investigation and sanctioning of cartel agreements and bid-rigging, which are extremely damaging to the market structure, and the competitive process between undertakings.

6. The specific sectors subject to a priority scrutiny by the CPC include the health sector, energy, fuels, food production and trade. In the CPC's view, these sectors must be given priority in its enforcement activities due to their structural importance to the Bulgarian economy and their likelihood of significantly affecting the competitive process in other economic sectors, thus directly affecting consumer's welfare.

7. In 2022, the CPC further prioritised antitrust monitoring and enforcement in the field of the digital economy as well as with regards to sustainability agreements. Indeed, the CPC takes into account the fact that these emerging markets are the subject of particular attention and action by the competition authorities of a number of EU Member States due to their high importance for developing the competitiveness of national economies, innovation and promoting sustainable infrastructure.

8. Another major priority for the CPC is enforcement against anticompetitive conduct (Chapter 7 of the LPC) and unloyal trade practices in the agriculture and food supply chain (the new Chapter 7B of the LPC). Priority is further given to allegations of misleading advertising of food supplements, medicines and medical devices applied to viral diseases, and the alleged effects and properties of such products when advertised. Further scrutiny is foreseen in the tourism, restaurant, and amusement outlets branches, the e-commerce sector and other fields of the digital economy.[11]

---

9 Regulation 2022/2065 of the European Parliament and of the Council of 19 October 2022 on a Single Market for Digital Services and amending Directive 2000/31 (the Digital Services Act or DSA) [2022] OJ L277/1, art 9 and art 21.

10 Commission for Protection of Competition Priorities for 2022 (n 6).

11 Commission for Protection of Competition Priorities for 2022 (n 6).

9. Further, by Decision No 101/26.01.2023 and Decision No 79/25.01.2024, the CPC laid down its enforcement priorities in 2023[12] and 2024[13] respectively. Among others, the CPC continues to prioritise antitrust compliance in the dynamic digital economy (including e-commerce) and sustainability agreements. The CPC explains that observations in recent years have shown that the 'opening up' of certain markets and services to new entrants and new services can foster even more innovation and greater benefits for consumers in a far more dynamic and competitive technological environment, but also the possibility of monitoring new and less well-known forms of anti-competitive behaviours that seek the exclusion of competitors from the relevant markets.

2. Supply of Digital Content and Digital Services

10. On 19 March 2021 the Act on the Supply of Digital Content and Digital Services and on the Sale of Goods (the "Act") was promulgated.[14] The Act implements into Bulgarian law the requirements laid down by Directive 2019/770 on certain aspects concerning contracts for the supply of digital content and digital services[15] and Directive 2019/771 on certain aspects concerning contracts for the sale of goods.[16] Entered into force on 1 January 2022, the Act introduces amendments to the existing consumer protection framework, including the exercise of rights to reclamation due to the lack of conformity of goods outside of digital content and digital services.

11. The scope of the Act is limited only to contractual relationships between providers and consumers. It lays down the rights of consumers with regard to contracts for both the supply of digital content and digital services and the sale of goods whereas matters related to the delivery of goods and unfair commercial practices remain within the current scope of the Bulgarian Consumer Protection Act.[17] Further, the Act provides that the parties should agree on any arrangements, which restrict existing consumer rights or envisage less favourable terms and conditions, including references to the governing law of a non-EU state.

12. These standards apply regardless of whether a service is provided for consideration or in exchange for the consent of consumers to have their personal data used by a digital content provider. They are also applicable to scenarios where a provider acts in accordance with a consumer's preferences and where content or a service is supplied on a tangible medium. However, the Act does not apply to cases in which content or a service is provided free of charge and the provider uses consumer data only for the purposes of the supply. Moreover, it introduces rules on the lack of conformity of provided digital content and services, such as the incompatibility with the operating system of a consumer's device and incomplete installation instructions.

---

12 Commission for Protection of Competition Priorities for 2023 (n 5).

13 Commission for Protection of Competition Priorities for 2024 (n 4).

14 Act on the Supply of Digital Content and Digital Services and on the Sale of Goods, State Gazette No 23/2021.

15 Directive 2019/770 of the European Parliament and of the Council of 20 May 2019 on certain aspects concerning contracts for the supply of digital content and digital services [2019] OJ L136/1.

16 Directive 2019/771 of the European Parliament and of the Council of 20 May 2019 on certain aspects concerning contracts for the sale of goods, amending Regulation 2017/2394 and Directive 2009/22, and repealing Directive 1999/44 [2019] OJ L136/28.

17 Consumer Protection Act, State Gazette No 99/2005 as amended up to 8 December 2023.

The specific standards introduced by the Act also include providers' obligation to supply the content or service without undue delay. Furthermore, providers should maintain the content or services, including the supply of updates to consumers, for the period covered by the contract or, in cases of contracts without any fixed term, for the period in which the consumer could reasonably expect such maintenance.

13. Where content or a service is accessible for a specific period of time, providers may change it only under certain conditions, i.e. where this is needed to ensure conformity with a supply agreement. For that purpose, supply agreements should contain clauses explicitly laying down such conditions. Further, such changes should not entail any additional costs for consumers. Should they limit consumers' opportunities to use the content or service provided, consumers are entitled to terminate the contract, unless the providers have authorised them to access the content or service in its previous version. Any breach of these rules will enable consumers to seek compensation from the person responsible for the breach, the liability for damage being not limited to the provider having entered into an agreement with the consumer concerned.

14. The Act thus reiterates the requirements of the Consumer Protection Act regarding the conformity of goods with commercial and contract guarantees. The burden of proof is borne by the providers. In the case of lack of conformity, consumers may request the supply of content or a service and, in the event of non-performance, terminate the contract. Alternatively, consumers may request the content or service in question to be brought into conformity or alternatively ask for a proportionate reduction of the price. Some differences to the provisions of the Consumer Protection Act regarding the compensation of damage may appear less straightforward since it can be legitimately assumed that these provisions shall apply to scenarios within the scope of the Act.[18] Indeed, this is an example of the issues resulting from splitting consumer protection rules in various legislative acts, leading to problems in terms of coherence and consistency.

15. The Act lays down completely new rules on digital content and digital services that should be reflected in the general terms and conditions of all providers concerned. Further, e-stores and other platforms that have the obligation to comply with this new framework will have to revise their general terms and conditions.

3. Developments Regarding the Enforcement of the Digital Services Act

16. On 15 December 2023, the Bulgarian Council of Ministers published a draft proposal (the 'Proposal') amending the Electronic Communications Act, aiming to implement the provisions of the Digital Services Act (DSA). The Proposal was subject to public consultation from the date of its publication until 15 January 2024.

17. The DSA aims at harmonising national regulations for intermediary services in the information society. It introduces measures based on their size, and impact as well as potential risks. Unlike the Digital Markets Act that is only enforced by the European Commission (the 'Commission'), the DSA provides for the creation of

18 Act on the Supply of Digital Content and Digital Services and on the Sale of Goods, State Gazette No 23/2021.

enforcement mechanisms at both the EU and national levels. Moreover, Member States have to designate a national Digital Services Coordinator (DSC) in charge of the enforcement of rules for intermediary services providers, while the surveillance of the conduct of very large online platforms and search engines is conferred to the Commission supported by the competent authorities of the Member States.[19]

18. The Proposal[20] lays down the role of the Bulgarian DSC. It further designates the Communications Regulation Commission (CRC) as a national DSC. The CRC is thus in charge of monitoring non-video-sharing intermediary service providers whereas the Council for Electronic Media (CEM) oversees compliance with the Radio and Television Act[21] by providers of video-sharing platforms. The process of personal data pursuant to the DSA, in particular under Articles 26 and 28 on the advertisement on online platforms and online protection of minors, is monitored by the Commission for Personal Data Protection.

19. The Proposal further provides for a procedure for the designation of trusted flaggers and vetted researchers under the DSA as well as a mechanism for handling complaints by users against intermediary service providers. Applicants for the status of 'trusted flagger' must submit a request to the CRC, providing information and declarations on their expertise, activity and independence from any online platform service provider pursuant to Article 22 of the DSA. Moreover, they should provide evidence of compliance and/or references to public registers.

20. Under the Proposal, a vetted researcher status is to be granted specifically for investigations requiring access to data from very large online platforms or search engines in Bulgaria. Applicants, (both individuals or entities) must submit applications containing evidence of compliance or provide information from public registries.

21. The Proposal grants the CRC the power to initiate scrutiny into trusted flaggers and vetted researchers. Should an inquiry indicate non-compliance with the DSA, the CRC shall issue a decision, allowing the parties concerned to present their observations within a seven-day period. The CRC may then set a one-month deadline for aligning activities with the DSA. The Proposal further contains provisions regarding the trusted flagger status, including rules on the acquisition and the revocation of this status. The CRC may initiate compliance investigations into trusted flaggers, potentially resulting in temporary suspension, permanent revocation or reinstatement of this status.

22. The Proposal also lays down a regulatory framework regarding the certification of bodies for out-of-court dispute settlement between service recipients and online platform providers under the DSA. It contains detailed provisions regarding the certification and revocation procedures, as well as the authority of the DSC to initiate investigations into its implementation and compliance with the requirements of the DSA.

---

19 Digital Services Act art 9 and art 21.

20 Draft Proposal of 15 December 2023 for a Law Amending and Supplementing the Electronic Communications Act.

21 Radio and Television Act, State Gazette No 138/1998 as amended up to 30 December 2023.

III. Conclusion: the DMA as a Piece of a Wider Cosmos of EU and Bulgaria's Legislative Initiatives for Digital Transformation?

23. Just like the DSA, Directive 2019/770, and Directive 2019/771, the DMA will doubtlessly affect the regulatory and enforcement landscape in Bulgaria since it imposes a number of duties and obligations on designated gatekeeper platforms. Similarly to the DSA and both directives, the DMA provides for a reversed burden of proof imposed on digital platform providers. The list of specific obligations and the reversed burden of proof will result in faster and smoother proceedings and a more efficient enforcement of competition rules. At the same time, similarly to the above-mentioned acts, the DMA provides for better protection of consumer interests by keeping digital markets open, fair and contestable. In that sense, it is a follow-up of the Platform to Business (P2B) Regulation[22] that lays down rules regarding the contractual relationships between platform providers and business users.

24. On the other hand, the DSA protects consumer interests and their fundamental rights by laying down clear and proportionate rules granting them more control over content and choice, guaranteeing a stronger protection of children online and limiting consumers' exposure to illegal content. At the same time, the DSA provides for greater democratic control and oversight of platforms while mitigating systemic risks, such as disinformation or the manipulation of public opinion, especially in the context of crisis management and elections. Thus, it fosters innovation, growth and competitiveness while assuring transparency and accountability.

25. Consumer protection and welfare are also major objectives pursued by Directive 2019/770 and Directive 2019/771 implemented into Bulgarian law through the Act. The latter introduces amendments to the consumer protection framework, including the exercise of the right to reclamation due to the lack of conformity of goods outside of digital content and digital services and reiterates the requirements of the Consumer Protection Act regarding the conformity of goods with commercial and contract guarantees. Together with these legislative initiatives, the DMA will guarantee the establishment and the better functioning of a single market for digital services while removing artificial barriers resulting from anticompetitive conducts and aggressive takeovers by major players.

---

22 Regulation 2019/1150 of the European Parliament and of the Council of 20 June 2019 on promoting fairness and transparency for business users of online intermediation services (Platform-to-Business Regulation or P2B-Regulation) [2019] OJ L186/57.

Croatia on its Path to Digital Market Regulation

Croatia

Mirta Kapural*
Croatian Competition Agency

Abstract

Doing business and providing services on line on digital market followed by spreading use of artificial intelligence posed challenges for legislators and for national institutions such as competition authorities implementing the competition rules. The introduction of EU Digital Market Act as the first EU legal document regulating the big on line players-digital platforms provided useful framework for national legislators and practitioners.

The purpose of this chapter is to present Croatian path to adjustment its laws and practices to digital market and new digital instruments.

Firstly, the paper gives the overview of most important legislation and national strategic documents adopted in Croatia in order to foster digitalisation as a priority in business and other areas. The digital Strategy Croatia until 2032 is examined as particularly important because is sets clear goals for digital transformation in the next ten years and defines priority areas of public policies in all segments of the digital ecosystem. From legislation, the Electronic Commerce Act is the main law that regulates business on internet or e-commerce in Croatia and at the same time it transposed the Digital Services Act.

---

* Mirta Kapural PhD is President of Croatian Competition Council.

Secondly, this paper looks at current practice of Croatian Competition Agency (CCA) in digital market. Considering the CCA still does not have concrete cases and thus, relevant decisions applying Competition Act or Articles 101 and 102 TFEU in digital markets, two relevant sector inquires are presented. The latest sector inquiry looked at digital platforms for online food delivery services in Croatia conducted in 2021/2022 and the first sector inquiry in digital sector conducted by the CCA, the provision of online hotel booking services in Croatia commenced at the end of 2019.

Finally, the author presents the efforts of Croatia to implement DMA and coordinating role of the CCA. In that respect, Regulation on the implementation of the DMA empowers the CCA as the designated coordinating body for the implementation of the Digital Markets Act (DMA) at national level. The paper ends with concluding that next steps on the EU and national level are putting into practice DMA Regulation and making the best use of new digital technologies such as AI. One should also note that in this process of digital transformation, competition law remains fulfilling its role with traditional tools but that the NCAs should also be equipped with new knowledge, new experts and should follow new future approaches in competition law.

I. Introduction: General Views from an EU Member State

26. The emergence of digital market as the new type of market providing services and selling goods in online space alongside or as an alternative to traditional shops and the rise in e-commerce has consequently created the need for different practical and legislative approaches both at EU and national level. Croatia like other EU Member States started to adjust its legislation and business practice to this digital reality. To that end, several important strategic documents have been adopted establishing digitalisation as a priority and as an important goal and recognising the need to create a stimulating regulatory and investment environment which has positive effects on development of technology and innovation. To achieve this, it is necessary to enhance digital competences and increase the number of experts such as data analysts and communication technology experts in the private and public sector and by application of advanced technologies in business market activities. The initiatives taken by the Croatian Government are in line and follow the European Digital Agenda for 2020–2030 aimed at fair economy which enhances competition as one of the three key goals. The statistics showed satisfactory levels of digitalisation in Croatian business. According to the Digital Economy and society Index (DESI), Croatian companies use the opportunities offered by internet sales as follows: 29% of small and medium enterprises sell their products on the internet and 13% of revenues come from the internet sales segment.[1] Advanced digital technologies are becoming more and more popular among Croatian companies: 35% are using cloud solutions, 43% use e-invoices and 9% use technologies based on artificial intelligence.[2] In addition, another relevant

---

1 Small and medium enterprises make of 99.8% of economic subjects, undertakings in Croatian economy. Data from Croatian Bureau of Statistics: <https://podaci.dzs.hr/2022/hr/29182> accessed 12 July 2024.

2 See, <https://digital-strategy.ec.europa.eu/hr/policies/desi> accessed 12 July 2024.

factor is the IT industry in Croatia which is constantly growing, it constitutes around 5% of national GDP.

27. The e-commerce in Croatia is well developed with the intention of growing, the current estimation is that Croatian e-commerce market is worth more than 1.3 billion euros in 2024. The estimation is for further growth in e-commerce in coming years, in 2024 it is predicted to grow for more than 13% compared to the previous year. Some of most successful Croatian internet search engines for online sales include *e-kupi.hr* with the largest net income of 51 million euros in 2022, *pevex.hr* online store for home décor and *Konzum* online supermarket for sale of groceries.[3] The majority of popular digital platforms widely used in Croatia are Booking, Wolt, Glovo, Microsoft, Meta, Apple, Alphabet (designated also as gatekeepers in line with the DMA).

28. From the perspective of competition and its rules, e-commerce and digital platforms for use of different services with their special characteristics (interoperability, multisided effects, network effects etc.), in Croatia as in many other EU Member States, it became clear that a new approach in competition law regarding this new market was required. Hence, in Croatia, the Croatian Competition Agency (CCA) started to follow digital markets more closely, including the adoption of the Digital Markets Act (DMA) at the EU level with the aim of setting rules for the big platform-gatekeepers.[4]

1. National Legislative Initiatives Adopted (or Incoming) for the Digital Sector

29. In Croatia, further digitalisation and regulation of the digital sector is recognised as a priority in business, public administration, labour market, education and research and development. For that purpose, several national strategic documents and legal texts were adopted.

A. *Digital Strategy of Croatia until 2032*[5]

30. The Croatian Digital Strategy determines guidelines for accomplishing targeted national transformation towards a green and digital way of life as preconditions for future sustainable economic growth. The strategy sets clear goals for digital transformation in the next ten years and defines priority areas of public policies in all segments of the digital ecosystem: infrastructure, technology, science, education, innovation and competitive markets. This strategy assumes the implementation of advanced technologies such as artificial intelligence (AI), machine learning,

---

3 Goran Pavlović, 'Croatian eCommerce is a growing market with numerous possibilities' (*Hrvatska*, 2024) <https://ecommerce.hr/hrvatski-ecommerce-je-rastuce-trziste-s-brojnim-mogucnostima/> accessed 12 July 2024. See also 'Croatia eCommerce Country Commercial Guide' (2024) <https://www.privacyshield.gov/ps/article?id=Croatia-eCommerce> accessed 12 July 2024.

4 Regulation 2022/1925 of the European Parliament and of the Council of 14 September 2022 on contestable and fair markets in the digital sector and amending Directives 2019/1937 and 2020/1828 (Digital Markets Act or DMA) [2022] OJ L265/1

5 Digital Croatia Strategy for the Period until 2032, Official Gazette No 2/23 16 December 2022 <https://narodne-novine.nn.hr/clanci/sluzbeni/2023_01_2_17.html> accessed 12 July 2024.

cloud computing, big data and blockchain in the public and private sectors. At the same time, it stays open for the implementation of new future technologies which may be developed in this period. The content of the strategy is aligned with the priorities and goals of relevant EU documents, such as the document of the European Commission, 'A Europe Fit for the Digital Age'.[6]

31. One goal of the strategy is to develop and innovate the digital economy through digitalisation and digital transition of the whole economy including industry and services with special emphasis on small and medium enterprises which are on the lower level of digitalisation, which affects their competitiveness.[7]

32. The National Development Strategy of Croatia until 2030 also recognises digitalisation of society and the economy as an important goal to be achieved.[8]

B. *Smart Specialisation Strategy until 2029*

33. This strategy was prepared by Croatian Ministry of the Economy at the end of 2023 and it encompasses also digital products and digital platforms.[9] The focus is on the development of technologies based on artificial intelligence (AI), blockchain via existing companies or new start-ups. The aim of the strategy is to direct development on new innovative and competitive solutions which can be applicable to most world markets. The strategy recognised the need to move away from traditional specific solutions adapted for one user which is neither competitive nor adjustable for competition on the market.

34. Besides the aforementioned national strategic documents, relevant legislation includes the law on e-commerce: the Act on the Implementation of the Regulation 2019/1150 on promoting fairness and transparency for business users of online inter-mediation services and regulation on the transposition of the DMA.

C. *The Electronic Commerce Act*

35. Business on internet or e-commerce in Croatia is regulated by the Electronic Commerce Act,[10] that has transposed the Digital Services Act (DSA) into the Croatian legal system[11]. This Act regulates the obligation of informing and providing commercial communications, e-documents, form and validity of e-contracts, responsibility of the provider of information society services, as well as inspection, supervision and penal provisions. Besides the Electronic Commerce Act,

---

6 European Commission, 'A Europe Fit for the Digital Age' (2024) <https://commission.europa.eu/strategy-and-policy/priorities-2019-2024/europe-fit-digital-age_en> accessed 12 July 2024.

7 Digital Croatia Strategy for the period until 2032, https://rdd.gov.hr/UserDocsImages/SDURDD-dokumenti/Strategija_Digitalne_Hrvatske_final_v1_EN.pdf 24, 32-40.

8 National Development Strategy 2030 of Republic of Croatia; Official Gazette No 13/21. https://digital-skills-jobs.europa.eu/en/actions/national-initiatives/national-strategies/croatia-national-development-strategy-2030

9 National Development Strategy of Croatia until 2030 <https://mingo.gov.hr/UserDocsImages/slike/Vijesti/2022/S3%20do%202029%20Tekst%20VRH%202023%2012%2013.pdf> accessed 12 July 2024. https://digital-skills-jobs.europa.eu/en/actions/national-initiatives/national-strategies/croatia-national-development-strategy-2030

10 Electronic Commerce Act, Official Gazette Nos 173/03, 67/08, 36/09, 130/11, 30/14, 32/19.

11 Regulation 2022/2065 of the European Parliament and of the Council of 19 October 2022 on a Single Market for Digital Services and amending Directive 2000/31 (Digital Services Act or DSA) [2022] OJ L277/1.

e-commerce is also regulated by provisions of the Electronic Money Act, the Trade Act and the Civil Obligations Act. The establishment of digital businesses in Croatia is regulated by the Electronic Commerce Act and the Companies Act. Croatian legislation does not distinguish the requirements and procedures for the establishment of digital businesses from those governing the establishment of brick-and-mortar businesses. Conclusion of agreements on the Internet in business to customer agreements is also regulated by the Electronic Commerce Act providing the obligation of the information society to confirm the receipt of the email containing the offer or the acceptance of the offer to conclude the contract, while in the case of business-to-business contracts this is prescribed only as a possibility.

36. Furthermore, the Act on the Implementation of Regulation 2019/1150 on promoting fairness and transparency for business users of online intermediation services, entered into force on 12 December 2020.[12] It aims to ensure that business users of online intermediation services and corporate website users in relation to online search engines are granted appropriate transparency, fairness and effective redress possibilities, creating at the same time predictable, a sustainable and trusted online business environment within the internal market open to innovation.

2. Landmark National Cases (by NCAs and Courts) in the Digital Realm Backstage of the DMA

37. Although there are still no significant competition cases in the digital market in Croatia, the CCA is closely following digital cases at EU level prior and post adoption of the DMA.

38. Moreover, the CCA conducted two sector inquiries on digital platforms. The latest one is on digital platforms for food delivery conducted in 2021.

A. *Market Study into Online Food Delivery Services in Croatia*[13]

39. In November 2021 the Croatian Competition Agency (CCA) launched a market investigation into the provision of food delivery services via digital platforms in Croatia with the aim of determining all the relevant facts relating to the pricing method for the provision of online food delivery services, inspecting the mutual relations between digital platforms and their most important partners – restaurants and catering establishments, and the mutual relations between the digital platforms and the food delivery workers (mandataries). The reason for carrying out this

---

12 The Act on the Implementation of Regulation 2019/1150 on promoting fairness and transparency for business users of online intermediation services (Zakon o provedbi Uredbe (EU) 2019/1150 o promicanju pravednosti i transparentnosti za poslovne korisnike usluga internetskog posredovanja) , Official Gazette 138/20, 19.12.2020.; Regulation 2019/1150 of the European Parliament and of the Council of 20 June 2019 on promoting fairness and transparency for business users of online intermediation services (Platform-to-Business Regulation or P2B-Regulation) [2019] OJ L186/57.

13 See, 'CCA Carries Out a Market Study into Online Food Delivery in Croatia' (*Aztn*, 2024) <https://www.aztn.hr/en/cca-carries-out-a-market-study-into-on-line-food-delivery-in-croatia/> accessed 12 July 2024.

sectoral inquiry has been the fast-emerging influence of digital platforms in the provision of food delivery services in Croatia. The emphasis of the research was additionally focused on the general terms and conditions used by individual digital platforms that actively provide food delivery services, as well as the contractual relations with restaurants and other catering establishments.

40. The analysis covered the legislative framework and the implementation in the provision of online food delivery services. General indicators of the online food delivery market in Croatia have been determined, such as the turnover of the individual digital platforms, the number of mentioned service users (restaurants and catering facilities) and the pricing and price calculation in the provision of online food delivery services. The understanding of the comparative practice of the European Commission and individual national competition authorities has also been included in the market analysis.

41. With respect to the legislative framework applicable in the provision of food delivery services via digital platforms in Croatia, the research results showed that there are no special provisions regulating the sector concerned. The main source of law in this area is the Electronic Commerce Act.

42. Furthermore, the CCA found that there have been no legal and/or factual entry barriers to the market concerned, that is, the market has not been subject to any detailed *ex ante* regulation. No significant infrastructure is required because the activity is primarily performed through a digital application and the people who work as delivery workers, do this by using their own means of transport. These are services that cannot be performed by just one undertaking in the market.

43. For the purpose of this inquiry, the CCA created a sample of undertakings that primarily provide online food delivery services, i.e. three digital platforms that are dominant in the market concerned: Wolt Zagreb d.o.o., Zagreb, Bolt Services HR d.o.o., Zagreb and GlovoApp Technology d.o.o., Zagreb.

44. The research showed that at the end of 2021 one digital platform provided online food delivery services in the area of 27 towns and cities and covered the territory from the western to the southern part of Croatia, including the four biggest cities: Zagreb, Split, Rijeka and Osijek. The second surveyed digital platform provided these services in the area of 11 towns and cities, also including the cities of Zagreb, Split, Rijeka and Osijek, whereas the third provider of these services has been active in the area of three cities (Zagreb, Split and Osijek) with an expansion plan.

45. Furthermore, based on the statements given by the above-mentioned undertakings active in the provision of online food delivery services, in the second phase of the analysis, the CCA surveyed the users of online food delivery services, i.e. the restaurants and other catering establishments. The survey included a total of the top ten undertakings – restaurants and catering facilities, that have been the partners–service users of the surveyed food delivery digital platforms, according to their turnover from food delivery and/or the number of deliveries in 2020.

46. In relation to the structure of the online food delivery market in Croatia in the period from 2019 to 2021, the research results showed that the undertaking Wolt represented the most significant online food delivery platform. Regarding the importance of the use of digital platforms as an intermediary in comparison with

the total sales of a particular restaurant, the research showed that the share of online food delivery ranged from 14% to 90% and more in the total sales of an individual restaurant.

47. In the part that referred to the way in which the relations with delivery workers (mandataries) as an important stakeholder in the food delivery chain have been regulated, the research results showed that digital platforms used general terms of business and contracts with delivery workers (mandataries). All three digital platforms stated that they perform their activities exclusively as intermediaries between the restaurants, the delivery workers and the persons who orders food. In the research referring to the requirements that must be met by delivery workers, the results of the research have essentially been the same for all three digital platforms.

48. In the research related to the pricing method applied by the digital platforms concerned, the results of the research based on the statements of the three surveyed digital platforms showed that food prices have been regulated by agreement and that the final price has been set independently and freely by the restaurants and other food service providers. There has been an obligation imposed on the restaurants and catering establishments to guarantee the price, concretely, the restaurant (partner) guarantees that the price of service of a particular digital platform would not exceed the price the partner applies when selling its products at its own point of sale, or that the price should not exceed the price offered on competing platforms. In their statements to the CCA, the surveyed restaurants and catering establishments stated that they freely set the final price of food on digital platforms and that the price of the product is identical to the price in their physical stores. In relation to possible restrictions by the digital platform service providers on restaurants related to food prices, delivery conditions and priority of delivery, the research found that there have been no such restrictions.

49. With respect to intermediary fees that online food delivery service providers charge the restaurants and catering establishments, the research results showed that intermediary fees differ between the surveyed digital platforms. As for the way in which the intermediary fee is defined, the interviewed undertakings, owners of restaurants and catering establishments responded that the intermediary fee is subject to contracting or negotiation.

50. Furthermore, the research also covered the fees that online food delivery service providers pay to food delivery workers and the way in which these fees have been calculated. In the case of one of the surveyed digital platforms the fee consisted of three parts: the basic fee, which is the same for each order in a particular delivery area depending on the means of transport, the additional fee for the air distance in kilometres, and in some cities, the bonuses that the courier gets if they meet a certain number of deliveries. The second platform calculated its fees similarly to the first digital platform, although it has described the individual parts of the fee differently. There have been weekly bonuses, additional promotion coefficients and additional top ups in case of unfavourable weather conditions, which has enabled the delivery workers to increase the final remuneration for the services they have provided. The third digital platform has also calculated the remuneration amount based on the distance travelled per kilometre at the same time defining the amount for pick-up and delivery of the order. A minimum pay per delivery has also been defined.

51. In addition, there have been weekly and weekend incentives. These bonus payments have been calculated based on the number of deliveries made by the courier or delivery person during the incentive period. Also, the research revealed a possibility of increasing the pay of the delivery person by the attributable bonus payment multiplier per delivery. Thus, in the case of one of the digital platforms, the highest multiplier has been applied in the evening hours, but it has differed in individual cities although the order has been made through the digital application of the same digital platform. In the case of second digital platform, bonus approval has been additionally elaborated depending on the acceptance rate of the order. One of the surveyed digital platforms has applied the same bonus system for delivery workers, depending on the number of deliveries and the means of transport, but it has made no difference between the places orcities where delivery has been made. The same platform, unlike the other two, has paid different bonuses for different means of transport.

52. Regarding the advertising on digital platforms and the conditions for advertising the restaurants on these platforms, the application and the functioning of the rating systems for individual restaurants, the research results showed that out of three surveyed digital platforms, one of them has not been engaged in advertising restaurants at all. On the other hand, seven out of ten surveyed restaurants confirmed that they have been using the advertising services on the digital platform. There have been no special advertising requirements for restaurants and the advertising campaigns have been carried out within the regular advertising campaigns of the digital platform concerned.

53. All three surveyed digital platforms have a rating system in place. The rating has been based on those given by the users of the individual digital platform. The surveyed restaurants essentially responded that the rating system has been based on the ratings or experience of the end users and not of the digital platform itself.

54. In this market study, the CCA carried out the analysis of the comparative practice of the European Commission and national competition authorities in the provision of online food delivery services. In that sense, it examined the relevant research studies in online food delivery market made by some national competition authorities.

B. *Sector Inquiry in Online Hotel Booking Services in Croatia*[14]

55. The first sector inquiry in digital area conducted by the CCA was a market inquiry into the provision of online hotel booking services in Croatia. The market inquiry was commenced at the end of 2019 and was carried out during 2020 with all the relevant market indicators in the period between 2017 and 2018.

56. The reason for the market inquiry was, amongst others, the growing influence of the digital economy in the provision of accommodation services globally and

---

14 See 'CCA carried out a market inquiry in the on-line hotel booking sector in the Republic of Croatia' (*Aztn*, 2024) <https://www.aztn.hr/en/cca-carried-out-a-market-inquiry-in-the-on-line-hotel-booking-sector-in-the-republic-of-croatia/> accessed 12 July 2024.

also in the territory of Croatia as a tourist destination country, and the effect of this trend on competition in the relevant market. In the past ten years, the European Commission and a number of national competition authorities (NCAs) and governments have intervened in the online hotel booking sector in the form of market studies, antitrust proceedings and legislation.

57. The aims of the CCA market inquiry were to analyse the legislative framework and its implementation in the provision of online hotel booking services, to define the main indicators of the market position in the provision of hotel online booking services in Croatia and to establish the relevant facts regarding the pricing policy in hotel on-line booking services in the country. Additionally, the aim of the inquiry was to investigate the contractual relationships between the online travel agents and their accommodation partners (hotels, boutique hotels and hostels). The CCA sector inquiry also included the comparative analysis of the relevant inquiries of the European Commission and the NCAs concerned. The CCA sector inquiry included all the actors in the provision of hotel online booking and sales services, the chain including the accommodation facility, the online travel agent and the final customer.

58. The market inquiry was based on a survey including all the categories of stakeholders in the relevant online hotel booking market in the Republic of Croatia (28 accommodation service providers, including the largest hotel chains). In the category of the providers of the accommodation services (hotels etc.) the sample of undertakings included in the survey was based on the data from the publicly available database of the Financial Agency, including the undertakings engaged in the provision of accommodation and food services. For the purposes of obtaining a better sample, the undertakings concerned have been grouped depending on their size (large and medium-sized undertakings) and the locality of the accommodation facilities. The geographic locations included the territory from Istria County to Dubrovnik-Neretva County, as well as the continental part of Croatia (Zagreb and the north and south of Croatia).

59. For the sample to be more representative the criterion regarding the type of the accommodation (hotels, boutique hotels, hostels and spa resorts) was also included. The survey also included the online travel agents (OTA).

60. With respect to the structure of the hotel online booking market in Croatia, the market inquiry showed that the undertaking Booking.com has been the most significant OTA, holding a market share, based on bookings made through OTAs, of 60–70% in 2017 and 70–80% in 2018 with a rising trend. Booking.com was followed by the undertaking Expedia with a market share of 20–30% in 2017 and 10–20% in 2018. These were then followed by other OTAs or platforms, such as Hotelbeds.com, HRS, Prestigia.com, Kuoni Global Travel Services and others, whose market shares were lower than 5%.

61. For the purpose of its market inquiry into the hotel on-line booking sector in Croatia, the CCA also compared its own indicators relating to OTA market shares with the figures indicated in the paper of the findings of the European number one and the world's number three ranking hotel distribution technology provider in hospitality, D-EDGE from October 2019. The latter inquiry involved the evaluation, on the

European level, of more than 200 distribution channels and 680 hotel properties in Europe. Based on this, the comparison of the results showed that the market share of the leading operator in this market, the undertaking Booking.com, but also the market shares of other hotel online booking service providers essentially matched.

62. Relating to the sales channels and hotel booking services used by the accommodation partners in Croatia, the results of the sector inquiry revealed that, as a rule, all undertakings that were included in the survey use the traditional sales channels, such as call centres, walk-in bookings and sales at the reception of the accommodation facility, as well as their own digital platforms on their websites, the direct sales channels. However, the participants of the survey reported that they generally increasingly use sales via OTAs, i.e. indirect sales channels. They reported successfully leveraging other channels – allotment purchase from a tour operator, traditional travel agencies, group rates, a global distribution system (GDS), congress and event sales such as (MICE – Meetings, Incentives, Conferences and Exhibitions) and DMC (Destination Management Companies).

63. Regarding the comparison between the accommodation facilities' own digital platforms and OTA platforms in hotel sales and booking, the CCA sector inquiry showed that in general the individual hotels and chains made more bookings via OTAs than via their own platforms. In addition, in 2018 most of the providers of accommodation facilities that took part in the survey recorded a rise in both online sales channels – on their own web platforms and OTA platforms in comparison with 2017. The number of online bookings via OTAs increased by 42% in 2018 in comparison with 2017, whereas the rise in online bookings on the platforms of the accommodation facilities themselves increased 24% in 2018 compared with 2017.

64. Considering the OTA commission rates for online hotel bookings, the results of the CCA sector inquiry showed that they differentiated among individual OTAs. Some OTAs charged the same commission rate to a hotel for the invoiced accommodation price payable by the final consumer, whereas some of OTAs applied the commission rate that ranges between certain percentages. The amount charged depends on the size of undertakings.

65. Furthermore, in its sector inquiry the CCA wanted to establish whether there had been an upfront number of accommodation units (rooms) within the total accommodation capacity that had been reserved by the accommodation provider for online booking, and if so, how this share had been determined. All but one of the participants of the survey stated that there had been no upfront shares of accommodation capacity in the total facility capacity that would be intended or reserved for online booking.

66. In addition, the CCA sector inquiry included a thorough analysis of the general terms of business of OTAs and the provisions contained in the agreements that OTAs concluded with the accommodation partners (hotels etc.).The investigation into the application of the parity clauses (most-favoured nation clause, MFN) in the contracts OTAs concluded with the hotels showed that the parity clauses are a constituent part of the general terms of business and/or the agreements with accommodation partners. A number of general terms of business and contracts with OTAs contained either a wide parity clause or a narrow party clause.

67. The comparative approach to the EU practice included the study of all the recent and relevant activities of the European Commission and the NCAs in the online hotel booking market.

3. Overlapping Issues between EU and National Regulations for the Digital Sector

68. In the process of preparing the legislation to adopt the regulation for implementation of the DMA in Croatia there were no overlapping issues that emerged. Explaining to the public what the DMA is regulating and who is competent for what, in other words, understanding that EC will be competent for DMA implementation and what will be the role of the CCA, is more the issue.

69. However, there is one good example in the sector inquiry in online hotel booking and its relevance for DMA. In 2024, after the DMA entered into force and started its implementation, Booking.com was designated as a gatekeeper which has special importance for Croatia as a tourist country with tourism being a very significant branch of economy.[15] This means that now Booking.com will have to align its business activities and practices with the provisions of the DMA and it will be unified in the whole EU territory and not as was previously the case, i.e. individually from one EU country to another. In that respect, there is no doubt that Croatia will strongly benefit from alignment of Booking.com's business with the new DMA rules.

II. Actions Undertaken by the EU Member State to Facilitate the Integration and Enhance Synergies between EU and National Legislation for the Digital Sector

1. Best Practice in the Application of Articles 1(5), 1(6), 38(7) and 39 of the DMA

A. *The Tools for Collaboration in the Implementation of the DMA*

70. Within the ECN several good mechanisms are established for the collaboration in the implementation of the DMA: the High-level Group, Digital Markets Advisory Committee and ECN Digital Working Group, including data science and AI. The CCA is included in the last two, there is one representative from the CCA in the advisory committee on the level of vice-president of the Competition Council and one representative of the relevant Ministry of the Economy. The expert team of the CCA are members of the ECN Digital Working Group. All three tools and especially the High-level Group consisting of relevant EU regulators are excellent examples of collaboration between the EC and national authorities of

15 National revenue from tourism in 2023 amounted to 14,6bn EUR and 19,6% GDP. Croatian National Bank, 'Record Revenues from Tourism in the Third Quarter of 2023' (29 December 2023) <https://www.hnb.hr/-/rekordni-prihodi-od-turizma-u-trecem-tromjesecju-2023> accessed 12 July 2024.

the EU Member States, helping to create the best possible practice, and expertise with the aim of ensuring that the DMA and other sectoral regulations applicable to gatekeepers are implemented in a coherent and complementary manner.[16] The ECN High-level Group recognised the need for a coordinated enforcement through the choice of appropriate regulatory instruments and other means to support cooperation fostering a consistent approach to ensure effective cooperation within the DMA and other instruments. In addition to that, many NCAs of EU Member States regularly publish useful papers on digital market topics and ECN has started to organise dedicated conferences about DMA.[17] The CCA is closely following such papers and attending national and international events on digital markets and their regulation.

B. *Coordination between EU Asymmetric Regulation and Public and Private Enforcement by NCAs and National Courts*

71. Considering that the DMA will not affect the competence of the NCAs to apply Articles 101 and 102 TFEU, the CCA has already investigated, and will continue to investigate general terms of contracts applied by digital platforms containing such contractual terms towards its business-to-business users of services in the context of the implementation of Articles 101 and 102 TFEU or corresponding national provisions.[18]

72. In relation to private enforcement at national courts, in Croatia there are practically no cases for breach of competition rules and damages claims based on the breach of competition law at competent commercial courts.[19] This applies not specifically to the digital sector where there are still no competition cases at national level but to the whole set of competition enforcement. Hence, in that sense there is a certain asymmetry between prevailing public enforcement by the competition authority and weak private enforcement by courts applying to all sectors including the digital sector.

C. *Legislative Mechanisms Provided at National Level to Ensure Coordination with EU Regulations*

73. Whereas the EC will have the role of the enforcer, the NCAs in many EU countries will have the role as designated body for coordination and support to the EC in applying DMA and will deal more with digital cases. In Croatia, regulation on the implementation of the DMA empowers the CCA as the designated coordinating

---

16 Commission Decision of 23.3.2023 on setting up the High-level Group for the Digital Markets Act C(2023) 1833 final <https://competition-policy.ec.europa.eu/system/files/2023-03/High_Level_Group_on_the_DMA_0.pdf> accessed 12 July 2024.

17 For example, ACM, 'Registration for the ECN Digital Markets Act Conference 2024 is now open' (8 May 2024) <https://www.acm.nl/en/publications/registration-ecn-digital-markets-act-conference-2024-now-open> accessed 12 July 2024.

18 Croatian Competition Act, arts 8 and 13, Official Gazette Nos 79/09, 80/13, 41/21.

19 For more detailed analysis see Jasminka Pecotic Kaufman, 'How to Facilitate Damage Claims? Private Enforcement of Competition Rules in Croatia – Domestic and EU Law Perspective' (2012) 7 Yearbook of Antitrust and Regulatory Studies.

body for the implementation of the Digital Markets Act (DMA) at national level.[20] The Croatian regulation has been adopted in order to safeguard the harmonised application and enforcement of this regulation, ensuring proper implementation framework for the implementation of the EU *acquis Communautaire.* This legal solution is in line with Article 38, paragraph 7 of the DMA and the obligation of EU Member States to ensure the implementation of the DMA with cooperation of the competent national authority by the application of national competition rules against gatekeepers.

74. The Croatian Regulatory Authority for Network Industries (HAKOM) has been elected as coordination body for the implementation of the Digital Services Act (DSA) in addition to its role as the regulatory body responsible for internet access tariffs and charges.[21]

75. The issues of personal data protection are supervised by the Croatian Personal Data Protection Agency (AZOP).

III. Conclusion: The DMA-the first legal instrument for broader digital transformation in the EU

76. The platforms for digital services and new technologies such as artificial intelligence (AI) strongly impact societies and economies. The innovations in question have redefined the way people communicate, shop, conduct business or access information on internet. Consequently, this has led to the need to regulate digital platforms based on digital strategy aiming to create more secure and open single digital markets in the EU with emphasis on rights of users and fair competition. The regulation was accomplished with the adoption of two important legal acts modernising EU legislation on digital services (DSA) and digital markets (DMA) Acts. The DMA sets the rules for undertakings designated as gatekeepers more sensitive to unfair practices including services such as internet search engines, social media and cloud computing. The DMA can be absolutely considered as the most important piece of legislation for the further digital transformation of law and procedures and regulation in the EU. Such wider EU legislative initiatives have already been developed soon after the DMA in the form of the Act on artificial intelligence (AI) and Act on cyber security. The new EU AI Act can be considered as a very comprehensive and risk-based legislative framework.[22] The goal of the AI Act is to address different risks that can occur by AI (health, safety and fundamental rights) and at the same time to promote innovation and benefits of AI.

---

20 Regulation 2022/1925, Official Gazette No 131/2023 (2 November 2023) <https://narodne-novine.nn.hr/clanci/sluzbeni/2023_11_131_1799.html> accessed 12 July 2024.

21 Regulation 2022/2065, Decision of the Government on the coordinator for digital services, Official Gazette Nos 19/24 (15 February 2024) <https://narodne-novine.nn.hr/clanci/sluzbeni/2024_02_19_306.html> accessed 12 July 2024.

22 Regulation (EU) 2024/1689 of the European Parliament and of the Council of 13 June 2024 laying down harmonised rules on artificial intelligence and amending Regulations (EC) No 300/2008, (EU) No 167/2013, (EU) No 168/2013, (EU) 2018/858, (EU) 2018/1139 and (EU) 2019/2144 and Directives 2014/90/EU, (EU) 2016/797 and (EU) 2020/1828 (Artificial Intelligence Act), OJ L, 2024/1689, 12.7.2024.

77. In relation to competition and application of the DMA, from the competition enforcement aspect it is positive that the possibility to conduct proceedings based on the Articles 101 and 102 TFEU or corresponding national provisions still remains in practice because it should not be forgotten that DMA is *ex ante* regulation and tools used in antitrust cases are complementary with the DMA but at the same time the DMA with its tools cannot replace traditional tools and goals of competition law. Another benefit of the DMA for the NCAs is that they will be able to save their resources and direct their investigation and research to other undertakings in a dominant position, but which are not designated as gatekeepers, and which are outside of scope of the DMA. Moreover, in situations with suspicion that certain practices might be harmful, the task of the NCAs will include concrete investigation considering that in every national market there are active digital platforms which might be dominant but that are not at the same time designated as gatekeepers. The national competition authorities will also have an important role filling the gaps caused by the introduction of the DMA. In order to be able to do that properly, NCAs have to be stronger and better equipped with more resources for education in digital markets for its staff and with the new types of experts necessary for future digital cases, such as data analysts or IT engineers.

78. The implementation of the DMA is still in its early stage, hence there is sas yet no case law on DMA so it remains to be seen how successful its application will be. The success of DMA will depend on the contribution of the business community and on clear guidelines for undertakings on how to best comply with its rules. Here the role of national digital coordinator between the different bodies could also be helpful for their implementation. The High-level Group for the DMA will continue to exchange enforcement experience and regulatory expertise relevant to the implementation and enforcement of the DMA and also with regard to AI. The level of development of national strategies in digital or AI areas will also have significant impact on the success of the DMA and the implementation of the AI Act.

79. In Croatia the number of companies dealing with aspect of digital business is constantly growing as are new digital platforms and apps, so too is the interest for all digitally related topics like digital market, IA, platforms and data management which can be observed from many public events (lectures, roundtables, conferences) dedicated to those issues where different experts discuss them. One especially interesting example is the launch of the Academy for AI for undertakings in the Croatian Chamber of Commerce in March 2024. The aim is to educate undertakings and their employees how to use AI more successfully and adequately in their business activities. This education is support by the digital transformation of the Croatian economy. Croatia has legislation in place with legal frameworks and strategic documents such as the Digital Strategy and as an EU Member State it must follow EU legislation and adapt its national legislation. In the Digital Strategy of Croatia until 2032, all mentioned areas are covered and taken into account with the priority of creating a developed and innovative digital economy. For example, on cybersecurity: 'In further development of digital economy and

society it is necessary to permanently include cyber security and, in that manner, to ensure the trust in digital technology and in process of digital transformation'.[23]

80. From everything outlined above it is clear that with the adoption of first important legislation on EU and national level, a new era of the digital world and market, has taken place. The next stage would be to put this regulation into practice and to control and direct large digital platforms from potentially harmful practices for consumers and the economy. At the same time, it is very important to put new digital technologies such as AI to good use, in order to benefit from them, especially in the field of health, education, labour, the environment and business in general. In that process of digital transformation, competition law with its traditional tools should remain in place but the NCAs should also be equipped with new knowledge, new experts and should follow new approaches in competition law if such an approach is developed over time. Croatia will continue its path to digital regulation in all sectors by supporting its digital business and continuously following best EU practices.

23 Digital Croatia Strategy until 2032, page 37.

Digital Markets not a Clear Priority

Czech Republic

MICHAL PETR*
Palacky University

Abstract

The digital economy is not a priority of Czech competition law. It does not have any specific legislation addressing the gatekeepers or other significant undertakings in digital markets. The number of cases from digital economy is very limited. The adoption of the Digital Markets Act did not change anything in this regard. Implementation of the DMA is very brief. The Czech Competition Authority will not be empowered to carry out investigations of compliance with the DMA. Among professionals, there does not seem to be a demand for a stronger national competition policy vis-à-vis the digital markets.

* Dr Michal Petr, Professor of law and head of the Centre for Competition Law at Palacky University in Olomouc, Czech Republic. He specialises in competition law since 2003, when he joined the Czech Competition Authority; he has worked as its Vice Chairman from 2010–2015. He has widely published on the issues of Czech and EU competition law. Email: michal.petr@upol.cz.

I. Introduction

1. In the Czech Republic, the digital economy does not seem to be a priority of competition policy. Czech competition law does not have any provisions concerning specifically digital markets. There is no Czech legislation addressing gatekeepers in a way similar to the Digital Markets Act (DMA).[1] Over the last ten years, enforcement activities of the Czech Competition Authority (CCA) focused on only two 'digital' cases. Private enforcement is almost non-existent in the Czech Republic, even though digital markets stand for a significant exception.

2. In this report, the next section will provide an overview of Czech application of competition law in digital markets; both legislation and enforcement activities will be discussed. The third section will be concerned with implementation of the DMA and its potential interaction with other pieces of Czech legislation.

II. Overview of Czech Legislation and Enforcement

3. In this section, Czech competition legislation will first be briefly outlined. Thereafter, we will discuss relevant policy statements of the CCA and the most notable cases of Czech public and private enforcement.

1. Legislation

4. Czech competition law is codified in the Act on the Protection of Competition (APC).[2] It prohibits anticompetitive agreements[3] and abuse of dominance[4] in a way fully compatible with Articles 101 and 102 TFEU;[5] indeed, Czech courts maintain, that the interpretation of Czech competition law needs to be fully in line with EU legislation even in cases without the EU dimension, when only the Czech law is applied.[6] The Czech law is not stricter than EU law in any regard. Thus, the provisions of Czech law on anticompetitive agreements and abuse of dominance may thus be considered the national competition rules in the meaning of Article 1(6) b) of the DMA.

5. The APC is applicable in all areas of the economy; it does not contain specific rules for any sector, including the digital economy. Thus, there are no national competition rules prohibiting other forms of unilateral conduct in the meaning of Article 1(6)(c) of the DMA.

---

1 Regulation 2022/1925 of the European Parliament and of the Council of 14 September 2022 on contestable and fair markets in the digital sector and amending Directives 2019/1937 and 2020/1828 (Digital Markets Act or DMA) [2022] OJ L265/1.

2 Act on the Protection of Competition (APC) No 143/2001 Coll., as amended. English translation of the APC may be found on the CCA's website <https://uohs.gov.cz/en/legislation.html> accessed 8 July 2024.

3 APC s 3.

4 APC ss 10 and 11.

5 Michal Petr, *Vztah českého a unijního soutěžního práva (The Relationship between Czech and EU Competition Law)* (CH Beck 2018).

6 Judgment of the Supreme Administrative Court No 7 Afs 78/2008, 25 February 2008.

6. For the sake of completeness, it may be added that even in case of merger review, the Czech system is fully aligned with the EU model. The notification criteria are based on annual turnover of the undertakings concerned;[7] the CCA cannot review any concentration where the criteria are not met. The CCA would prohibit a concentration that would significantly distort competition in the market, especially by creating or strengthening dominant position of the undertakings concerned.[8] There are no specific rules and no exemptions for any area of the economy.

7. In addition to these, the APC also contains a prohibition on public authorities to distort competition by the exercise of their powers;[9] this provision has nonetheless been used so far only for municipal regulation of gambling,[10] never for digital markets.

8. The APC was significantly amended in 2023,[11] the changes were however concerned with the implementation of the ECN+ Directive and with strengthening the investigatory powers of the CCA. The DMA was implemented only in the most minimalistic way: the APC only states that the CCA is entitled to require cooperation of undertakings necessary for the exercise its duties pursuant to the DMA.[12]

9. There is no specific regulation of gatekeepers outside the scope of competition law and no specific rules on the functioning of digital markets in addition to the transposition of relevant EU directives.

2. CCA's Policy Statements Towards Digital Markets

10. The CCA broadly outlines its priorities in its annual reports,[13] albeit in very general terms. In the annual report for 2022, the CCA suggests as its agenda for 2023 that it 'will continue combating hardcore cartel agreements [...] [and] abuse of dominant position through exclusionary practices'.[14] Digital markets are mentioned only indirectly, with regard to vertical agreements: the CCA shall 'continue to sanction in particular the minimum price agreements or restrictive practices relating to limiting the use of the Internet as a distribution channel'.[15]

11. It may be observed in the annual reports that the CCA generally does not identify digital markets as its enforcement priority. It dedicated most attention to them

---

7 APC s 13.

8 APC s 17(2).

9 APC s 19(a).

10 Michal Petr, 'To What Extent might (and should) the Competition Law Apply to Public Authorities' (2022) 2 Journal of Administrative Sciences 67.

11 APC No 226/2023 Coll., amending the Act on the Protection of Competition and Act on the Competencies of the Office for the Protection of Competition.

12 Directive 2019/1 of the European Parliament and of the Council of 11 December 2018 to empower the competition authorities of the Member States to be more effective enforcers and to ensure the proper functioning of the internal market [2019] OJ L11/3. APC s 20a(3)(i).

13 See the annual reports of the APC: <https://uohs.gov.cz/en/information-centre/annual-reports.html> accessed 8 July 2024.

14 CCA, 'Annual Report 2022' 61.

15 *Ibid.*

in its annual report for 2017, which mentioned the digital economy as its likely focus for the future:

> "The Office is going to concentrate on the enforcement of new phenomena in the field of competition law that follow from the developing digitalisation across all business sectors. Such digitalisation can be observed especially in the case of digital platforms, which disrupt and change the current thinking on the functioning of present economic relations. A big challenge in this regard will be the assessment of the functioning and behaviour of digital algorithms which have the ability of autonomous learning and which substitute human decision-making in some sectors. That will bring about a number of questions, for example, who would be liable for the potential infringement of competition law: the user of the algorithm or its designer; or how to assess a mutual agreement between two or more algorithms which would be contrary to competition law principles. The interest of the Office will also be focused on the issues of digital sales whether it be certain kind of production or services, or potentially on the internet price comparison websites".[16]

12. Despite this ambitious proclamation, the actual enforcement has not shifted towards digital markets. Similarly, there was no visible change in enforcement after the CCA suggested in the annual report for 2021 that it 'will also closely monitor developments in digital markets and platforms'.[17]

13. Policy statements concerning the digital economy cannot be found on other fora either. For example, the CCA did not file any submission in the OECD roundtable debates concerned with digital markets. If digital markets are discussed at conferences organised by the CCA, it tends to be as a part of the Commission's policy, and not that of the CCA.[18] Similarly, academic articles focus in this regard on EU practice, not on that of the Czech Republic.

3. CCA's Enforcement Activities

14. As is evident from its annual reports, the CCA's enforcement is directed at specific practices rather than specific markets; over the last ten years,[19] the focus has been on anticompetitive agreements, specifically on bid rigging and resale price maintenance. Thus, even though the CCA investigated anticompetitive practices concerning digital markets, e.g. bid rigging in the area of digitalisation of regional

---

16 CCA, 'Annual Report 2017' 84.

17 CCA, 'Annual Report 2021' 57.

18 For example, in 2022, the CCA hosted the European Competition Day, where the first panel was dedicated to new challenges to competition enforcement in a much more online and greener world. Except for the moderator, all the speakers were from other competition authorities and international institutions. Information on this event is available at <https://uohs.gov.cz/en/information-centre/conferences-and-workshops/past-events/european-competition-day-2022.html> accessed 8 July 2024.

19 For a detailed discussion of the years 2014–2019, see Jiří Kindl and Michal Petr, 'Czech Republic' in Daniel Mandrescu *EU Competition Law and the Digital Economy: Protecting Free and Fair Competition in an Age of Technological (R)evolution.XXIX FIDE Congress, Congress Proceedings vol 3* (Eleven International Publishing 2020).

administration[20] or resale price maintenance on e-shops,[21] the actual analysis was identical to similar practices in any other markets.

15. Over the last ten years, only two cases may be regarded as specifically connected to digital markets: the putative abuse of dominance in the market of digital timetables by CHAPS and the MFN clauses used by Booking.com.

A. *Chaps*

16. According to Czech regulation, all the providers of public transportation services were required to submit information concerning their timetables, including any modifications, to a private company Chaps Spol SRO which operated the National Information System on Timetables (NIST) and which thus held a legal monopoly on access to this information. On the basis of this data, Chaps created a public search engine for timetables and connections by public transport. It refused to provide this data to other companies, including Google and Seznam.cz, the Czech equivalent to Google.

17. In the *Chaps* decision,[22] the CCA found that Chaps had abused its dominant position. The CCA defined three very narrow relevant markets which follow each other in the downstream chain. The first relevant market was defined as the 'market of up-to-date data on timetables submitted to NIST'. The second relevant market was defined as the 'market with information on existing variants of transport connections' and the third one as the 'market of services of automated search of transport connections with full national coverage'. According to the CCA, the abuse of dominance consisted in refusal to provide access to data on timetables as submitted to NIST to Chaps' downstream competitor Seznam.cz, which led to a restriction of competition on the downstream services markets to the detriment of Seznam.cz and consumers.

18. The CCA's decision was annulled by the courts, essentially for procedural reasons.[23] It was issued anew in 2023.[24] The case is currently pending before the Regional Court in Brno.

B. *Booking.com*

19. In the *Booking.com* case, the CCA investigated – as did most other EU competition authorities – the parity clauses applied by Booking.com to the providers of accommodation. The CCA concluded that the wide parity clauses (which guaranteed that the offer the provider of accommodation made via Booking.com are at least

---

20 One of the most prominent cases concerned a bid rigging cartel concerning digitalisation of a regional authority. Decision of the Chairman of the CCA No R11/2022/HS and others, 12 April 2022 and the previous first-instance decision of the CCA No S191/2017/KD, 17 January 2022. This decision was recently annulled by the Regional Court in Brno in a judgment No 29 Af 63/2021, 19 February 2024.

21 One of the most prominent cases concerns the resale price maintenance for online sales for Electrolux, AEG and Zanussi products. CCA decision No S187/2023/KD, 1 January 2024.

22 Decision of the Chairman of the CCA No R12/2016/HS, 16 January 2018 and the previous first-instance decision of the CCA No S669/2013/DP, 22 December 2015.

23 Judgment of the Regional Court in Brno No 30 Af 28/2018, 25 November 2020; judgment of the Supreme Administrative Court No 6 As 4/2021, 18 May 2022. For more details to the case, see Kindl and Petr (n 19).

24 Decision of the Chairman of the CCA No R163/2022/HS, 1 January 2023.

as favourable as the most favourable offer made to anybody else) are anticompetitive vertical agreements that have the effect of restricting competition. By contrast, the narrow parity clauses (which enable the providers of accommodation to make a more favourable offer via other online platforms or via offline distribution channels) were found to be compliant with competition law. The CCA's findings of 2019[25] were thus mostly in line with those of the French, Italian and Swedish competition authorities, which in parallel negotiated the commitments of Booking.com in 2015.

20. The *Booking.com* case was also peculiar as far as the commitments are concerned. The CCA opened the proceedings only after Booking.com committed itself to switch from wide parity clauses to narrow ones, which resulted in closure of the proceedings before French, Italian and Swedish competition authorities. As the commitments were Europe-wide, it was generally believed that further investigation was not necessary, and indeed, other competition authorities in the EU brought their investigation to an end after the commitments were approved in France, Italy and Sweden. Conversely, the CCA was the only country to open formal investigation thereafter. As Booking.com had already modified its behaviour, no commitments were possible in the proceedings before the CCA. The CCA concluded that Booking.com's conduct before the commitments (i.e. wide parity clauses) was anticompetitive and imposed a fine; it also scrutinised its conduct after the commitments (i.e. narrow parity clauses) and concluded that the conduct was not anticompetitive. Unlike other NCAs, the CCA also imposed a fine on Booking.com.

21. The judicial appeal against this decision was dismissed by the Regional Court in Brno in 2022,[26] the appeal before the Supreme Administrative Court is still pending.

C. *Private Enforcement*

22. Private enforcement of competition law is very limited in the Czech Republic. Over the last 20 years, there have only been a few reported cases.[27] The implementation of the Damages Directive[28] into Czech legal order[29] has not brought about any significant change.

23. One of the few high-profile cases is nonetheless connected with digital markets. In 2020, Heureka, a company operating on the market in sales price comparison

---

25 Decision of the Chairman of the CCA No R0219/2018/HS, 1 November 2019 and the previous first-instance decision of the CCA No ÚOHS-S664/2015/KD, 22 December 2018.

26 Judgment of the Regional Court in Brno No 30 Af 2/2020, 31 January 2022.

27 Michal Petr and Eva Zorková, '*Soukromé prosazování v České republice*' (Private Enforcement in the Czech Republic) (2016) 2 ANTITRUST; Michal Petr and Eva Zorková, '*Zkušenosti se soukromým prosazováním soutěžního práva v České republice*' (Experience with Private Enforcement of Competition Law in the Czech Republic) (2020) 3 ANTITRUST.

28 Directive 2014/104 of the European Parliament and of the Council of 26 November 2014 on certain rules governing actions for damages under national law for infringements of the competition law provisions of the Member States and of the European Union [2014] OJ L349/1.

29 APC No 262/2017 Coll., on Competition Damages and on amendment of the Act on the Protection of Competition. English translation of the act is available at: <https://uohs.gov.cz/en/legislation.html> accessed 8 July 2024.

services in the Czech Republic, brought an action for damages against Google before the Prague City Court. That action sought compensation for the harm allegedly suffered by Heureka as a result of the abuse of a dominant position in which Google, according to the Commission's *Google Shopping* decision,[30] engaged in the Czech Republic for the period from February 2013 to 2017. Heureka claimed that Google had positioned and displayed its own sales price comparison service in the best possible place amongst the results in its general search services, which reduced the number of visits to the sales price comparison portal Heureka.cz.

24. The case is still pending. The court however addressed the Court of Justice of the European Union with a request for a preliminary ruling, concerning the temporal application of the Damages Directive;[31] so far, the opinion of AG Kokott has been published.[32]

25. Allegedly, another action against Google has been submitted by Google's Czech competitor Seznam.cz,[33] following the Commission's *Google Android* decision.[34]

III. Implementation of the DMA and Synergies with other Legislation

26. As discussed above in section II.1, there is no Czech legislation addressing the digital markets in a way similar to the DMA. On a plus side, there are thus no overlaps and potential conflicts of legislation; at the same time, there are no synergies either.

27. In this section, we will discuss the potential rules on unilateral conduct targeting the gatekeepers and the implementation of the DMA.

1. Other Rules on Unilateral Conduct

28. There is no Czech legislation targeting gatekeepers specifically within the meaning of the DMA; thus, the gatekeepers are subject to general legislation, as are all the other undertakings. Of these, only the price regulation deserves closer attention.

---

30 Case AT.39740 – *(Google Search (Shopping))* Decision of 27 June 2017 relating to a proceeding under Article 102 TFEU and Article 54 of the EEA Agreement C(2017) 4444 final <https://eur-lex.europa.eu/legal-content/EN/TXT/?uri=CELEX%3A52018XC0112%2801%29&qid=1720456993009> accessed 8 July 2024.

31 Case C-605/21 *Heureka Group (Comparateurs de prix en ligne)* ECLI:EU:C:2023:695, Opinion of AG Kokott, see Eugenia Muscolo, Myrane Malanda and Ambroise Simon, *The EU Court of Justice clarifies national limitation periods and upholds parties' right to compensation in follow-on damages actions (Heureka Group / Google)*, E-COMPETITIONS April 2024, art. No. 118622.

32 Jiří Kindl and Martin Holásek, 'AG's Opinion in Heureka – On The Temporal Application of EU Damages Directive and Why Does it (Not) Matter' (*Wolters Kluwer*, 2023) <https://competitionlawblog.kluwercompetitionlaw.com/2023/10/11/ags-opinion-in-heureka-on-the-temporal-application-of-eu-damages-directive-and-why-does-it-not-matter/> accessed 8 July 2024.

33 *Ibid.*

34 Case AT.40099 – *(Google Android)* Decision of 18 July 2018 relating to a proceeding under Article 102 of the Treaty on the Functioning of the European Union and Article 54 of the EEA Agreement C(2018) 4761 final <https://eur-lex.europa.eu/legal-content/EN/ALL/?uri=CELEX:52019XC1128(02)> accessed 8 July 2024.

A. *Stricter National Rules*

29. The Price Act[35] *inter alia* prohibits a misuse of advantageous market position in order to extract unfair purchasing or selling prices.[36] The advantageous market position is defined in a way similar to dominant position,[37] which may lead to overlaps with competition law. Indeed, in one case concerning the energy markets that overlap has led to a competency dispute between the CCA and the Energy Authority, responsible for the application of the Price Act in energy markets. It was argued by the affected party (an energy company) that the CCA and the Energy Authority could not have parallel powers to assess similar conducts under both the Price Act and the APC. The Supreme Administrative Court disagreed and accepted the possibility of parallel investigations due to differences in the applicable laws and different public interests being protected by those two authorities.[38] Similar parallel cases were also dealt with in respect to various other energy companies and one heavy industry company. The overlap concerned was that unfair pricing practices were claimed to be both an infringement of the Price Act and also an abuse of dominant position under the APC. The price-related practices of gatekeepers would also be subjected to the Price Act.

30. But for the Price Act, there are no provisions in Czech law imposing additional obligations on gatekeepers, as foreseen by Article 1(5) of the DMA.

B. *Stricter Competition Law*

31. Czech competition law may be applied in parallel with the DMA according to Article 1(6)(a) of the DMA. It has already been observed that the Czech competition law is practically identical to the EU law; there are no national competition rules prohibiting other forms of unilateral conduct, as foreseen by Article 1(6)(b) of the DMA.

2. Implementation of the DMA

32. There is no specific act implementing the DMA. When an amendment of the APC implementing the ECN+ Directive was discussed by the Parliament, a single provision concerning the DMA was added. Because this provision was proposed in the Parliament, not by the Czech Government, there is no explanatory memorandum accompanying it.

33. According to the new provision, the CCA is entitled to require cooperation of undertakings necessary for the exercise the duties pursuant to the DMA.[39] This presumably implements Article 21(5) of the DMA.

34. Concerning the DMA's specific provisions on cooperation among the Commission and the NCAs, most of Article 38 of the DMA does not need any implementation

---

35 Price Act No 526/1990 Coll., on Prices, as amended.

36 Price Act s 2(3)

37 Price Act s 2(3)

38 See the judgment of the Supreme Administrative Court No Komp 3/2006-511, 18 December 2007.

39 APC s 20a(3)(i).

as it is directly applicable. Conversely, Article 38(7) of the DMA, allowing NCAs to investigate non-compliance with the DMA, requires authorisation under national law. No such regulation was adopted in the Czech Republic, and the CCA is thus not empowered to investigate compliance with the DMA on its own initiative.

35. The same applies to the cooperation with courts, as Article 39 of the DMA is not implemented at all. Most of Article 39 of the DMA is directly applicable and does not need any implementation. Conversely, Article 39(2) of the DMA, concerning the forwarding of court judgments to the Commission, is addressed to Member States, and a national authority responsible for this thus needs to be designed. This has not been done yet.

IV. Conclusions

36. The digital economy is clearly not a priority for Czech competition policy. There is no specific regulation addressing it and the DMA was implemented only in the briefest way imaginable. The number of enforcement cases specifically targeting the digital economy is negligible.

37. The reason for this situation may be the smallness of Czech markets. These are fully implemented into the EU markets and the global gatekeepers approach them under a Europe-wide strategy; there does not seem to be much space for purely national solutions.

38. On the other hand, Czech Republic has its own internet platforms with significant position in Czech markets, which are however not caught by the DMA. It might be advisable to concentrate on them, the CCA nonetheless lacks any specific tools in this regard. The public debate does not suggest that there would be demand for such an increase in the CCA's powers.

A Smaller Country in Terms of Size, but a Larger Member State in Terms of Digitalisation

Denmark

SIGURD SLOT JACOBSEN*

Naviair

Abstract

The chapter introduces Denmark's initiatives, strategies and work in the digital sector over the past decades. The important role of the Danish Competition and Consumer Authority is covered, and illustrative examples of judicial decisions in the digital realm are given. Denmark may be a smaller country in terms of size, but one of the larger member states in terms of digitalisation. This is also reflected in Denmark's high prioritisation of the area with the establishment of robust mechanisms and institutional frameworks for coordination and implementation of EU regulation, including the Digital Markets Act (DMA).

---

* Sigurd Slot Jacobsen is Chief Legal Officer at Naviair (the Danish Air Navigation Service Provider) and has previously been Chief Special Advisor at the Danish Competition and Consumer Authority and Senior Associate at Bech-Bruun Law Firm within Competition Law. All views expressed in this chapter are those of the author and not necessarily those of the Danish authorities.

I. Introduction: General Views from an EU Member State

1. The digital sector is developing rapidly, and this places great demands on the regulation of the sector. On one hand, regulation must contribute to a well-functioning market framework and support the significant benefits that come with the development, such as the creation of new business models and user platforms, increased automation, efficiency and accessibility, increased innovation and growth as well as a potentially larger customer base and audience across borders. On the other hand, regulation must also contribute to the effective management of the various risks and challenges that the development also brings with it. For example, increased exposure to cyber threats in the form of hacking and data breaches.

2. However, this development also poses challenges in relation to the so-called Tech giants, who in a short period of time have achieved a dominant market position through the spread of their platforms and services, and thus occupy an almost unchallengeable status due to their volume. This can entail risks of monopolisation and unfair competition, for example, as a result of Tech giants unilaterally setting the rules of the game under which the users of their platforms and services have to operate.

3. This chapter introduces Denmark's initiatives, strategies and work in the digital sector. Examples of specific initiatives are given, with a particular focus on the Danish implementation of the Digital Markets Act[1] and the role of the Danish Competition and Consumer Authority[2] in this context. However, it is important to note that a lot has happened during these past few years in terms of regulation of the digital sector in addition to the DMA, and that the overall regulation must contribute to ensuring the best possible utilisation of the benefits of digital development while managing the risks and challenges of that development.

1. National (Danish) Strategic and Legislative Initiatives Adopted or Incoming for the Digital Sector and Overlapping Issues between EU and National Regulations for the Digital Sector

4. Denmark is a small country in terms of size and does not have any national Tech giants on the scale of the seven gatekeepers that the European Commission (the Commission) has appointed as of August 2024[3] under the DMA. However, Denmark is generally recognised as one of Europe's most digitalised countries[4] and as a heavy user of digital services, including services offered by the gatekeepers. Denmark has a high degree of digitalisation across areas including infrastructure, public services, education and business. Digitalisation in Denmark

---

1 Regulation 2022/1925 of the European Parliament and of the Council of 14 September 2022 on contestable and fair markets in the digital sector and amending Directives 2019/1937 and 2020/1828 ('Digital Markets Act' or DMA) [2022] OJ L265/1.

2 The national independent competition authority of Denmark (together with the Danish Competition Council).

3 The current seven gatekeepers covering 24 core platform services are listed on the European Commission website: <https://digital-markets-act.ec.europa.eu/gatekeepers_en> accessed 9 July 2024.

4 Denmark was ranked second among Member States in the Digital Economy and Society Index (DESI) 2022.

is well-functioning and widely available throughout the country. Furthermore, Denmark has a strong tradition of digital innovation and entrepreneurship, which further contributes to the country's position as a digitally advanced society.

5. Digitalisation in Denmark has been underway for several decades. As far back as the 1980s and 90s, public and private institutions began implementing computerised systems and automated work processes.

6. Milestones in the further digital development in Denmark include the establishment of *e-Boks*[5] in 2001, which introduced a digital mailbox for secure communication between citizens, businesses and public authorities. The joint public health portal, *Sundhed.dk*,[6] was established in 2003 as a national portal for health information, digital health services and access to personal health data. The joint public payment system, *NemKonto*,[7] was also established in 2003 and enabled payments from the public sector to citizens and businesses simply by knowing their CPR/CVR number.[8] Several digital self-service solutions were launched, such as *Virk*[9] in 2003 and *Borger.dk*[10] in 2007, which made it possible for businesses and citizens to access and perform digital self-service in relation to the public sector. *NemID*[11] was launched in 2010 and allowed users to access public and private online services, such as SKAT and online banking. Another example is *Digital Post*,[12] which became mandatory for all companies in 2013 and all citizens in 2014, and which gave authorities the right to send messages, documents, etc. digitally with the same legal effect as traditional paper mail.

7. The list of milestones is purely exemplary, but it is also illustrative of the development of the many cross-cutting digital solutions in Denmark, which generally have in common that they stem from joint public digitalisation strategies. The latest strategy covers the years 2022–2025.[13]

8. Specifically on the Danish efforts in relation to Tech giants, the Danish Government issued a proposal in 2021 under the heading 'Tech giants: Fairer competition and better consumer protection'.[14] In it, the government presented a total of 22 initiatives to ensure a better framework for fair competition and consumer safety

---

5 The functionality of e-Boks has been continuously expanded, and e-Boks is represented in several countries and has a total of 23.6 million users globally, see e-Boks website: <https://corporate.e-boks.com/> accessed 9 July 2024.

6 Sundhed.dk has since been supplemented with an app, MinSundhed, which provides an overview and easy access to the healthcare system and own health information, see Sundhed.dk's website: <https://www.sundhed.dk/> accessed 9 July 2024.

7 Initially the Act on public payments etc., Act No 1203 of 27 December 2003.

8 Equivalent to VAT/CPR number.

9 Virk is the digital gateway to the public sector for businesses. Virk provides unified access to self-service across the public sector, see Virk's website: <https://virk.dk/> accessed 9 July 2024.

10 Borger.dk is a joint public portal that provides access to the authorities' self-services and information about the public sector in one place, see Borger.dk's website: <https://www.borger.dk/> accessed 9 July 2024.

11 NemID was phased out on 31 October 2023 and replaced by MitID, cf. initially Act No 783 of 4 May 2021.

12 Initially Act No 528 of 11 June 2012.

13 A total of six Joint Government Digital Strategies have been published since 2001, and they can all be accessed on the Danish Agency for Digital Government's website: <https://en.digst.dk/strategy/the-joint-government-digital-strategy/> accessed 9 July 2024.

14 The government proposal from August 2021 can be accessed via the Ministry of Industry, Business and Financial Affairs' website: <https://www.em.dk/aktuelt/temaer/tech-giganter> accessed 9 July 2024.

online. The initiatives were presented under the headings 'A digital world – the role and responsibility of tech giants', 'Better competition conditions', 'Safe online shopping for consumers' and 'Responsible use of data and algorithms'.

9. Among the initiatives in the proposal was the establishment of an external expert group to support the work of setting the framework for the Tech giants. The expert group has so far submitted two interim reports, in June 2023[15] and February 2024, respectively.[16] In the June report, the expert group identified a number of challenges associated with the Tech giants' platforms and on that basis made 13 recommendations regarding the Tech giants' business models. The Danish Government has expressed agreement with the recommendations and will work to implement them in both Denmark and the EU. In the February report, the expert group presented recommendations on the framework for Tech giants' development and use of artificial intelligence.

10. The government proposal from 2021 and the interim reports from 2023 and 2024 are supplemented by other publications, including articles and analyses from the Danish Competition and Consumer Authority,[17] which support the Authority's great interest and high prioritisation of tech companies and digital platforms, and the markets they operate in. This is also evident in the Authority's internal organisation with a separate competition centre that specifically handles tasks involving tech companies and digital platforms.[18]

11. In recent years, the Danish Competition and Consumer Authority has intensified its supervision and efforts in the digital area, and this has come in line with the great and increasing political attention in the area and in line with the expansion of the Authority's enforcement powers. Recently, changes to the Danish Competition Act have resulted in the Danish Competition and Consumer Authority expanding its powers.

12. In 2021, through the implementation of an EU directive,[19] the Danish Competition and Consumer Authority was given the opportunity to conduct interviews, carry out inspections in private homes and issue structural injunctions. The Authority's independence was clarified and the possibility of civil fines against companies was introduced. In addition, the option was introduced to bring appeals against the Authority's substantive decisions to the Danish Competition Appeals Board or directly to the courts.[20] These expanded powers are also relevant to the Authority's supervision and efforts in the digital area.

---

15 The interim report can be accessed on the Ministry of Industry, Business and Financial Affairs' website: 'Democratic Control over Big Tech Business Models' (1 July 2023) <https://www.eng.em.dk/publications/2023/publicationpage> accessed 9 July 2024.

16 The interim report can be accessed on the Ministry of Industry, Business and Financial Affairs' website: 'Boundaries for Big Tech's Development and Use of Artificial Intelligence' (9 February 2024) <https://www.eng.em.dk/publications/2024/boundaries-for-big-techs-development-and-use-of-ai> accessed 9 July 2024.

17 The Danish Competition and Consumer Authority's articles and analyses can be accessed on the Authority's website: <https://kfst.dk/konkurrenceforhold/tech-virksomheder/udgivelser/> accessed 9 July 2024.

18 Competition division Tech, responsible for enforcing the competition rules in tech, finance and insurance, IT and payment services: <https://en.kfst.dk/competition/contact-a-competition-division/> accessed 9 July 2024.

19 Directive 2019/1 of the European Parliament and of the Council of 11 December 2018 to empower the competition authorities of the Member States to be more effective enforcers and to ensure the proper functioning of the internal market [2019] OJ L11/3.

20 Act No 207 of 15 February 2021, cf. Consolidation Act No 360 of 4 March 2021.

13. On 28 February 2024, a bill was introduced to amend the Danish Competition Act with the aim of ensuring (even) more effective competition. The bill had its first reading in the Danish Parliament on 14 March 2024 and contains several extended powers for the Danish Competition and Consumer Authority. Among other things, it was proposed that the Danish Competition and Consumer Authority may require certain mergers below the established turnover thresholds to be notified in order for the Authority to assess whether a merger will significantly impede effective competition, in particular as a result of the creation or strengthening of a dominant position. This possibility is already recognised in other Member States, and several are considering introducing similar rules.[21] Furthermore, Article 14 of the DMA requires gatekeepers to inform the Commission of any intended mergers, irrespective of the merger being notifiable under EU or national merger rules. It was also proposed to introduce the possibility for the Authority to initiate a market investigation into behaviour or structures in one or more sectors of the economy to determine whether there are circumstances that clearly impair effective competition with harmful effects on consumers or other undertakings. In order to ensure that fines for competition law infringements better reflect the economic harm caused by certain offences, it was also proposed to change the principles for calculating fines for undertakings and natural persons.

14. The bill was passed by the Danish Parliament on 21 May 2024, and entered into force on 1 July 2024. The expanded powers apply horizontally (i.e. they are not sector-specific) and are therefore potentially useful tools for the Danish Competition and Consumer Authority's supervision and efforts in the digital area, including in relation to tech companies and digital platforms.

15. There is thus a close connection between, for example, the DMA and the competition rules, and this already follows from the fact that the DMA aims to complement the enforcement of the competition rules.[22] This also implies that extended enforcement powers under the competition rules could strengthen enforcement in the digital area.

2. National cases (by NCAs and Courts) in the digital realm in the backstage of the DMA

16. In Denmark, the national independent competition authority consists of the Danish Competition Council and the Danish Competition and Consumer Authority,[23] where the Authority is responsible for the day-to-day administration of the competition rules, and the Council has overall responsibility for the Authority's work with the administration of the rules. An enforcement case in the competition area of fundamental or particular importance is generally decided by the Danish Competition Council. A decision from the Council or the Authority can be appealed to the Danish Competition Appeals Board as the final administrative authority.[24] Decisions can then be brought before the Maritime and Commercial

---

21 Germany, Hungary, Latvia and Norway (EEA) have introduced similar rules, and France, Ireland and Sweden, among others, are considering the same.

22 DMA recital 10.

23 Consolidation Act No 360 of 4 March 2021, Chapter 6, initially Act No 1371 of 16 December 2014.

24 Consolidation Act No 360 of 4 March 2021, Chapter 7.

Court with the possibility of appeal to the High Court, however, to the Supreme Court in cases of fundamental importance.

17. In recent years, Denmark has seen several cases involving the digital sector, including cases concerning digital platforms. Some of the cases have been settled by binding commitments from the companies in question, while others have been settled by actual decisions in either administrative or judicial proceedings. The following decisions are only examples from recent years, and all relate to administrative decisions.

A. *Case about platform tendering*[25]

18. The Danish Competition Council ruled that Ageras, via its digital platform in the period from 7 March 2018 to 26 June 2018, had violated the prohibition against agreements restricting competition, partly by using a price normalisation mechanism that, among other things, indicated the 'estimated market price' and gave the providers (typically auditors but a range of other professional services were also available) the opportunity to adjust their bids, and partly by using minimum prices in job descriptions that were made available to the providers prior to the submission of bids.

19. Ageras' platform is a procurement portal that connects buyers of e.g. auditing services with providers of these services. The platform has a page for potential buyers and a page for potential providers, called partners. The way the platform works is that buyers post tasks for which partners compete. Buyers can get up to three offers for a posted task.

20. The case was prompted by a complaint from one of Ageras' former partners, and the complaint was followed by a verification investigation. Material from the investigation showed that the partners did not compete openly with each other. If a partner submitted a low bid, a message window would inform the partner of Ageras' 'estimated market price' and give them the opportunity to adjust their bid. Ageras had also organised its fee model so that the payment to Ageras depended on the size of the bid, unless it was below the 'estimated market price'. In that case, the fee was calculated based on the estimated price. In addition, there were examples of Ageras adding minimum prices to clients' job descriptions, which all partners, but not buyers, could see before submitting a bid.

21. The Danish Competition Council assessed that Ageras – both with the 'estimated market price' in the message windows and the minimum prices in the job descriptions – sought to influence one of the most important competition parameters, namely the price of the service provided via Ageras' platform. Ageras' announcements were likely to have a normalising effect on the partners' prices in the bidding process.

22. At the same time, it was also assessed that Ageras' announced 'estimated market price' in this case functioned as a signal and benchmark that reduced the uncertainty for the partners in bidding for the tasks on the platform. The announcements

---

25 The Danish Competition Council's decision of 30 June 2020, case 18/19827 *Ageras*.

meant that the partners did not independently decide on their pricing policy, and Ageras' and the partners' practices were thus likely to have a price normalising effect. The price normalisation mechanism could be expected to cause prices to rise and, seen in isolation, lead to increased margins for Ageras.

23. Overall, it was an unlawful practice aimed at appreciably restricting horizontal competition between partners on the platform.

24. Subsequently, on 9 July 2021, Ageras adopted a fine of DKK 1,275,000 (~ EUR 170,000) for the infringement.

B. *The case for minimum prices on platforms*[26]

25. The Danish Competition Council intervened against the companies behind the platforms Hilfr and Happy Helper, which had set a minimum hourly rate (minimum prices) for the providers' cleaning services.

26. Hilfr and Happy Helper are both digital platforms that connect providers and buyers of cleaning services.

27. The Danish Competition and Consumer Authority became aware of the platforms' use of minimum prices in connection with a general mapping of the platforms' prevalence in Denmark in December 2018. On this basis, the Ayhority conducted an inspection of Hilfr and Happy Helper in January 2019.

28. The Danish Competition and Consumer Authority had concerns about minimum prices as they could create a 'price floor' and eliminate the part of competition that took place below the minimum prices. Restrictions on independent traders' pricing are generally considered to be among the most anti-competitive behaviours, as the conditions do not correspond to normal market conditions where companies independently decide on their own prices and policies.

29. It was the Danish Competition and Consumer Authority's immediate assessment that there was an anti-competitive concerted practice between Hilfr and Happy Helper on the one hand and the providers of cleaning services on the other hand regarding minimum prices for the sale of the providers' cleaning services via the platforms.

30. Hilfr and Happy Helper offered to address the competition concerns by submitting commitments to remove the minimum prices. After an overall assessment, the Danish Competition and Consumer Authority found that the cases were suitable for closure with commitments, and the Danish Competition Council accepted the closure with commitments, which are binding and without time limit.

31. The overall assessment included the fact that the market for digital platforms is rapidly evolving, and the number, business models and forms of digital platforms are changing relatively quickly. A pledge solution would contribute to increased focus on platform pricing and thus provide similar platforms with faster clarification.

---

26 The Danish Competition Council's decisions of 26 August 2020, joined cases 19/05552 and 19/05554 *Minimum prices on Hilfrs and Happy Helpers platforms*, see Frederik Haugsted and Morten Nissen, *The Danish Competition Authority accepts commitments from a digital platform to remove a mandatory minimum hourly fee for regular cleaning services providers on the platform (Hilfr)*, E-COMPETITIONS 26 August 2020, art. No 96757.

C. *Case of collective boycott of platform*[27]

32. The Danish Competition Council ruled that Peugeot Forhandler Foreningen (PFF) in the period from the end of 2012 to at least August 2014 had violated the prohibition against anti-competitive agreements by having adopted a collective boycott of the digital platform Bilbasen.dk to promote the competitor Biltorvet.dk.

33. PFF is an association of independent car dealers in Denmark who sell and/or service cars of the Peugeot brand. The members of PFF sell used cars, among other things.

34. The car portals Bilbasen.dk and Biltorvet.dk are digital platforms for advertising primarily used cars. The car portals act as a link between potential car buyers on the one hand and professional car dealers and private individuals selling used cars on the other.

35. The case was prompted by an investigation carried out in April 2018. Material from the control investigation (dawn raid) showed that e-mails had been exchanged between independent Peugeot dealers and one or more members of the board of directors of PFF and between members of the board of directors of PFF to the effect that Peugeot dealers should not advertise on bilbasen.dk in order to promote the competitor biltorvet.dk.

36. The Danish Competition Council found that the objective purpose of the adoption in PFF was to restrict competition on the market for advertising on car portals in Denmark by placing bilbasen.dk at a competitive disadvantage and eliminating ordinary competition parameters such as quality and price. The adoption of the PFF was thus intended to restrict competition between Peugeot dealers in the market for the sale of used cars in Denmark by removing or reducing the uncertainty that would otherwise have existed between Peugeot dealers as to where they each advertised, and at the same time, the adoption could have led to fewer choices for potential car buyers (consumers).

37. PFF admitted to violating the prohibition against anti-competitive agreements and on 20 April 2022, PFF agreed to a fine of DKK 500,000 (~ EUR 67,000) for the violation.

D. *Platform Price Fixing Case*[28]

38. The Danish Competition Council ruled that Autobutler, via its digital platform, in the period from at least March 2016 to October 2021, had violated the prohibition against anti-competitive agreements by having agreements with several hundred workshops on fixed prices for certain services.

39. Autobutler's platform is a supply portal that connects buyers of motor vehicle repair and maintenance services (car owners) with providers of these services (repair shops) online.

---

27 The Danish Competition Council's decision of 23 February 2022, case 20/05735 *Collective boycott of Bilbasen in Peugeot Forhandler Foreningen*, see Rebecca Fink Joensen and Martin André Dittmer, *The Danish Competition Authority decides that the boycott of a digital marketplace by an association of car dealers constitutes an anti-competitive agreement (Peugeot Forhandler Foreningen)*, E-COMPETITIONS 23 February 2022, art. No 106301.

28 The Danish Competition Council's decision of 28 June 2023, case 22/03002 *Faste priser på Autobutlers platform.*

40. The case was prompted by an inquiry in January 2021 from a car owner about possible fixed prices on Autobutler's platform, and the inquiry was followed by a control investigation in October 2021. Material from the control investigation showed that several workshops had for a number of years offered similar prices on Autobutler's platform for at least nine services consisting of air conditioning service with or without cleaning, basic service, car check, brake, wheel change with or without tyre storage, oil change and MOT check.

41. The Danish Competition Council assessed that Autobutler and some of the garages on Autobutler's platform had entered into bilateral, vertical agreements on fixed prices for selected services. The individual workshop could choose whether it wanted to participate in the fixed price for a certain period and sign up with Autobutler.

42. The Danish Competition Council found that the objective purpose of the agreement on fixed prices was to restrict competition between repair shops on the Danish market for repair and maintenance of motor vehicles. The agreement prevented the participating repair shops from competing on price by setting a lower price than the other participating repair shops and thereby attracting customers. The agreement thus supported less customer mobility between the participating repair shops and weakened competition for customers, which in general could lead to higher prices, lower quality, etc.

43. The case has been brought before the courts in order for Autobutler to be fined for the offence.

II. Actions Undertaken by Denmark to Facilitate the Integration and to Enhance Synergies between EU and National Legislations for the Digital Sector

1. Introduction to DMA

44. The DMA entered into force on 1 November 2022 and applied from 2 May 2023. The regulation is of general application and directly applicable in all Member States, including Denmark, and therefore does not require transposition into national law.

45. The purpose clause states that the DMA must contribute to the proper functioning of the internal market by laying down harmonised rules to ensure fair and effective competition in digital markets with the presence of gatekeepers.[29] In this context, the regulation allows for a number of requirements to be imposed on gatekeepers, such as access to data and the use of fair and non-discriminatory terms and conditions.

46. A gatekeeper is an undertaking providing core platform services designated by the Commission pursuant to the regulation.[30] An undertaking is designated as a gatekeeper if: (i) it has a significant impact on the internal market; (ii) it provides

---

29 DMA art 1(1).

30 DMA art 3.

a core platform service that is an essential gateway for business users to reach end users; and (iii) it has an entrenched and durable position in its activities or it is likely to acquire such a position in the near future.

47. On 6 September 2023, the Commission designated six companies (Tech giants) as gatekeepers, respectively Alphabet, Amazon, Apple, ByteDance, Meta and Microsoft.[31] Furthermore, based on the quantitative thresholds of the regulation, the Commission identified 22 core platform services offered by the six gatekeepers, including social media such as Facebook, Instagram, LinkedIn, TikTok, and intermediary services such as Amazon Marketplace, App Store and Google Maps.

48. Designated gatekeepers have six months (until March 2024 for the appointees of September 2023) to comply with the full set of requirements under the regulation and to submit a compliance report detailing the solutions they have put in place.

49. On 7 March 2024, the Commission issued a press release on the gatekeepers' obligation to comply with the DMA,[32] followed on 25 March 2024 by another press release stating that the Commission had opened an investigation into three of the six gatekeepers, namely Alphabet, Apple and Meta, for non-compliance with the regulation.[33]

50. On 29 April 2024, the Commission added iPad OS to the list of Apple's designated platform services[34] and on 13 May 2024, the Commission designated Booking as gatekeeper for its intermediary service Booking.com,[35] summing up to the current seven gatekeepers and 24 core platform services.[36]

51. On 24 June 2024, the Commission sent preliminary findings (that is, similar to a statement of objections) to Apple regarding its steering rules for the App Store,[37] and on 1 July 2024 to Meta regarding its "Pay or consent" model for Facebook.

52. If a gatekeeper fails to comply with the obligations of the regulation, the Commission can impose fines of up to 10% of the company's total worldwide turnover, and in case of repeated infringements, these can be increased to 20%.[38] In case of systematic infringements, the Commission also has the possibility to adopt several remedial

---

31 European Commission Press Release, 'Digital Markets Act: Commission designates six gatekeepers' (6 September 2023) <https://ec.europa.eu/commission/presscorner/detail/en/IP_23_4328> accessed 9 July 2024.

32 European Commission Press Release, 'Designated Gatekeepers Must Now Comply with all Obligations under the Digital Markets Act' (7 March 2024) <https://ec.europa.eu/commission/presscorner/detail/en/ip_24_1342> accessed 9 July 2024.

33 European Commission Press Release, 'Commission Opens Non-Compliance Investigations against Alphabet, Apple and Meta under the Digital Markets Act' (25 March 2024) <https://ec.europa.eu/commission/presscorner/detail/en/ip_24_1689> accessed 9 July 2024.

34 European Commission Press Release, 'Commission designates Apple's iPadOS under the Digital Markets Act' (29 April 2024) <https://ec.europa.eu/commission/presscorner/detail/en/ip_24_2363> accessed 9 July 2024.

35 European Commission Press Release, 'Commission designates Booking as a gatekeeper and opens a market investigation into X' (13 May 2024) <https://ec.europa.eu/commission/presscorner/detail/en/ip_24_2561> accessed 9 July 2024.

36 The European Commission website: <https://digital-markets-act.ec.europa.eu/gatekeepers_en> accessed 9 July.

37 European Commission News Article, 'Commission sends preliminary findings to Apple and opens additional non-compliance investigation against Apple' (24 June 2024) <https://digital-markets-act.ec.europa.eu/commission-sends-preliminary-findings-apple-and-opens-additional-non-compliance-investigation-2024-06-24_en> accessed 9 July.

38 DMA art 30.

measures such as obliging a gatekeeper to sell a business or parts thereof or prohibiting the gatekeeper from acquiring additional services related to the systemic non-compliance.

53. The DMA states that the Commission is the only authority authorised to enforce the regulation.[39] However, to support the Commission in its enforcement, Article 38(7) of the regulation allows Member States to authorise the competent competition enforcement authorities to conduct own-initiative investigations into possible non-compliance by gatekeepers with obligations under Articles 5, 6 and 7 of the DMA.[40]

54. The DMA does not affect the application of competition rules, neither Articles 101 and 102 TFEU nor national competition rules.[41] On the contrary, the regulation complements the enforcement of competition rules.[42]

2. Best Practice in the Application of DMA Articles 1(5), 1(6), 38(7) and 39: the Danish Implementation of DMA

55. In order to support the Commission's sufficient and effective enforcement of the DMA, Denmark has passed a law giving the Danish Competition and Consumer Authority competence and powers in relation to the regulation. The law entered into force on 1 January 2024.[43]

56. The purpose of the Act is to ensure that the Danish Competition and Consumer Authority has the competence and powers to conduct investigations into possible non-compliance by gatekeepers with the obligations in Articles 5, 6 and 7 of the DMA in Denmark. The purpose is also to establish that the Danish Competition and Consumer Authority is the competent authority in Denmark that – possibly together with other Member States – may request the Commission to initiate a market investigation pursuant to Article 41 of the regulation.

57. The Act relates to core platform services provided or offered by gatekeepers designated by the Commission pursuant to Article 3 of the regulation to business users established in Denmark or end users established or located in Denmark, regardless of the establishment or domicile of the gatekeepers and regardless of the legislation otherwise applicable to the provision of services. The Act thus complements the regulation and contributes to supporting the Commission's enforcement of the DMA.

58. The Act states that the Danish Competition Council has overall responsibility for the Danish Competition and Consumer Authority's administration of the Act,[44] and this entails a statutory confirmation of the independence and impartiality of the Danish Competition Council and the Danish Competition and Consumer Authority, similar to what applies under the competition rules.[45]

---

39 DMA recital 91 and art 38(7).
40 DMA art 38(7).
41 DMA art 1(6).
42 DMA recitals 10 and 11.
43 Act No 1533 of 12 December 2023.
44 Act No 1533 of 12 December 2023 s 2(1), equivalent to Consolidation Act No 360 of 4 March 2021 s 15(3).
45 Consolidation Act No 360 of 4 March 2021 s 14(a)(1).

59. It also states that the Danish Competition and Consumer Authority is the national competent authority under Article 38 (referring to Article 1(6)) of the regulation,[46] which means that the Danish Competition and Consumer Authority is the Danish authority that is competent to cooperate and coordinate with the Commission under Article 38 of the regulation.

60. Furthermore, in Denmark, the Danish Competition and Consumer Authority is the competent authority that can make a request to the Commission to initiate a market investigation under Article 41 of the regulation.[47] Such a request must be authorised by the Danish Competition Council,[48] and documentation in support of the request must be provided.

61. The Act also states that the Danish Competition and Consumer Authority may conduct an investigation of a possible failure to comply with Articles 5, 6 and 7 of the regulation,[49] and that this may be done on its own initiative or on the basis of a complaint.[50] However, according to Article 38(7) of the regulation, the Authority is obliged to inform the Commission before launching an investigation either on its own initiative or on the basis of a complaint. Notification must be made before the Authority takes the first formal investigative measure, such as a request for information or a request to conduct an interview. The purpose of the notification obligation is to avoid overlapping investigations under the regulation.[51]

62. The Danish Competition and Consumer Authority decides whether such an investigation should be carried out or whether the investigation should be temporarily or permanently discontinued.[52] This means that the Authority has broad powers to handle a case on its own initiative and to refuse to handle a complaint, which is similar to what applies under the competition rules.

63. After conducting an investigation into a possible non-compliance with Articles 5, 6 and 7 of the DMA, the Authority may inform the Commission of its conclusions, subject to prior approval by the Danish Competition Council.[53] The Commission, as the sole enforcement authority, may then choose to initiate proceedings to investigate a possible non-compliance with the rules of the regulation. Thus, it is not possible for the Danish Competition and Consumer Authority, on the basis of a completed investigation, to decide on any non-compliance with Articles 5, 6 and 7 of the regulation.

64. In connection with the performance of the tasks assigned to the Danish Competition and Consumer Authority under the Act, the Authority may demand all information, including access to algorithms and information about tests, and demand explanations regarding these as deemed necessary.[54] The Authority itself determines

---

46 Act No 1533 of 12 December 2023 s 2(2).
47 Act No 1533 of 12 December 2023 s 2(3).
48 Act No 1533 of 12 December 2023 s 2(4).
49 Act No 1533 of 12 December 2023 s 3(1).
50 Act No 1533 of 12 December 2023 s 3(2).
51 DMA recital 91.
52 Act No 1533 of 12 December 2023 s 3(3), equivalent to Consolidation Act No 360 of 4 March 2021 s 15(3).
53 Act No 1533 of 12 December 2023 s 3(4).
54 Act No 1533 of 12 December 2023 s 4(1) equivalent to Consolidation Act No 360 of 4 March 2021 s 17(1).

which information and explanations are considered necessary for the Authority's conduct of investigations under the Act, however, taking into account, among other things, the general principle of proportionality and the prohibition against self-incrimination.

65. The Danish Competition and Consumer Authority may also conduct interviews with any legal or natural person who gives consent, when such legal or natural person is assessed to be in possession of relevant information pursuant to Section 3 of the Act.[55] The consent requirement means that the Authority cannot require a person to cooperate in an interview.

66. It has been clarified that the Danish Public Access to Information Act does not apply to cases and investigations under the Act.[56] Companies must be able to act in confidence that information provided to the Danish Competition and Consumer Authority can be kept confidential. However, the Authority may publish information about an investigation under Section 3 of the Act and documents included in cases and investigations that require a third party's comments,[57] as long as it does not involve, for example, operational and business secrets of significant economic importance.[58]

67. It is also clarified that the rules in the General Data Protection Regulation[59] on the obligation to provide information and the right of access do not apply to cases and investigations under the Act.[60] The provision means that there is no access to documents under the Danish Public Access to Information Act or access under the General Data Protection Regulation when the Danish Competition and Consumer Authority performs the tasks assigned to the Authority under the Act.

68. Finally, the law states that daily or weekly fines can be imposed for failure to provide complete and correct information to the Danish Competition and Consumer Authority, or for failure to provide such information within the established timeframe.[61] Daily fines are intended for urgent cases. The calculation is based on the daily setup, and therefore weekly fines will be equivalent to seven daily fines.

69. The DMA allows Member States to impose obligations on undertakings, including undertakings providing core platform services, in areas outside the scope of the regulation, provided that the obligations in question are compatible with EU law and do not result from the gatekeeper status of the undertakings in question.[62] Denmark has not introduced stricter rules for the undertakings in question, but has merely made use of the opportunities for cooperation and coordination with the Commission, harmonising with the regulation.

---

55 Act No 1533 of 12 December 2023 s 5 equivalent to DMA art 22(1).

56 Act No 1533 of 12 December 2023 s 6(1).

57 Act No 1533 of 12 December 2023 s 6(2).

58 Equivalent to Consolidation Act No 145 of 24 February 2024 s 30.

59 Regulation 2016/679 of the European Parliament and of the Council of 27 April 2016 on the protection of natural persons with regard to the processing of personal data and on the free movement of such data, and repealing Directive 95/46 (General Data Protection Regulation) [2016] OJ L119/1, arts 15-17, cf. art 23.

60 Act No 1533 of 12 December 2023 s 7.

61 Act No 1533 of 12 December 2023 s 8(1) equivalent to Consolidation Act No 360 of 4 March 2021 s 22.

62 DMA art 1(5).

3. Legislative Mechanisms Provided at National Level to Ensure Coordination with EU Regulations

70. Overall, Denmark's position on EU matters is determined in what is known as the 'Danish EU decision-making procedure'[63]. During the process, the Danish ministries, the Danish Parliament and relevant interest organisations are involved. The aim is to reach agreement on the Danish position internally in Denmark and externally in relation to the EU. The Danish EU decision-making procedure runs in parallel with the EU decision-making procedure in Brussels.

71. Specifically in relation to the implementation of EU regulation in the digital area, Denmark has, as described, in December 2023 passed a law,[64] which gives the Danish Competition and Consumer Authority competence and powers in relation to the DMA. Similarly, in December 2023, Denmark passed an Act,[65] which gives the Authority competence and powers in relation to the Digital Services Act (DSA),[66] which is a regulation that addresses the broader societal challenges of digital services, including requirements for content on digital platforms.

72. A few years earlier, a law was passed,[67] which also gave the Competition and Consumer Authority competence and powers to enforce the Platform to Business (P2B) Regulation,[68] which gives business users access to transparency, fairness and effective redress when selling goods or services on large and small digital platforms.

73. These examples of enforcement laws are illustrative of the Danish coordination and implementation of EU regulation in the digital area.

74. A further significant part of the coordination at Community level takes place in the European Competition Network (ECN), where the Commission and the national competent authorities (competition authorities) cooperate, inform and coordinate with each other and have the possibility to provide each other with all factual and legal information, including confidential information.[69]

75. In addition, in connection with the DMA, the Commission has established a High-level Group,[70] which is tasked with providing advice and expertise to the Commission on the regulation and other sectoral rules applicable to gatekeepers in order to ensure harmonised and future-proof implementation. Denmark is *inter alia* represented in the High-level Group as one of six representatives of the ECN.

---

63 Ministry of Foreign Affairs, 'The Danish EU Decision Procedure' (2024) <https://eu.um.dk/en/info-about-denmark-and-the-eu/decision-procedure-in-denmark-and-the-eu> accessed 9 July 2024.

64 Act No 1533 of 12 December 2023.

65 Act No 1765 of 28 December 2023.

66 Regulation 2022/2065 of the European Parliament and of the Council of 19 October 2022 on a Single Market for Digital Services and amending Directive 2000/31 (the Digital Services Act or DSA) [2022] OJ L277/1.

67 Act No 740 of 30 May 2020.

68 Regulation 2019/1150 of the European Parliament and of the Council of 20 June 2019 on promoting fairness and transparency for business users of online intermediation services (Platform-to-Business Regulation or P2B-Regulation) [2019] OJ L186/57.

69 DMA art 38(1).

70 European Commission Press Release, 'Digital Markets Act: Commission Creates High-level Group to Provide Advice and Expertise in Implementation' (23 March 2023) <https://digital-strategy.ec.europa.eu/en/news/digital-markets-act-commission-creates-high-level-group-provide-advice-and-expertise-implementation> accessed 9 July 2024.

76. Overall, Denmark has established robust mechanisms and institutional frameworks for the coordination and implementation of EU regulation, including in relation to the digital area.

III. Conclusion: the DMA as a Piece of a Wider Cosmos of EU and National Legislative Initiatives for Digital Transformation

77. The digital sector is developing rapidly, and this is also reflected in the increasing regulation in the area. Tech companies and digital platforms are cross-border in their structure, and it is therefore both natural and appropriate for initiatives and efforts to converge internationally, including at EU level.

78. It is therefore also pertinent for Denmark – as one of the smaller member states in terms of size, but one of the more advanced member states in terms of digitalisation – to be actively involved in further regulation at EU level.

79. Enforcement of competition rules, respectively enforcement of anti-competitive agreements and abuse of dominant position, may involve extensive legal and economic investigations of often complex facts on a case-by-case basis,[71] and may entail longer case handling times. This is particularly challenging in fast-growing markets, as exemplified by the digital sector. Such *ex post* enforcement may thus be insufficient when the whole idea is a well-functioning market framework.

80. Therefore, a regulation such as the DMA is particularly important as an example of *ex ante* enforcement, which should, as far as possible, contribute to address behaviour that actually or potentially harms competition and free market access. In this sense, the DMA is precisely an important piece of a wider cosmos of EU.

81. The combination of *ex ante* and *ex post* enforcement will be fundamental for further action and regulation in the digital area, precisely because the area is rapidly evolving.

82. The effectiveness of the DMA will rely heavily on swift and effective follow-up of compliance, with the Commission leading the way as the sole enforcement authority under the regulation, but under the influence and in close co-operation with Member States. A coherent, effective and complementary enforcement of the available legal instruments will be crucial.[72]

83. To this purpose, Denmark has prepared itself by utilising the regulation's possibilities to conduct investigations to support the Commission under the DMA, and with the Danish Competition and Consumer Authority's high prioritisation of the digital area, it is expected that the Authority will make use of its expanded powers.

---

71 DMA recital 5.

72 DMA art 37(1).

Estonia and the Digital Markets Act: A Minimalist Yet Proactive Approach

Estonia

ELO TAMM*
Cobalt Law Firm

Abstract

Estonia is recognized as a pioneer in digital innovation, with initiatives such as the e-Estonia program and e-Residency, which have fostered a strong digital infrastructure and attracted tech entrepreneurs. Estonia has also been at the forefront of cryptocurrency regulation, balancing a lean regulatory approach with swift action when necessary. The Estonian National Competition Authority has been vigilant in monitoring digital markets, addressing various specific cases involving digital services. The Digital Markets Act (DMA) has been supported by Estonia, though the country has opted for minimal national regulation, preferring EU-wide governance to avoid market fragmentation. Estonia's approach to the DMA emphasizes ensuring fundamental procedural rights and appropriate enforcement mechanisms. While the Estonian NCA is preparing to align with DMA requirements, practical implementation has been limited due to the lack of significant gatekeeper presence in the country. The broader implications of the DMA for Estonia's digital market, particularly for startups, remain to be fully realized. The author supports Estonia's stance of relying on EU-level regulation rather than introducing additional national rules.

---

* Partner, Cobalt Law Firm, located at Pärnu mnt 15, Tallinn, Estonia.

I. Introduction: General Overview from Estonia

1. E-Estonia Initiatives

1. Estonia is often acknowledged as a pioneer in building up a digital society and a hub for the start-up world. International and domestic, larger and smaller players of the digital economy are welcome to provide their services in Estonia or to use the Estonian digital hub to build new services with global impact.

2. The initiatives of the government have been primarily directed at creating national digital infrastructure. There have been many important building blocks for the creation of e-Estonia, and one of the most important has been the digital identification of all Estonian residents based on mandatory ID cards in 2002. Currently 98% of Estonians have an ID card and thus a digital identity. In 2014 Estonian e-Residency was launched to global citizens to attract tech-savvy entrepreneurs to use Estonia as the digital headquarter country for their businesses.[1]

3. Though not directly relevant to the regulation of digital giants under DMA, the boom and regulation of cryptocurrencies in Estonia provides interesting experiences in regulating novel sectors. Estonia is one of the pioneers in blockchain technology and was one of the first countries to offer cryptocurrency business licenses in 2017. This followed by a boom of more than 1000 global cryptocurrency companies applying and receiving licenses in Estonia by 2019 and the subsequent tightening of financial and anti-money-laundering regulations ensuring Estonia continued as a sustainable hub for cryptocurrency businesses. This example demonstrates Estonia's generally lean approach towards regulating, but also its readiness to react swiftly and set regulatory measures in place, once needed.

4. The Estonian National Competition Authority (Estonian NCA) has been watchful of the new digital market players emerging, however so far there have been no major interventions in their activities.

2. Estonian NCA Interferences in the Digital Realm

5. The Estonian NCA noted in its 2021 Yearbook that more and more competition concerns are emerging in different digital markets, both in Estonia and in many other countries. The Estonian NCA referred to the threat of high market concentration in digital markets and the need to tackle these concerns both with the traditional monopoly approach to competition law as well as evolving EU regulatory competition law in digital markets, in particular in relation to the global digital giants.[2]

6. The year 2021 was marked by a number of Estonian NCA decisions in local digital markets and services.

---

[1] More information on the creation of e-Estonia available here: <https://e-estonia.com/story/> accessed 9 July 2024.

[2] Estonian Competition Authority, 'Annual Report 2021' (2021) <https://aastaraamat.konkurentsiamet.ee/index.php/en/annual-report-2021/competition-supervision> accessed 9 July 2024.

7. With regard to narrow price parity clauses, the Estonian Competition Authority took a preliminary view that they required individual exemption analysis in two cases – by a food courier app Wolt[3] and insurance mediator IIZI.[4] Both companies removed price parity clauses from their terms and thus the clauses were not reviewed in great detail by the Authority.

8. The Estonian NCA has also handled several cases concerning access to online classifieds portals. In real estate classifieds cases (*kv.ee* and *city24.ee*[5]) the conditions for the automatic exchange of data by the real estate portals were under investigation based on a complaint from real estate agencies. The Estonian NCA considered the availability of automatic exchange necessary to ease the use by real estate agencies and thus viability of multiple classifieds portals in a small market like Estonia. As a result of the investigation several restrictions for the data exchange were removed, including the restrictions on the free use of the XML service for automatic data exchange (initially this service was available only to larger real estate agencies); restriction of export of advertisements via XML; export of data to competing portals via XML; inclusion of portal trade mark on customers photos that prevented the use of such photos in competing portals. The case was closed by the Estonian NCA following compliance by the real estate portals.[6]

9. In the car classifieds case (*auto24.ee*) the restriction of transmission of data and advertisement in XML format was under investigation. The service was not available to all interested parties due to claimed technical and commercial limitations of the existing technical platform. The case was closed following the investments by the car classifieds portal enabling the extension of the XML service to all interested parties.[7]

10. The Estonian NCA has assessed the market position of leading local digital learning materials portal OPIQ which offers almost the entire curriculum in all subjects and classes for Estonian basic education using modern information technology opportunities. The case was initiated based on the complaint by Tartu municipality, who alleged that there were no substitutes for the local digital learning materials for schools after OPIQ had reached wide use during the COVID-19 e-schooling period. The Estonian NCA however did not establish dominance by the portal and thus there was also no need to look into claims of infringement since after the pandemic the use of learning materials on paper resumed.[8]

---

3 Estonian Competition Authority 19 March 2021, Decision No 5-5/2021-023 *Wolt Eesti OÜ* in Estonian: <https://www.konkurentsiamet.ee/sites/default/files/juhtumid/2021/teade_menetluse_lopetamisest_wolt_eesti_ou_19.03.2021_ilma_ak.pdf> accessed 9 July 2024

4 Estonian Competition Authority 9 September 2021, Decision No 5-5/2021-056 *Iizi Kindlustusmaakler AS* in Estonian: <https://www.konkurentsiamet.ee/sites/default/files/juhtumid/2021/as-ta_teade_menetluse_lopetamisest_iizi_kindlustusmaakler_09_09_2021.pdf> accessed 9 July 2024.

5 Estonian Competition Authority 18 April 2024, Decision No 5-5/2024-021, *Allepal OÜ and Kinnisvaraportaal OÜ,* in Estonian: <https://www.konkurentsiamet.ee/media/786/download> accessed 5 August 2024.

6 More details of the case are published in the Estonian Competition Authority Annual Report 2021 (n 2).

7 Estonian Competition Authority 11 March 2021, Decision No 5-5/2021-021 *Allepal OÜ (Auto24)* in Estonian: <https://www.konkurentsiamet.ee/sites/default/files/juhtumid/2021/teade_menetluse_lopetamisest_allepal_ou_auto24_11.03.21_arakiri.pdf> accessed 9 July 2024.

8 Estonian Competition Authority 30 December 2021, Decision No 5-5/2021-075 *Star Cloud OÜ* in Estonian <https://www.konkurentsiamet.ee/sites/default/files/juhtumid/2021/teade_menetluse_lopetamisest_30.12.21_star_cloud_ou_arakiri.pdf> accessed 9 July 2024.

11. The following years of 2022–23 did not see as active engagement by the Estonian NCA in the digital sector. Interestingly, the Estonian Competition Authority decided not to join its Baltic neighbours, when Latvia and Lithuanian initiated a sector inquiry into online marketplaces to learn more about its mechanisms, as well as identifying any competition risks. Based on informal discussions, the Estonian NCA decided to pass this opportunity since it had gained sufficient knowledge of the operation of these markets through its own practice.

II. Use of DMA at the Domestic Level

1. Position of Estonia in Relation to Draft Digital Markets Act Prior to its Adoption

12. The discussion around the enforcement of Digital Markets Act (DMA) in Estonia has been rather lean. The Estonian Government prepared its position in relation to the draft Digital Markets Act prior to its adoption, on 1 April 2021. Estonia supported the draft Digital Markets Act in most of its substance and only noted with regard to concentrations in the digital sector that there should be no special procedure and referred to a need to ensure that penalties for non-compliance can only be imposed based on *ultima ratio* principle and that fundamental procedural rights need to be ensured to the market players subject to DMA.[9]

2. Enforcement of DMA in Estonia

13. As always with EU regulations, there is no need to take legislative action by a Member State to give legal force to the provisions of the DMA on a national level. In relation to the DMA however, it has been noted by the Ministry of Justice that certain implementing provisions will need to be added to Estonian legislation to enable Estonian authorities to issue requests for information, conduct inspections and other measures, which are to a large extent similar to the powers that the Estonian NCA has in competition proceedings. The Ministry of Justice is planning amendments to Estonian Competition Act to provide the Estonian NCA with the proper tools, however such draft amendments of local legislation have not yet been prepared. The authorities appear to have an understanding that there is no immediate rush with granting the Estonian NCA such tools, since it is unlikely that there would be a need to conduct such measures in relation to gatekeepers in Estonia. This is probably an accurate understanding since the gatekeepers that have been designated so far, do not have their headquarters in Estonia.

14. The Estonian Competition Authority has indicated its willingness to act as the Estonian representative to the Digital Markets Advisory Committee, so far Estonia has been represented by the Ministry of Justice. Amendments to the Estonian Competition Act are further needed in order to empower the Estonian NCA with this task.

---

9 Republic of Estonia Government Office, Estonian position on the draft EU Digital Markets Act (1 April 2021) in Estonian: <https://www.riigikogu.ee/tegevus/dokumendiregister/dokument/9f1372ba-f13d-4d44-9f78-8a130d6d042c/eesti-seisukohad-euroopa-liidu-digiturgude-oigusakti-eelnou-kohta-com2020-842/> accessed 9 July 2024.

15. Due to the novelty of the DMA and the small number of gatekeepers, we are not yet aware of any practical local implementation of the DMA in Estonia, including the use of DMA Articles 1(5), 1(6), 38(7) and 39. Also we are not aware of any challenges or disputes in relation to the implementation of the DMA.

III. Conclusion: the DMA as a Piece of a Wider Cosmos of EU and National Legislative Initiatives for Digital Transformation?

16. The opportunities arising from the DMA to the Estonian start-up business community have not yet been well recognised. DMA can ensure smaller digital market players better opportunities to be competitive alongside larger companies. When preparing the Estonian position in relation to the draft DMA, it was acknowledged that the adoption of the DMA can result in smaller companies using the services of the gatekeepers to gain better access to the data generated on the gatekeepers' platforms. This, in turn can foster the development and marketing of new products and services. Companies can also start communicating with their customers in ways that are currently hindered by contractual or technical restrictions imposed by gatekeepers. Increasing business freedom in the digital environment is certainly important for Estonian companies, and the DMA also provides them with the opportunity to contribute to start-up businesses.[10]

17. The author supports the position of Estonia not to initiate specific country-level regulation of digital markets. One of the aims of the DMA is to avert the fragmentation of the internal market by preventing Member States from applying national rules which are within the scope of the DMA and to pursue the same objectives. Digital markets are global and thus regulating it at EU level is appropriate and should not be complicated with additional national layers.

---

10 *Ibid* Explanatory *memorandum* 8.

The DMA and its Interaction with French Regulations

France

IRÈNE LUC*
French Court of Cassation

Abstract

In France, alongside the DMA to which the Authority and the specialized courts contribute, competition law applies to digital, as well as sectoral regulations. The success of the interaction between competition law and the DMA and between all regulatory laws in the digital sector in the years to come will largely depend on our ability to coordinate effectively. This is undoubtedly one of the major challenges facing us and we must work together to achieve more competitive, contestable and fairer digital markets.

---

* Irène Luc is First Advocate General at the Commercial Chamber of the French Court of Cassation since 2025. She has previously been Vice President of the French Competition Authority.

I. Introduction: General View from France

1. National Legislative Initiative Adopted for the Digital Sector

18. The purpose of the Security and Regulation of the Digital Space SREN Act of 21 May 2024 aimed at securing and regulating the digital space (SREN Act) is to provide better protection for minors and improve the fight against cyber harassment. It also includes provisions adapting French law to the Digital Markets Act (DMA) and Digital Services Act (DSA). Under the terms of the new Article L. 442-12 of the French Commercial Code relating to cloud computing, a cloud computing service provider may only grant a cloud computing credit for a limited period, and without attaching any condition of exclusivity of any kind whatsoever on the part of the beneficiary vis-à-vis the credit provider. Failure to comply with these obligations will incur an administrative penalty of up to €1 million for legal entities (€2 million in the event of a repeat offence), to be imposed by the relevant unit of the General Directorate for Competition Policy, Consumer Affairs and Fraud Control France (DGCCRF). It is also prohibited for any person to make the sale of a product or service conditional on the simultaneous conclusion of a contract for the provision of cloud computing services, which constitutes an unfair commercial practice.

19. In addition, the Autorité de la concurrence has been given new powers in relation to self-preferencing practices. It may, either on its own initiative or at the request of the Minister for Digital Affairs or any legal entity concerned, investigate any reports of such practices, sanction them or adopt any necessary measures, on the basis of its traditional powers.

20. Lastly, under Article 27 of the SREN Act, all cloud computing service providers are prohibited from charging, under the contracts they enter into with a customer, switching fees in excess of the costs incurred by the provider and directly linked to the switch, subject to a ceiling regulated under the supervision of the telecom sector regulator.

21. Other developments in the law will be discussed below.

2. Landmark National Cases in the Digital Realm Backstage of the DMA

22. As early as 2004 (Decision 04-D-54), the Competition Council (the Autorité's predecessor) received a complaint from Virgin, which claimed that music loaded onto its platform could not be played on Apple iPods. The issue of 'closed ecosystems' of platforms was emerging. But in this case, there were doubts about the essential infrastructure of these tools, so the case was dismissed.

23. The Autorité's first proactive intervention dates back to 2010. In Decision 10-MC-01, it upheld the request of, NaVX, a company that had been delisted from Google's Adwords services. The Autorité did not base its decision on the refusal of access to an essential infrastructure, for which the conditions of application are very demanding, but on the discriminatory implementation of the conditions of referencing by Google, a practice of exploitative abuse. Google was ordered to revise its Adwords rules so that the conditions of access would henceforth be objective, transparent and non-discriminatory.

24. The Autorité has resolutely continued along the path of exploitative abuse, sanctioning Google again in 2019 on this same basis, in the *Gibmédia* case (Decision 19-D-26). The dereferencing policy implemented by Google Ads to protect consumers from illegal sites, which was not objective and was discriminatory, was deemed to be disproportionate to its purpose. The Autorité defined Google's position on the online search advertising market as 'largely dominant', and emphasised its 'extraordinary' aspects, in the same way that the Commission had described Microsoft's position in 2004.

25. In addition, Google's refusal to apply fairly the law protecting the related rights of press agencies and publishers in France led to a decision in 2020 (Decision 20-MC-01), following complaints from these market players, whereby the Autorité found it had likely imposed unfair trading conditions and issued a number of orders toward a fair negotiation of the remuneration legally owed to them

26. Another example is the Autorité's new use of the abuse of economic dependence in Decision 20-D-04, upheld on this point by the Paris Court of Appeal. In this decision, the Autorité sanctioned Apple's abuse of the situation of dependence in which Apple Premium Resellers were placed in relation to it, through a series of interlocking contracts.

27. In addition to exploitative abuse and abuse of dependence, the Autorité has also sanctioned exclusionary abuses, in particular practices whereby a company favours its own services over those of its competitors on related markets, i.e. self-preferencing. In Decision 21-D-11, *Google News Corporation Inc*, the Autorité sanctioned abusive self-preferencing practices implemented by Google to favour its own intermediation technologies. A penalty of €220 million was imposed on Google in a settlement procedure.

28. Finally, in Decision 22-D-12, the Autorité accepted and made binding commitments from Meta, to put an end to competition concerns regarding the transparency and fairness of relations between the platform and advertising technology suppliers.

29. Opinion 14-A-18, issued following a referral to the Court of Appeal in the *Bottin Cartographe* case, illustrates the difficulty for a competition authority to demonstrate the existence of predatory pricing on the free side of platforms, in this Google case.

30. Other practices have been sanctioned as cartels. Some of these were classic decisions relating to distribution channels. In Decision 08-MC-01, the Competition Council ordered interim measures against Apple on the grounds that the exclusive distribution clauses for the iPhone, granted to Orange, were problematic.

31. It should be remembered that the rules on vertical agreements apply to platforms, as the new Vertical Block Exemption Regulation (VBER) has clearly shown. In Decision 15-D-06, the Autorité accepted commitments to put an end to the parity clauses implemented by Booking.com. It also sanctioned Apple for limiting the commercial freedom of its wholesalers in the aforementioned Apple decision, which was upheld on this point.

32. It should be emphasised that abuses by digital platforms often take the form of contracts. In this respect, France has an effective commercial system of civil

penalties. For example, the offence of 'significant imbalance' (*déséquilibre significatif*) makes it possible to penalise operators who take advantage of the dependence of user companies or consumers to impose unbalanced contractual clauses (Article L. 442-1 of the French Commercial Code). The Minister for the Economy may refer this infringement to the commercial courts, which was done successfully in several cases. Several commercial court rulings can be cited in this regard, such as a ruling of 2 September 2019, sanctioning Amazon, and a ruling of 28 March 2022 sanctioning Google.

33. The Minister for the Economy may also issue administrative injunctions, if necessary subject to a fine, to put an end to the practices, on the basis of Articles L. 470-1, L. 470-2 and R.470-2 of the French Commercial Code. The DGCCRF fined Amazon €3.33 million for its delay in bringing its contracts in line with the new conditions, which were not implemented until 28 April 2022.

II. Actions Undertaken by France to Facilitate the Integration and to Enhance Synergies between EU and National Legislation for the Digital Sector

1. Articulation with Competition Law and Others Economic Laws

34. The rationale behind the Commission's *ex ante* regulation of gatekeepers, with its power to impose sanctions in the event of non-compliance by companies, is identical to the rationale behind the creation of specialised sectoral authorities in France and Europe since the early 2000s. At the time, in markets newly opened to competition, the aim was to guarantee the contestability of markets dominated by incumbent operators in a dominant position and to establish asymmetrical competition to the benefit of new entrants: *ex ante* obligations were imposed on former monopolies, such as the ATR obligation (third party access to networks, accounting separation, etc.).

35. The purpose of the DMA is to ensure the contestability of certain digital markets, such as essential platform services provided by gatekeepers.

36. In terms of principles, the coexistence of competition law and sector-specific regulation does not pose any more difficulties than it has in other sectors.

37. Competition law will continue to play a central role to regulate digital markets:
   - Platforms not included in the list of gatekeepers will still be outside the scope of the DMA.
   - Only the obligations in Articles 5 and 6 DMA are concerned.

38. Within the scope of Articles 5 and 6, nothing prohibits the parallel application of competition law to the practices referred to in the DMA.

39. Under Article 1.6 of the DMA, EU competition law, national competition law and national competition rules prohibiting other forms of unilateral conduct as well as merger control rules will remain fully applicable in parallel with the DMA (*provided that decisions taken by NCAs do not run counter to Commission decisions* – see Articles 1, 7), insofar as the legal bases, and therefore the objectives

pursued, are different and each regulation is based on distinct assessment methods (i. e. competition law, unlike the DMA, is based on an individual assessment of market positions and conduct, including its possible effects and the precise scope of the prohibited conduct, and provides for the possibility for undertakings to objectively justify the conduct in question on efficiency grounds).

40. National rules prohibiting other forms of unilateral conduct, such as certain commercial practices (under Article L. 442-1 of the French Commercial Code for example), are compatible if they target undertakings other than gatekeepers or impose other obligations than those of the DMA on them.

2. Cooperation of the Autorité and of the DGCCRF

41. In practical terms, cooperation and coordination between the Commission and the National Competition Authorities is governed by Article 38 DMA, when the NCAs act whether on the basis of EU or national competition law or other unilateral practices.

42. First, according to point 1 of Article 38, the Commission and the NCAs cooperate and exchange information through the ECN.

43. According to point 2, NCAs are obliged, where they 'intend to open an investigation into gatekeepers', to 'inform the Commission in writing of the first formal investigative measure before or immediately after the start of that measure'. In practical terms, this indication will appear on the equivalent of Article 11(3) *fiches* under Regulation 1/2003.

44. According to point 3, if the NCA intends to impose obligations on gatekeepers, on the same basis as point 3 of Article 38, 'it shall communicate the draft measure and its reasons to the Commission no later than 30 days before its adoption'. This is the equivalent of Article 11(4) *fiches* under Regulation 1/2003, which provides for communication of the proposed decision.

45. From this point of view, the European Commission will be informed of all investigations and measures concerning gatekeepers in the Member States.

46. The bridges that already exist between NCAs and the Commission will therefore be used for DMA information.

47. Under Article L. 450-11 of the French Commercial Code, the Autorité de la concurrence and the French Minister for the Economy are 'the national authorities responsible for enforcing the rules referred to in paragraph 6' of Article 1 of the DMA Regulation.

48. The authorities will be able to conduct their own investigations into the DMA.

49. Under Article 38(7) DMA, national competition authorities, where empowered to do so under their national law, may on their own initiative conduct investigations into possible breaches of the obligations set out in the DMA. This power will be particularly relevant where it is not immediately clear whether the practices in question are potentially contrary to the DMA, competition law, or both. The information transmitted on the basis of Article 38 will possibly enable the Commission, duly informed, to open a litigation procedure and adopt a decision within the framework of the DMA, which will de facto relieve the NCA in question.

50. NCAs will be required to assist in investigations carried out by the Commission, for example Article 23 ESMA inspections, or market investigations (Article 38(6) DMA).

51. In this capacity, the Autorité and the DGCCRF cooperate with the Commission in the enforcement of this text. In accordance with Article L. 450-12 of the French Commercial Code, they have the same powers of investigation as those granted to them for the investigation of anticompetitive practices. They cooperate with the Commission to verify that companies comply with the obligations of the DMA, in accordance with Article 27 of the DMA (Article L. 462-9-2 of the French Commercial Code).

52. They may be informed of non-compliance by third parties.

53. Under Article 27(1), all third parties, including user undertakings, competitors or end-users of essential platform services may inform the Autorité or the DGCCRF, or the Commission directly, of any practice of gatekeepers falling within the scope of the regulation. The authorities are not obliged to act on them. If they believe that there is a breach of the Regulation, they forward the information to the Commission.

54. Finally, the DGCCRF may ask the Commission to conduct investigations, in accordance with Article 41 of the DMA (Article L. 490-9 of the French Commercial Code).

3. Cooperation of Courts

55. The behaviours foreseen in Articles 5 and 6 DMA are prohibited conduct. As such, private actions may be brought before the courts, seeking compensation or nullity. Those actions could follow a Commission decision finding the infringement (follow-on action) or be directly lodged before the courts, without any decision of the Commission.

56. For the moment, the designation of gatekeeper services subject to the DMA and the monitoring of their compliance with the obligations it sets out are at different stages of development. Some designations are being challenged before the EU courts. However, proceedings before the national courts could be imminent.

57. Article 39 DMA provides for cooperation between the Commission and the courts of the Member States. As with litigation concerning anticompetitive practices, the private actions based on the DMA in France are heard by the same specialised courts as those applying competition law, under Articles L. 420-7 and R. 420-3 to R. 420-5 of the French Commercial Code, i.e. eight judicial courts and eight commercial courts, with appeals centralised before a specialised chamber of the Paris Court of Appeal.

58. However, unlike in the case of anti-competitive practices, there is currently no specific text governing cooperation between the national courts and the Commission. In France, no text comparable to the law transposing the 'Damage Directive' has been passed to regulate issues of access to files, rules on evidence or relations with the Autorité or the DGCCRF.

III. Conclusion: the DMA as a Piece of a Wider Set of EU and National Initiatives for Digital Transformation?

59. For the application of the DMA, the European Competition Network provides the natural framework for exchange.

60. The Autorité's participation, via the ECN, in a high-level expert group bringing together the networks of European regulators will make it possible to provide technical expertise and recommendations to the Commission on issues relating to the application of this regulation, as well as on questions relating to the interaction of the DMA with relevant sector regulations.

61. Alongside the DMA, which involves several players, other digital regulations have been introduced.

62. In France, the aforementioned SERN Act of 21 May 2024 also transposed the DSA into French law. Several regulators are involved:
   - The audiovisual and digital communication regulator (Arcom) is designated as the coordinator of digital services under the DSA;
   - The DGCCRF is responsible for monitoring compliance with the obligations of marketplace providers;
   - The data privacy regulator (Cnil) verifies compliance by platforms with restrictions on advertising profiling;
   - As mentioned above, the telecom regulator (Arcep) is responsible for regulating cloud services.

63. The SREN Act of 21 May 2024 Article 7–4) creates a 'national coordination network for the regulation of digital services', which comprises the three abovementioned regulators Arcom, Cnil and Arcep, as well as the Autorité de la concurrence, the national agency for information systems security, the authority for employment platforms labour relations and the relevant government departments.

64. The list of government departments that are members of this national coordination network for the regulation of digital services is defined by decree.

65. According to the law, 'The national coordination network for the regulation of digital services is responsible for exchanging information and encouraging coordination between its members. It shall ensure synergies in the work of the bodies mentioned in this chapter with regard to the regulation of information society services, while respecting their respective remits and, where applicable, their independence'. 'It shall promote a global vision of the regulation of digital services that incorporates the issues of fairness, protection, innovation and competitiveness. It leads reflection and comparative analysis of regulatory practices in other European Union Member States'.

66. In conclusion, the success of the interaction between competition law and the DMA and between all regulatory laws in the digital sector in the years to come will largely depend on our ability to coordinate effectively. This is undoubtedly one of the major challenges facing us and we must work together to achieve more competitive, contestable and fairer digital markets.

The Digital Markets Act and Competition Law Enforcement in the Digital Economy: A German Perspective

Germany

SIMON REETZ AND ALEXANDER IKEN*

DG COMP, European Commission

Abstract

The German Federal Cartel Office (Bundeskartellamt) has been at the forefront of enforcing competition law in the digital economy, addressing the challenges posed by dominant platforms and gatekeepers. This paper explores the interplay between Germany's competition law framework, particularly Section 19a of the German Competition Act (GWB), and the EU's Digital Markets Act (DMA). It examines the Bundeskartellamt's case practice in the digital economy aimed at curbing anti-competitive practices like self-preferencing, data exploitation, and market-entry barriers, and often serving as an inspiration for the DMA. The paper further discusses the complementary yet distinct roles of national competition authorities and the European Commission in enforcing the

* Both authors are case handlers in the Directorate for the Regulation of Digital Platforms in the Directorate-General for Competition of the European Commission. The content of this article does not reflect the official position of the European Commission. Responsibility for the information and views expressed lies entirely with the authors.

DMA and competition law, emphasising the need for coordinated enforcement and cooperation to avoid fragmentation. By analysing Germany's unique contributions and case precedents, the study underscores the potential for harmonised regulatory approaches to foster fair competition and innovation in digital markets across the EU.

I. Introduction: The Bundeskartellamt's Work in the Digital Economy

1. The Bundeskartellamt, Germany's Federal Cartel Office, plays an important role in maintaining fair competition within the digital economy. As digital markets grow increasingly complex, the agency has prioritised monitoring and addressing anti-competitive practices by major technology companies. It focuses on ensuring that digital platforms, such as online marketplaces, search engines, and social media networks, do not misuse their market power to the detriment of smaller competitors or consumers. Under the provisions of the German Competition Act (GWB)[1], the Bundeskartellamt is empowered to investigate and curb practices such as self-preferencing, discriminatory access to data, and the leveraging of dominance across different markets.

2. A key aspect of the Bundeskartellamt's work in the digital economy is its proactive approach to new regulatory challenges. This is particularly relevant for the increasingly complex challenges faced by competition law enforcers in digital markets. As early as 2016, the Bundeskartellamt published a working paper on the market power of platforms and networks.[2] Since then, the German legislator has empowered the agency with multiple amendments to the GWB to be able to enforce competition law in the digital markets more effectively. The 10th amendment to the GWB, also known as the 'GWB Digitalisation Act', has expanded the agency's authority to identify and address behaviours by companies deemed to have 'paramount significance for competition across markets'. This new framework allows the Bundeskartellamt to act pre-emptively against large digital companies that could harm competition, even before their practices lead to significant market distortions. Furthermore, the 11th amendment to the GWB has implemented the competences foreseen for national competition agencies (NCAs) under the Digital Markets Act (DMA)[3] into the GWB. Most importantly, the amendment has designated the Bundeskartellamt as the national competent authority enforcing the rules referred to in Article 1(6) DMA within the meaning of Article 38(7) DMA.

---

1 German Competition Act in the version published on 26 June 2013 (Bundesgesetzblatt (Federal Law Gazette) I, 2013, p 1750, 3245), as last amended by art 1 of the Act of 25 October 2023 (Federal Law Gazette I, p 294) <https://www.gesetze-im-internet.de/englisch_gwb/englisch_gwb.html>.

2 See Bundeskartellamt, 'Market Power of Platforms and Networks' (Working Paper, June 2016) <https://www.bundeskartellamt.de/SharedDocs/Publikation/EN/Berichte/Think-Tank-Bericht-Langfassung.pdf?__blob=publicationFile&v=2d>.

3 Regulation 2022/1925 of the European Parliament and of the Council of 14 September 2022 on contestable and fair markets in the digital sector and amending Directives 2019/1937 and 2020/1828 (Digital Markets Act or DMA) [2022] OJ L265/1.

II. Competition Law Enforcement in the Digital Economy in Germany

1. Important Cases Before the Entry into Force of the DMA

3. For more than 15 years, the Bundeskartellamt has been actively conducting proceedings focusing on the digital economy. Some of these have had an effect beyond Germany and inspired certain DMA provisions.

4. One notable case involved Facebook (now Meta) and its data processing practices.[4] In 2019, the Bundeskartellamt found that Facebook abused its dominant position in the social media market by collecting user data from third-party sources (such as Instagram, WhatsApp, and other websites) without adequate user consent, linking it to Facebook accounts. The agency ordered Facebook to change its practices, a decision that sparked extensive legal debate and set a precedent for certain data-related obligations of the DMA, notably Article 5(2) DMA.

5. The Bundeskartellamt has also conducted several investigations into best price clauses, particularly in the online hotel booking sector, where such clauses were used by platforms like Booking.com and HRS to prevent hotels from offering lower prices on competing platforms or their own websites. The Bundeskartellamt argued that these clauses restricted competition by limiting price differentiation and market entry for smaller platforms, thereby reinforcing the dominant positions of larger platforms. For instance, in its 2015 decision against Booking.com,[5] the authority prohibited the use of so-called narrow best price clauses (which restricted lower pricing only on the hotel's own website), following a similar prohibition of 'wide' clauses (which applied to all channels). The prohibition of all such parity clauses is now included in the DMA.

6. Another high-profile case concerned Amazon,[6] focusing on its role as both a marketplace operator and a competitor to the sellers on its platform. The Bundeskartellamt investigated Amazon's alleged abuse of its dual role, including unfair terms for sellers, such as unclear account suspensions and restrictions on pricing strategies. The investigation was concluded in 2019 after Amazon committed to changing its terms of service. Among other cases, this investigation highlighted the need for closer scrutiny of dominant platforms acting as gatekeepers and imposing unfair business conditions on other market participants.

7. Furthermore, the Bundeskartellamt conducted a sector inquiry into non-search online advertising. The results of this inquiry were published in 2023.[7] The main findings of this sector inquiry were, i.a., that Google/Alphabet occupies a significant

---

4 Bundeskartellamt, Case B6-22/16, 6 February 2019.

5 Bundeskartellamt, Case B9-121/13, 22 December 2015.

6 Bundeskartellamt, Case B2-88/18, 17 July 2019; see Philipp Westerhoff, 'The German Competition Authority reaches an informal settlement with an online marketplace and closes investigation into the company's commercial practices (*Amazon*)' (2019) e-Competitions, art no 96435.

7 See Bundeskartellamt, 'Sector inquiry on online advertising' (30 May 2023) <https://www.bundeskartellamt.de/SharedDocs/Publikation/DE/Sektoruntersuchungen/Sektoruntersuchung_Online_Werbung_Abschlussbericht.html?nn=298202> (in German).

market position in the market for non-search online advertising and that programmatic advertising is not sufficiently transparent.[8]

8. The Bundeskartellamt has therefore played a significant role in advancing the enforcement of competition law in digital markets, and its enforcement practices have inspired several provisions of the DMA.

2. Relationship between German Competition Law Enforcement and the DMA

9. The DMA foresees that the enforcement of the Regulation and competition law enforcement by the Bundeskartellamt work in tandem to ensure fair digital markets, with the DMA focusing on proactive *ex ante* regulation of designated gatekeepers and specific services across the EU and the Bundeskartellamt addressing broader competition issues within Germany. The Bundeskartellamt continues to apply German and EU competition law to conduct that may also fall under the DMA.

10. The relationship between the DMA, on the one hand, and European as well as national competition rules, on the other hand, is governed by Article 1(5), (6) and (7) DMA. According to Article 1(5) DMA, '[i]n order to avoid the fragmentation of the internal market, Member States shall not impose further obligations on gatekeepers by way of laws, regulations or administrative measures for the purpose of ensuring contestable and fair markets'. However, the norm does allow Member States to impose (further) obligations on gatekeepers 'for matters falling outside the scope of [the] Regulation'. Furthermore, according to Article 1(6) DMA, the DMA is 'without prejudice to the application of Articles 101 and 102' of the Treaty on the Functioning of the European Union (TFEU) as well as to the set of equivalent national competition rules defined in Article 1(6)(a), (b) and (c) DMA.[9] Article 1(6) DMA thus clarifies the scope of the limitations imposed by Article 1(5) DMA. In our view, it is thus possible that a gatekeeper's behaviour, in addition to being relevant under the DMA, may also violate national or European competition law and that the latter could be enforced by competent national authorities. This point is further underlined by the wording in Recital 91 (speaking of the possibility of behaviour violating 'both'). In addition, as indicated by the recital, it may not be known from the outset which set of rules may be relevant. The Bundeskartellamt will therefore continue to enforce German competition law as well as Articles 101 and 102 TFEU in digital markets, including for gatekeepers, in parallel to the European Commission's enforcement of the DMA.

11. The ratio for the parallel enforcement of both sets of rules can be explained by taking a look at their different goals and designs respectively. While traditional competition law looks at the individual conduct of an undertaking in order to prohibit anti-competitive behaviour, the DMA has a service-based perspective and

---

[8] See Bundeskartellamt, 'Inquiry into non-search online advertising: significant market position of Alphabet/Google, insufficient transparency in programmatic advertising' (Press Release, 2 June 2023) <https://www.bundeskartellamt.de/SharedDocs/Meldung/EN/Pressemitteilungen/2023/31_05_2023_SU_Online_Werbung.html?nn=298202>.

[9] See section III.2. of this chapter on the classification of s 19a GWB as a competition law instrument and the subsequent applicability of art 1(6)(b) DMA.

intends to ensure contestable and fair (digital) markets. The type of behaviour that falls under each set of rules may partially overlap, but may also vary significantly. Further, while traditional competition law has an *ex post* approach, meaning that competition authorities look at the market conduct of a particular undertaking after the fact, the DMA has introduced an *ex ante* approach, with certain relatively clearly defined obligations and prohibitions to compel gatekeepers to adopt a certain type of behaviour in advance to ensure contestable and fair markets. Consequently, the DMA will not be able to cover all types of anti-competitive behaviour in digital markets, whereas competition law enforcement is more flexible, being able to address behaviour not foreseen by the lawmakers at the time of the adoption of the DMA. Competition law enforcement in digital markets (at the national and EU level) will therefore continue to be important, in order to address these types of behaviour not covered under the DMA and avoid gatekeepers making use of the gaps in the DMA to undermine its goals. In addition, such cases in digital markets under competition law could also serve as an important indicator of the need for potential updates to the DMA under Article 12 DMA. The above was also reaffirmed by the Bundeskartellamt, stating that '[c]ompetition law will thus continue to play a significant role in the digital economy', including the enforcement by the Bundeskartellamt.[10]

12. Nevertheless, due to this potential overlap between competition law and DMA enforcement, some commentators have voiced concerns about potential over-regulation of gatekeepers or even the possibility of violations of the *ne bis in idem* principle. The need for the consideration of the principles of proportionality and *ne bis in idem* when enforcing the DMA has also been reaffirmed in Recital 86 DMA, which stipulates that in order to ensure that those principles are respected, the Commission and the relevant national authorities should coordinate their enforcement efforts, in particular when it comes to the imposition of fines and penalties under the DMA and other (EU or national) rules for the same fact. However, this stipulation, in line with established principles of EU law (see *bpost* and *Nordzucker* rulings of the European Court of Justice – ECJ),[11] shows that the same behaviour may well violate both the DMA and other (European and national) rules and that in case these rules address different aspects of harmful behaviour to society, enforcement under both sets of rules is possible against the same gatekeeper, including by NCAs.

13. Beyond the duty to respect the principle of *ne bis in idem*, Article 1(7) DMA also mandates the Commission as well as the Member States to 'work in close cooperation and coordinate their enforcement actions'. This duty is specified in Articles 37 and 38 DMA, which further set out the principles and mechanisms by which 'coherent, effective and complementary enforcement of available legal

---

10 See Bundeskartellamt, 'Rules for the digital economy' <https://www.bundeskartellamt.de/EN/Digital_economy/RulesDigital_economy/rulesdigitaleconomy_node.html>.

11 Case C-117/20 *bpost SA v Autorité belge de la concurrence* ECLI:EU:C:2022:202 and Case C-151/20 *Bundeswettbewerbsbehörde v Nordzucker AG and Others* ECLI:EU:C:2022:203; see Andreas Reindl and Margot Vogels, 'The EU Court of Justice preliminarily rules that the *ne bis in idem* principle provides limited protection against sanctions following investigations of the same infringements of competition law (*bpost*) (*Nordzucker*)' (2022) e-Competitions, art no 107729.

instruments applied to gatekeepers'[12] shall be ensured. The Bundeskartellamt has publicly reaffirmed these principles, stating that 'the Bundeskartellamt will continue to cooperate closely with the European Commission and other authorities'.[13] In addition, to avoid fragmentation and in particular contradicting obligations for gatekeepers, Article 1(7) DMA further prohibits national authorities from taking 'decisions which run counter to a decision adopted by the Commission' under the DMA.

III. New Powers of the Bundeskartellamt in the Digital Economy: Section 19a GWB

1. Legal Framework

14. In 2021, the 10th amendment to the German Competition Act modernised and expanded the framework for controlling abusive practices in the digital economy. This reform enables the Bundeskartellamt to act more swiftly and effectively against anti-competitive behaviour by major digital companies. It grants the Bundeskartellamt the authority to prohibit companies deemed to have 'paramount significance for competition across markets' from engaging in practices that harm competition. Importantly, interventions can now take place even in markets where these companies are not yet dominant. This marks a significant shift from traditional abuse control, allowing the Bundeskartellamt to act pre-emptively to preserve market openness, foster innovation, and safeguard consumer choice.

15. According to the newly introduced Section 19a GWB, companies with 'paramount significance for competition across markets' pose a particularly serious threat to competition. Under the new framework, this status is attributed to firms whose economic power spans multiple markets, granting them a degree of influence that cannot be sufficiently constrained by competition. The risk arises from their ability to strengthen their position or entrench their dominance across various markets, particularly as operators of expansive digital ecosystems. To determine whether a company falls into this category, several factors are considered, including:

- the company's market position,
- its financial resources or access to other critical assets,
- the breadth and interconnection of its activities across multiple markets,
- its access to competition-relevant data, and
- the significance of its activities for market access and their influence on third parties.

16. After the Bundeskartellamt has established that a company is of paramount significance for competition across markets, it can prohibit such a company from engaging in the following practices:

- Favouring its own offers over the offers of its competitors;
- 'Penetrating' new markets;

---

12 See DMA, art 37(1).

13 See Bundeskartellamt (n 9).

- Impeding competitors in cases where the company can rapidly expand its own position in the markets affected by using tying or bundling strategies;
- Exploiting the power it has gained based on data;
- Creating or raising barriers to market entry by processing data relevant to competition that have been collected by the company;
- Refusing the interoperability of products or services or data portability or making this more difficult.

2. Relationship with the Digital Markets Act

17. Section 19a GWB and the DMA both aim to regulate powerful digital platforms' behaviour. Both legal instruments are applicable to large digital companies and overlap regarding certain types of conduct covered, such as self-preferencing of a group's own services. However, there are several differences between the scope, legal approach, and implementation of both legal frameworks.

18. The DMA is a regulatory tool that applies to companies subject to presumption rules based on turnover figures, user numbers and market capitalisation, and generally focuses on individual, central platform services. Section 19a GWB, on the other hand, is based more strongly on a cross-service and cross-market perspective. With regard to the practices covered, the DMA includes a more specific list of rules and prohibitions, which apply directly to the services listed for each gatekeeper. In contrast, Section 19a GWB provides for a case-by-case examination of practices, which includes the possibility for companies to provide an objective justification for their conduct. Finally, Section 19a GWB only applies in Germany, while the DMA establishes a uniform framework applicable across the EU.

19. Section 19a GWB applies in parallel to the DMA subject to the rules for the interplay between the DMA and national competition law outlined in section II.2. above. When the DMA entered into force, it was initially debated under which rules Section 19a GWB would fall, namely, either Article 1(5) or Article 1(6)(b) DMA. Which rule would be applicable to the instrument depends on the classification of the legal nature of Section 19a GWB. It was discussed whether this section constitutes a competition law instrument or whether it should rather be classified as a type of regulatory law. The outcome of this legal assessment has significant consequences for the applicability of Section 19a GWB in parallel to the DMA. While a competition law tool dealing with the unilateral conduct of an undertaking falls under Article 1(6)(b) DMA (and therefore continues to find applicability besides the DMA insofar as it applies to undertakings other than gatekeepers or amounts to the imposition of further obligations on gatekeepers), a regulatory law falls under Article 1(5) DMA, meaning that Member States are not able to rely on this law to impose further obligations on gatekeepers for matters not falling outside the scope of the DMA. This question was addressed by the Bundesgerichtshof (Germany's Federal Court of Justice – BGH) on 23 April 2024, ruling that Section 19a GWB indeed constitutes a competition law instrument and therefore should fall under Article 1(6)(b) DMA.[14] Based on this ruling, the

14 Bundesgerichtshof (Federal Court of Justice), Case KVB 56/22, 23 April 2024 (in German).

Bundeskartellamt continues to be able to rely on Section 19a GWB in parallel to the DMA, with the limitation of only being applicable to undertakings other than gatekeepers or rules that amount to the imposition of further obligations on gatekeepers.

3. Implementation and Cases

20. To date, the Bundeskartellamt has identified Meta, Alphabet, Amazon, Apple, and Microsoft as companies of paramount significance for competition across markets pursuant to Section 19a GWB. Apple and Amazon have appealed their designation. Amazon's appeal was rejected by the BGH, while Apple's is still pending. The Bundeskartellamt has launched a total of seven substantive proceedings under Section 19a GWB: three against Alphabet, of which two have been concluded, two against Amazon and one against each Apple and Meta.

21. In the first closed case against Alphabet,[15] the Bundeskartellamt examined whether Google's News Showcase service, a licensing programme where Google pays publishers to feature curated news content on its platform, involves anti-competitive practices, such as self-preferencing or imposing unfair terms on publishers. In reply to these proceedings, Google made a number of important adjustments to the benefit of publishers.

22. The second closed case against Alphabet[16] focuses on Google's data processing practices and whether they harm competition by giving the company an unfair advantage. The investigation examined how Google collects and processes user data across its services, including whether users have sufficient control over their data. In reply to these proceedings, Google committed to provide its users with the possibility to give free, specific, informed and unambiguous consent to the processing of their data across services. While Google is already subject to such an obligation pursuant to Article 5(2) DMA for the core platform services listed in its designation decision (Google Shopping, Google Play, Google Maps, Google Search, YouTube, Google Android, Google Chrome and Google's online advertising services), the commitments to the Bundeskartellamt concern more than 25 other services (including Gmail, Google News, Assistant, Contacts and Google TV). The Bundeskartellamt and the European Commission coordinated closely during this investigation and will continue to do so to facilitate an effective interplay between competition law and the DMA. This case serves as a good example of how the principles of cooperation and coordination explained in section II.2. of this chapter can work in practice. Throughout the German case, the Bundeskartellamt and the European Commission cooperated closely to ensure that the outcome of the case was consistent with the obligations under Article 5(2) DMA. Concretely, the Bundeskartellamt confirmed that by cooperating closely, the Bundeskartellamt and the European Commission also intend to give Google the possibility to proceed in a uniform manner under the implementation of Article 5(2) and the commitments. In addition, the case shows that Member States are able to make use of

---

[15] Bundeskartellamt, Case V-43/20, 21 December 2022.

[16] Bundeskartellamt, Case B7-70/21, 6 October 2023.

their powers under Article 1(6)(b) DMA[17] without contravening the goals of the DMA or jeopardising the principles of proportionality or *ne bis in idem*. In fact, the Bundeskartellamt stated that '[t]he proceeding is a testament to the close cooperation between the Bundeskartellamt and the European Commission on the way to achieving more competition and fair markets in the digital sector'.[18]

23. The Bundeskartellamt's ongoing cases pursuant to Section 19a GWB cover the following aspects:[19]

   - Google's licensing practices of services for infotainment systems and terms of use of the Google Maps Platform;
   - Amazon's use of price control mechanisms or algorithms to potentially influence retailer prices on Amazon Marketplace;
   - Amazon's rules for marketplace sellers to obtain permission to sell branded products, for example, due to agreements between Amazon and (brand) manufacturers;
   - Apple's tracking policy for third-party apps and requirement of user consent to the potential favour of Apple's own services;
   - Meta's rules for the use of its VR headset, in particular the accounts that can be used and the combination of data processed in the context of Meta's various services.

IV. The Role and Competences Foreseen for Member States in the Enforcement of the DMA

24. Unlike in the case of competition law, the DMA empowers the European Commission as the 'sole enforcer' of the DMA (Recital 91 DMA). This centralised enforcement approach was adopted by EU lawmakers in particular to avoid fragmentation in the application of the DMA. However, the DMA nevertheless provides several ways in which NCAs can contribute to the enforcement of the DMA.

25. Articles 37 and 38 DMA set out the parameters of cooperation between the Commission and national authorities in the enforcement of the DMA. According to Article 37(1) DMA, '[t]he Commission and Member States shall work in close cooperation and coordinate their enforcement actions to ensure coherent, effective and complementary enforcement of available legal instruments applied to gatekeepers within the meaning of [the DMA]'. In addition, Article 38(1) DMA

---

17 For an in-depth discussion on whether s 19a GWB qualifies as competition law within the meaning of art 1(6) DMA, see eg the following publication by the German Parliament (Bundestag) (2022) <https://www.bundestag.de/resource/blob/880748/856d83cb24c61822c508aa47f27e18e7/WD-7-114-21-PE-6-067-21-pdf.pdf> (in German).

18 See Bundeskartellamt, 'Bundeskartellamt gives users of Google services better control over their data' (Press Release, 5 October 2023) <https://www.bundeskartellamt.de/SharedDocs/Meldung/EN/Pressemitteilungen/2023/05_10_2023_Google_Data.html>.

19 For a summary published by the Bundeskartellamt, see <https://www.bundeskartellamt.de/SharedDocs/Publikation/EN/Downloads/List_proceedings_digital_companies.pdf?__blob=publicationFile&v=14> (last updated December 2024).

stipulates that the European Commission and NCAs 'shall cooperate with each other and inform each other about their respective enforcement actions through the European Competition Network (ECN)'. Specifically, the DMA foresees the following roles for Member States and NCAs in the enforcement of the DMA.

26. First and foremost, Article 38(7) DMA stipulates that national competent Member State authorities may, on their own initiative, conduct an investigation into a case of possible non-compliance with Articles 5, 6 and 7 DMA on their territory.[20] As specified in Recital 91 DMA, this could be particularly 'relevant for cases where it cannot be determined from the outset whether a gatekeeper's behaviour is capable of infringing [the DMA], the competition rules which the national competent authority is empowered to enforce, or both'. However, even for cases where a gatekeeper's behaviour is only capable of infringing the DMA, the involvement of NCAs in DMA non-compliance investigations allows the NCAs to contribute their additional capacities as well as their own expertise to the enforcement of the DMA. In the case of the Bundeskartellamt, this may be particularly relevant given the Bundeskartellamt's significant experience and expertise in enforcing competition rules in digital markets (see section I of this chapter). The NCA shall report to the European Commission the findings of its investigation, which remains solely competent for any final findings on the investigated conduct under the DMA.

27. In order to avoid overlapping investigations under the DMA, the national competent authority concerned should inform the European Commission before taking its first formal investigative measure into a possible non-compliance by gatekeepers, according to Recital 91 and Article 38(7) DMA. Should the European Commission decide to open a formal investigation into the same gatekeeper practice as well, the NCA would be relieved of the possibility to conduct a separate investigation under Article 38(7) DMA.

28. Germany has made use of the possibility to determine the national competent authority responsible for conducting investigations under Article 38(7) DMA by way of the 11th amendment to the GWB, which entered into force on 7 November 2023. According to the newly introduced Section 32g(1) GWB, the Bundeskartellamt is empowered as the national competent authority to conduct non-compliance investigations under the DMA. For the purpose of such investigations, the Bundeskartellamt may make use of the investigative powers that the GWB grants to the agency for the enforcement of competition law, including the issuance of requests for information and the execution of searches of premises (see Section 32g(2) GWB). In case the non-compliance investigation concerns Article 7 DMA (related to the interoperability of number-independent interpersonal communications services), the Bundeskartellamt must also give the German Federal Network Agency a chance to express its opinion on the matter (see Section 32g(2) GWB). It will be interesting to see how the Bundeskartellamt, if at all, will make use of these powers, in particular in cases where a gatekeeper's

---

[20] It is worth noting that art 38(7) DMA was included, ia, at the initiative of the German government; see eg the German Federal Ministry for Economic Affairs and Climate Action's website <https://www.bmwk.de/Redaktion/DE/Schlaglichter-der-Wirtschaftspolitik/2022/06/12-digital-market-act.html> (in German).

behaviour may violate the DMA as well as Section 19a GWB or other national competition law rules. The German NCA has not made use of the investigative powers of Section 32g GWB as of January 2025.

29. Second, in addition to the possibility of non-compliance investigations at the NCA's own initiative under Article 38(7) DMA, the DMA also allows the Commission to ask national competent authorities of the Member States to support any of its market investigations under the DMA (see Article 38(6) DMA). This tool further allows the Commission to take advantage of an NCA's expertise and resources, contributing to a more efficient allocation of resources in the enforcement of the DMA. In the case of Germany, the Bundeskartellamt will also function as the national competent authority for requests by the European Commission under Article 38(6) DMA.

30. Third, Article 41 DMA provides Member States (either individually or in combination with at least two other Member States) with the right to request the Commission to open market investigations for the purpose of potential designations (para 1), non-compliance findings (para 2) or expansion of the Regulation under Article 19 DMA (para 3). Unlike Article 38(7) DMA, Article 41 DMA notably goes beyond non-compliance investigations.

31. Fourth, the DMA also foresees the private enforcement of DMA provisions in national Member State courts, with Article 39(1) DMA referring to 'proceedings for the application of this Regulation' in front of national courts. While any private enforcement possibility will increase the risk of fragmentation in the application of a regulatory system, the DMA addresses this risk under Article 39(5), stipulating that '[n]ational courts shall not give a decision which runs counter to a decision adopted by the Commission under this Regulation' and further requiring national courts to avoid giving decisions that would conflict with a contemplated future Commission decision under an ongoing proceeding.

32. The German lawmakers have incorporated the possibility of private DMA enforcement into the above-mentioned GWB amendment, introducing the following changes to the GWB. First and foremost, the now-amended Section 33a GWB expressly stipulates the civil liability of any gatekeeper for damages resulting from a violation of Articles 5 to 7 DMA. Further, the newly amended Section 33b GWB declares the Commission's decision to designate a certain company as a gatekeeper to be binding for German civil courts. In addition, the GWB amendment declares many of the GWB provisions relating to the private enforcement of antitrust damages also applicable to the private enforcement of the DMA. This also includes claims for removal and injunctive relief under Section 33 GWB. Lastly, the GWB amendment also determines the German courts responsible for private enforcement matters of the DMA. Concretely, the amendment exclusively tasks district courts (*Landgerichte*) with such matters, the same chambers tasked with the enforcement of actions under the Damages Directive (Directive 2014/104/EU)[21] and which already have gathered experience

---

21 Directive 2014/104/EU of the European Parliament and of the Council of 26 November 2014 on certain rules governing actions for damages under national law for infringements of the competition law provisions of the Member States and of the European Union [2014] OJ L349/1.

in private enforcement in the digital sector.[22] Overall, Germany has therefore aligned the private enforcement of the DMA with that of Articles 101 and 102 TFEU violations (Section 87 GWB).

33. Fifth, Article 40 DMA foresees the establishment of the 'high-level group', a body made up of representatives of the following European bodies and networks:
    - the Body of the European Regulators for Electronic Communications;
    - the European Data Protection Supervisor and European Data Protection Board;
    - the European Competition Network;
    - the Consumer Protection Cooperation Network;
    - the European Regulatory Group of Audiovisual Media Regulators.

34. The high-level group is tasked with providing the Commission with advice and expertise related to DMA enforcement and in particular with the goal to ensure a consistent approach across different regulatory instruments. Germany has the possibility to participate in the high-level group indirectly, as its agencies and bodies may serve as representatives of the European bodies and networks represented in the high-level group. In this function, the Bundeskartellamt has already been present at the high-level group multiple times.

35. Sixth, according to Article 27 DMA, in addition to the European Commission, the Bundeskartellamt, as the national competent authority of the Member State enforcing the rules referred to in Article 1(6) DMA, also functions as one of the potential contact points for third parties who wish to relay information about any practice or behaviour by gatekeepers that falls within the scope of the DMA. According to Article 27(2) DMA, the Bundeskartellamt has 'full discretion as regards the appropriate measures and [is] under no obligation to follow-up on the information received'. Should the Bundeskartellamt, based on the information received, determine that there may be an issue of non-compliance with the DMA, 'it shall transfer that information to the Commission' according to Article 27(3) DMA.

36. Lastly, Article 50 DMA foresees the participation of every Member State NCA in the decision-making procedure under the DMA as members of the Digital Markets Advisory Committee (DMAC), which will have to be consulted for several types of decisions under the DMA (including designation decisions and findings of non-compliance).

37. In light of these various ways in which Germany and other EU Member States can participate in the enforcement of the DMA, it remains to be seen how the cooperation foreseen under the DMA will be implemented in practice. In particular, it will be interesting to see the role of established structures such as the ECN, which is also explicitly referenced in Article 38(1) DMA as the appropriate

---

[22] See ia the following judgments by German courts: Landgericht München, Case 37 O 15721/20, 10 February 2021, see Thomas Höppner, 'The Munich Regional Court bans the preferential display within a search engine of information exclusively drawn from a state-run health portal (*Google / German Ministry of Health*)' (2021) e-Competitions, art no 100162; and Hanseatisches Oberlandesgericht Hamburg, Case 15 U 18/23 Kart, 31 August 2023.

venue for enforcement cooperation between the European Commission and the NCAs, in complementing new structures such as the high-level group as well as several bilateral avenues for cooperation foreseen by the DMA as set out above.

V. Conclusion

38. The Bundeskartellamt's expertise in enforcing competition law in the digital economy has played a crucial role in the past, even serving as an inspiration for the DMA, and continues to play an important role – alongside and complementing the enforcement of the DMA. Competition law and the DMA, as well as the work of NCAs and the European Commission, complement each other. The unique features of digital markets, such as rapid innovation, network effects, and data monopolies, require careful coordination to ensure the effective application of these rules. The DMA has struck a delicate balance between the limitations imposed on Member States under Article 1(5) DMA and the European Commission being appointed as the 'sole enforcer' of the DMA, and the enforcement space granted to Member States under Article 1(6) DMA as well as the principles set out in Articles 37 and 38 DMA. In order to make this balanced structure work in practice, close cooperation and coordination between Member States and the European Commission are critical to avoid legal fragmentation, maximise impact and provide clarity for businesses.

39. Such cooperation may also maximise the opportunity for the DMA to influence global standards for digital markets, for example by encouraging gatekeepers to adopt uniform policies within the EU but also beyond due to operational efficiency or in response to public pressure. Germany's recent *Google data* case illustrates how close collaboration can resolve concerns about overlapping enforcement, particularly regarding the *ne bis in idem* principle preventing double jeopardy. The case demonstrated that Member States can effectively enforce their own laws alongside the DMA. The *Google data* case, as well as the investigative powers conferred to NCAs under Article 38(7) DMA, also shows that the resources and expertise of NCAs can be leveraged in parallel to as well as within the structure of the DMA to deal with the unique challenges faced in the digital economy most effectively.

Digital Markets Act and Relevant Developments in Greece

Greece

Dimitrios Kyriazis*
Aristotle University of Thessaloniki

Abstract

This chapter seeks to describe the main digital law developments in Greece in the past few years, especially in relation to the Digital Markets Act (DMA). It introduces the general views from Greece, then proceeds to analyse various digital initiatives, and concludes with an overall assessment of the DMA as a key piece of the EU's digital transformation.

* Dimitrios Kyriazis (DPhil, Oxon) is an assistant professor of EU law at the Aristotle University of Thessaloniki Law School.

I. Introduction: General Views from Greece

1. The Digital Markets Act (DMA) – namely, Regulation (EU) 2022/1925[1] – forms part of the European Union's broader strategy to regulate the digital economy, focusing on creating a fair and open digital market. It primarily aims to address the market power of large tech companies, referred to as 'gatekeepers', and ensure that smaller players can compete fairly.

2. According to the European Commission's ('Commission') own description,[2] the DMA 'establishes a set of clearly defined objective criteria to qualify a large online platform as a "gatekeeper" and ensures that they behave in a fair way online and leave room for contestability'. The DMA thus 'is one of the centrepieces of the European digital strategy'.

3. As we will see in the following sections, Greece has been active in relation to initiatives in the digital sector. *Inter alia*, the Greek competition authority, i.e. the Hellenic Competition Commission (HCC), was designated – by an amendment to its governing law – the national competent authority for the implementation of the DMA.

4. The structure of this chapter is as follows. In section II, we explore some of the initiatives undertaken by Greece to facilitate the integration and to enhance synergies between EU and national legislations for the digital sector. The focus there is twofold: on digital matters more generally and on the DMA and competition law more specifically. In section III, we ponder the DMA as a piece of a wider cosmos of EU and national legislative initiatives for digital transformation, and then we conclude.

II. Actions Undertaken by the EU Member State to Facilitate the Integration and to Enhance Synergies between EU and National Legislations for the Digital Sector

5. This section is divided into two parts. In part 1, we explore the room for cooperation that exists between national authorities and the EU under the DMA itself, i.e. we peruse the main DMA provisions leaving scope for action by Member States and national authorities, so as to better understand Greek initiatives in this context. In part 2, we present and analyse the principal actions undertaken by Greece in order to facilitate digital integration and enhance synergies between EU and national legislations.

---

[1] Regulation 2022/1925 of the European Parliament and of the Council of 14 September 2022 on contestable and fair markets in the digital sector and amending Directives 2019/1937 and 2020/1828 (Digital Markets Act or DMA) [2022] OJ L265/1.

[2] European Commission, 'The Digital Markets Act: ensuring fair and open digital markets' <https://commission.europa.eu/strategy-and-policy/priorities-2019-2024/europe-fit-digital-age/digital-markets-act-ensuring-fair-and-open-digital-markets_en>.

1. Room for Cooperation between National Authorities and the EU in Accordance with the DMA

6. Starting off with the DMA's preamble, according to Recital 91, '[t]he Commission is the sole authority empowered to enforce this Regulation'. Still, '[i]n order to support the Commission, it is [made] possible for Member States to empower their national competent authorities enforcing competition rules to conduct investigations into possible non-compliance by gatekeepers with certain obligations under [the DMA]'. Moreover, in order to avoid overlapping investigations under the DMA, the preamble states that the national competent authority concerned – in our case, the HCC – 'should inform the Commission before taking its first investigative measure into a possible non-compliance by gatekeepers with certain obligations under [the DMA]'. Additionally, it should closely cooperate and coordinate with the Commission when enforcing national competition rules against gatekeepers.

7. Moving to the actual text of the DMA, there are various provisions that are of interest. One of the initial provisions is Article 1(6) and (7) DMA, where it is stated that the DMA is 'without prejudice to the application of Articles 101 and 102 TFEU [Treaty on the Functioning of the European Union]'. It is also, *inter alia*, without prejudice to the application of national competition rules mirroring Articles 101 and 102 TFEU or prohibiting other forms of unilateral conduct insofar as they are applied to undertakings other than gatekeepers or amount to the imposition of further obligations on gatekeepers. Still, national competition authorities are not allowed to take decisions that 'run counter to a decision adopted by the Commission under this Regulation. The Commission and Member States shall work in close cooperation and coordinate their enforcement actions'.

8. Even if the DMA did not specifically provide for this, such an obligation would arguably emanate directly from the principle of sincere cooperation, as set out in Article 4(3) of the Treaty on European Union (TEU):

> Pursuant to the principle of sincere cooperation, the Union and the Member States shall, in full mutual respect, assist each other in carrying out tasks which flow from the Treaties.
>
> The Member States shall take any appropriate measure, general or particular, to ensure fulfilment of the obligations arising out of the Treaties or resulting from the acts of the institutions of the Union.
>
> The Member States shall facilitate the achievement of the Union's tasks and refrain from any measure which could jeopardise the attainment of the Union's objectives.

9. According to Article 16(5), '[t]Commission may ask one or more national competent authorities to assist it in its market investigation'. Moreover, according to Article 23, the Commission is empowered to 'conduct all necessary inspections of an undertaking or association of undertakings' and it may request the assistance of the national competent authority. According to Article 27(3), where the national competent authority of the Member State – in our case, the HCC – determines that there may be an issue of non-compliance with the DMA, it shall transfer that information to the Commission. Please note that there is no discretion here, but a clear obligation.

10. Finally, Articles 37 and (especially) 38 are key in this context. Article 37 makes it clear that the Commission and Member States shall work in close cooperation and coordinate their enforcement actions to ensure coherent, effective and complementary enforcement of available legal instruments applied to gatekeepers within the meaning of the DMA. Moreover, the Commission is allowed to consult national authorities where appropriate, on any matter relating to the application of the DMA.

11. Still, the truly important DMA provision in relation to the relationship between the Commission and the national competition authority – in our case, the HCC – is Article 38. The first duty is to keep each other informed, since the Commission and the HCC 'shall cooperate with each other and inform each other about their respective enforcement actions through the European Competition Network (ECN). They shall have the power to provide one another with any information regarding a matter of fact or of law, including confidential information'. Secondly, where a national competition authority 'intends to launch an investigation on gatekeepers based on national [competition] laws..., it shall inform the Commission in writing of the first formal investigative measure, before or immediately after the start of such measure'. Thirdly, where a national competition authority 'intends to impose obligations on gatekeepers based on national [competition] laws..., it shall, no later than 30 days before its adoption, communicate the draft measure to the Commission stating the reasons for the measure'. For interim measures, it has to communicate to the Commission the draft measures envisaged 'as soon as possible, and at the latest immediately after the adoption of such measures'. Fourthly, the Commission may ask the HCC to support any of its market investigations pursuant to this Regulation.

12. Paragraph 7 deserves its own honourable mention, as it is the most substantive provision in this context. It states that, '[w]here it has the competence and investigative powers to do so under national law', a national competition authority 'may, on its own initiative, conduct an investigation into a case of possible non-compliance with Articles 5, 6 and 7 [DMA] on its territory. Before taking a first formal investigative measure, that authority shall inform the Commission in writing'. However, the opening of proceedings by the Commission pursuant to Article 20 DMA shall relieve the national authorities of the 'possibility to conduct such an investigation or end it where it is already ongoing. Those authorities shall report to the Commission on the findings of such investigation in order to support the Commission in its role as sole enforcer of [the DMA]'.

2. Greek Developments in the Digital Sector

A. *Greek Developments in the Digital Sector More Generally*

13. Before delving into DMA-specific developments in Greece, which are not numerous, it is worth surveying the broader horizon of digital initiatives in Greece in the past few years.[3]

---

[3] To showcase Greece's commitment to AI, the author utilised ChatGPT, an AI language model developed by OpenAI, to assist in generating content and refining language in certain parts of this chapter.

14. Firstly, the implementation of the General Data Protection Regulation (GDPR) was the initial (obvious) step in this context. The Greek Data Protection Authority plays a crucial role in enforcing the GDPR, thus ensuring compliance. It has already issued a significant number of decisions based on the GDPR and has been very active in informing natural and legal persons of their obligations. No digital transformation can start without due respect to data protection, which is these days also guaranteed by Article 8 of the EU Charter of Fundamental Rights.

15. Secondly, the Greek government put together its so-called Digital Transformation Bible (2020–2025). This Bible is a record of the necessary interventions in the state's technological infrastructure, as well as in the education and training of the population for the acquisition of digital skills. The Greek government wishes to improve the way in which digital technology is utilised in all sectors of the economy and public administration. The main role of the Bible is to describe the vision, philosophy and goals of the national strategy for the country's digital transformation, while also keeping government ministers accountable in case the goals are not reached by 2025.

16. Many targets have already been achieved since the Bible was published, for instance, the digital ID and driver's licence for all Greek citizens, the digital vaccination certificate and the overhaul of the government portal Gov.gr. This central online portal provides access to a wide range of government services, allowing citizens to complete tasks such as tax filings, health registrations, and social security applications online. Moreover, the Greek government has launched various mobile apps that facilitate easier access to services, such as scheduling appointments, accessing health records, and receiving notifications about public services.

17. The text of the Digital Transformation Bible, however, goes much deeper, describing the guiding principles, the model of governance and implementation, as well as the strategic axes of digital transformation. It further describes more than 400 specific projects, classified into short- and medium-term, horizontal and sectoral. It identifies a variety of specific projects, classified into short- and medium-term, that affect all areas of public policy (e.g. Health, Education, Justice, Economy, Environment, and Energy), seeking to modernise the operation of public and private sectors. Obviously, the effective implementation of the new digital strategy requires continuous monitoring of the implementation of the interventions and the projects included in it. In this context, it is worth noting that the Ministry of Digital Governance monitors the implementation of the Digital Transformation Bible.

18. Thirdly, significant investments have been made in digital infrastructure, including high-speed internet access across urban and rural areas. The Greek government has been working with the EU to secure funding for broadband expansion, particularly in underserved regions. Furthermore, Greece actively participates in EU programmes such as Horizon Europe, thus engaging in research and innovation projects that promote digital technologies, and the Digital Europe Programme, thus seeking funding for projects that enhance digital skills, infrastructure, and public services.

19. Fourthly, Greece has endeavoured to create a conducive environment for technology and innovation through various policies, including funding programmes for the digital transformation of small and medium-sized enterprises (SMEs) and tax incentives for tech investments and research and development activities. In this context, the Greek government has launched initiatives aimed at reskilling the workforce in areas like coding, digital marketing, and data analytics.

20. Fifthly, Greece has developed a national cybersecurity strategy in line with the EU's cybersecurity framework. Its focus is twofold. First, to initiate awareness campaigns with the goal of educating citizens and businesses about cybersecurity risks and best practices. This way, citizens can protect themselves from cyber threats and not fall into the hands of fraudsters. Secondly, to strengthen the capabilities of the Greek police force and the Greek judicial system so as to deal with such crimes more effectively.

21. Finally, Greece has launched a series of Public-Private Partnerships (PPPs or 'ΣΔΙΤ' in Greek) to facilitate dialogue between the public sector and private enterprises and ensure that national policies reflect industry needs. In this way, the Greek state can also collaborate with private companies to carry out a series of important digital infrastructure projects. This way the Greek State can also work together with private companies to bring to completion a series of important projects of digital infrastructure.

B. *Greek Developments in Relation to the DMA and Competition Law*

22. In this section, we will endeavour to mention some Greek competition law developments in relation to the digital sector, as well as peruse some relevant legislative amendments.[4]

23. Firstly, starting off with the DMA specifically and relevant national law developments in Greece, Article 14(1A) of Law 3959/2011 (the law that governs the competences of the HCC) was added by Article 83 of Law 5019/2023, with effect from 14 February 2023.

24. This new provision reads as follows:

> 1A. The Hellenic Competition Commission is the national competent authority for the implementation of Regulation (EU) 2022/1925 of the European Parliament and of the Council of 14 September 2022 'on enforceable and fair markets in the digital sector and amending Directives (EU) 2019/1937 and (EU) 2020/1828 (Digital Marketplaces Act)' (L 265/1), and in particular par. 7 of Article 38 thereof, without prejudice to the specific arrangements concerning the competences of the National Telecommunications and Postal Commission. In order to fulfil this competence, it may make use of the powers provided for in Articles 38 and 39 hereof [meaning of Law 3959/2011].

---

4 The following analysis is non-exhaustive, since the aim is to identify certain flagship initiatives/changes.

25. Article 38(7) DMA, to which the aforementioned provision refers, provides for the following:

> 7. Where it has the competence and investigative powers to do so under national law, a national competent authority of the Member States enforcing the rules referred to in Article 1(6) may, on its own initiative, conduct an investigation into a case of possible non-compliance with Articles 5, 6 and 7 of this Regulation on its territory. Before taking a first formal investigative measure, that authority shall inform the Commission in writing.
>
> The opening of proceedings by the Commission pursuant to Article 20 shall relieve the national competent authorities of the Member States enforcing the rules referred to in Article 1(6) of the possibility to conduct such an investigation or end it where it is already ongoing. Those authorities shall report to the Commission on the findings of such investigation in order to support the Commission in its role as sole enforcer of this Regulation.

26. It is obvious that this new provision in the Greek law serves multiple purposes. First, it designates the HCC as the national competent authority for the DMA. Second, it empowers the HCC to conduct, on its own initiative, an investigation into cases of possible non-compliance with the DMA on Greek territory. Of course, before taking a first formal investigative measure, the HCC shall inform the Commission in writing and, if the Commission opens proceedings, the HCC will need to halt its own investigation. Thus, the combined text of the Greek law and Article 38 DMA provides us with much-needed legal certainty and creates useful synergies.

27. It is worth noting that the HCC has been involved in the DMA project from the beginning. When the European Commission adopted a decision to establish a High-Level Group on the DMA, Professor Ioannis Lianos, professor of global competition law and public policy at UCL Laws and (then) president of the HCC, was selected, along with five other heads of competition authorities (from the 27 Member States), to participate in the High-Level Group representing the ECN.[5] The role of this High-Level Group was to provide the Commission with advice and expertise to ensure that the DMA and other sectoral regulations applicable to gatekeepers are implemented in a coherent and complementary manner.

28. Secondly, moving on to 'pure' competition law matters, the approval of the first major digital sector merger in Greece came in 2022 with the *Delivery Hero* case.[6] In that case, the HCC unanimously approved Delivery Hero's acquisition of sole control over companies (a) Alfa Distributions SA, (b) Inkat SA, (c) Delivery.gr Single Member P.C., and (d) E-table Online Restaurant Reservations Single

---

5 'Professor Ioannis Lianos appointed to EU High Level Group on the Digital Markets Act' (*UCL Faculty of Laws*, 18 April 2023) <https://www.ucl.ac.uk/laws/news/2023/apr/professor-ioannis-lianos-appointed-eu-high-level-group-digital-markets-act>.

6 Decision no 775/2022 – approval of Delivery Hero's acquisition of companies Alpha Distributions SA, Inkat SA, Delivery.gr Single Member P.C. and E-Table Single Member P.C.

Member P.C. ('E-table Single Member P.C.') subject to commitments offered by Delivery Hero.[7]

29. In Greece, Delivery Hero operates the online delivery platform e-food, through which consumers connect with restaurants, supermarkets, convenience stores and other local stores, as well as the online convenience store e-food market. After imposing certain key conditions, the HCC found that, following the transaction, the combined entity's e-food and delivery.gr platforms would have a high combined market share in the market for online intermediation for the sale of groceries. However, given the bargaining power of other supermarkets, it was estimated that the merged entity would not be able to substantially restrict competition in the market, compared with the pre-merger situation. Therefore, the merger was approved.

30. Thirdly, it is worth noting that the HCC, acting in the context of its responsibilities by virtue of Article 40 of Law 3959/2011, took the initiative in April 2020 to investigate in depth the competitive conditions prevailing in the market for financial technology services, in order to enhance consumer welfare and to promote innovation through the sector's digital transformation ('FinTech sector inquiry'). The inquiry was concluded in December 2022, and the final report was published (only in Greek).[8]

31. Still, according to the report's executive summary (available in English), many interesting issues were flagged.[9] It was, for example, concluded that the current situation of the markets was still 'volatile and taking shape'. For this reason, it was 'premature to draw definitive conclusions about the existence of restrictions or distortions of competition'.

> In this respect, despite the extensive regulation of the relevant markets, which may occasionally create barriers to entry, any proposals for its modification or restriction are made without prejudice to the special role that regulation plays in these markets, in view of their particular characteristics and of the paramount importance of legal certainty. In any case, the experience and know-how of the sectoral regulator and the competent supranational organisations [*inter alia* the European Commission] should be also taken into account.[10]

32. Moreover, it was stated in the final report of the FinTech sector inquiry, which was published before the entry into force of the DMA, that the entry and operation of FinTechs in the Greek market were expected to be further facilitated by the DMA (which entered into force on 2 May 2023). Among the various obligations imposed upon gatekeepers, it was noted that 'the DMA contains a provision (Art. 5(7)) the purpose of which is to safeguard [third party providers]

---

7 HCC, 'The HCC approves Delivery Hero's acquisition of four companies subject to commitments' (Press Release, 20 April 2022) <https://epant.gr/en/information/press-releases/item/2189-press-release-the-hellenic-competition-commission-approves-delivery-hero-s-acquisition-of-four-companies-subject-to-commitments.html>.

8 HCC, FinTech sector inquiry, *Final Report* (2022) (in Greek) <https://www.epant.gr/files/2022/fintech/FINTECH_Final_Report_EL.pdf>.

9 HCC, FinTech sector inquiry, 'Executive Summary' (2022) <https://www.epant.gr/files/2022/fintech/executive_summary_EN.pdf>.

10 *ibid* [49].

from possible anti-competitive conduct by Big Tech firms, thus facilitating their integration into the latters' ecosystems'.[11]

33. Fourthly and finally, it is worth briefly focusing on the internal workings of the HCC. Since 2020/2021, the HCC has had a directorate that also deals with digital markets, an important step in the right direction. Moreover, its own digital transformation remains a key priority for the HCC. By way of example, in the HCC Strategic Plan 2024–2025,[12] it is stated its strategy focuses on three key goals, namely (i) 'effective intervention in the market to protect competition'; (ii) 'enhancing a competition culture among consumers and undertakings'; and (iii) 'internal organizational refinement, with an emphasis on digital transformation and innovation'. It is also noted that the HCC's work is 'supported by modern technological tools and innovative and interdisciplinary methodological approaches to control and prevent anti-competitive practices, while at the same time ensuring the use of [its] resources with a sense of responsibility and due regard to sustainable development'. It is evident that the HCC seeks to become, and has partly already become, a model enforcer of competition law rules in the digital sector.

III. Conclusion: the DMA as a Piece of a Wider Cosmos of EU and National Legislative Initiatives for Digital Transformation?

34. It has been correctly observed that there has not been much public debate over the DMA in Greece.[13] Greek newspapers have devoted little coverage to the DMA since it does not directly impact Greek companies, which, on average, are smaller than their average EU counterparts. Moreover, no Greek company risks being identified as a gatekeeper.

35. However, as seen in the previous sections of this chapter, certain things have been made abundantly clear. First, the DMA is a key part of the European Union's broader strategy to regulate the digital economy, focusing on creating a fair and open digital market. The annual report on the DMA's implementation sheds more light on these matters and the significant progress made.[14] Second, Greece has made strides in the right direction, both in digital matters more generally and in competition law more specifically. Finally, the HCC has taken important steps to effectively enforce competition law in the digital sector and possesses the necessary know-how and highly skilled personnel to successfully discharge all of its duties and competences set out in the DMA.

---

11 *ibid* [48].

12 HCC, *Strategic Plan 2024–2025* <https://www.epant.gr/en/ea/strategic-plan.html>.

13 George Tzogopoulos, 'Europe's DMA: The Cloudy View From Athens' (*CEPA*, 22 March 2024) <https://cepa.org/article/europes-dma-the-cloudy-view-from-athens/.

14 European Commission, 'Annual report on Regulation (EU) 2022/1925 of the European Parliament and of the Council on contestable and fair markets in the digital sector and amending Directives (EU) 2019/1937 and (EU) 2020/1828 (Digital Markets Act)' COM(2024) 106 final <https://eur-lex.europa.eu/legal-content/EN/TXT/HTML/?uri=CELEX:52024DC0106>.

Ireland's Choices in Implementing the Digital Markets Act: Narrow or Wide?

Ireland

PAUL K. GORECKI[*]

Department of Economics, Trinity College Dublin

Abstract

Under the Digital Markets Act (DMA), the European Commission (the Commission) is the 'sole enforcer' with limited discretion accorded to the Member State in the administration of the DMA. Member States can, however, enforce competition rules with respect to the Commission-designated gatekeepers. The Member State's discretion under the DMA is circumscribed by the necessity of informing and making decisions consistent with the Commission's previous decisions and stated preferences. Even within the limited choice set of DMA-delegated responsibilities confronting the Member State, Ireland opted to exercise discretion towards the minimum end of the spectrum. The Competition and Consumer Protection Commission (CCPC), which has been designated as the national competent authority under the DMA, does not have a substantial track record of competition law

---

[*] Doctor Paul K Gorecki, Adjunct Lecturer 2013–2019 in Trinity College Dublin. The author was a member of the Competition Authority (2000–2008), a Research Professor at the Economic and Social Research Institute (2009–2013), a member of the Council of the Pharmaceutical Society of Ireland (2014–2022); and is a Non-Governmental Advisor to the International Competition Network, on the Regulatory Decisions Panel of the Central Bank of Ireland and an Adjudicator under the Communications Regulation & Digital Hub Development Agency (Amendment) Act 2023. He has not acted in any capacity in relation to the gatekeepers designated by the Commission. Sean Lyons and Francis O'Toole provided helpful comments on the chapter while the CCPC and the Department of Enterprise, Trade and Employment clarified the application of the DMA to Ireland. The usual disclaimer applies.

enforcement in the digital sector in general or with respect to the gatekeepers in particular. There are sound reasons for these CCPC enforcement choices. In terms of future competition law and DMA enforcement, while any predictions are somewhat speculative, it seems reasonable to assume that the CCPC's main involvement will be referring third-party information on non-compliance with the DMA to the Commission, assisting the Commission conducting inspections and making requests to the Commission under Article 41 of the DMA.

I. Introduction

1. Notwithstanding the fact that Article 38 of the Digital Markets Act (DMA)[1] states that the European Commission (the Commission) is the 'sole enforcer'[2] of the DMA there is a limited role for the Member States in the DMA's administration and enforcement. The DMA also permits Member States to continue to enforce existing competition law against the Commission-designated gatekeepers (the gatekeepers) and to enact legislation that goes beyond the DMA with respect to the gatekeepers. The purpose of this chapter is to examine the scope of the legislative discretion accorded to a Member State under the DMA and the choices made by Ireland in exercising that discretion.

2. Section II briefly describes the DMA and the options accorded Member States under that legislation. The choices made by Ireland in exercising that discretion are outlined in Section III, together with selected recent digital sector regulatory developments in Ireland that impact the gatekeepers. The record of competition law enforcement by Ireland's national competition authority (NCA) with respect to the digital sector and gatekeepers in particular is analysed in Section IV.

3. The focus of competition law enforcement by Ireland's NCA on sectors other than the digital sector does not necessarily presage future sectoral enforcement. Section V thus assesses the prospects for competition law enforcement with respect to the gatekeepers and the wider role that Ireland's NCA might play with respect to the DMA's administration and enforcement. Section VI considers the question posed in the title of this chapter: whether or not the choices made by Ireland in relation to the discretion accorded to it under the DMA have been narrow (i.e. the minimum necessary required under the DMA) or wide (i.e. the maximum possible under the DMA). The conclusion is that Ireland's choices lean, for quite understandable and rational reasons, towards the minimum necessary to satisfy the DMA requirements.

II. The DMA & the Member State

1. Introduction

4. After a brief description of the designation and regulation of gatekeepers together with the associated core platform services under the DMA, the section outlines the roles that the Member States *may* play under this legislation. In other words,

---

1 Regulation 2022/1925 of the European Parliament and of the Council of 14 September 2022 on contestable and fair markets in the digital sector and amending Directives 2019/1937 and 2020/1828 (Digital Markets Act or DMA) [2022] OJ L265/1.

2 DMA recital 91.

these roles are largely discretionary. Attention will also be paid to the factors that might influence a Member State's participation in these roles. The section concludes with some general comments.

2. *Ex Ante* Regulation: The Digital Markets Act (DMA)

5. The purpose of the DMA, as set out in its title, is 'to ensure contestable and fair markets in the digital sector.' The DMA applies to gatekeepers: undertakings 'providing core platform services'[3] (e.g. online search engines, online social networking services, video-sharing platform services, web browsers, cloud computing services and online advertising services that are linked to another core platform service) that have 'a significant impact on the internal market,' that 'provides a core platform service which is an important gateway for business users to reach end users' and 'enjoys an entrenched and durable position…'.[4] An undertaking is presumed to meet the requirement to be designated a gatekeeper by the Commission if the undertaking satisfies certain quantitative thresholds such as annual European Union (EU) turnover of at least €7.5 billion in each of the last three years[5] and provides a core platform service that in the last financial year has at least 45 million monthly active end users and at least 10,000 active business users in the EU.[6] Any consultation with the Member States on the designation of a gatekeeper is solely at the discretion of the Commission.[7]

6. Once the Commission has designated an undertaking as a gatekeeper with respect to one or more core platform services the gatekeeper shall comply with certain obligations specified in Articles 5, 6 and 7 of the DMA. The gatekeeper must report to the Commission 'at least annually' on how it satisfies these obligations.[8] The Commission may commence market investigations into systematic non-compliance by a gatekeeper with its obligations under Articles 5, 6 and 7.[9] Failure to comply by the gatekeeper with the obligations in Articles 5, 6 and 7 may result in fines and other sanctions being imposed by the Commission.[10]

7. On 6 September 2023 the Commission designated the following six undertakings as gatekeepers: Alphabet; Amazon; Apple; ByteDance; Meta and Microsoft – covering 22 core platform services.[11] The gatekeepers had six months (i.e. until 6 March 2024) to ensure full compliance with Articles 5, 6 and 7 of the DMA. The gatekeepers also had to file, under Article 11, compliance reports to the

---

3 DMA art 2(1).

4 DMA art 3(1).

5 DMA art 3(2)(a).

6 DMA art 3(2)(b).

7 DMA art 37(2).

8 DMA art 11. These are annual updates of the initial compliance reports referred to in the next paragraph for the first six Commission-designated gatekeepers.

9 DMA art 18. The Commission also has the power to issue requests for information (art 21) and conduct inspections (art 23).

10 DMA arts 29–33.

11 For details, including steps to conduct market investigations with respect to whether or not other gatekeeper core platform services should be designated, see European Commission Press Release, 'Digital Markets Act: Commission Designates Six Gatekeepers' (6 September 2023) <https://ec.europa.eu/commission/presscorner/detail/en/ip_23_4328> accessed 31 July 2024.

Commission describing 'in a detailed and transparent manner the measures' taken to comply with these articles. The Commission held six compliance workshops, based on these compliance reports, between 18 and 26 March 2024, one workshop for each gatekeeper.

8. The Commission opened non-compliance investigations against Alphabet, Apple and Meta in March/June 2024. Preliminary Commission findings of non-compliance with the DMA were sent to Apple on 24 June 2024, concerning its steering rules for the App Store, and to Meta on 1 July 2024, with respect to its 'pay or consent' advertising model.

9. In 2024 the Commission also designated one new gatekeeper and two new core platform services: 'On 29 April 2024, (it) designated Apple with respect to its iPadOS, its operating system for tablets, as a gatekeeper under the DMA. On 13 May 2024, (it) also designated under the DMA, Booking (Booking.com BV) as a gatekeeper for its online intermediation service Booking.com. In total, 24 core platform services provided by those (seven) gatekeepers have been designated.'[12]

10. At least three of the designated gatekeepers have instituted legal proceedings in the General Court disputing their designation under the DMA by the Commission: Apple,[13] Meta[14] and ByteDance.[15] In contrast to Apple and Meta, ByteDance requested that the General Court grant Interim Measures that would suspend the Commission designation decision of its TikTok services. On 9 February 2024 the General Court dismissed, under an expedited procedure, ByteDance's application for Interim Measures.[16] On 17 July 2024 the General Court dismissed ByteDance's application to annul the Commission's designation decision.[17]

11. The DMA is a form of *ex ante* regulation. Once a gatekeeper has been so designed by the Commission with respect to one or more core platform services then the gatekeeper has to comply with the obligations in Articles 5, 6 and 7 and furthermore via compliance reports to the Commission, demonstrate how those obligations are being satisfied. There is no need for the Commission – as in a unilateral conduct case under Article 102 – to define a relevant market, that the gatekeeper is dominant in that market, has abused its dominant position and cannot provide a credible objective justification for its market behaviour.

---

12 European Commission, 'Gatekeepers' (*European Commission*, 29 July 2024) <https://digital-markets-act.ec.europa.eu/gatekeepers_en> accessed 31 July 2024.

13 Case T-1079/23 *Apple v Commission*, and Case T-1080/23 *Apple v Commission*. Both actions were brought on 16 November 2023.

14 Case T-1078/23 *Meta Platforms v Commission*, action brought on 15 November 2023.

15 Case T-1077/23 *ByteDance v Commission*, action brought on 16 November 2023.

16 For discussion and links see Alba Ribera Martinez, 'The General Court Dismisses TikTok's Request for Interim Measures Against its DMA Designation Decision: Better to be Safe than Sorry (Case T-1077/23 R)' (*Kluwer Competition Law Blog*, 20 February 2024) <https://competitionlawblog.kluwercompetitionlaw.com/2024/02/20/the-general-court-dismisses-tiktoks-request-for-interim-measures-against-its-dma-designation-decision-better-to-be-safe-than-sorry-case-t-1077-23-r/> accessed 31 July 2024.

17 For discussion and links see Alba Ribera Martinez, 'The DMA's Little Piece of heaven: The General Court Dismisses ByteDance's Appeal Against its Designation Decision (Case T-1077/23, ByteDance Ltd v. European Commission)" (*Kluwer Competition Law Blog*, 18 July 2024) <https://competitionlawblog.kluwercompetitionlaw.com/2024/07/18/the-dmas-little-piece-of-heaven-the-general-court-dismisses-bytedances-appeal-against-its-designation-decision-case-t-1077-23-bytedance-ltd-v-european-commission/> accessed 31 July 2024.

3. National Competent Authorities May Enforce Competition Rules Against Gatekeepers

12. The DMA is, under Article 1(6), 'without prejudice to the application of Articles 101 and 102'; national competition rules prohibiting anticompetitive agreements, unilateral conduct and mergers; and 'national competition rules prohibiting other forms of unilateral conduct (but not with respect to agreements or mergers) insofar as they are applied to undertakings other than gatekeepers or amount to the imposition of further obligations on gatekeepers.' In other words, the Member State can continue to enforce competition rules with respect to the gatekeepers.

13. There are constraints, however, on the national competent authority on the application of these competition rules. The national competent authority 'shall not make a decision which runs counter to a decision adopted by the Commission' under the DMA.[18] The national competent authority shall inform: the European Competition Network (ECN) of actions taken under Article 1(6);[19] the Commission 'in writing of the first formal investigative measure, before or immediately after the start of such measure;'[20] and the Commission if it 'intends to impose obligations on gatekeepers based on national laws referred to in Article 1(6)'.[21]

14. Furthermore, if the Commission were to open proceedings under the DMA against a gatekeeper for non-compliance with its obligations, as discussed immediately below, then the Commission under Article 38, shall relieve the national competent authorities of the Member State enforcing the rules referred to in Article 1(6) of the possibility to conduct such an investigation or end it where it is already ongoing. Those authorities shall report to the Commission on the findings of such investigation in order to support the Commission in its role as sole enforcer of this Regulation (the DMA).

15. It would thus appear that were a national competent authority to undertake an investigation under national competition rules with respect to a gatekeeper it would be well advised to consult extensively with the Commission in order to ensure that its actions are consistent with the views and decisions (both past and prospective) of the Commission.

16. There is, of course, the prior question as to whether or not a national competent authority is likely to commence an investigation into whether a gatekeeper has breached competition rules. This is not an idle question. One of the important motivations behind the creation of the DMA was that 'enforcement (in the digital sector against dominant firms) occurs *ex post* and requires an extensive investigation of often very complex facts on a case by case basis.'[22] To the extent that the DMA, by shifting to an *ex ante* form of regulation of the conduct of such dominant (and in some instances non-dominant) gatekeepers, then the DMA lessens, if not removes, the necessity of enforcing competition rules by national competent authorities.

---

18 DMA art 1(7).
19 DMA art 38(1).
20 DMA art 38(2).
21 DMA art 38(3).
22 DMA recital 5.

17. It has been argued that in some instances enforcement of competition law complements *ex ante* regulation (e.g. telecommunications).[23] However, in the case of the DMA it contains mechanisms such as market investigations that offer the opportunity to extend both the range of core platform services, currently set out in Article 2(2), as well as the obligations set out in Articles 5 and 6. In other words, the DMA is not a static but rather a dynamic form of *ex ante* regulation that is likely to limit the scope of complementary competition law enforcement actions compared to more conventional forms of *ex ante* regulation.

4. National Competent Authorities May Investigate Non-Compliance of Gatekeepers with DMA Obligations

18. Under Article 38(7) of the DMA,

> Where it has the competence and investigative powers to do so under national law, a national competent authority of the Member States enforcing the rules referred to in Article 1(6) may, on its own initiative, conduct an investigation into a case of possible non-compliance with Articles 5, 6 and 7 of this Regulation (the DMA) on its territory. Before taking a first formal investigative measure, that authority shall inform the Commission in writing.

19. The national competent authority must, however, be given the required 'competence and investigative powers' in order for it to exercise the discretion under Article 38(7) under national law.

20. Since the Commission is the sole enforcer of the DMA, a national competent authority's role is confined to *investigating* whether or not a gatekeeper is complying with its obligations under the DMA. It is up to the Commission to decide whether the gatekeeper is non-compliant and the appropriate sanction, not the national competent authority.

21. The DMA contains a number of mechanisms for the Commission to investigate non-compliance by a gatekeeper with its obligations set out in Articles 5, 6 and 7. The Commission may, for example, institute a market investigation under Article 18 of the DMA into systematic non-compliance.

22. It is not at all clear that a national competent authority is well (or best) placed or has an incentive to conduct an investigation into the non-compliance by a gatekeeper of its obligations under the DMA. The Commission has extensive powers in this regard, has the expertise and is familiar with the operations of the gatekeepers in a way that is less likely to be the case with respect to the national competent authority of a smaller Member State (e.g. Ireland), if not necessarily for a larger Member State (e.g. France and Germany). Furthermore, Member States can, under Article 41(2), either on their own or together with other Member States, request the Commission to conduct a market investigation 'because they consider that there are reasonable grounds to suspect that a gatekeeper has systematically infringed one or more of the obligations laid

[23] Pablo Ibanez Colomo, *The New EU Competition Law* (Hart 2023) ch 3 73-99.

down in Articles 5, 6, and 7…'. The Member State shall submit evidence to support the request, while the Commission within four months of receiving the request shall examine the merits of the request and 'shall publish the results of its assessment.'

23. It should be noted that if a third-party informs a national competent authority that there is an issue of non-compliance under the DMA then under Article 27(3) the national competent authority 'shall transfer that information to the Commission.' There is no obligation on the Commission to publish a report of its assessment of the third-party information.

5. Member States May Impose Further Obligations on Gatekeepers Outside of the Scope of the DMA

24. Although under Article 1(5) of the DMA Member States 'shall not impose' on gatekeepers 'further obligations' designed to achieve the DMA's 'purpose of ensuring contestable and fair markets,' this does not preclude Member States from 'imposing obligations on undertakings, including undertakings providing core platform services, for matters falling outside the scope' of the DMA. These latter obligations must be compatible with other legitimate public interest objectives set out in the Treaty on the Functioning of the European Union (TFEU) or for purposes set out in case law of the Court of Justice of the European Union (CJEU).

25. If a Member State were to impose such additional obligations on a gatekeeper, the Member State would probably need to provide a legislative basis for such a course of action together with an enforcement mechanism, whether through a national competition or competent authority or another mechanism such as a government department.[24]

6. Member States May Request the Commission to Conduct Market Investigations into Gatekeeper and Core Platform Designation and Gatekeeper Systematic Non-Compliance with Obligations in Articles 5, 6 and 7 of the DMA

26. Under Article 41 three or more Member States: (i) 'may request the Commission to open a market investigation pursuant to Article 17 because they consider that there are reasonable grounds to suspect that an undertaking should be designated as a gatekeeper;' and/or (ii) 'may request the Commission to conduct a market investigation pursuant to Article 19 because they consider that there are reasonable grounds to suspect that "one or more services should be added to the list of core platform services set out in Article 2(2)."' Furthermore, as noted above, one or more Member States may request that the Commission undertake a market investigation because of a belief that a 'gatekeeper has systematically infringed one or more of the obligations laid down in Articles 5, 6, and 7.' In all instances the Member States shall provide evidence to the Commission supporting their

24 See Section III.5.D below for discussion of such obligations.

request, while the Commission has four months in which to assess and respond to the request of the Member State(s) for a market investigation.

27. The Article 41 mechanism for instituting a Commission market investigation is a low-cost method by which Member States can bring to the attention of the Commission the designation of gatekeepers, core platform services and systematic infringements by a gatekeeper of its obligations under the DMA. The threshold for reference is 'reasonable grounds', and must be made by one or more or at least three Member States depending on the nature of the request.

7. The Commission Shall Establish the DMA High-level Group

28. Article 40 states that the Commission 'shall establish a high-level group for the' DMA to be known as the High-level Group. Membership is drawn from five 'European bodies and networks' including the European Competition Network (ECN), Consumer Protection Cooperation Network (CPCN), Body of European Regulators for Electronic Communications (BEREC), the European Data Protection Supervisor and European Data Protection Board. The Commission 'shall' chair the High-level Group which 'shall' meet at least once a year upon request of the Commission. However, if a majority of the members of the High-level Group request a meeting to address a specific issue, the Commission shall convene a meeting.

29. The High-level Group 'may provide advice and expertise in the areas falling within the competences of its members.' The High-level Group 'may, in particular, identify and assess the current and potential interactions between… (the DMA) and the sector-specific rules applied by the national composing bodies of the European bodies and networks' that comprise the High-level Group and submit an annual report on such 'trans-regulatory issues' to the Commission, with, if necessary, recommendations.

30. The High-level Group was set up in March 2023. It has met three times to date (July 2024): for the first time on 12 May 2023,[25] the second on 27 November 2023 and the third on 22 May 2024. The High-level Group comprises thirty representatives nominated by various European bodies and networks referred to above. At its second meeting, according to BEREC the 'participants exchanged views on practical issues concerning the DMA implementation, discussing ways to efficiently address key challenges.'[26] The issue of the challenge posed by Artificial Intelligence (AI) was the subject of the High-level Group's most recent meeting.[27]

---

[25] DG-Comp and DG-Comm Networks Press Release, 'Inaugural Meeting of DMA High-Level Group' (12 May 2023) <https://digital-markets-act.ec.europa.eu/inaugural-meeting-dma-high-level-group-2023-05-12_en> accessed 31 July 2024.

[26] BEREC Press Release, 'BEREC Participates in the Second DMA High-Level Group Meeting' (28 November 2023) <https://www.berec.europa.eu/en/news-publications/news-and-newsletters/berec-participates-in-the-second-dma-high-level-group-meeting> accessed 31 July 2024.

[27] DG-Comp and DG-Comm Networks Press Release, 'High-Level Group for the Digital Markets Act Public Statement on Artificial Intelligence' (22 May 2024) <https://digital-markets-act.ec.europa.eu/high-level-group-digital-markets-act-public-statement-artificial-intelligence-2024-05-22_en> accessed 31 July 2024.

8. Private Enforcement by Business and End Users of Gatekeeper Core Platform Services May Be Instituted in National Courts Against Gatekeepers for Non-Compliance with DMA Obligations

31. Although there is no explicit reference in the DMA to private enforcement actions (proceedings) against gatekeepers for non-compliance with their obligations under, for example, Articles 5, 6 and 7, either as a standalone action or as a follow on from a Commission non-compliance decision, it 'becomes clear from the Regulation (the DMA) that its effectiveness implicitly relies on private enforcement activities by, for example, business users and end users.'[28] A successful private action could result in an injunction and damages.

32. Business users and end users will often be in the best position to determine and furnish evidence of whether or not the obligations under Articles 5, 6 and 7 are being adhered to, given that the obligations apply directly to these users (e.g. 'the gatekeeper shall not prevent business users from offering the same products or services to end users through third-party online intermediation services…' or the 'gatekeeper shall not restrict technically or otherwise the ability of end users to switch between, and subscribe to different software applications and services that are accessed using the core platform services of the gatekeeper…').

33. Private enforcement actions appear to be brought before national courts within the framework of cooperation with national courts set out in Article 39 (in conjunction with Recital 42) of the DMA. Under this framework, national courts may ask the Commission to transmit information in its possession or 'its opinion on questions concerning the application of' the DMA. Member States 'shall' forward to the Commission written judgments that decide on the application of the DMA. 'Where the coherent application' of the DMA requires, the Commission may, on its own initiative, 'submit written observations to national courts' and, with permission of the national court, 'make oral observations.' National courts 'shall not give a decision that runs counter to a decision adopted by the Commission' under the DMA and 'shall also avoid giving decisions which would conflict with a decision contemplated by the Commission in proceedings which it had initiated' under the DMA.

34. The degree to which private actions take place before national courts depends on: the extent to which private enforcement is, in general, facilitated by national courts;[29] whether a Member State introduces legislation or similar measures

---

28 Giulia Rurali and Martin Seegers, 'Private Enforcement of the EU Digital Markets Act: the Way Ahead After Going Live' (*Kluwer Competition Law Blog*, 20 June 2023) <https://competitionlawblog.kluwercompetitionlaw.com/2023/06/20/private-enforcement-of-the-eu-digital-markets-act-the-way-ahead-after-going-live/> accessed 31 July 2024. See also Magnus Strand, 'Private Enforcement Under the Digital Markets Act: Rights and Remedies' (2024) 7 Nordic Journal of European Law 120.

29 The first claims in the EU for follow-on damages arising from the July 2016 Commission settlement decision that seven truck manufacturers had been involved in a price-fixing cartel between 1997 and 2011 occurred in Ireland when, on 25 April 2017, 51 High Court claims that were brought by truck owners were entered into the Competition List of the High Court. Due to various procedural and jurisdictional issues these claims – now around 150 – have yet to come to trial. Suggestions have been made that a representative set of cases should proceed to trial. On the twists and turns in these cases see *National Truck Rental Company Ltd v Man Importers Ireland Ltd and Others* [2022] IEHC 404 (which may be accessed on <https://www.courts.ie/>) and

designed to encourage private enforcement of the DMA; and whether or not the 'Commission introduces a DMA-specific tool similar to the Damages Directive in the future.'[30] In Germany, for example, an amendment to its competition law came into effect on 7 November 2023 that included proposals to facilitate the private enforcement of the DMA:

35. The law facilitates follow-on damages by providing that European Commission decisions finding an infringement of these DMA rules are legally binding for German courts. That also applies to the designation of a gatekeeper by the Commission, i.e., a designation decision can be used for stand-alone claims (that the gatekeeper infringes the DMA and/or for damages).[31]

36. To date there is no indication as to whether or not the Commission will take any action to facilitate private enforcement of the DMA.

9. Commentary

37. Under the DMA the national competent authority *may*:
    - Enforce competition rules against gatekeepers; and
    - Investigate non-compliance of gatekeepers with their DMA obligations, providing the national competent authority has the competence and investigative powers under national law.

38. Although not stated explicitly in the DMA the national competent authority is likely to be the NCA. The NCA almost certainly already has the legal authority to investigate gatekeepers for breaking competition rules, while Article 38(7), quoted above, appears to give the NCA authority under the DMA to investigate allegations of non-compliance by gatekeepers of their DMA-mandated obligations, subject to the qualification concerning competence/investigative powers under national law.

39. Nonetheless, for reasons set out above, an NCA may have little incentive to pursue competition cases, almost certainly unilateral infringements, which overlap with or substitute for issues dealt with under Articles 5, 6 and 7 of the DMA for a gatekeeper's designated core platform services. The substantial resources that may be involved in such cases is likely to weigh especially heavily for NCAs in smaller Member States. Equally, NCAs may be reluctant to investigate allegations of non-compliance gatekeepers under the DMA when only the Commission can determine whether or not the gatekeeper is in fact non-compliant or impose any sanction.

---

on the recent moves for a representative sample see, 'High Court Told of Dozens of Actions Brought Over Anti-Competitive Conduct Linked to Alleged Truck Overcharging' (*Irish Times*, 6 March 2024) <https://www.irishtimes.com/business/2024/03/06/high-court-told-dozens-of-actions-deal-with-truck-market-overcharging-due-to-anti-competitive-conduct/> accessed 31 July 2024.

30 See, 'Private Enforcement of the Digital Markets Act: Germany as a Frontrunner' (*Norton Rose Fulbright*, March 2023) <https://www.nortonrosefulbright.com/en/knowledge/publications/41cb9705/private-enforcement-of-the-digital-markets-act-germany-as-a-frontrunner> accessed 31 July 2024.

31 For details see Silke Heinz, 'Main Developments in Competition Law and Policy 2023 – Germany' (*Kluwer Competition Law Blog*, 5 March 2024) <https://competitionlawblog.kluwercompetitionlaw.com/2024/03/05/main-developments-in-competition-law-and-policy-2023-germany/> accessed 31 July 2024. See also Bundeskartellamt, 'Rules for the Digital Economy' (*Bundeskartellamt*, 2024) <https://www.bundeskartellamt.de/EN/Digital_economy/RulesDigital_economy/rulesdigitaleconomy_node.html> accessed 31 July 2024.

40. The Member State *may*:
   - Impose further obligations on gatekeepers outside of the scope of the DMA;
   - Request the Commission to conduct market investigations into gatekeeper and core platform designation and/or gatekeeper systematic non-compliance with obligations in Articles 5, 6 and 7 of the DMA; and
   - Facilitate private enforcement by business users and end users of gatekeeper non-compliance with their DMA-mandated obligations.

41. The first and the third possible actions by the Member State are likely to require legislation to effect. A request by the Member State for the Commission to conduct market investigations while unlikely to require legislation, nevertheless, requires the preparation of an evidentiary basis for the request. This is likely to require the involvement of the NCA, given its probable role in investigating alleged non-compliance by gatekeepers of their DMA-mandated obligations. Indeed, the Member State might delegate such power to the NCA.

42. Notwithstanding the fact that the DMA as a regulation has direct legal effect, Member States are nonetheless likely to clarify, by various legal instruments, the application of the DMA. Such clarity ensures that there is little or no ambiguity over, for example, what precisely an NCA is responsible for under the DMA and perhaps more importantly what legislative steps might be taken to assist in facilitating private damages. It is to these issues that attention now turns with respect to one Member State, Ireland.

III. Ireland: Implementing the DMA and Related Digital Sector Regulation

1. Introduction

43. The purpose of this section is to describe and analyse recent EU legislation in relation to the digital sector and how Ireland has given effect to that legislation to its institutions and legal order. While attention is primarily focussed on the DMA, reference is made to two other EU legislative acts in relation to the digital sector (i.e. the P2B Regulation and the Digital Services Act). These earlier legislative acts have been chosen because 'the P2B Regulation is a first step towards a fairer and more predictable online environment for businesses and consumers, with further legislative developments such as the Digital Services Act and the Digital Markets Act coming into force.'[32]

44. An overview of the EU legislation together with the legal instrument used in Ireland to implement this legislation together with the relevant national competent authority is presented in Table 1. Prior to considering Panels A, B and C of the table a brief description of the two national competent authorities – Coimisiún na Meán (CNAM)

---

[32] Competition and Consumer Protection Commission, 'Business Feedback to the CCPC Highlights a Range of Issues When Using Online Platforms to Sell to Consumers' (*CCPC*, 27 January 2023) <https://www.ccpc.ie/business/business-feedback-to-the-ccpc-highlights-a-range-of-issues-when-using-online-platforms-to-sell-to-consumers/> accessed 31 July 2024.

and the Competition and Consumer Protection Commission (CCPC) – referred to in the table, is presented. The Department of Enterprise, Trade and Employment (DETE), within the Irish Government, is responsible for preparing the legislation referred to in Table 1. It is also the parent department of Ireland's NCA, the CCPC.

Table 1. EU Legislation, Ireland Implementing Legal Instrument, Agency Responsible for Administration & Enforcement, Digital Sector, 2020 to 2024

Panel A: Platform to Business (P2B) Regulation
EU Legislation: Regulation 2019/1150 of the European Parliament and of the Council of 20 June 2019 on promoting fairness and transparency for business users of online intermediation services [2019] OJ L186/57
Ireland Legislation: SI Instrument No 256 of 2020, European Union (Promoting Fairness and Transparency for Business Users of Online Intermediation Services) Regulations 2020
Agency Responsible: CCPC
Panel B: Digital Services Act
EU Legislation: Regulation 2022/2065 of the European Parliament and of the Council of 19 October 2022 on a Single Market for Digital Services and amending Directive 2000/31/EC (Digital Services Act) [2022] OJ L277/1
Ireland Legislation: Digital Services Act 2024 (DSA 2024); SI No 53/2024 – Digital Services Act 2024 (Commencement) Order 2024.
Agency(s) Responsible: (i) Coimisiún na Meán (Digital Services Coordinator, lead national competent authority for DSA 2024); and (ii) CCPC (national competent authority with specific responsibility for online marketplaces, Articles 30, 31 and 32 of the Digital Services Act).
Panel C: Digital Markets Act
EU Legislation: Regulation (2022/1925 of the European Parliament and of the Council of 14 September 2022 on contestable and fair markets in the digital sector and amending Directives 2019/1937 and 2020/1828 (Digital Markets Act) [2022] OJ L265/1
Ireland Legislation: SI No 117 of 2024 European Union (Contestable and Fair Markets in the Digital Sector) Regulations 2024.
Agency Responsible: CCPC

Notes: SI = statutory instrument.
Source: see text.

2. National Competent Authorities

45. There are two national competent authorities in Ireland with responsibility for enforcing the digital sector regulations referred to in Panels A to C in Table 1.

46. First, the CCPC which 'is the statutory body responsible for promoting compliance with, and enforcing, competition and consumer protection law in Ireland.' The CCPC 'was established on 31 October 2014 after the National Consumer Agency and the Competition Authority (established in 2002) were amalgamated;'[33]

47. Second, the CNAM which regulates broadcasting in Ireland and is responsible for establishing a 'regulatory framework for online safety,' updating 'the regulation of television broadcasting and audiovisual on-demand services,' and transposing

---

33 Competition and Consumer Protection Commission, 'About Us' (*CCPC*, 16 February 2024) <https://www.ccpc.ie/consumers/about/about-us/> accessed 31 July 2024.

'the revised Audiovisual Media Services Directive into Irish law.'[34] The CNAM was established in 2022 and took over the functions of the Broadcasting Authority of Ireland. The CNAM has no competition law enforcement powers.

48. As can be readily observed from Table 1, while the CCPC is a national competent authority under all three pieces of EU digital regulation in Panels A to C, CNAM is a national competent authority in one instance (Panel B).

3. Platform to Business (P2B) Regulation

49. The CCPC has been designated, effective 12 July 2020, as the body responsible for discharging Ireland's responsibilities under Article 14(5)(b) of the P2B Regulation 'on promoting fairness and transparency for business users of online intermediation services.'[35] These services include online marketplaces such as that of Amazon, app stores such those of Google Play and Apple and social media sites such as Facebook and Instagram, all entities that are also designated as gatekeepers under the DMA. An undertaking subject to the P2B Regulation must comply with certain rules, including transparency with respect, for example, of terms and conditions and ranking of goods and services. Entities subject to the P2B Regulation are required to set up complaint procedures. Business users that meet certain conditions can take legal action to prevent non-compliance by undertakings subject to the P2B Regulation. In 2022 the CCPC 'engaged with the operators of 23 online platforms to improve compliance with the P2B Regulation.'[36] The CCPC is required by law to keep a register of unlawful acts subject to an order before the Circuit Court or High Court under Section 71 of the Consumer Protection Act 2007. At the time of writing (July 2024) no such unlawful acts were registered on the CCPC's website.

4. Digital Services Act (DSA)

50. The Digital Services Act (DSA) came into force in EU law in November 2022 and applied in full across all Member States from 17 February 2024. According to the DETE the DSA

51. aims to contribute to the proper functioning of the EU's internal market for online intermediary services by setting out harmonised rules for a safe, predictable and trusted online environment that facilitates innovation and in which fundamental

---

34 Coimisiún na Meán, 'About Us' (*CNAM*, 30 March 2024) <https://www.cnam.ie/about-us/> accessed 31 July 2024.

35 Regulation 2019/1150 of the European Parliament and of the Council of 20 June 2019 on promoting fairness and transparency for business users of online intermediation services (Platform-to-Business Regulation or P2B-Regulation) [2019] OJ L186/57. For details of the involvement by the CCPC in the P2B Regulation see CCPC, 'Platform to Business (P2B) Regulation' (*CCPC*, 2024) <https://www.ccpc.ie/business/help-for-business/guidelines-for-business/platform-to-business-regulations/> accessed 31 July 2024. The paragraph draws heavily on this source and that contained in the next footnote.

36 Competition and Consumer Protection Commission, 'Business Feedback to the CCPC Highlights a Range of Issues When Using Online Platforms to Sell to Consumers' (*CCPC*, 27 January 2023) <https://www.ccpc.ie/business/business-feedback-to-the-ccpc-highlights-a-range-of-issues-when-using-online-platforms-to-sell-to-consumers/> accessed 31 July 2024.

rights enshrined in the EU Charter of Fundamental Rights, including the principle of consumer protection, are effectively protected.[37]

52. Ireland enacted the Digital Services Act 2024 (DSA 2024) to provide for the supervision and enforcement of its obligations under the DSA. The DSA 2024 was signed into law on 16 Febuary 2024 and put into operation – commenced – on 17 February 2024.

53. Although the lead agency designated by the DSA 2024 for supervising and enforcing Ireland's obligations under the DSA is CNAM there is a role for the CCPC with respect to the investigation and enforcement of Articles 30 (the traceability of traders),[38] 31 (compliance by design)[39] and 32 (right to information)[40] of the DSA. These articles are concerned with certain obligations that providers of online marketplaces must furnish to consumers. Under the DSA 2024, in relation to these three articles, the CCPC has, *inter alia*, investigative as well as fining powers, subject to confirmation by the courts.[41] However, it is the online marketplaces that are responsible under Articles 30, 31 and 32 to ensure, for example, that sellers using the platform must provide certain information to be displayed in a readily accessible way to consumers using the online marketplaces as well as removing illegal products and services from the online marketplace.

54. It should be noted that under the DSA the Commission shall supervise and enforce the DSA in relation to certain categories of online marketplaces: Very Large Online Platforms (VLOP) and Very Large Online Search Engines (VLOSE), defined in both instances as having at least 45 million users per month.[42] On the 14 March 2024 the Commission designated all of the seven gatekeepers either a VLOSE or a VLOP or both in the case of Alphabet and Microsoft. There were several other VLOSEs or VLOPs in addition to the seven gatekeepers such as Twitter International Unlimited Company (now X.com).[43] The CCPC's remit (and that of UNAM) is thus confined to online platforms and search engines that: fall below the 45 million monthly user threshold; and have their main establishment in Ireland (i.e. the country-of-origin principle).

---

37 Regulation 2022/2065 of the European Parliament and of the Council of 19 October 2022 on a Single Market for Digital Services and amending Directive 2000/31 (the Digital Services Act or DSA) [2022] OJ L277/1 (*DETE*, March 2024) <https://enterprise.gov.ie/en/what-we-do/the-business-environment/digital-single-market/eu-digital-single-market-aspects/digital-services-act/> accessed 31 July 2024.

38 Article 30 states that providers of online platforms shall allow consumers to conclude contracts with traders and shall ensure the traceability of traders.

39 Article 31(1) reads as follows: 'Providers of online platforms allowing consumers to conclude distance contracts with traders shall ensure that its online interface is designed and organised in a way that enables traders to comply with their obligations regarding pre- contractual information, compliance and product safety information under applicable Union law.'

40 Article 32(1) reads as follows: 'Where a provider of an online platform allowing consumers to conclude distance contracts with traders becomes aware, irrespective of the means used, that an illegal product or service has been offered by a trader to consumers located in the Union through its services, that provider shall inform, insofar as it has their contact details, consumers who purchased the illegal product or service through its services of the following: (a) the fact that the product or service is illegal; (b) the identity of the trader; and (c) any relevant means of redress.'

41 For details of these powers see Part 3 of the DSA 2024.

42 This is consistent with the criteria used to define a gatekeeper under the DMA. For details see Section II.2 above.

43 European Commission, 'Supervision of the Designated Very Large Online Platforms and Search Engines Under DSA' (14 March 2024) <https://digital-strategy.ec.europa.eu/en/policies/list-designated-vlops-and-vloses> accessed 31 July 2024.

55. On its website the CCPC states that while it is the competent authority for enforcement of Articles 30, 31 and 32, CNAM 'is Ireland's Digital Services Coordinator with responsibility for the enforcement and application of the DSA.' The CCPC under the heading 'Complaints' also states that: 'If you believe that an online marketplace provider has contravened the DSA, you can flag this issue directly with the online marketplace. For further information in relation to making a complaint under the DSA please refer to the website of Ireland's Digital Services Coordinator, CNAM.'[44] This arrangement reflects the fact that *all* complaints with regard to the DSA are made or referred to the CNAM as Ireland's Digital Services Coordinator, which then refers complaints relevant to the Articles 30, 31 and 32 to the CCPC.[45]

5. Digital Markets Act (DMA)

A. *Introduction*

56. The DMA was given effect in Ireland by SI No 117 of 2024, European Union (Contestable and Fair Markets in the Digital Sector) Regulations 2024, dated 27 March 2024. These will be referred to as the DMA Regulations. It is a short document, slightly over three pages in length. The DMA Regulations are confined almost exclusively with the powers and responsibilities of the CCPC under the DMA.[46]

B. *Designation of the CCPC as the National Competent Authority*

57. The DMA Regulations designate the CCPC as 'the national competent authority that is enforcing the rules referred to in Article 1(6)'[47] of the DMA. This issue, concerning the enforcement by the national competent authority of the competition rules against gatekeepers, was discussed above in Section II.3.

58. Notwithstanding the CCPC's designation under Article 1(6) the agency has not under the DMA Regulations been given "the competence and investigative powers" to investigate the non-compliance of gatekeepers with their DMA obligations. Such a policy position is consistent with the discussion in Section II.4 above that suggests the Commission is better placed than smaller Member States such as Ireland to investigative the non-compliance of gatekeepers with their DMA obligations.

---

44 CCPC, 'Digital Services Act' (*CCPC*, 2024) <https://www.ccpc.ie/business/help-for-business/guidelines-for-business/the-digital-services-act/> accessed 31 July 2024.

45 If the online marketplace being complained of under arts 30, 31 or 32 falls below the thresholds to be considered a VLOSE or VLP and is headquartered in a Member State other than Ireland then the CNAM refers the complaint to the Digital Services Coordinator of that Member State. For details see CNAM, 'The Right to Complain Under the Digital Services Act' (*CNAM*, 2024) <https://www.cnam.ie/onlinecomplaints/> accessed 31 July 2024.

46 One exception is that s4 of the DMA Regulations states that: 'The Minister for Enterprise, Trade and Employment shall designate an expert for the purposes of Article 49(4)' of the DMA. Under art 49(4) before the Commission adopts a delegated act it is required to consult experts designated by each Member State.

47 DMA s 3.

59. Nonetheless, the DMA Regulations state specifically that: 'Any third-party may inform the… (CCPC) in accordance with Article 27 of any practice or behaviours that fall within the scope of' the DMA.[48] If the CCPC, based in this information, determines that there may be an issue on non-compliance 'it shall transfer that information' to the Commission. The wording implies that the CCPC will assess the information provided and, where appropriate, seek further information from the third-party and possibly other market participants in order to determine whether or not the practice or behaviours falls within the scope of the DMA. Smaller Irish-based firms adversely affected by gatekeeper behaviour are one third-party group that may well provide information to the CCPC.

60. The DMA Regulations also permit the CCPC 'either alone or with another Member State, (to) request the European Commission to open a market investigation in accordance with Article 41.'[49] Section II.6 above discussed how Article 41 can be used by the Member States to request the Commission to conduct market investigations into gatekeeper and core platform designation as well as market investigations into gatekeeper systematic non-compliance with their obligations under Articles 5, 6 and 7 of the DMA.

C. *CCPC Authorised to Assist the Commission in Conducting Inspections*

61. Article 23(8) of the DMA states that:

> Where the officials and other accompanying persons authorised by the Commission find that an undertaking or association of undertakings opposes an inspection ordered pursuant to this Article, the Member State concerned shall afford them the necessary assistance, requesting, where appropriate, the assistance of the police or of an equivalent enforcement authority, so as to enable them to conduct their inspection.

62. The DMA Regulations provides the statutory basis for the CCPC's authorised officers 'to provide the necessary assistance for the purposes of Article 23(8).'[50] These regulations give authorised officers, for example, the power to use reasonable force in order that the Commission can conduct the inspection, enter premises on production of a warrant issued by a judge of the District Court, while setting out the penalties should an authorised officer be obstructed from conducting the inspection.

63. All of seven of the gatekeepers bar Booking have extensive operations in Ireland, measured in terms of employment, profits, and sales, while all bar Amazon (i.e. Luxembourg) and Booking (i.e. the Netherlands) have their EU operations centred in Ireland.[51] Thus if the Commission were to conduct inspections of one or more of the gatekeepers under the DMA it is likely that the CCPC will be called upon to a much greater extent than any other national competent authority.

---

[48] DMA s 8.

[49] DMA s 9.

[50] DMA ss 6 and 7. For a discussion of the appointment, role and powers of authorised officers see Philip Andrews, Paul Gorecki and David McFadden, *Modern Irish Competition Law* (Wolters Kluwer 2015) 77–80.

[51] The magnitude of gatekeeper operations in Ireland are set out in Annex A below.

D. *No Further Obligations Imposed on Gatekeepers nor Measures to Facilitate Private Enforcement*

64. There are no provisions in the DMA Regulations for the imposition of further obligations on the gatekeepers outside of the scope of the DMA (discussed in Section II.5 above) and/or measures to facilitate private enforcement by business and end users of gatekeeper core platform services against gatekeepers for non-compliance with their DMA obligations (discussed in Section II.8 above). There is no indication that Ireland intends to introduce legislation in either of these respects.[52]

65. While it may not be entirely clear what additional obligations might be appropriate to impose on gatekeepers reference to the experience of Germany which since 2021 has introduced measures 'which take into account the specificities of digital business models,'[53] might have provided a useful precedent.[54] In terms of private enforcement, Ireland could have followed Germany, referred to in Section II.8, with respect to facilitating follow-on damages against gatekeepers for non-compliance with the DMA. Making Commission decisions finding an infringement of the DMA rules by a gatekeeper legally binding for Irish courts, for example, would be analogous to Ireland's implementation of the Damages Directive.[55]

E. *Ireland Legislative DMA Choices*

66. Based on the above analysis of what is and what is not in the DMA Regulations, compared to the choices that could have been made by Ireland from the menu of possibilities outlined in Section II, it appears that Ireland has adopted only a subset of the DMA options. In this regard the CCPC can administer and enforce competition law with respect to the gatekeepers, refer to the Commission third-party information on non-compliance by a gatekeeper with the DMA, assist the Commission in conducting inspections and request, either on its own or with other Member States, that the Commission undertake market investigations.

IV. The CCPC's Record of Competition Law Enforcement in the Digital Sector

1. Introduction

67. In order to gain an insight into the likely response of the CCPC to enforcement of competition rules against gatekeepers and/or other CCPC responsibilities under the DMA Regulations some context is needed. What has been the record of

---

52 Based on an examination of the DETE website: <https://enterprise.gov.ie/en/what-we-do/the-business-environment/digital-single-market/eu-digital-single-market-aspects/> accessed 31 July 2024.

53 Bundeskartellamt (n 31).

54 It appears that Austria, Greece and Italy, as well as Germany, 'have introduced or are considering legislative changes under their national competition law, with provisions applying specifically to the digital sector.' European Competition Network, 'How National Competition Agencies Can Strengthen the DMA' (22 June 2021).

55 European Union (Action for Damages for Infringements of Competition Law) Regulations 2017, SI 43 of 2017, states, for example, in s 8(1) that 'An infringement of competition law found by a final decision of a national competition authority or by a review court is deemed to be irrefutably established for the purposes of an action for damages brought before a court for an infringement of competition law.'

enforcement by the CCPC with respect to the digital sector in the recent past? What might explain the CCPC pattern of enforcement? Building on this description and analysis Section V considers future prospects for CCPC enforcement of competition law, including under the DMA Regulations, in the digital sector.

2. A Preliminary Consideration

68. The CCPC does not have a monopoly of public competition law enforcement in Ireland. The Commission for Communications Regulations (ComReg) has since 2007 had concurrent powers with the CCPC with respect to Articles 101 and 102 and the corresponding sections of the Competition Act 2002 as amended (the 2002 Act). ComReg, which was established on 1 December 2002, 'is the statutory body responsible for the regulation of the electronic communications sector (telecommunications, radio communications, broadcasting transmission and premium rate services) and the postal sector in Ireland.'[56] ComReg has, however, had little involvement in the enforcement of competition law since 2007; it has conducted only two investigations, neither of which involved the digital sector.[57] The core platform services specified in the DMA do not appear to overlap to any great extent with the electronic communications sector. Article 1(3) specifically states that the DMA shall not apply to 'electronic communications networks' and 'electronic communications services... other than those related to number-independent interpersonal communications services.' Hence attention is confined here to the record of CCPC competition law enforcement in the digital sector.

3. CCPC Enforcement in the Digital Sector

69. There is little in the recent record of CCPC enforcement of competition law that impinges on the digital sector or on any of the seven gatekeepers, with two limited exceptions noted below.[58] Since the CCPC came into existence in 2014 there have been two criminal cartel prosecutions: one has been successfully completed (i.e. a bid-rigging for commercial flooring in the Dublin area);[59] while the other case is still before the courts (i.e. bid-rigging for tenders for school bus transport).[60] The CCPC has instituted no civil Court cases seeking a declaration and/or an injunction. There have been three cases – two concerning resale price maintenance, one in Fitflop branded footwear and the other Coach House furniture, with the third concerning Ticketmaster Ireland's ticketing arrangements – where the CCPC has reached an agreement with undertakings memorialised in Court Orders.[61] If a

---

56 Commission for Communications Regulation, 'What We Do' (*ComReg*, 30 March 2024) <https://www.comreg.ie/about/what-we-do/> accessed 31 July 2024.

57 For details see ComReg, 'Competition Law Enforcement' (*ComReg*, 2024) <https://www.comreg.ie/industry/electronic-communications/regulated-markets-competition/competition-law-enforcement/> accessed 31 July 2024.

58 Unless otherwise stated reference here is to the CCPC's record since its inception in October 2014.

59 For a discussion of this case see, for example, Paul Gorecki, 'Cartel Enforcement in Ireland Post the Court of Appeal's Bid-Rigging Judgment: A Bleak Future?' (2019) 40 ECLR 299. The Court of Appeal judgment is dated June 2018.

60 Thirteen suspects were charged in 2021.

61 For a discussion of the use of this mechanism by the CCPC see Paul Gorecki, 'Section 14B Court Orders and Civil Enforcement of Competition Law in Ireland: A New Direction?' (2019) 40 ELCR 63. The two cases cited in the text took place after 2019. For details see: <https://www.ccpc.ie/>.

somewhat more expansive approach is taken of what constitutes a civil enforcement then, for example, price signalling in private motor vehicle insurance can be added to the list of CCPC civil cases.[62] An examination of extended Phase I and all Phase II mergers notified to the CCPC since 2017 suggests that none involved the digital sector.[63] Although the CCPC has a market inquiry function, these studies and reports have not addressed competition issues in the digital sector.[64]

70. Nonetheless, there have been two areas where there has been some, albeit limited, involvement by the CCPC in the digital sector. First, the agency has followed a number of Commission merger investigations involving the gatekeepers: (case M.8228 – *Facebook/WhatsApp*); (case M.10262 – *Meta/Kustomer*); and (case M/10920 – *Amazon/iRobot*).[65] In (case M.10262 – *Meta/Kustomer*) the CCPC was one of several NCAs that referred the transaction to the Commission under Article 22 of the EU Merger Regulation.[66] Second, the CCPC 'agreed (in November 2015) with Booking.com that it would change the terms and conditions it requires of hotels and other accommodations listed on Booking.com.'[67]

4. CCPC Enforcement in a Member State Context

71. The record of the lack of competition law enforcement in the digital sector by the CCPC is consistent with the EU-wide survey of involvement by NCAs in the digital economy by Christophe Carugati.[68] Involvement was defined broadly to include enforcement of competition law (i.e. antitrust and mergers), advocacy (i.e. articles, initiatives, market investigations, position papers and reports) over the period 2010 to 2021. There was no involvement recorded by Ireland's NCA over that period, with the NCAs of Germany, France and the Netherlands accounting for approximately two-thirds of all 182 actions in the digital sector by NCAs over that period.[69]

---

62 For a discussion of this case see Paul Gorecki, 'Price Signalling Ireland: Leading the Way?' (2022) 6 CoRe 294. Details of the other cases (e.g. concerning nursing homes, sharing potentially ant-competitive information amongst private motor insurers via a software product provided by an intermediary software services provider, Relay Software Limited) may be found on <https://www.ccpc.ie/>, under 'Civil Competition Enforcement,' 'Closed Cases.'

63 Based on the cases highlighted in the CCPC Mergers & Acquisitions Reports, which have been issued annually since 2017 by the CCPC.

64 Based on a search of the CCPC website, <https://www.ccpc.ie/>, using the following terms: 'studies,' 'reports' and 'market inquiries'.

65 The CCPC lists the Commission merger investigations that it follows closely in the annual CCPC Mergers & Acquisitions Reports.

66 Regulation 139/2004 of 20 January 2004 on the control of concentrations between undertakings (the EC Merger Regulation) [2004] OJ L24/1.

67 CCPC, 'Booking.com investigation' (*CCPC*, 9 November 2015) <https://www.ccpc.ie/business/enforcement/civil-competition-enforcement/closed-investigations/booking-com-investigation/> accessed 31 July 2024. Booking.com notified the Commission that their services might meet the DMA thresholds to be designated a gatekeeper. For details see European Commission, 'Booking, ByteDance and X Notify their Potential Gatekeeper Status to the Commission under the Digital Markets Act' (1 March 2024) <https://digital-markets-act.ec.europa.eu/booking-bytedance-and-x-notify-their-potential-gatekeeper-status-commission-under-digital-markets-2024-03-01_en> accessed 31 July 2024.

68 Christophe Carugati, 'The Role of National Authorities in the Digital Markets Act' (21 October 2021) <https://papers.ssrn.com/sol3/papers.cfm?abstract_id=3947037> accessed 31 July 2024.

69 It is not clear whether or not Carugati (n 68) took into account the CCPC's involvement in booking.com (Section IV3) while France's booking *MFN* case was taken into account.

5. An Explanation for the Pattern of CCPC Enforcement

72. There are good grounds for arguing that it is a rational allocation of resources by the CCPC to concentrate its competition law activities in areas other than the digital sector. The resources and expertise required to bring complex and time-consuming enforcement action in the digital sector might be difficult to fund/retain expertise for a smaller NCA. To these difficulties are added the fact that Ireland has a judicial model of competition enforcement, in which courts not the CCPC make findings concerning whether or not there is a breach of competition law.[70] Larger NCAs and the Commission are likely to be better placed to deal with the competition law and policy issues arising in the digital sector which often have EU-wide implications. Ireland is thus a beneficiary of such policy interventions. Nonetheless, this is perhaps only a partial explanation. After all NCAs of smaller Member States such as Denmark, Cyprus, Austria and others did record at least some actions in the digital sector over the 2010 to 2021 period.

V. Future Prospects of Competition Law and DMA Enforcement in the Digital Sector

1. Introduction

73. Under the DMA Regulations, the CCPC may enforce competition rules against gatekeepers, refer to the Commission third-party information on non-compliance by a gatekeeper with the DMA, assist the Commission in conducting inspections and request, either on its own or with other Member States, that the Commission undertake market investigations into, for example, whether an undertaking should be designated as a gatekeeper. How is the CCPC likely to exercise these powers? In this section several factors are identified that are likely to assist in answering this question from improvements in Ireland's competition enforcement model to budgetary measures designed to increase the CCPC's effectiveness. Taking these factors into account the section concludes by making a judgment as to whether or not past CCPC involvement in the digital sector is likely to be a guide to future involvement in this sector.

2. Ireland's Competition Model: Moving Towards the Administrative Option

74. In contrast to most other Member States the courts, rather than the CCPC decide all criminal and civil law competition cases. Under the 2002 Act the CCPC is responsible for investigating alleged breaches of competition law using various powers such as inspections (aka dawn raids) and issuing witness summons.[71] The courts are in turn responsible for determining whether competition law has been breached and imposing a sanction. Fines and jail can only be

---

70 For further discussion of this issue see Section V.2 below.

71 See Andrews, Gorecki and McFadden (n 50) for a description and analysis of competition enforcement structures, administration and enforcement prior to the 2022 reforms discussed in the next paragraph.

imposed for criminal breaches; for civil breaches a declaration that the conduct infringes competition law and/or an injunction prohibiting the anticompetitive conduct. The exception is mergers where the CCPC is the decision-maker of first instance, although its determinations can be appealed to the courts, which have wide-ranging powers of review.[72] These institutional arrangements for the application of competition law are characterised by the 'judicial', as compared to the much more common 'administrative' model across the EU. In the latter model 'a single administrative authority investigates cases and takes enforcement decisions subject to judicial control.'[73] Ireland is moving, nonetheless, closer to the administrative model.

75. The Competition (Amendment) Act 2022 (the 2022 Act) transposes into Irish law the ECN+ Directive.[74] The 2022 Act permits for 'the first time in Irish law, breaches of competition law can be enforced through administrative actions taken by competition authorities, with maximum fines of up to €10 million or 10% of total worldwide turnover, whichever is the greater.'[75] Criminal sanctions are retained and as at present will be confined to hard-core cartels, while the merger control regime remains largely unchanged. It may, however, be some time before the first case is heard under the 2022 Act and administrative fines imposed.

76. While the 2022 Act was signed into law on 29 June 2022, it did not come into force until 27 September 2023. An essential part of the administrative architecture is the appointment of Adjudication Officers with responsibility for assessing Statements of Objections from the CCPC and recommending fines to be confirmed by the High Court. The relevant secondary legislation setting 'out the requirements governing certain independence and employment terms relating to the adjudication officers'[76] was also put in place on 27 September 2023. The appointment of a Chief Adjudication Officer is currently (July 2024) underway, with a panel of Adjudication Officers expected to follow in due course.

77. Once the institutional architecture is in place this should facilitate the CCPC bringing cases against the gatekeepers under the competition rules, particularly unilateral conducts cases. The CCPC will outline its case in a Statement of Objections, which is heard before an Adjudication Officer who is more likely than a High Court judge to have the expertise required to assess complex unilateral conduct cases and impose the appropriate sanction.

---

72 The Competition Authority assumed control of mergers on 1 January 2003. There has been only one appeal from a Competition Authority/CCPC merger determination since that date, despite several prohibition determinations. For a discussion of this case see Paul Gorecki, 'The Kerry/Breeo Merger' (2009) 5 ECJ 585.

73 European Commission Enhancing Competition Enforcement by Member States' Competition Authorities: Institutional and Procedural Issues SWD(2014) 231/2 para 10.

74 Directive 2019/1 of the European Parliament and of the Council of 11 December 2018 to empower the competition authorities of the Member States to be more effective enforcers and to ensure the proper functioning of the internal market [2019] OJ L11/3.

75 Competition (Amendment) Act 2022 (*DETE*, 27 September 2023)' <https://enterprise.gov.ie/en/legislation/competition-amendment-act-2022.html> accessed 31 July 2024.

76 Competition Act 2002 (Adjudication Officers) Regulations 2023, SI 476 of 2023.

3. The CCPC and Digital Sector Priorities

78. The CCPC Strategy Statement for 2024–26, released in November 2023, provides an obvious starting point for gauging the CCPC's likely reaction to the exercise of its responsibilities under the DMA Regulations. The DMA is dated 14 September 2022, while the Commission designated the initial six gatekeepers on 6 September 2023. In other words, when the CCPC prepared its Strategy Statement for 2024–26 it would have been aware of the broad contours of its likely new powers contained in the DMA Regulations and the identity of the gatekeepers.

79. The CCPC in the Strategy Statement for 2024–26 addresses the issue of its role in the digital space as follows:

> In terms of digital and data, modern life and commerce is increasingly conducted online. Information about our preferences and interests are harvested and monetised in ways that would have seemed like science fiction only decades ago. AI and how it may impact on consumer interests and competition raise important issues. As the European Union moves to level the playing field in relation to digital and data, the CCPC has recently received, and expects to receive more, new responsibilities and powers across a range of new and existing functions for the purpose of tackling issues in digital and data markets. The CCPC has to ensure it already to take on these roles and to make robust decisions that will be upheld if they are subjected to judicial scrutiny. The preparations in some areas have been ongoing over our previous strategy but in other areas a significant amount of work is required to draft legislation, establish parameters with other agencies and put structures in place to be able to deliver on new functions.[77]

80. Apart from these essentially administrative and process issues the Strategy Statement provides no indication as to what priority the agency attaches to enforcement in the digital sector (or any other sector for that matter). In other words, the Strategy Statement provides maximum discretion to the CCPC with regard to its sectoral enforcement priorities. It is only *ex post* by observing where the CCPC allocated resources in terms of cases is it possible to infer what were in fact the agency's priorities.

81. Not all NCAs are reluctant to identify sectoral priorities. France's *Autorité de la Concurrence* in its Priorities 2023–24 states 'The digital economy in all its forms continues to be one of the Autorité's priorities for action. The increasing complexity of the issues and the diverse range of activities involved require this long-term commitment.' Germany's Bundeskartellamt identifies the digital sector as a key enforcement priority,[78] in part driven by various legislative reforms in the digital sector referred to above. The Netherland's Authority for Consumers

---

[77] CCPC, 'Strategy Statement 2024–2026' (November 2023) 4. Similar statements appear in the most recent CCPC Annual Report: CCPC, 'Annual Report 2022' (*CCPC*, 2023) 4, 33 <https://www.ccpc.ie/business/about/annual-reports/?csyear=2022> accessed 31 July 2024.

[78] Bundeskartellamt, 'Annual Report 2022–2023' (May 2023) 6–7.

and Markets (ACM) stated that for 2023 it had 'three key priorities: the energy transition, the digital economy, and the sustainability transition.'[79]

4. CCPC Organisational and Budgetary Issues

82. The CCPC's responsibilities under the DMA Regulations will be included in the remit of the CCPC's Competition Enforcement and Mergers Division (CEM). The CEM is responsible for 'the CCPC's merger review function and its administrative competition enforcement function as it relates to vertical and unilateral conduct and the EU Digital Markets Act (DMA).' This seems a sensible allocation. Unilateral conduct cases is typically the area in which the gatekeepers are likely to breach competition rules. In contrast, to the arrangements with respect to the DMA Regulations, the CCPC has set up within the Consumer Protection Division a digital, EU and International Cooperation Unit to deal 'with traders established/headquartered in Ireland who operate across EU Member State borders selling goods and services to EU consumers' which includes the agencies' P2B and DSA responsibilities.[80] No doubt as the CCPC gains experience with the operation of the DMA Regulations changes in the organisational structure may follow.

83. The DMA Regulations increase the responsibilities of the CCPC and hence a concomitant budgetary settlement is required for effective enforcement of these regulations. The CCPC's budget has been increased substantially but not only to fund the agency's new digital responsibilities set out in Table 1, but also for the implementation of the 2022 Act. There was a €4.9 million increase the CCPC's budget for 2024 compared to 2023 or approximately a quarter, with a sanctioned staff of 207 persons.[81] In the past year or so the CCPC has approved a number of new posts related to digital markets. Once these are filled the agency will be in a much better position for dealing with the challenges posed by the DMA.

5. Inter-Agency Cooperation in the Digital Sector

84. Responsibility for the digital sector is shared across a number of different agencies. As noted in Table 1 UNAM and to a much lesser extent the CCPC share responsibility for the administration and enforcement of the DSA 2024. Although ComReg is not designated a national competent authority for the purposes of the DMA Regulations, nevertheless, as noted in Section II.7, BEREC is a member of the High-level Group that advises the Commission on the DMA and ComReg is a member of BEREC. Given these interconnections there is within Ireland coordination across the various regulators concerned with the digital sector through the Digital

---

79 ACM, '2023 ACM Annual Report: New Rules and Duties Call for a New Form of Oversight' (*ACM*, 2024) <https://www.acm.nl/en/publications/2023-acm-annual-report-new-rules-and-duties-call-new-form-oversight> accessed 31 July 2024.

80 The information concerning the allocation of responsibilities within the CCPC is derived from recent job descriptions posted on the CCPC website <https://www.ccpc.ie/> under 'Current Opportunities' for deputy Director (Mergers) and Deputy Director, Consumer Protection Division, the closing dates for which were 2 April 2024 and 4 April 2024.

81 Dara Calleary, 'Consumer Protection, Written Answers, Q21' (*Houses of the Oireachtas*, 23 November 2023) <https://www.oireachtas.ie/en/debates/question/2023-11-23/section/52/> accessed 31 July 2024.

Regulators Group (DRG) whose membership includes the CCPC, ComReg, the Data Protection Commission (DPC)[82] and UNAM. The DRG was established in 2022 and held its first meeting in 2023. According to the CCPC the DRG's 'primary purpose is to develop strong cross-functioning communications between Regulators whose work has direct ramifications for Ireland's digital economy, so that current and future digital legislation is applied in a consistent and cohesive manner.'[83]

6. Conclusion

85. Notwithstanding the discussion above, it is still somewhat speculative as to the what the CCPC will do with the new powers it has under the DMA Regulations. Based on past performance with respect to the digital sector outlined in Section IV and the resources required to launch a complex unilateral conduct case against a gatekeeper it seems reasonable to assume that the CCPC will confine most of its attention – until the reforms under the 2022 Act are bedded down – under the DMA Regulations to referring to the Commission third-party information on non-compliance by a gatekeeper with the DMA, assisting the Commission in conducting inspections and making requests to the Commission for market investigations under Article 41 of the DMA (analogous to the Article 22 references in merger cases referred to in Section IV.3 above).

VI. Choice and Discretion: Narrow or Wide?

86. As noted in Section I the Commission is the 'sole enforcer' under the DMA, with limited discretion accorded to the Member State in the administration of the DMA. Member States can, however, enforce competition rules with respect to the Commission-designated gatekeepers. The Member State's discretion under the DMA is circumscribed by the necessity of informing and making decisions consistent with Commission's previous decisions and stated preferences. Even within the limited choice set of DMA-delegated responsibilities confronting the Member State, Ireland opted to exercise discretion towards the minimum end of the spectrum. The CCPC, which has been designated as the national competent authority under the DMA, does not have a track record of competition law enforcement in the digital sector in general or the gatekeepers in particular. There are sound reasons for the enforcement choices made by the CCPC. In terms of future competition law and DMA enforcement the evidence suggests that the CCPC will be much better resourced and staffed in the digital sector and hence able to successfully fulfil the mandate that it has been given under the DMA Regulations.

1. Annex A: The Operations of the Gatekeepers in Ireland

87. Of the seven firms designated as gatekeepers under the DMA by the Commission to date (July 2024) six – Alphabet, Amazon, Apple, ByteDance, Meta and

---

[82] The DPC is according to its website, 'the Irish supervisory authority for the General Data Protection Regulation'. In that regard the DPC is the supervisory authority for several of the gatekeepers whose county-of-origin is Ireland. For details see <https://www.dataprotection.ie/> accessed 31 July 2024.

[83] CCPC Annual Report 2022 (n 77) 35.

Microsoft – have extensive operations in Ireland in terms of employment, pre-tax profits and sales (see Table 2).[84] In 2022 gatekeeper employment in these six firms in Ireland varied from 2,600 (ByteDance) to 6,000 (Apple). The level of pre-tax profits exceeded a €1bn for all of these six gatekeepers except Amazon and ByteDance, reaching €65.8bn in the case of Apple. For all of these six gatekeepers, bar ByteDance, annual sales in 2022 exceeded a €1bn. In the case of Meta, its operations in Ireland accounted for slightly more than 50% of its global revenues in 2022.

Table 2. Gatekeepers Employment, Profits and Revenue, Ireland, 2022[85]

Gatekeeper	Employment	Pre-Tax Profits	Sales
Alphabet[86]	4,800	€2.0bn	€72.6bn
Amazon[87]	4,000	€50.7mn	€4.9bn
Apple[88]	6,000	€65.8bn	€211.6bn
ByteDance[89]	2,600	€11.2mn	€332.4mn
Meta[90]	2,700	€1.8bn	€58.1bn
Microsoft[91]	3,500	$41.8bn	$113.5bn

Source: see text.

88. A small number of foreign-owned corporations account for a significant and increasing percentage of Ireland's corporation tax receipts.[92] The ten leading corporate taxpayers accounted for around a third of total corporation tax receipts in 2008; but by 2022 this share reached 60%. Corporation tax receipts, in turn, accounted for a rising share of Ireland's overall tax receipts from all sources: in

---

84 The exception is Booking. Of Booking's worldwide revenue outside the US in 2022, 90% was ascribed to the Netherlands, while none of Booking's subsidiaries as of December 31, 2022 was incorporated in Ireland. For details see Booking Holdings Inc, Form 10-K, Annual Report Pursuant to Section 13 or 15(d0 of the Securities Exchange Act of 1934, p. 114 and Exhibit 21 <5704910b-d65d-4528-a869-e1e1216a1f8b.pdf> accessed 31 July 2024.

85 Refers to the gatekeepers' employment in Ireland (rounded to near 100) together with the pre-tax profits and revenue that accrues to the gatekeepers' operations irrespective of whether or not it is generated from customers in Ireland or elsewhere. Press reports of accounts filed at the Companies Registration Office <https://cro.ie/> accessed 31 July 2024.

86 Refers to the calendar year 2022 and to Alphabet's Google operations in Ireland.

87 Refers to the calendar year 2022 and to Amazon Data Services Ireland Ltd and Amazon Ireland Support Services Ltd.

88 Refers to the 12 months to September 2022 and Apple Operations International Ltd and its subsidiaries. The pre-tax profits and sales were converted from $ to € using the Central Bank of Ireland annual average exchange rate for 2022.

89 Refers to calendar year 2022 and to TikTok Technology Ltd. The pre-tax profits and sales were converted from $ to € using the Central Bank of Ireland annual average exchange rate for 2022.

90 Refers to the calendar year 2022 and to Meta Platforms Ireland Ltd, which accounts for slightly more than 50% of Meta's global revenues for 2022.

91 Refers to the 12 months to 30 June 2022, to Microsoft Ireland Operations Ltd and Microsoft Ireland Research Ltd. The latter's pre-tax profits included $15bn gain from the liquidation of some subsidiaries – Mojang Synergies, Microsoft Singapore Holdings and Microsoft Mopr Holdings Luxembourg.

92 All data in this paragraph is taken from Brian Cronin, 'Understanding Ireland's Top Corporation Taxpayers' (June 2023) Irish Fiscal Advisory Council Working Paper No 20.

2008 corporation tax receipts accounted for around 13% overall tax receipts, by 2022 it had risen to 25%.

89. Gatekeepers constitute an important component of the ten leading corporate taxpayers in Ireland.[93] The first three ranked corporate taxpayers are all gatekeepers – Apple, Microsoft and Alphabet – as is the seventh-ranked – Meta. Furthermore, the distribution of corporation tax among these ten leading corporation taxpayers is substantially skewed towards the leading payers. For example, while Apple paid in excess of €2bn in corporation tax, the tenth-ranked corporation payer was around €0.25bn.

93 The Revenue Commissioners which are the source of the information of the leading corporate taxpayers do not identify the individual payers, while the reference in the previous note which uses a variety of public sources also decided not to name the ten leading corporation taxpayers. The source for the information in the paragraph is drawn from an attempt to identify the leading ten corporation taxpayers from 'company filings, reports and other data.' It is 'by no means definitive' and is 'subject to a number of caveats'. The data refer to corporation tax paid in 2020. For details see, Eoin Burke-Kennedy, 'The State's Top 10 Corporate Taxpayers: Who Are They?' *Irish Times* (Dublin, 30 December 2021).

The DMA and the Digital Transformation: An Italian Perspective

Italy

ENRICO ADRIANO RAFFAELLI*
Rucellai & Raffaelli

Abstract

The chapter outlines the legislative framework in Italy with regard to digital markets, delving into the efforts made by the Italian legislature and authorities to strengthen the relationship between the EU and national tools in the digital realm. Some leading Italian cases are then examined, highlighting key initiatives and significant issues raised, in particular, by the activity and decisions of the Italian Competition Authority (ICA). The chapter concludes with reflections and observations about the interplay between the DMA and national digital transformation initiatives, offering insights on the interactions and implications of such initiatives for the evolving digital market landscape.

* Enrico Adriano Raffaelli is founding partner of Rucellai & Raffaelli. He taught European Law at the Milan Catholic University for several years. He is Honorary President of the European Lawyers Union and also President of the Competition Law Commission of the same association.

I. Introduction: General Views from Italy

1. Over the past few years, regulating the digital sector has become a key objective all over the world, including for the European Union (EU) and its Member States. This is because the digital sector stands at the core of important innovation initiatives and requires cooperation among many stakeholders and policymakers.

2. Italy is no exception in this regard: notably, some of its national initiatives relating to the digital sector predate the adoption of the Digital Markets Act (DMA),[1] while others were implemented or proposed subsequently. The Italian legislator has implemented a number of specific measures governing the conduct of players in digital markets. Moreover, as we will see, the Italian Competition Authority (*Autorità Garante della Concorrenza e del Mercato* – ICA) has dealt with several cases in which digital markets played an important role.

3. The present chapter will, first, outline the chief legislative initiatives adopted in Italy with respect to digital markets and the most significant cases decided by the ICA (Section I). Next, it will focus on the steps taken within the Italian legal system to facilitate the integration of and enhance the synergy between EU and national legislation for the digital sector (Section II). Finally, it will make some concluding remarks on the interactions between the DMA and national initiatives relating to digital transformation (Section III).

1. The Chief Legislative Initiatives Adopted in Italy with Regard to Digital Markets

4. In terms of national legislative initiatives, a significant step was taken with the passage of Law No 118/2022 (Annual Market and Competition Law 2021), which entered into force on 27 August 2022, through an amendment to the provision on the abuse of economic dependence (Article 9 of Law No 192/1998).[2] This provision

---

1 Regulation 2022/1925 of the European Parliament and of the Council of 14 September 2022 on contestable and fair markets in the digital sector and amending Directives 2019/1937 and 2020/1828 (Digital Markets Act or DMA) [2022] OJ L265/1.

2 The text of Law No 192/1998 art 9 was supplemented with three new sentences, indicated in italics: '1. Any abuse by one or more undertakings of a customer or supplier's state of economic dependence, in their or its regard, is prohibited. Economic dependence is a situation in which an undertaking is able to bring about an excessive imbalance of rights and obligations in its business relations with another undertaking. Economic dependence shall also be assessed taking into account the real possibility for the abused party to find satisfactory alternatives on the market. *Unless proven otherwise, economic dependence shall be presumed where an undertaking uses the intermediation services provided by a digital platform that plays a decisive role in reaching end users or suppliers, including in terms of network effects or data availability.* 2. Abuse may also consist in refusal to sell or refusal to buy, the imposition of unjustifiably onerous or discriminatory contractual terms, or the arbitrary termination of existing business relations. *The abusive practices carried out by the digital platforms referred to in paragraph 1 may also consist in providing insufficient information or data on the scope or quality of the service provided and in requesting undue unilateral performances not justified by the nature or content of the activity carried out, or in adopting practices that inhibit or hinder the use of a different provider for the same service, including through the application of unilateral conditions or additional costs not provided for in the contractual agreements or existing licenses.* 3. The agreement by which the abuse of economic dependence is realised is null and void. The competent ordinary courts have jurisdiction in actions for abuse of economic dependence, including actions for injunctions and for damages. *Civil actions available under this Article shall be brought before the chambers specialised in business matters referred to in Article 1 of Legislative Decree No 168 of 27 June 2003.* 3a. Without prejudice to the possible application of Article 3 of Law No. 287 of 10 October 1990, the Italian Competition Authority may, if it finds that an abuse of economic dependence

can be enforced by both the ICA (public enforcement) and private parties bringing actions before national courts (private enforcement). In particular, the amendment introduced a presumption of economic dependence for digital platforms with a decisive role in reaching customers or suppliers. The purpose of the amendment was to facilitate national authorities' application of the prohibition in specific sectors where large digital platforms enjoy significant market power.

5. The recent Italian reform is part of a broader trend to bolster the use of national rules on the abuse of economic dependence, which are generally easier to enforce than the rules prohibiting abuses of dominant position.[3] This is recognised by the ICA, which takes the position that taking full advantage of the potential of the prohibition will more effectively combat abuses of a 'non-dominant' position in digital markets, making the relevant provisions 'more appropriate and effective with regard to the characteristics and, in particular, the power of the large platform'.[4]

6. It bears noting that Article 9(1) of Law No 192/1998 generally defines the state of economic dependence on the basis of two criteria: an undertaking's capacity to give rise to an 'excessive imbalance of rights and obligations' in trade relations with another party, and the relative existence of a concrete possibility for the dependent company 'to find satisfactory alternatives on the market'.

7. Against this backdrop, the following sentences were added to paragraphs 1 and 2 of Article 9, respectively:

> Unless proven otherwise, economic dependence shall be presumed where an undertaking uses the intermediation services provided by a digital platform that plays a decisive role in reaching end users or suppliers, including in terms of network effects or data availability[5]

and

> The abusive practices carried out by the digital platforms referred to in paragraph 1 may also consist in providing insufficient information or data on the scope or quality of the service provided and in requesting undue unilateral performances not justified by the nature or content of the activity carried out, or in adopting practices that inhibit or hinder the use of a different provider for the same service, including through the application of unilateral conditions or additional costs not provided for in the contractual agreements or existing licences.[6]

---

is relevant for the protection of competition and the market, including upon report by third parties and following the activation of its powers of investigation and preliminary enquiry, proceed with the warnings and sanctions provided for in Article 15 of Law No. 287 of 10 October 1990 against the undertaking or undertakings that have committed such abuse. In the event of a widespread and repeated breach of the rules set forth in Legislative Decree No. 231 of 9 October 2002, carried out to the detriment of undertakings, with particular reference to small and medium-sized enterprises, abuse shall be found to have been committed regardless of the establishment of economic dependence'.

3 A Licastro, *La riscoperta dell'abuso di dipendenza economica nell'era dei mercati digitali* (4 May 2022).

4 ICA, 'Proposals for Competition Reform for the Annual Law on the Market and Competition Year 2021' (22 March 2021) ICA's Bulletin No 13/2021 99.

5 See Law No 118/2022 art 33(1-*bis*) (*Legge annuale per il mercato e la concorrenza* 2021) published in Gazzetta Ufficiale (12 August 2021) Serie Generale No 188. The law entered into force on 27 August 2022.

6 Law No 118/2022 art 33(1-*bis*).

8. As mentioned above, the reform introduced a rebuttable presumption (*iuris tantum*) of economic dependence. In particular, the new formulation of Article 9(1) relieves the allegedly abused undertaking of the burden of proving the existence of the two criteria mentioned above. Over the last decade, the Italian legislator has introduced presumptions in specific areas characterised by structural asymmetry of power between the parties[7] to relieve the lesser party of the burden of proving its state of economic dependence. In many cases, it was impossible or excessively difficult for them to produce such evidence. Similarly, the ICA reflects the conclusion that satisfying the burden of proving the anti-competitive significance of abuse, which the exercise of its powers in a given matter presupposes, could be excessively difficult.[8]

9. This notwithstanding, plaintiffs must still meet the burden of proving that the defendant platform plays a 'decisive role in reaching end users or suppliers'. This expression is not unrelated to showing economic necessity for the plaintiff undertaking, since it suggests that, without such basic platform services, the plaintiff company could not reach end users or suppliers on economically satisfactory terms.[9]

10. This requirement appears to overlap with the inability to find satisfactory alternatives on the market, which Article 9(1) of Law No 192/1998 indicates as a typical element of the relationship of economic dependence. As a consequence, many scholars and commentators have convincingly argued that the provision tends to be redundant, as the condition for the presumption would end up coinciding with a presumed fact, i.e. the economic dependence. To overcome this apparent contradiction, one proposed solution is to consider the 'decisive position' of the platform or provider vis-à-vis the market as a whole, accepting a presumption of individual dependence whenever it is demonstrated that access to the services of the digital platform constitutes an economically necessary choice for a 'reasonably efficient' company.[10]

11. In this context, it remains to be clarified what the provision means by the words 'decisive role', leading some authors to argue that the presumption may apply automatically to the so-called GAFAMs (Google, Amazon, Facebook, Apple, Microsoft). This notwithstanding, the presumptive technique is often used, by both the Italian and the European legislators, to rebalance the information asymmetry typically suffered by injured parties as a result of an antitrust violation. Moreover, it is a rebuttable presumption and, hence, it can always be overcome by offering evidence to the contrary. In this case, the defendant must prove the actual market

---

[7] In this regard see Decree-Law No 1/2012 art 17, para 3, according to which «conduct adopted by large companies that own petrol stations or supply fuel 'for the purpose of hindering, preventing or limiting, in practice or through contractual provisions, the use of fuel distribution facilities for the purpose of hindering, preventing or limiting the use of fuel, within the meaning of Article 9 of Law No. 192 of 18 June 1998'.

[8] See Law No 192/1998 art 9(3-*bis*).

[9] M Libertini, *La presunzione di dipendenza economica nei mercati digitali. Un commento all'art. 33 della l. 5 agosto 2022, n 118* in *Orizzonti del diritto commerciale* (2023) 9.

[10] *Ibid* para 3.1; V Bachelet, *Il rafforzamento del contrasto agli abusi di posizione 'non dominante' delle piattaforme digitali in Nuove leggi civili commentate* (2023) 39, para 4; S Lopopolo, *L'abuso di dipendenza economica alla prova dei mercati digitali tra presunzione e misure cautelari* in *Il Foro Italiano* (2023) 432.

position of that undertaking and the concrete absence of bargaining subservience to it. This kind of evidence should be easy for the defendant to provide, taking into account the fact that such platforms have superior technical and financial tools and have access to more information about the overall dynamics of the market.

12. The abovementioned reform provides for an extension of the types of abuse identified by the provision, adding them to those already contained in the original text. The new scenarios highlight the legislator's willingness to keep up with the specific needs of the digital markets. Nonetheless, it is important to note that these new scenarios should not be considered an exhaustive list, as the possibility remains that new provisions will be added in keeping with future developments in this ever-changing field.

13. Furthermore, Article 33(1)(c), of the abovementioned Law No 118/2022 (Annual Market and Competition Law 2021) sets new rules on the competence of national courts in civil actions in matters of abuse of economic dependence. This competence is now specifically conferred upon the Chambers specialised in business matters of the Italian civil courts. An important difference from the private enforcement of EU and Italian antitrust law (i.e. Articles 101 and 102 TFEU, as well as Articles 2 and 3 of Law No 287/90) should be underlined here. Competence for antitrust disputes is limited to the three Chambers specialised in business matters of the courts of Milan, Rome and Naples. On the contrary, civil actions concerning abuses of economic dependence pursuant to Article 9 of Law No 192/98 are dealt with by *all* Chambers specialised in business matters instituted in the different Italian courts, and not only by the three Chambers mentioned above. This differentiation between the private enforcement of abuse of economic dependence and antitrust law does not seem entirely reasonable and may rightly be criticised. Moreover, as explained in greater detail below, competence in the private enforcement of the DMA is not subject to any provision of Italian legislation, which adds to the confusion surrounding the competence of Italian courts in the enforcement of provisions relating to digital markets.

14. Lastly, the reform at issue – through the provision set out in Article 33(3) of Law No 118/2022 (Annual Market and Competition Law 2021) – provides that the Presidency of the Council of Ministers, in agreement with the Ministry of Justice and after having consulted the ICA, 'may adopt special guidelines aimed at facilitating the application of the provisions set forth in paragraph 1, in accordance with the principles of European law, also for the purpose of preventing litigation and promoting good market practices in the field of competition and the free exercise of economic activity'. However, the entry into force of the new rules is not conditional on the publication of such guidelines, the adoption of which is a simple faculty (and not a duty) of the Presidency of the Council of Ministers. Until now, no guidelines of this kind have been adopted.

15. Aside from the abovementioned new provisions on the abuse of economic dependence, on 30 December 2023, the Italian legislator adopted Law No 214/2023 (Annual Market and Competition Law 2022), laying down, inter alia, measures meant to ensure the implementation of the DMA. Indeed, Article 18 of Law No 214/2023 explains that the ICA guarantees coordination with the Commission and the network of authorities for the relevant public enforcement activities

envisaged by the DMA. The ICA will regulate the procedures and modalities for achieving this aim, since the procedure already in force for the application of competition law cannot be automatically applicable.[11] Article 18 demonstrates that Italy has begun to take active steps to facilitate the integration between EU and national legislation for the digital sector. An in-depth analysis of the article will be provided below, in Section II of the present chapter.

16. Finally, another novelty concerning digital markets that deserves to be mentioned is the transposition of Directive 2019/2161[12] on the better enforcement and modernisation of Union consumer protection rules. Italy has implemented this Directive mainly through Legislative Decree No 26/2023, which represents a significant innovation in strategies to address the challenges of modern contractual contexts, where direct interpersonal contact between service providers and consumers is decreasing. This Decree brings additions and modifications to the Italian Consumer Code, aimed at strengthening consumer protection online and enhancing the effectiveness of sanctions applicable to companies in case of violations. When it comes to consumer rights in contracts, the Decree primarily focuses on general definitions, updating them in light of the digital context and recent additions to the Consumer Code regarding guarantees for the supply of digital content and services. Notions such as 'online market' and 'online market provider' are introduced for the first time.

17. In addition, the scope of consumer rights regulations is extended to contracts where consumers provide or commit to providing personal data to professionals in exchange for digital content or services. Information obligations towards consumers before entering into contracts now include references to guarantees, as well as to functionality compatibility, and interoperability characteristics of digital goods and services.

18. The transposition of the Directive has created specific grounds for information obligations for contracts concluded in online markets (Article 49-*bis* of the Italian Consumer Code). Online market providers are required to clearly and comprehensibly indicate to the consumer, through appropriate means of distance communication, the following elements: general information about the main parameters that determine the classification of offers presented to consumers as a result of their search and the importance of these parameters compared to others; whether the third party offering goods, services or digital content is a professional or not, based on what that party has declared to the online market provider; in cases where the third party is not a professional, that the consumer rights deriving from EU law do not apply to the contract; and, if applicable, how the contractual obligations are divided between the third party and the online market provider.[13]

---

11 *Legge annuale per il mercato e la concorrenza 2022, Dossier XIX Legislatura a cura dei Servizi Studi di Camera e Senato A.C. 1555* (20 November 2023).

12 Directive 2019/2161 of the European Parliament and of the Council of 27 November 2019 amending Council Directive 93/13/EEC and Directives 98/6, 2005/29 and 2011/83 of the European Parliament and of the Council as regards the better enforcement and modernisation of Union consumer protection rules [2019] OJ L328/7.

13 A Palmieri, *Il codice del consumo si rinnova per raccogliere le sfide dei mercati digitali, in Altalex* (20 March 2023).

2. The Most Significant Cases Handled by the ICA and the Italian Courts in the Digital Realm

19. In recent years, the European Commission and the National Competition Authorities have had to face challenges coming from the digital markets. Their actions have focused particularly on the so-called GAFAMs (i.e. Google, Amazon, Facebook (now Meta), Apple, Microsoft). Indeed, these Tech giants have proven their ability to reshape entire sectors of the economy and create new competitive dynamics. Since an increasing number of businesses rely on these industry behemoths to connect with their customer base, the GAFAMs have also been called 'guardians' or 'gatekeepers' of the network.

20. The ICA has initiated several investigations against the GAFAMs for conduct violating competition law provisions. Such investigations have generally concluded with the imposition of sanctions that, in light of the turnover of the companies involved and the seriousness of distortions on the market, were particularly high.

21. One notable decision by the ICA targeted Google[14] for engaging in exclusionary abuse of its dominant position, in violation of Article 102 TFEU. Notably, the ICA considered the dominant position held by Google on two different markets: the first held through Android on the market for the licensing of operating systems for smart mobile devices, and the second held through Google Play, on the market for portals selling apps for Android. This case stemmed from a complaint filed by Enel X Italia, alleging that Google refused to allow the Juice Pass app (previously known as Enel X Recharge) on the Android Auto platform. The digital application, developed by Enel X Italia, offers various services related to electric car recharging, such as locating charging stations, navigation, booking sessions, managing payments, and more. Google's actions were allegedly aimed at excluding a competitor and enhancing user engagement with its popular navigation app, Google Maps, with expanded functionalities to include information on recharging stations. This case concerns the interoperability between the areas of smartphones and cars and the competitive comparison between apps.[15]

22. It is worth noting that Google had a dual role in this case, since it acted as both gatekeeper and competitor. Google, as the developer and controller of Android Auto, holds a significant position in the market alongside competitors in the realm of navigation and electric recharging services. Therefore, it is imperative for Google to adhere to regulations that promote fair competition while carrying out its duties as the overseer of Android Auto's features and advancements. It must ensure that it does not hinder the ability for third-party developers to introduce new and diverse applications and functionalities on Android Auto. This includes allowing competitors to offer services that may differ from those provided by Google's proprietary apps. Google's likely aim is to safeguard the established

---

14 ICA, Case A529/2021 *Google/Compatibilità app Enel X Italia con sistema Android Auto*, see Silvia Pietrini, *Italy: The Italian Competition Authority sanctions an Internet giant for abuse of dominant position (Google/Enel)*, CONCURRENCES No. 3-2021, art. No. 101661.

15 G Galasso, 'Digital Ecosystems between Competition and Regulation: The Italian Experience' in EA Raffaelli (ed), *Antitrust between EU Law and National Law* (Bruylant 2023) 229.

business model of Google Maps and its position as a vital access point for user engagement and data flow, while also facilitating the integration of competitors' services to enhance its data collection efforts.

23. The ICA deemed it necessary to impose not only sanctions, but also corrective measures, which generally consist of obligations intended to reconfigure the platform and its conduct on the market so as to guarantee competitors' access free of discriminatory conditions. In this particular case, the ICA imposed a cease and desist order[16] consisting of the release of 'the final version of the template for the development of apps for electric recharging' and, where the template does not allow the development of the Enel X Italia app, including the functions indicated as essential by the same ICA, ordered Google to 'proceed to the development of the missing functions by integrating the aforementioned template or by developing a new one'.[17]

24. These measures should contribute to a more vibrant European digital economy, given that they are aimed at safeguarding the contestability of the affected markets and, more importantly, protecting and facilitating the implementation of innovative markets initiatives. Finally, as the Italian judges remarked, the purpose of these measures is ensuring that, whenever a market was affected by an antitrust infringement, 'conditions similar to those that would have been found there in the absence of the infringement be restored'.[18]

25. Another case was initiated in July 2020, when the Authority, prompted by a complaint filed by a company named Digitech, began investigating an alleged breach of Article 101 TFEU by Apple and Amazon. The two companies had reached an agreement to restrict access to the marketplace for Apple and Beats branded products to a select group of operators, without consideration of qualitative attributes. These competitive constraints hindered retailers, other than Amazon and the specifically chosen operators, from utilising the Amazon.it sales platform, which holds prominence in the Italian marketplace. Notably, the investigation revealed that one of the exclusion criteria for retailers was their geographical origin, increasing the difficulty of integrating national markets, creating compartmentalisation and restricting parallel sales. The cartel detrimentally impacted consumers by limiting their choices and affecting retailers for whom the marketplace serves as a crucial tool for international business expansion. It is interesting to note that, in this case, too, the Tech giants involved acted as both the marketplace operator and direct seller of the products. In addition to imposing a fine, the Authority ordered Apple and Amazon to eliminate or amend the contractual clauses at issue. This order aimed to establish distribution mechanisms that enable legitimate operators engaged in marketing authentic Apple and Beats branded products to access the Amazon.it marketplace and utilise its intermediary services in a non-discriminatory manner, compared to Amazon and

---

16 Law No 287/90 art 15.

17 See ICA Decision No 29645 of 27 April 2021, *Enel X Italia S.r.l./Alphabet Inc/Google LCC/Google Italy S.r.l.* See also Michele Giannino, *The Italian Competition Authority fines a Big Tech company for abusively locking a SatNav rival out of their app store (Google/Enel X)*, E-COMPETITIONS April 2021, art. No. 100994.

18 Consiglio di Stato 8 April 2014 n 1673.

other approved sellers of Apple and Beats products on Amazon.it. These actions align with the objective criteria of a qualitative nature established for the sale of Apple and Beats products.[19]

26. It is also important to look at the so-called *Amazon case*, which was initiated *ex officio* and concluded by the Authority through the adoption of the final decision in November 2021. The ICA determined that Amazon had abused its dominant position, contravening Article 102 TFEU, by providing various advantages related to the visibility of its offerings and enhancing sales on the Amazon.com website exclusively for third-party sellers utilising its logistics service, known as 'Amazon Logistics' or 'Fulfilment by Amazon'. This link created by Amazon for exclusively favoured retailers utilising its logistics services gave rise to a competitive harm for the other logistics companies, since a significant portion of their potential demand was diverted. Similar to the aforementioned cases, in addition to imposing a fine exceeding one billion euros, the Authority made the noteworthy decision to include a cease-and-desist order. This order imposed a comprehensive set of obligations on Amazon, primarily focused on redefining the Prime program and ensuring equitable treatment between sellers utilising Amazon's logistics and third-party sellers not utilising Amazon's logistics.[20]

27. Among the cases recently dealt with by the ICA involving digital platforms, the interim measures adopted in the framework of a case between Meta Platforms Inc (a company managing several social networks and software, including Facebook, Instagram and WhatsApp) and the Italian Society of Authors and Publishers (SIAE) bears mentioning. The case was predicated on SIAE's presumed position of economic dependence with respect to Meta. As described above, the recent legislative amendment to Article 9 of Law No 192/1998 introduced a presumption of economic dependence when an undertaking uses the intermediation services of a digital platform that is decisive in reaching end users. Against this backdrop, the case at issue perfectly shows the need to balance economic asymmetry in negotiations.

28. The dispute between the two undertakings, as brought to the attention of the ICA, revolves around a licensing agreement for the use of copyrighted works. The Meta group is globally active in offering its users social digital platforms, functions, applications, services, technologies and software. Its most popular social networks are Facebook and Instagram. On the other hand, SIAE, an Italian Government entity, specialises in managing and providing access to copyrights by issuing licenses for protected works, collecting royalties and distributing the resulting revenues.

---

19 See ICA Decision No 29889 of 16 November 2021, *Apple Inc./Apple Distribution International Ltd/Apple Sales International/Apple Italia S.r.l./Apple Retail Italia S.r.l./Amazon.com Inc./Amazon Services Europe S.à r.l./Amazon Europe Core S.à r.l./Amazon EU S.à. r.l./Amazon Italia Services S.r.l.* See also Silvia Pietrini, *Italy: The Italian Competition Authority sanctioned two web giants for engaging in a cartel to restrict competition with authorized resellers of Apple and Beats branded products (Apple/Beats)*, CONCURRENCES No 1-2022, art. No. 105567.

20 See ICA Decision No 29925 of 30 November 2021, *Amazon Europe Core S.à r.l./Amazon Services Europe S.à r.l./Amazon EU S.à r.l./Amazon Italia Services S.r.l./Amazon Italia Logistica S.r.l.* See also Geoffrey Manne and Lazar Radic, *The Italian Competition Authority issues a record €1.128B fine against a Big Tech company for merging its platform marketplace and its distribution operations thereby shutting out rival distributors (Amazon)*, E-COMPETITIONS November 2021, art. No. 106075.

29. The users of Meta platforms, such as Facebook and Instagram, often use works protected by SIAE in content they post on these platforms. For this reason, Meta (then Facebook) and SIAE concluded an agreement in 2018, which was renewed in 2020. When the agreement expired in September 2022, renewal negotiations between the two entities revealed disagreements, particularly over remuneration. Despite multiple rounds of negotiations and interim arrangements, the parties were unable to reach a new agreement. Consequently, the ICA initiated proceedings for abuse of economic dependence under Article 9 of Law No 192/1998, resulting in the adoption of an interim measure. In its decision opening the proceedings, adopted on 4 April 2023, the ICA emphasised that Meta may have exploited its stronger bargaining position in relation to SIAE by engaging in practices that breached principles of good faith, fairness and transparency during the negotiations. For these reasons, the ICA quickly – on 20 April 2023 – adopted interim measures addressed to Meta, imposing the following obligations:
   - Restart negotiations, maintaining behaviour inspired by good faith and correctness;
   - Provide SIAE with the information necessary to enable SIAE to restore a balance in the whole commercial relationship with Meta;
   - Upon authorisation on the part of SIAE, promptly restore the availability of the musical content protected by SIAE on Meta's platform during the period necessary to conclude the negotiations;
   - In the event of disagreement between the parties about the amount and quality of the information referred to in point two above, appoint a trustee to be identified through a specific procedure.
30. The Meta group appealed the interim decision of the ICA before the Regional Administrative Court of Lazio (TAR Lazio), which confirmed the ICA's order obligating Meta to resume negotiations with SIAE. According to the TAR Lazio, the existence of a situation of economic dependence is clear, since Meta plays a crucial role in allowing its users to access the music works protected by SIAE. Essentially, without an agreement with Meta, SIAE cannot reach the members of the social networks managed by Meta.
31. The Meta group appealed the TAR Lazio's decision before the Italian Council of State. On 2 July 2024, the Council of State, overturning the TAR Lazio's judgment, annulled the decision issued by the ICA[21], as it found, in essence, that the conditions for granting an interim decision were not met in the case at hand. The Council of State's judgment, however, was limited to the review of the ICA's interim decision: the main proceedings on the merits is still pending before the ICA.[22]
32. Lastly, it is worth mentioning a case that represents an important step forward in the protection of user rights in Europe. As a preliminary matter, it bears recalling the contents of the right to data portability, as stated in Article 20 of Regulation 2016/679 (GDPR). This provision ensures users' freedom of choice and their

---

21 Council of State, judgment No. 5827 of 2 July 2024.

22 ICA Proceeding No. A559, Meta/Siae.

greater control over their own data, facilitating the transfer of data from one online service to another, thereby promoting competition between different companies.

33. Specifically, the right to data portability includes the freedom to obtain the data stored by a controller, as well as the possibility to transfer them to a second and different data controller, unhindered by the previous one. The same provision also covers the right to directly transmit personal data from one controller to another, at the request of the data user, provided this is technically feasible.

34. Data portability facilitates the circulation of data, enabling alternative operators to compete with entities like Google, which manage ecosystems relying on vast amounts of data, tailored exclusively to their own business model. In addition, the right to data portability, if accompanied by effective interoperability mechanisms, can offer users the possibility of obtaining the maximum economic potential from the use of personal data, including through alternative methods of exploitation to those currently practiced by the dominant operator.

35. Against this backdrop, on 14 July 2022, the ICA announced it was opening an investigation into Google for an alleged abuse of dominant position resulting from limitations imposed on the portability of data to other operators.[23] According to the Authority, Google held a dominant position in several markets, which allowed it to acquire large amounts of data by exploiting its many services such as Gmail and Maps: this resulted in an alleged abuse of dominant position to hinder interoperability in the sharing of data on its platform with other platforms.

36. In essence, Google's conduct was capable of limiting the right to data portability, consequently decreasing the advantages that users could derive from it and from free competition. This significantly reduced the ability of alternative operators to develop innovative forms of data use.

37. On these grounds, an undertaking named Hoda reported conduct by Google that would allegedly harm its business and constitute violations of Article 102 TFEU and Article 3 of Law No 287 of 10 October 1990. Hoda had developed a data investment bank app and the complementary technologies necessary to exploit the managed data on the market.

38. In particular, the reporting company developed an app database, called Weople, which allows subscribers to enter their data into a sort of account and to profit whenever companies request their data in statistical, aggregated and anonymous form. Companies often use this data for their own customer targeting activities or for other purposes, such as the creation of statistical databases. The individual users interested in exploiting their data through Weople can register themselves through the app. They then start a procedure of delegation in favour of Hoda allowing Hoda to collect the users' data wherever available on the main Internet platforms by placing them in digital storage areas called safety deposit boxes.

39. Hoda had been in contact with Google over a period of years in order to identify interoperability mechanisms, to enable Weople users to seamlessly transfer their

---

23 See ICA Decision No 30215 of 5 July 2022, *Hoda S.r.l./Google LCC/Alphabet Inc./Google Ireland Limited/ Google Italy S.r.l.*

data to their Weople account either through the app or via proxy.[24] The only way Google allows users to request and obtain a copy of their data is through its own data retrieval platform, Google Takeout, which can only be reached directly and individually by each Google user. Using Google Takeout, however, allegedly involves an elaborate and complicated procedure that discourages users from exercising data portability.

40. After the ICA opened its investigation, Google proposed a set of three commitments, two of which envisage supplementary solutions to the Google Takeout service, aimed at facilitating the export of data to third-party operators. The third commitment involves the opportunity to test a new solution, currently in development, that will enable direct data portability between services for third-party operators authorised by an end user who requests it. This pertains to the data provided by users themselves or generated through their activity on Google's online search engine and the YouTube platform.

41. The ICA considered Google's proposed commitments[25] to be adequate to eliminate competition concerns.[26] It determined that the commitments ensure significant streamlining of the procedure available for exporting data. They also improve an interoperability mechanism that makes the data available in the Google ecosystem accessible to third-party platforms. Users and third-party operators will, therefore, be able to take advantage of this mechanism until the release of a direct service-to-service portability solution, which, according to Google, will take place in the first quarter of 2024.

42. Overall, the cases before the ICA show that the Authority has paid specific attention to the main players in digital markets and the protection of consumers and competition on these markets, to the benefit of the economy at large. In this way the decisions by the ICA are in line with the general trend that can be seen at EU level and in many other Member States, reaffirming the well-known prominence of the ICA in the landscape of the European Competition Network.

3. Overlapping Issues between EU and National Regulations for the Digital Sector

43. Another important factor relating to Italian legislation in the digital sector concerns the possibility of overlap between the EU and national frameworks. Setting aside the general relations between the DMA and competition law to focus only on the Italian legal system, the question arises as to the relationship between the DMA and the national provisions on abuse of economic dependence examined above.[27] Indeed, particularly after the Italian legislative reform introducing specific rules on digital platforms, one may well question whether such rules have the potential

---

[24] Regulation 2016/679 of the European Parliament and of the Council of 27 April 2016 on the protection of natural persons with regard to the processing of personal data and on the free movement of such data, and repealing Directive 95/46 (General Data Protection Regulation – GDPR), art 20(2).

[25] See Law No. 287/1990 art 14-ter.

[26] See ICA Decision No 30736 of 18 July 2023, *Hoda S.r.l./Google LCC/Alphabet Inc./Google Ireland Limited/ Google Italy S.r.l.*

[27] See above Section I.1.

to overlap, or in any event interfere, with the application of the DMA. It bears noting that similar concerns have been expressed with regard to other EU Member States (such as Germany), which recently adopted similar rules on the abuse of economic dependence regarding digital platforms.

44. In general terms, Article 1(5) of the DMA prevents Member States from imposing 'further obligations on gatekeepers by way of laws, regulations or administrative measures for the purpose of ensuring contestable and fair markets', while national rules 'imposing obligations on undertakings, including undertakings providing core platform services, for matters falling outside the scope' of the DMA are allowed, provided that they are compatible with EU law and do not stem from the fact that the undertakings at issue are identified as gatekeepers under the DMA. Moreover, Article 1(6)(b) of the DMA provides that the enforcement of the DMA is without prejudice to the application of 'national competition rules prohibiting other forms of unilateral conduct insofar as they are applied to undertakings other than gatekeepers or amount to the imposition of further obligations on gatekeepers'.

45. A closer look at the overall structure of the DMA and the features of the Italian reform adopted through Law No 118/2022 (Annual Market and Competition Law 2021) reveals that some differences between the two sets of rules may serve to limit the areas of potential overlap, at least in part.[28]

46. First, from a subjective standpoint, the scope of application of the DMA is more limited than that of the Italian rules on the abuse of economic dependence on the part of digital platforms. Indeed, on the one hand, the DMA applies only to the large digital platforms designated by the European Commission as 'gatekeepers' pursuant to Article 3 of the same DMA. On the other hand, the national rules are not subject to any limitations on the identification of the digital platforms to which such rules may apply, provided that the general criteria of Article 9 of Law No 192/98 are met (i.e. the capability for an undertaking to give rise to an 'excessive imbalance of rights and obligations' in trade relations with the other party, and the relative existence of a concrete possibility for the dependent company 'to find satisfactory alternatives on the market'). Fulfilment of the criteria can be presumed – as seen above – where 'an undertaking uses the intermediation services provided by a digital platform that plays a decisive role in reaching end users or suppliers, including in terms of network effects or data availability'.[29] This difference in the subjective spheres of application clearly reduces the possibility of overlapping issues, which may arise only with regard to conduct of digital platforms designated as 'gatekeepers' by the European Commission.

47. Second, the approaches underlying the two sets of rules are different. The DMA is a regulatory tool that applies *ex ante* and lays down a detailed list of obligations and prohibitions for gatekeepers. This is one of the most innovative aspects of the DMA, which is well-known for having changed the approach to the conduct of large digital platforms completely, with the aim of effectively achieving the objective of ensuring contestable and fair markets in the digital

---

28 See, in particular, Bachelet (n 10) 76 ff.; Libertini (n 9) 13 ff.

29 Law No 192/98 art 9, as amended in 2022: see Section I.1 above.

sector. The Italian rules on the abuse of economic dependence, however, are applied on the basis of a more traditional *ex post* approach, like the one typical of competition law.

48. At the same time, it is not possible to deny that some overlap may be possible, considering that much of the conduct envisaged by the DMA was drawn from, or would be relevant also for, the enforcement of competition law (EU and national). Considering the Italian rules on the abuse of economic dependence, overlapping issues may arise, in particular, in the event that such abuse (relevant pursuant to the Italian provisions) was carried out by a gatekeeper designated by the Commission under Article 3 of the DMA and falling within the scope of application of Articles 5, 6 and 7 of the DMA (the provisions setting out the main obligations and prohibitions imposed on gatekeepers). In such a case, the relevant provisions of the DMA would apply, notably Article 1(7) DMA[30] and, for present purposes, Recital 10 of the DMA, which specifies that the DMA 'should apply without prejudice to Articles 101 and 102 TFEU, to the corresponding national competition rules and to other national competition rules regarding unilateral conduct that are based on an individualised assessment of market positions and behaviour'. The latter reference seems applicable to the Italian rules on the abuse of economic dependence, which, therefore, can be enforced, in principle, notwithstanding the entry into force (and full applicability) of the DMA. However, Recital 10 of the DMA also explains that the application of the rules mentioned above 'should not affect the obligations imposed on gatekeepers under (the DMA) and their uniform and effective application in the internal market'.

49. In light of the possibility of overlapping issues between the DMA and national regulations, the DMA introduced further provisions on the matter, which are fully applicable to the Italian rules concerning not only antitrust law in general, but also the abuse of economic dependence.[31] In addition to the aforementioned Article 1(7) of the DMA, reference is made, in particular, to Recital 86 of the DMA, recalling the importance of the principles of proportionality and *ne bis in idem*,[32] and to the detailed provisions on cooperation and coordination between the European Commission and National Competition Authorities, laid down in DMA Articles 37 (Cooperation with national authorities) and 38 (Cooperation and coordination with national competent authorities enforcing competition rules). The provision of the DMA on cooperation with national courts (Article 39) may also come into play, given that both the national rules on the abuse of economic dependence and the provisions of the DMA itself can be applied by national courts, in the form of actions brought by private parties, in the framework of so-called private enforcement.

---

30 According to which: 'National authorities shall not take decisions which run counter to a decision adopted by the Commission under this Regulation. The Commission and Member States shall work in close cooperation and coordinate their enforcement actions on the basis of the principles established in Articles 37 and 38'.

31 See Libertini (n 9) 13 ff.; Bachelet (n 10) 80 f.

32 On this issue, see, among others, A Andreangeli, 'The Digital Markets Act, EU Competition Enforcement and Fundamental Rights: Some Reflection on the Future of *ne bis in idem* in Digital Markets' in *CPI Antitrust Chronicle* (2022) 43; M Cappai and G Colangelo, 'Applying *ne bis in idem* in the Aftermath of *bpost* and *Nordzucker*: The Case of EU Competition Policy in Digital Markets' (2023) 60 CMLR 431.

50. In short, concerns about potential overlapping issues are partially justified, even though it remains to be seen to what extent such issues will concretely arise in practice. A more specific assessment will be possible on the basis of enforcement of the obligations and prohibitions set out by the DMA, which have just become fully applicable. One hopes that the DMA provisions will avoid (or, at least, substantially reduce) clashes between the enforcement of the DMA and the application of national rules on the abuse of economic dependence of digital platforms. This could happen in the light of the provisions facilitating cooperation and coordination between the European Commission and National Competition Authorities, as well as with national courts, and the ability of national courts to make references for preliminary rulings to the Court of Justice pursuant to Article 267 TFEU on the interpretation and/or validity of the provisions of the DMA.

II. Steps Taken within the Italian legal System to Facilitate the Integration of and Enhance the Synergy between EU and National Legislation for the Digital Sector

51. The Digital Markets Act establishes a centralised application and enforcement framework led by the European Commission. At the same time, however, it acknowledges the importance of national competition authorities in collaborating in the enforcement of its provisions through close cooperation and information sharing with the Commission. In particular, Article 38 of the DMA allows the Commission to request support from national competition authorities in conducting market investigations under the regulation. In addition, the national competition authorities, on their own initiative, can independently and autonomously investigate gatekeepers within their respective jurisdictions for potential violations of the DMA, and must report their findings to the Commission, which retains the power to adopt final decisions and impose remedies.

52. In order to better align the national regulatory framework to the provisions just described, the Italian legislator has begun to enhance synergies between EU and national legislation for the digital sector, by adopting internal rules specifically aimed at implementing – so to speak – some provisions of the DMA into the Italian legal order.

53. In this the key provision is Article 18 of Law No 214/2023 (Annual Law on Competition and Market 2022), which entrusts the ICA with all functions relating to public enforcement of the DMA at the national level. The legislator deemed this a necessary step due to the absence of an explicit Italian legislative authorisation enabling the ICA to act outside the scope of its specific competences as set out by the law. This would have hindered the ICA from carrying out the functions of national competition authorities as mandated by the DMA. It is worth noting that Article 18, which is entitled 'Measures for the implementation of Regulation (EU) 2022/1925 of the European Parliament and the Council of 14 September 2022', is divided into eight paragraphs.

54. Paragraph 1 of Article 18 establishes the ICA as the entity responsible for enforcing the DMA in Italy,

55. Paragraph 2 of Article 18 confirms that the ICA serves as the primary contact point for the Commission and the network of authorities in fulfilling the obligations set out in the DMA, including various forms of coordination and cooperation (e.g. for purposes of performing inspections).

56. Paragraphs 3 and 4 of Article 18 clarify that the ICA, in performing its functions under the DMA, enjoys the same investigation powers and can impose the same sanctions provided for by Law No 287/90, i.e. the national antitrust law. This clarification is important to avoid inconsistencies in the procedures governing the application of DMA provisions by the ICA.

57. Specifically, paragraph 5 of Article 18 of Law No 214/2023 explicitly entrusts the ICA with the power to conduct investigations within the national legal system to identify potential DMA violations. This requires the Authority to have investigative and sanctioning powers. The cooperation of the '*Guardia di Finanza*' (Italian Financial Police) is ensured to assist the ICA in carrying out its functions related to the DMA, including inspections. There are, however, limitations on the use of information collected during DMA investigations, aligning with the EU regulatory framework.

58. Paragraph 6 of Article 18 enables the ICA to use the information it collects through investigations carried out in application of the DMA for more general purposes as well, as long as this is compatible with the relevant EU legislation. In particular, the ICA is allowed to use this kind of information in the enforcement of the provisions concerning agreements restricting competition, abuse of dominant position, abuse of economic dependence and merger control.

59. According to paragraph 7 of Article 18, the ICA must perform its tasks with the resources available to it under existing legislation, which means that, in principle, no additional resources will be granted as a result of the new provisions concerning the implementation of the DMA.

60. Finally, Article 18 also underlines the role of the '*Garante per la protezione dei dati personali*' (Italian Data Protection Authority), to which general supervisory and control powers are conferred, particularly concerning personal data protection and confidentiality. This safeguard clause aims to prevent conflicts, overlapping of competences, and excessive administrative burdens on private entities under the supervision of the relevant authorities.

61. In general terms, the provision adopted by the Italian legislator to implement the DMA in the Italian legal order is clear and exhaustive from the perspective of public enforcement.

62. However, it must be noted that the legislator has remained completely silent on private enforcement of the DMA, i.e. its application, on the initiative of private parties, before national courts. No provision was adopted, for instance, on the important issue of competence, which gives rise to uncertainties about which courts will be competent when private parties bring actions against the gatekeepers designated under the DMA to seek injunctions, interim measures, and/or compensation for damages. In particular, the legislator did not include a provision like the one in Legislative Decree No 3/2017 (transposing Directive 2014/104, the Damages Directive), which concentrates the competence for the private enforcement of

competition law (Articles 101 and 102 TFEU, as well as Articles 2 and 3 of Law No 287/90, the national antitrust law) in only three courts, namely the Chambers specialised in business matters of the courts (and Courts of Appeal) of Milan, Rome and Naples. The silence of the Italian legislator in this respect has drawn criticism, particularly because it will create inconsistencies between the private enforcement of the DMA, on one side, and competition law on the other, despite the similarities between the two sets of rules.

III. Conclusion: the DMA as a Piece of a Wider Cosmos of EU and National Legislative Initiatives for Digital Transformation?

63. Recent years have witnessed a proliferation of European legislative initiatives relating to the digital transformation. Many sectors are undergoing a significant metamorphosis, driven by the integration of technology into their core operations. This evolution is reshaping traditional practices and normative frameworks. This general trend makes it imperative to reconsider the legislation governing various sectors, in light of the vital need for clear and up-to-date rules on the growing body of digital issues affecting citizens and undertakings.

64. In this regard, it is necessary to point out that the European Union, in the framework of its Digital Decade Policy Programme 2030,[33] set up an annual cooperation cycle among the Commission and the Member States in order to establish concrete targets and objectives to be reached in this field by 2030. This includes a transparent and structured monitoring system and an annual report in which the Commission assesses progress and makes recommendations for action. This system might help clarify the relationships identified by the DMA with the National Competition Authorities and overcome the concerns raised by the ICA after the adoption of the DMA proposal. At that time, the ICA stated that the DMA, by giving a central role to the European Commission, risked causing delays or even lack of intervention with reference to conduct that, albeit restricting competition, affects only some Member States and/or does not fall within the European Commission's priorities.

65. This concern was addressed by the Secretary-General of the Italian Antitrust Authority at the time, in his remarks during a hearing before a commission of the Italian Parliament in June of 2021.[34] On that occasion, the Secretary-General noted that National Competition Authorities are, in some cases, the best placed entities to deal with the competition issues raised by digital platforms. For that reason, he stressed the need to guarantee an effective application of the principle of subsidiarity and, hence, to adequately involve National Competition Authorities

---

33 See generally, the European Commission Website <https://futurium.ec.europa.eu/en/digital-compass/events/digital-decade-policy-programme-2030-way-forward> accessed 10 July 2024.

34 Hearing of the Secretary-General of the ICA, Avv. Filippo Arena, before the IX Commission of the Chamber of Deputies of the Italian Parliament (16 June 2021) < https://www.camera.it/application/xmanager/projects/leg18/attachments/upload_file_doc_acquisiti/pdfs/000/005/678/Audizione_parlamentare_AGCM_DMA_e_DSA_16.06.2021_FINALE.pdf>.

(NCAs) in the enforcement of the DMA, suggesting the adoption of a cooperation model similar to the one designed by Regulation 1/2003.[35]

66. More recently, the President of the Italian Antitrust Authority, in his presentation of the annual report on the activities carried out by the Authority in 2022, highlighted that the ICA has already successfully handled cases relating to digital markets which resulted in positive synergistic effects.[36] This – in the words of the President – demonstrates the Authority's ability to act promptly and proactively. Additionally, the decision to start an investigation often shows the unique characteristics of the national context and the specific behaviours of an undertaking towards a particular locale. These factors suggest that the NCA is well-prepared to actively participate in implementing the DMA, including by collaborating with the Commission as outlined in Articles 37 and 38 of the DMA's regulatory framework.[37]

67. Relatedly, one may conclude, in principle, that the DMA will not affect the Italian Antitrust Authority's ability to bring its own competition law-based cases against large digital platforms. However, in practice, the centralisation of powers in the hands of the Commission and the *ex-ante* application of the new set of rules may reduce the relevance, or at least the promptness, of the Italian Antitrust Authority's actions against such platforms.

68. Over the past few years, the Italian Government and the Italian Parliament have elaborated several draft laws aiming to foster a secure and sustainable digital transformation that puts people at the centre, protecting their rights and ensuring that all digital players act responsibly in a fair online environment.

69. Among these initiatives, one noteworthy example is Draft Law No 908/2023, entitled 'Provisions on the annual digital law', which was presented on 12 October 2023. This draft law envisages the introduction of a national annual law for the digital sector, aimed at 'taking a snapshot of the progress in policy adoption, identifying and removing technological and regulatory barriers to access and deployment of digital innovation to strengthen protections and guarantees for users of digital services and workers and to update, where necessary, the regulatory framework as to guarantee the access of businesses, users, consumers and workers to a digital ecosystem that protects their rights and spreads its benefits equitably'.[38]

70. Although Draft Law No 908/2023 is structured as a single article, it identifies all the essential elements of the envisaged annual digital law. In particular, it foresees the institution of a Committee for Digital Development and Regulation, consisting of one representative each from the ICA, the Communications Regulatory Authority, the Energy, Networks and Environment Regulatory Authority, the Transport Regulatory Authority, the Personal Data Protection Authority, the National Cyber Security Agency and the Agency for Digital Italy.

---

[35] Regulation 1/2003 of 16 December 2002 on the implementation of the rules on competition laid down in Articles 81 and 82 of the Treaty [2003] OJ L1/1.

[36] See, for example, Case A552 *Google-ostacoli alla portabilità dei dati*.

[37] President of the ICA, 'Presentation of the ICA's Annual Report 2022' (2023) <https://www.agcm.it/dotcmsdoc/relazioni-annuali/relazioneannuale2022/AGCM_Relazione_annuale_2023.pdf> accessed 10 July 2024.

[38] Draft Law No 908/2023, 'Provisions on the annual digital law' (*Senate of the Republic XIX Legislature*, 2023) <https://www.senato.it/service/PDF/PDFServer/DF/428582.pdf> accessed 10 July 2024.

71. By 30 September of each year, the Committee is to submit to the government an annual report on the state of digital development in the country, highlighting all the relevant technological obstacles still in place. Thereafter, the government is required to submit an annual digital law to the parliament, divided into several sections and followed by an illustrative report highlighting, among other things, the state of conformity of the internal system with the European principles on digital policy and the European policies on competition, as well as the state of implementation of the measures provided for in previous national laws and the effects they are expected to have on citizens. The law must also contain rules of immediate application in order to remove obstacles to digital innovation, based in part on the opinions of the various independent authorities and government bodies indicated in their annual reports, as well as one or more delegations to the government for the issuance of legislative decrees.

72. Another proposal worth mentioning is a draft law entitled 'Measures on the transparency of content generated by artificial intelligence',[39] which was communicated to the Italian Parliament on 19 October 2023. The aim of this proposal is to promote transparency in the field of artificial intelligence (AI) by encouraging accountability on the part of content creators or those responsible for its spread. The proposal provides that stakeholders must ensure that AI content is immediately recognisable to users by indicating, at the beginning and end of the content, that it is AI generated, by means of labelling and watermarking systems.

73. The draft law on the transparency of content generated by AI also instructs the Italian Communications Regulatory Authority (*Autorità per le garanzie nelle telecomunicazioni* – AGCOM) to first define the modalities for implementing its provisions and then to monitor their correct application. Lastly, it also identifies the means of reporting and removing content published in violation of the provisions, as well as the sanctions regime to be applied.

74. Another related step is the new 'Cybersecurity draft law', approved in January 2024 by the Council of Ministers.[40] This draft law is aimed at suppressing and inhibiting the conduct of cybercriminals by encouraging post-attack cooperation.[41] The growing adoption of generative AI technologies has made it crucial to envision a security system that incorporates dynamic and adaptable measures, tailored to safeguard the technologies they are designed to protect.

75. While the combined use of cybersecurity and AI solutions on the global market has clearly entailed big advantages, such as data protection enforcement and data loss prevention, it has also facilitated a significant increase in cyberattacks, with a worrying focus on public infrastructure. Cybercriminals may exploit AI to improve

---

39 Draft Law No 917/2023, 'Measures on the transparency of content generated by artificial intelligence' (*Senate of the Republic XIX Legislature*, 2023) <https://www.senato.it/service/PDF/PDFServer/BGT/01393060.pdf> accessed 10 July 2024.

40 Draft Law No 1717/2024, 'Provisions regarding the strengthening of cybersecurity national and computer crimes' (*Chamber of Deputies XIX Legislature*, 2024) <https://documenti.camera.it/leg19/pdl/pdf/leg.19.pdl.camera.1717.19PDL0077340.pdf> accessed 10 July 2024.

41 L Di Giacomo, 'Approvato il ddl cybersecurity: prima risposta alle sfide future' (*Diritto.it*, 2024) <https://www.diritto.it/?s=Approvato+il+ddl+cybersecurity%3A+prima+risposta+alle+sfide+future> accessed 10 July 2024.

the algorithms they use to crack passwords faster and more accurately, enabling hackers to become more efficient and profitable. And the use of crypto-virological malware like 'ransomware' to block access to an organisation's personal data indefinitely unless a ransom is paid is ongoing. These kinds of attacks usually gain access to an organisation's system and identify points of weakness.

76. The draft law represents an opportunity for Italy to reinforce its set of tools to fight against these practices, as harsher punishments would contribute to better protection of health data and improved security for citizens and public infrastructure. Given the high potential public-sector impact, it is no coincidence that the regulatory framework emphasises the importance of cybersecurity not only for companies but also for public institutions.

77. The Cybersecurity draft law doubles the penalties for unauthorised access to computer systems from one to five years to two to ten years in prison, and provides for up two years in prison plus fines for those who possess or distribute malicious software. It also reinforces the responsibilities falling to the Public Administration, which it obliges to report cyberattacks to the National Cybersecurity Agency within 24 hours of an incident. It charges that agency with preventing attacks and coordinating with the judiciary. It also requires public entities to appoint a cybersecurity contact person responsible for the management and governance of cybersecurity issues, in line with the European NIS2 Directive. Finally, the Cybersecurity draft law identifies specific offences, such as cyber extortion (e.g. ransomware), which involve an attack or threat of attack coupled with a demand for money or some other response in return for stopping or remediating the attack.

78. Although the Cybersecurity draft law would be a marked improvement in the response to cyberattacks conduct and disciplinary provisions, it is important to note that this draft law does not focus on prevention, which remains a crucial and yet partially unexplored approach.

79. In analysing the potential increase in innovation spurred by regulation that put digital transformation at its core, the parliamentary 'Digital Health and Digital Therapeutics' Intergroup, set up in May 2023 within the Italian Parliament, introduced an initial draft law on digital therapeutics in June 2023[42] (also known as 'DTx'). As a background matter, it bears noting that the life sciences industries continue to grow in global importance. With the digitalisation of healthcare, the world has witnessed the explosion of digital health with the emergence of social media platforms, mobile applications, cloud-based data and so on. General well-being and health monitoring are gradually extending to the widespread digital world through various smartphone applications.

80. In this regard, the above-mentioned DTx draft law initially defines the expression 'digital therapeutics' by establishing that they are '[...] software-mediated therapeutic interventions with specific treatment instructions designed to prevent, manage or treat a medical condition by modifying the patient's behaviour in order to improve clinical outcomes'. In Italy, no digital therapy is yet available through

---

[42] Draft Law No 1208/2023, 'Provisions on digital therapies' (*Chamber of Deputies XIX Legislature*, 2023) <https://documenti.camera.it/leg19/pdl/pdf/leg.19.pdl.camera.1208.19PDL0040170.pdf> accessed 10 July 2024.

the healthcare system, unlike in other countries, where there are already initiatives and pathways in this regard.[43]

81. The DTx draft law defines, among other things, the fields of action for which DTx can be used (cardio-metabolic diseases, endocrinology and diabetology, neuroscience and mental health, respiratory diseases, rehabilitation areas and oncology). The same draft law also envisages the institution of an evaluation committee and provides for the establishment of a permanent observatory on DTx by the National Agency for Regional Health Services, in order to monitor and update any scientific and technological developments of digital treatment.

82. All of these proposals reveal a national tendency towards the adaptation of the regulatory framework to the digital age. Despite these recent signs of change, doubts and concerns still remain with regard to how such interventions should be designed and how the inevitable risks the digital revolution brings with it might be minimised. Therefore, while the various initiatives reveal an encouraging degree of attention to several digital issues on the part of the legislator, clear legislative action remains necessary to find the right balance between market regulation and innovation, in order to foster – and, at least to some extent, govern – the digital transformation.

---

43 See, e.g. the German Digital Healthcare Act (DVG), which entered into force on 9 December 2019.

DMA in Lithuania: All Quiet, So Far

Lithuania

Šarūnas Keserauskas*
Ellex

Abstract

This article examines Lithuania's approach to the Digital Markets Act (DMA) and related digital sector regulations. Lithuania has not introduced a national equivalent to the DMA but has adopted two pieces of enabling legislation: DMA-related amendments to the Law on Competition and the Law on Supervision of Online Intermediation Services and Search Engines. The DMA's adoption received minimal public attention in Lithuania, with little political engagement. The national competition authority, Konkurencijos taryba (KT), has been the most involved actor, consistently signaling the need for more resources to address digital market challenges. While there are no DMA-specific cases yet, three notable digital market cases are highlighted: the Eturas case involving an online travel booking platform, the Diginet case investigating alleged abuse of dominance in online real estate advertising, and the Snowball.xyz/Šviesa merger in the digital education sector. Lithuania has not introduced national digital sector regulations that could overlap with the DMA, and coordination between EU and national legislation relies on existing mechanisms, primarily through KT's role in supporting the European Commission's DMA enforcement efforts. A EU-funded and OECD-led joint market study with Latvian and Polish authorities on online marketplaces and ecosystems is underway, which may inform future regulatory approaches in the digital sector.

---

* Partner at Ellex Valiunas; Partnership Professor at Vilnius University.

I. Introduction: General Views from an EU Member State

1. National Legislative Initiatives Adopted (or Incoming) for the Digital Sector

1. Lithuania has no national equivalent of the Digital Markets Act (DMA)[1] and there are no initiatives or debates to introduce similar legislation. Still, the EU ambitions to regulate the digital sector have resulted in the adoption of two pieces of enabling national legislation: the DMA-related amendments to the Law on Competition (LOC and 2023 LOC Amendments),[2] and the Law on Supervision of Online Intermediation Services and Search Engines (P2B Law).[3]

2. Starting with the DMA, its birth was not a remarkable event in Lithuania. It was observed and debated by a small group of professionals but failed to trigger significant public interest.

3. Most notably, the DMA's adoption and its later entry into force went largely unnoticed by political bodies. Future PhD researchers would waste their time trying to find any public statements explaining the origins of the DMA, the negotiations that led to its adoption, the aims that it wants to achieve and what Lithuanian political decision-makers thought about this. There was only a passing reference to the DMA in a press release issued by the Ministry of the Economy and Innovation in early March 2022, following the Minister's meeting with Google representatives.[4] In that meeting, the Minister suggested moving Google's Moscow office to Vilnius, stressing the importance of fighting against Russian disinformation in the context of the Russian invasion into Ukraine, and explaining the important contribution that both Lithuania and Google had to make in achieving fairness as the DMA goal.

4. The politicians had exposure to the DMA in 2023 when the bill introducing, among other things, some DMA-related amendments to the Law on Competition went to the Lithuanian Parliament (Seimas). The DMA aspects of the bill raised neither interest nor debates, and the amendments were adopted without anyone objecting.

5. To be fair to politicians, the 2023 LOC Amendments themselves gave no reason for anyone to get excited, as the DMA-related provisions were kept to a bare technical minimum and can be summarised by dividing them in four groups:

   - *The national competent authority enforcing the rules referred to in Article 1(6) DMA*. The 2023 LOC Amendments confirm the national competition authority (*Konkurencijos taryba* or KT) as the national competent authority of the Member State enforcing the rules referred to in Article 1(6) DMA.[5]

---

1 Regulation 2022/1925 of the European Parliament and of the Council of 14 September 2022 on contestable and fair markets in the digital sector and amending Directives 2019/1937 and 2020/1828 (Digital Markets Act or DMA) [2022] OJ L265/1.

2 1999 Law No. VIII-1099 on Competition, as modified by 2023 LOC Amendments (2023 Law No. XIV-2035).

3 2024 Law No. XIV-2855 on Supervision of Online Intermediation Services and Search Engines.

4 Lithuanian Government, Press Release, "Minister Armonaitė proposes Google to move their representation office from Moscow to Vilnius" (4 March 20222) <https://sena-eimin.lrv.lt/en/news/minister-armonaite-proposes-google-to-move-their-representation-office-from-moscow-to-vilnius> accessed 25 November 2024.

5 LOC art 54(2).

As such, KT operates under the national competition rules to the extent that its functions are not defined by DMA.[6]

- *Police assistance in carrying out inspections.* Article 56 LOC allows the Commission officials and the authorised officials of *Konkurencijos taryba* assisting them, to employ, when carrying inspections under DMA, the police to keep public order and for potential application of coercive measures.[7] The authorisation to use coercive measures (as they are foreseen in Article 23(8) DMA) is issued by the administrative court of the first instance[8] on the application of the Commission or KT.[9]
- *Informing competition authorities about court judgments.* Article 57 LOC demands that, after their announcement, court judgments in cases where DMA provisions have been applied must be forwarded without delay to the Commission and *Konkurencijos taryba.*[10]
- *Renewal of court proceedings to avoid conflicting decisions.* Article 57 LOC allows the court to renew proceedings if it emerges that after the adoption of the court judgment, in which the DMA provisions have been applied to a conduct, the Commission issues its own decision applying the DMA provisions to the same conduct and the result of such application fundamentally differs.[11]

6. Given the limited scope of the DMA-related provisions in the 2023 LOC Amendments, it is hardly surprising that in the explanatory note accompanying the bill, the Lithuanian Government succinctly noted that amendments would have a positive effect on business, and, for reasons of unpredictability, no extra funding for courts and authorities involved in the DMA enforcement would be allocated.[12]

7. Despite not being promised an increase in funding for the DMA-related activities, *Konkurencijos taryba* has been the most engaged actor with an understandable interest in the DMA enforcement. References to the DMA appear in each of the authority's annual reports starting from 2020, whereas e-commerce and/or digital markets have been among the authority's sectorial priorities since 2022. The authority's consistent signalling that more human and financial resources are necessary to face the challenges of the digital markets has been rewarded when, in 2024, a portion of KT's annual budget increase was specifically dedicated to dealing with digital markets.[13]

8. There is a good chance the funding for KT's activities in relation to digital markets will continue to grow as in June 2024 the authority was entrusted with enforcement powers under the Law on Supervision of Online Intermediation Services and Search Engines (P2B Law).[14] The P2B Law and the KT's designation as its enforcer came

---

6 LOC art 54(3).

7 LOC art 56(1).

8 LOC art 56(2).

9 LOC art 56(4).

10 LOC art 57(2).

11 LOC art 57(3).

12 Lithuanian Government, Explanatory Note (in Lithuanian) https://e-seimas.lrs.lt/portal/legalAct/lt/TAK/e73f76e0e25f11eda305cb3bdf2af4d8?jfwid=-laib937el .

13 KT's overall budget increased from €2.91 million in 2023 to €3.09 million in 2024.

14 2024 Law No. XIV-2855 on Supervision of Online Intermediation Services and Search Engines.

in response to the Commission's concerns, expressed by way of sending a reasoned opinion to Lithuania,[15] about the lack of enforcement of Regulation 2019/1150 on promoting fairness and transparency for business users of online intermediation services (P2B Regulation).[16] Under the P2B Law, which enters into force on 1 January 2025, KT has powers to carry investigations of suspected violations of the P2B Regulation, establish infringements and impose financial sanctions. The sanctions – set from €300–€15,000 – are small compared to what the authority has available in case of antitrust violations, while the level and effect of enforcement is yet to be seen. Crucially, however, the authority's role as enforcer of the P2B Law and the P2B Regulation gives it an opportunity to gain additional resources[17] and accumulate experience in the digital sector, both of which are currently lacking.

9. Beyond the boundaries of the public sector, the Lithuanian Free Market Institute was the only non-governmental body that was actively involved in the debate before and after the adoption of the DMA. As the private think-tank promoting, in its own words, "ideas of individual freedom and responsibility, free market, and limited government intervention", the Institute surprised no one when it stuck to its usual line, arguing that "the proposed regulation will inevitably hurt SMEs and the end-users".[18] More specifically, the Institute's experts predicted potential negative consequences to include, among other things, distorted competitive conditions of digital technology services, decreasing incentives for innovation, risk of market concentration, higher service prices or lower service quality, and less consumer choice".[19]

10. Overall, in relation to the DMA, the stakeholders involved behaved as expected: politicians wasted no time on the topic that was of no great interest to the voters, the enforcement authority cared about the resources, and the free-market think-tank criticised yet another overreaching State intervention.

2. Landmark National Cases (by NCAs and Courts) in the Digital Realm Backstage of the DMA

11. Neither KT, nor the national courts have experience in dealing with issues that are currently being targeted by the DMA. In a broader digital realm, the *Eturas* case stands as a landmark. Two other cases, *Diginet* and *Snowball.xyz/Šviesa* – also involve competition issues in digital markets.

---

[15] For more on the Commission's reasoned opinion to Lithuania, European Commission, Press Release, "November Infringement Package: Key Decisions" (16 November 2023) <https://ec.europa.eu/commission/presscorner/detail/en/inf_23_5380> accessed 25 November 2024.

[16] Regulation 2019/1150 on promoting fairness and transparency for business users of online intermediation services (P2B Regulation) [2019] OJ L186/57–79.

[17] According to the Explanatory Note, accompanying the P2B bill in Parliament, the KT's new enforcement will demand an annual increase of the authority's budget by €355,000. This constitutes around 11% of the KT's 2024 budget.

[18] See Dr Guoda Azguridienė, "Report on the Digital Market Act: Competition, Property, Innovation And User Interests" (January 2022) <www.llri.lt/wp-content/uploads/2022/02/Paper-On-Digital-Market-Act_LFMI-2021-12-14.pdf> accessed 25 November 2024.

[19] See Lithuanian Free Market Institute, "Policy Brief, DMA" (2023) <www.llri.lt/wp-content/uploads/2023/06/Policy-brief-DMA.pdf> accessed 25 November 2024.

A. *The Eturas Case*

12. The *Eturas* case, which started as the KT's investigation and found its international fame after the ECJ preliminary ruling,[20] addresses the intersection of competition law and digital markets, particularly focusing on the role of digital platforms in potentially facilitating anti-competitive behaviour. The case revolves around Eturas, an online travel booking platform used by multiple travel agencies in Lithuania. The central issue was whether Eturas had facilitated a concerted practice among travel agencies by implementing a system-wide restriction on discounts offered to consumers.

13. Eturas operated as a shared booking system for travel agencies, streamlining their online booking processes. In 2010, Eturas sent a message through the platform's internal messaging system, notifying the agencies of the introduction of the technical restriction on the platform capping the maximum allowable discount on services at 3%. Some of the agencies claimed not to have seen or taken notice of the message, while others argued that they did not intend to comply with the restriction. Nonetheless, *Konkurencijos taryba* launched an investigation and concluded that the agencies had engaged in concerted practices to limit competition through the imposed discount cap.[21]

14. The Lithuanian administrative court of first instance reduced some of the fines, but essentially upheld the authority's findings. On appeal, the Lithuanian Supreme Administrative Court (LSAC) referred the matter to the ECJ, which delivered a preliminary ruling in 2016.[22]

15. In its ruling, the ECJ clarified the concept of "concerted practices" in the context of digital platforms.

16. First, the ECJ considered whether the travel agencies could be presumed to have been aware of the content of the message sent by Eturas about the discount cap. According to the ECJ, in line with the presumption of innocence, the mere dispatch of the message through the platform was not sufficient to infer awareness of its content.[23] The Court added that the dispatch of the message could nonetheless be used in combination with other objective and consistent indicia to establish a rebuttable presumption of awareness, provided that the travel agencies could still rebut it[24] and that the rebuttal was not excessively difficult.[25] Ultimately, however, the ECJ left this question to be decided by the national court, seeing it as an evidential issue rather than one that follows from the concept of "concerted practice".[26]

---

20 Case C-74/14 *Eturas UAB v Lietuvos Respublikos Konkutencijos Taryba* ECLI:EU:C:2016:42, see Gintarė Surblyte-Namaviciene, *The EU Court of Justice gives a preliminary ruling for an alleged collusion among a number of travel agencies through an online travel booking system (Eturas)*, E-COMPETITIONS January 2016, art. No. 82628.

21 See KT Decision No 2S-9, 7 June 2012.

22 *Eturas* (n 20).

23 *Ibid* para 39.

24 *Ibid* para 40.

25 *Ibid* para 41.

26 *Ibid* para 34.

17. Then, turning to the concept of "concerted practice", the ECJ stressed that if it cannot be established that a travel agency was aware of that message, its participation in a concertation cannot be inferred from the mere existence of a technical restriction implemented in the system, "unless it is established on the basis of other objective and consistent indicia that it tacitly assented to an anticompetitive action".[27]

18. The ECJ also observed that rebutting the presumption of participation in a concerted practice in circumstances, such as those in the main proceedings, where concertation does not involve an anti-competitive meeting, has certain peculiarities. First, when it comes to public distancing, a travel agency cannot be required to make the declaration of its intention to distance itself "to all of the competitors which were the addressees of the message at issue in the main proceedings, since that agency is not in fact in a position to know who those addressees are".[28] Then, as regards the possibility of rebutting the presumption by means other than public distancing or reporting it to the administrative authorities, this can be done by "evidence of a systematic application of a discount exceeding the cap in question".[29]

19. Following the ECJ's guidance, LSAC rendered its final judgment in May 2016.[30] LSAC upheld the authority's findings concerning the Eturas platform itself and the 11 travel agencies (including one that applied for leniency), which knew of the discount cap and did not oppose it. LSAC annulled the infringement decision for the remaining 19 travel agencies. Some of these agencies knew of the restriction, but opposed it, while in relation to others the evidence of their knowledge was lacking.

20. The *Eturas* case remains relevant for digital markets. In line with *AC Treuhand*,[31] the *Eturas* judgment by the ECJ highlights the potential liability of platform operators, as intermediaries, for facilitating anti-competitive behaviour among users. The case also underscores how digital tools can be used to restrict competition without traditional forms of communication. By embedding anti-competitive restrictions into a platform's software, companies can limit competition with minimal direct interaction.

B. *Diginet*

21. On 28 December 2020, *Konkurencijos taryba* terminated its investigation into Diginet LTU, the owner of a classified real estate advertising website, without finding an infringement.[32] The investigation was launched in 2018 following a complaint that the company was abusing its dominant position by way of charging unfairly high prices to customers.

---

27 *Ibid* para 45.

28 *Ibid* para 47.

29 *Ibid* para 49.

30 See LSAC judgment in administrative Case No. A-97-858/2016, 2 May 2016.

31 Case C-194/14 *AC-Treuhand AG v European Commission* ECLI:EU:C:2015:717, see Michel Debroux, *Facilitator: The Court of Justice of the European Union confirms, against the opinion of Advocate General Nils Wahl, the sanction of a cartel facilitator, who is not active on the market of the cartel, on behalf of the "full effectiveness" of article 101 § 1 TFEU (AC-Treuhand)*, CONCURRENCES No. 1-2016, art. No. 77646.

32 See KT Decision No 1S-137, 28 December 2020.

22. KT found Diginet LTU had been consistently maintaining very high market shares in a market characterised by high entry barriers. The authority considered there to be sufficient evidence to establish dominance but felt there was no need to reach a definitive conclusion on that issue, as that would not have changed the ultimate assessment of the company's conduct.[33]

23. While investigating the allegations, KT used several methods to test the hypothesis of unfairly high prices. However, as KT admits in its decision, the use of such methods could not lead to the conclusion that the prices applied by the company to the business and private customers were consistently excessive and unfair.[34] With that statement, the authority closed the case.

24. The *Diginet* case and the authority's decision to terminate the investigation exemplifies the complexity of analysis and a high threshold for proving abuse of dominance in digital markets.

C. *Snowball.xyz/Šviesa Merger*

25. The *Snowball.xyz/Šviesa* merger, conditionally cleared by *Konkurencijos taryba* in 2022,[35] concerned digital services in the education sector. Snowball.xyz was the largest provider of electronic diary services to schools, and Šviesa was a leading publisher of educational materials, including printed textbooks and digital educational content.

26. As established by the authority, the merging parties already faced limited competitive pressure from other market participants, as schools that were required to purchase electronic diary services were more likely to choose the most popular products offered on the market by the merging parties instead of the products sold by competitors.

27. In articulating competition concerns, KT relied on a conglomerate theory of harm, arguing that the merger would give the merging parties ability and incentive to engage in sales and technical tying of their respective products, thus resulting in foreclosure of their existing competitors and raising prices to schools.[36] As to potential new entry, KT saw that as unlikely given the need for any such potential competitor to offer both digital diary and digital educational content services.[37]

28. KT conditionally cleared the merger by accepting time-limited behavioural remedies proposed by the parties. The remedies were time-limited to 15 years, with potential extension for another five years. The key conditions included:

- Non-discriminatory access: Snowball.xyz and Šviesa were required to give their existing and potential competitors non-discriminatory access to the digital diary and digital educational tools. This was important in ensuring that other publishers and digital tool providers could integrate their products with the services offered by the merging parties and compete effectively.

---

33 *Ibid* para 42.
34 *Ibid* paras 151-152.
35 KT Decision in *Snowball.xyz/Šviesa*. 9 September 2022
36 *Ibid* para 231.
37 *Ibid* para 208.

- No tying or bundling: the merging parties committed to not linking digital diary and digital educational content sales. This condition was crucial in preventing the merged company from using its combined market power to restrict access to educational materials for schools.
- Monitoring compliance: a monitoring mechanism was established, and a trustee appointed to ensure that the conditions were adhered to, and that the merger did not result in anti-competitive behaviour over time.

29. The *Snowball.xyz/Šviesa* decision is of double rarity: not only did KT based its theory of harm on conglomerate effects, but, rather exceptionally, it also accepted behavioural remedies as being capable of addressing the authority's competition concerns.

3. Overlapping Issues between EU, the DMA and New Competition Tools Adopted at National Level

30. There is no national digital sector regulation – and none is planned – that could create overlaps with DMA.

II. Actions Undertaken by the EU Member State to Facilitate the Integration and to Enhance Synergies between EU and National Legislations for the Digital Sector

1. Best Practices in the Application of Articles 1(5), 1(6), 38(7) and 39 DMA

A. *The Tools for Collaboration in the Implementation of the DMA*

31. The DMA and DMA-related provisions of the 2023 LOC Amendments have introduced little change to the powers of *Konkurencijos taryba* and to the way it collaborates with the Commission.

32. To start with, Lithuania has no national equivalent to the DMA and thus there is no clear danger of the fragmentation of the internal market, to which Article 1(5) DMA refers.

33. The 2023 LOC Amendments have not given the national competition authority the competence and investigative powers allowing it, on its own initiative, as foreseen by Article 38(7) DMA, to investigate a case of possible non-compliance with Articles 5, 6 and 7 of the DMA on the territory of Lithuania.

34. What remains are the two lines of cooperation between *Konkurencijos taryba* and the Commission. The first aims for complementarity between the DMA and the application of competition rules in the digital sector – this is covered in Section II.1.B below. The other gives *Konkurencijos taryba* a role in supporting the Commission's DMA enforcement efforts.

35. National laws do not elaborate on either of the two lines of cooperation. The Law on Competition succinctly states that KT operates under the national competition

rules to the extent that its functions are not defined by DMA.[38] Thus the tools for cooperation in the implementation of the DMA are those envisaged by the DMA itself, with a few details appearing in the LOC also:

- The Commission consulting with national authorities, including KT, on any matter relating to the DMA application;[39]
- The Commission asking KT to support its market investigations under the DMA;[40]
- KT playing a role in Lithuania as the Member State making a request for a market investigation;[41]
- The Commission asking for KT's assistance and KT providing assistance to the Commission carry out inspections under the DMA.[42] In relation to such inspections, Article 56 LOC allows the Commission officials and the authorised officials of KT assisting them, to employ the police to keep public order and for potential application of coercive measures.

36. Beyond the DMA-specific collaboration, the rules that specify the mechanism of the KT's cooperation with competition and other competent authorities of the EU Member States (the Rules on Cooperation) were adopted by KT itself, back in 2020, to implement the ECN+ Directive.[43] Those rules provide details on handling the requests for assistance submitted or received by KT. The Rules on Cooperation, however, have a narrow focus on inter-agency mutual assistance in competition cases and do not cover the DMA-related matters. At the time of writing (November 2024), KT has made no public announcements as to whether it intends to amend the Rules on Cooperation to cover the authority's collaboration under the DMA.

B. *Coordination between EU Asymmetric Regulation and Public and Private Enforcement by NCAs and National Courts*

37. The national laws are very laconic in describing the interactions between the Commission as the DMA enforcer, on the one hand, and *Konkurencijos taryba* as competition enforcer, on the other.

38. The situations of these two enforcers coordinating their actions are envisaged in the DMA itself:

- KT sharing information with other national competition authorities and the Commission about its respective enforcement actions through the European Competition Network;[44]

---

38 LOC art 54(3).

39 DMA art 37(2).

40 DMA arts 16(5) and 38(6).

41 DMA arts 41(1)-(3).

42 DMA art 23(3).

43 Rules for cooperation with competition or other competent authorities of the EU Member States, approved by KT Resolution No 1S-80 (2020). See also Directive 2019/1 of the European Parliament and of the Council of 11 December 2018 to empower the competition authorities of the Member States to be more effective enforcers and to ensure the proper functioning of the internal market (ECN+ Directive) [2019] OJ L11/3.

44 DMA art 38(1).

- KT informing the Commission in writing of its first formal investigative measure in case KT intends to launch an investigation, based on national competition rules, on gatekeepers;[45]
- KT communicating to the Commission interim measures – envisaged or adopted;[46]
- KT communicating to the Commission draft measures to be imposed on gatekeepers based on national competition rules.[47]

39. As mentioned before, the KT-approved Rules on Cooperation explain the mechanism of KT's cooperation with other competition enforcers, but the application of these rules does not extend to include the DMA.

40. Unlike *Konkurencijos taryba,* whose role in the DMA enforcement is very limited, the national courts can directly apply the DMA in cases of private enforcement. As such, national courts must follow certain rules to ensure coherent application of the DMA. Those rules are mostly present in Article 39 DMA, with LOC adding some details:
    - National courts may ask the Commission to transmit to them information in their possession or their opinion on questions concerning the application of the DMA;[48]
    - While the Commission does not have a general right to request information from national courts, it may intervene, on its own initiative, by submitting written observations to national courts if the coherent application of the DMA so requires.[49] In Lithuanian competition cases, such interventions, foreseen by Article 15(3) of Regulation 1/2003, have been absent,[50] and one may wonder if or why this may change in relation to the DMA.
    - When preparing to submit its observations – and for that purpose only – the Commission may request the relevant national court to transmit the necessary documents for the assessment of the case;[51]
    - After a national court issues a judgment that involves application of the DMA, a copy of such judgment must without delay be forwarded to the Commission.[52] That duty is imposed on the Member State – and not directly on the national court concerned – which leaves some doubt as to whether this mechanism of keeping the Commission informed will work. By way of example, a similar mechanism envisaged in Article 15(2) of Regulation 1/2003 has failed and, in the case of Lithuania, resulted in just two court judgments – out of many in which Articles 101 and 102 TFEU

---

45 DMA art 38(2).
46 DMA art 38(3).
47 DMA art 38(3).
48 DMA art 39(1).
49 DMA art 39(3).
50 While direct Commission interventions are not known, in two cases, the Commission sent its observations to *Konkurencijos taryba* and the latter presented them to administrative courts.
51 DMA art 39(4).
52 DMA art 39(2).

have been applied – being reported to the Commission.[53] It may not help that Article 57(2) LOC requires judgments involving application of the DMA and of Articles 101 and 102 TFEU to be forwarded to the Commission and, in addition, to *Konkurencijos taryba* since the same provision in the national law fails to name a person or an institution that is a bearer of such duty.

- National courts are required not to give a decision which runs counter to a decision adopted by the Commission.[54]
- National courts may renew proceedings if it emerges that after the adoption of the court judgment, in which the DMA provisions have been applied to a conduct, the Commission issues its own decision applying the DMA provisions to the same conduct and the result of such application fundamentally differs.[55]

2. Legislative Mechanisms Provided at National Level to Ensure Coordination with EU Regulations

41. The mechanism for coordination with EU regulations is provided by the Rules on Coordination of the European Union Affairs (Rules on Coordination).[56]

42. In accordance with the Rules on Coordination, ministries, government agencies and other designated institutions are responsible for the implementation of the EU legal acts in their areas of competence. Specialists working in these institutions prepare national legislation implementing the EU legislation and take other measures that help ensure proper implementation and operation of the EU legislation in Lithuania.

43. The DMA and its implementation come within the competences of two ministries. The Ministry of Economics and Innovation is responsible for competition policy and the digital agenda (including in relation to the EU). Meanwhile, the Ministry of Justice coordinates the processes of transposition and implementation of EU law.

III. Conclusion: the DMA as a Piece of a Wider Cosmos of EU and National Legislative Initiatives for Digital Transformation?

44. As mentioned at the beginning of this chapter, the adoption of the DMA failed to create any significant debate in Lithuania. *Konkurencijos taryba*, as the country's competition authority, remains a public body that is by far the most engaged in DMA-related matters and has past examples of enforcement in the digital sector.

45. In its recent initiative, the authority joined efforts with the Latvian and Polish competition authorities to carry out a market study of online marketplaces and

---

53 See the list of reported judgments, <https://ec.europa.eu/competition/elojade/antitrust/nationalcourts/?ms_code=ltu> accessed 25 November 2024.

54 DMA art 39(5).

55 LOC art 57(3).

56 2004 Government Resolution No 21 on the Coordination of the European Union Affairs.

their ecosystems in Poland, Latvia and Lithuania. The market study was financed by the EU and led by the OECD.[57]

46. The study will focus on potential issues related to national or regional digital platforms that are not covered by the DMA. The study will also aim to establish whether there is a regulatory gap which could prevent the competition authorities from solving the identified issues.

47. The market study is scheduled to last 21 months, with the final report, including recommendations, expected to be published in spring 2026. It is unlikely that any significant national legislative initiatives will come up before that date.

---

57 See OECD, "Competition Market Study: Digital Sector in Poland, Latvia and Lithuania" (forthcoming, 2026) <www.oecd.org/en/about/projects/oecd-competition-market-study-digital-sector-in-poland-latvia-and-lithuania.html> accessed 25 November 2024.

DMA Enforcement Paradise?

The Netherlands

JASPER VAN DEN BOOM*
FRISO BOSTOEN AND GIORGIO MONTI**
Heinrich-Heine-Universität Düsseldorf
Tilburg University

Abstract

The Dutch Authority for Consumers and Markets (ACM) has played a major role in supporting the enactment of the Digital Markets Act (DMA). In this paper we trace how the Dutch have influenced the DMA and then examine how the ACM is gearing itself up to play a major role it its enforcement by considering the current legislative proposal, which would confer on the ACM more powers than required by the DMA. This, combined with the ACM's active enforcement of competition law in the digital space, its eagerness to explore synergies with other regulators via the Digital Regulation Cooperation Platform, and a healthy system for collective redress which can stimulate private enforcement, suggests that the Netherlands may well become a significant actor in the regulation of digital markets. Combined with a cooperative approach vis-à-vis the European Commission, the Dutch case-study provides valuable lessons for other national competition authorities.

---

* Jasper van den Boom, Postdoctoral researcher, Heinrich-Heine-Universität Düsseldorf, SCiDA Project.

** Friso Bostoen, Assistant professor of competition law and digital regulation; Giorgio Monti, Professor of competition law, Tilburg University.

I. Introduction

1. The Digital Markets Act (DMA) heralds a new era in the regulation of digital markets, as it complements the competition law toolbox with a set of specific and targeted rules for this sector. The implementation of the DMA is moving full steam ahead, and the first entities designated under the DMA – the gatekeepers – have begun to comply with the obligations imposed on them since 7 March 2024. This process of implementing new competition-adjacent rules raises questions about the role of general competition law in digital markets, especially the *ex post* enforcement tools. It particularly raises questions about the role of national competition authorities (NCAs) in regulating competition in the digital economy. While the European Commission (Commission) is the sole enforcer of the DMA, there is still room for NCAs to be active in digital markets, even with respect to gatekeepers. NCAs can still enforce their own competition laws, introduce new national rules for competition in digital markets and participate in the enforcement of the DMA in a supporting role. This chapter examines the relationship between the DMA and enforcement by the Dutch competition authority (*Autoriteit Consument & Markt* – ACM).

2. The ACM has evolved significantly since its inception 26 years ago. Up until the 1990s, the Netherlands had a reputation as a cartel paradise, with weak competition laws, even weaker enforcement and a general preference for coordination.[1] The EU Merger Regulation included what was known as the 'Dutch clause' to compensate for the absence of national merger rules.[2] Things have changed radically since then. Today, the ACM is an active enforcer eager to use its powers to scrutinise big tech firms, as evidenced by its ongoing case against Apple. Furthermore, private enforcement via class actions has been encouraged by the 2020 Resolution of Mass Damage in Collective Action Act (*Wet afwikkeling massaschade in collectieve actie* – WAMCA). The Netherlands is a major jurisdiction where collective follow-on cartel damages claims are brought. We may see claims against big tech as well in the near future. This raises the question how will the ACM evolve further in its role in enforcing competition laws and the DMA? Will the Netherlands go from a cartel paradise to an enforcement paradise?

3. When the DMA was proposed, the ACM took great interest.[3] It presented itself as one of the 'Friends of an Effective DMA' and pushed for affording NCAs more powers to apply these new rules. It also insisted on the continued relevance of NCAs in enforcing competition law as a complement to the DMA. In this chapter, we first sketch the ways in which the ACM contributed to influencing the content of the DMA by making the case for an enhanced role for national laws and NCAs (Section II). We then examine the proposed Dutch law to implement the DMA and the current state of play (Section III). We continue by discussing the ways

---

1 Bram Bouwens and Joost Dankers, 'The Invisible Handshake: Cartelisation in the Netherlands, 1930–2000' (2010) 84 Business History Review 751.

2 Leon Brittan, *Competition Policy and Merger Control in the Single European Market* (Grotius Publications 1991) 41–42, observing that Italy and Belgium joined the Netherlands in requesting this provision.

3 Proposal for a Regulation of the European Parliament and of the Council on contestable and fair markets in the digital sector (Digital Markets Act) COM(2020) 842 (final) (DMA proposal).

the ACM has used its enforcement powers in the digital space and by reviewing the prospects for private enforcement (Section IV), before concluding (Section V).

II. The Ambitions of the Netherlands in Shaping the DMA and Expanding the Role of Member States

4. The Netherlands was one of the most active Member States throughout the process of developing and implementing the DMA. Following the initial proposal, it published together with the other friends of the DMA (Germany and France) a brief non-paper entitled 'Strengthening the Digital Markets Act and Its Enforcement'.[4] With respect to the relationship between the DMA and national orders, the document stressed three points.[5] First, that the DMA should allow Member States to enact additional rules to address the conduct of digital gatekeepers because there may be national peculiarities that require local intervention. Second, one Member State should be entitled not only to request a market investigation for the purposes of designating a gatekeeper but also to request market investigations into systematic non-compliance and the identification of new services and practices. This would enhance the role of Member States in making the DMA future-proof. Third, and more vaguely, national authorities should support the Commission in its enforcement efforts to ensure there is sufficient capacity and expertise.

5. This non-paper and a follow-up by the same three governments,[6] which set out more detailed suggestions in the form of amendments, proved influential in strengthening the role of national law and enhancing the role of the NCAs in enforcing the DMA. Below, we compare the original proposal with the final text and gauge the impact of the proposals by the friends of the DMA.

6. First, Article 1(5) DMA was amended to allow Member States to impose further regulatory obligations on providers of core platform services, provided that these obligations are not imposed on a firm because it has been designated as a gatekeeper under the DMA.[7] This amendment tallies with the non-paper's position. It provides Member States with ample room to regulate digital undertakings according to their wishes. In Germany, Section 19a of the *Gesetz Gegen Wettsbewerbsbeschranküngen* (GWB) imposes additional rules on undertakings if they are of 'paramount significance across markets'. These new competition rules are applied predominantly (and for now exclusively) against digital platforms that are also gatekeepers under the DMA. It seems that in the Netherlands, there are currently no plans to introduce additional regulation specifically aimed at

---

[4] Germany, France & The Netherlands 'Strengthening the Digital Markets Act and Its Enforcement' (May 2021). A non-paper is an informal document designed to test the reactions of other parties, online; https://open.overheid.nl/documenten/ronl-536668e07519d9e6032ef0097ba01145bcdcb4bb/pdf.

[5] *Ibid* paras 3–5.

[6] Germany, France & The Netherlands, Strengthening the Digital Markets Act and its Enforcement, September 2021, online: https://www.bmwk.de/Redaktion/DE/Downloads/XYZ/zweites-gemeinsames-positionspapier-der-friends-of-an-effective-digital-markets-act.pdf?__blob=publicationFile&v=4

[7] All references to 'DMA', in the main text and footnotes, refer to Regulation 2022/1925 of the European Parliament and of the Council of 14 September 2022 on contestable and fair markets in the digital sector and amending Directives 2019/1937 and 2020/1828 (Digital Markets Act or DMA) [2022] OJ L265/1.

regulating large digital undertakings or gatekeepers. However, nothing in the DMA precludes the Netherlands from doing so as long as they adhere to the conditions set out in Articles 1(5) and (6) DMA. The ACM's chief economist, Paul de Bijl, has observed that existing competition law instruments are insufficient and has suggested that powers to carry out market investigations and impose remedies on the basis of a finding of anticompetitive effects, akin to those enjoyed by the UK's Competition and Markets Authority, may be desirable.[8]

7. Second, according to Article 41 DMA, three or more Member States may request that the Commission open market investigations on designation and the addition of other services or new obligations, while one or more Member States may request the Commission to open a market investigation into systematic non-compliance. This also coincides with the wishes of the friends of the DMA.

8. Third, the friends of the DMA were partially successful in securing amendments that would empower the NCAs to apply the DMA. The Commission's original proposal made no effort to involve the NCAs, but the friends sought to empower NCAs to carry out investigations on their own initiative and, upon referral by the Commission, to enforce the DMA on the same basis as the Commission.[9] The test for conferring enforcement powers on an NCA would have been whether it is well placed to apply enforcement measures. One immediate defect of a proposal conferring enforcement powers is that NCAs lack the power to impose remedies that have extraterritorial effects.[10] Therefore, the friends of the DMA suggested a provision allowing the Commission to extend the territorial scope of an NCA decision to the whole of the EU. However, in the final version of the DMA, Article 38 only gives Member States the power to grant investigative powers to a national competent authority to 'conduct an investigation into a case of possible non-compliance with Articles 5, 6 and 7 of this Regulation in its territory'.[11] The power ends when the Commission decides to open proceedings at which stage the authority is required to report its findings to the Commission, who remains 'sole enforcer of this Regulation'.[12]

9. The Commission is also empowered to recruit NCAs to increase enforcement capacity. In the Commission's original proposal, the Commission was only able to extend requests for information to Member States and national authorities.[13] According to the final version, the Commission may also request Member States to aid them in their market investigations,[14] to aid in conducting inspections within their territory[15] or to help monitor the obligations and measures imposed under the

---

8 ACM, 'Blog Paul de Bijl: A New Phase for Competition Supervision' (*ACM*, 25 May 2023) <https://www.acm.nl/nl/publicaties/blog-paul-de-bijl-een-nieuwe-fase-voor-mededingingstoezicht> accesses 10 July 2024. See also Jasper van den Boom and others, 'Towards Market Investigation Tools in Competition Law: The Case of the Netherlands' (2023) 14 Journal of European Competition Law & Practice 553.

9 Strengthening the Digital Markets Act and its Enforcement (n 6) arts X1 and X2.

10 Giorgio Monti 'Managing Decentralised Antitrust Enforcement: Toshiba' (2014) 51 CMLR 261.

11 DMA art 38(7), para 1.

12 DMA art 38(7), para 2.

13 DMA Proposal art 19(6); now DMA art 21(5).

14 DMA art 16(5).

15 DMA art 23.

DMA.[16] This implements the friends of the DMA's views that national capacities should be used to maximise the Commission's enforcement capacity.

10. The Netherlands has expressed the ambition to fully cooperate within the limited discretion offered to them under the DMA. Martijn Snoep, president of the ACM, has charted a course for the Dutch authority in helping to enforce the DMA and other pieces of EU legislation related to digital markets.[17] In a blog post, he sets out ambitious ideas for the role of the ACM in helping to regulate digital markets. With respect to DMA enforcement, for instance, he envisages the creation of Joint Supervisory Teams, where NCAs and the Commission would collaborate to enforce the DMA. The ambition of the ACM is supported by the Ministry of Economic Affairs and Climate. According to a public letter issued by the ACM, the ACM and the Ministry have collaborated closely in developing the implementation strategy for the DMA in the Netherlands and to organise the appointment of the ACM as the relevant authority tasked with implementing the DMA. In its letter, the ACM further requests the Ministry to grant them the power to enter and search private residences of natural persons involved with the investigated undertaking, as well as an expansion of its resources to enforce the DMA (7 FTE and €20.000 for reimbursements for international travel).[18] The Ministry has granted the ACM an expansion of its capacity to ensure that it can effectively fulfil its duties under the DMA.[19]

III. The Implementation of the DMA in the Netherlands

11. In this section, we discuss the substantive implementation of the DMA in the Netherlands and the powers granted to the ACM. We elaborate on the ambitions of the ACM as a partner in enforcing the DMA and the design of the Dutch DMA Implementation Act (Section III.1) and discuss the advice of the Dutch Legislative Advisory Body on the Act (Section III.2). Finally, we examine initiatives to expand enforcement cooperation and coordination within the Netherlands and beyond (Section III.3).

1. Setting up the ACM as an Active Partner in DMA Enforcement

12. The appointment of the ACM to enforce the DMA and the related expansion of its powers has been implemented in the Netherlands through the proposed DMA Implementation Act (*Uitvoeringswet digitalemarktenverordening*).[20] At the time of

---

16 DMA art 26(2).

17 ACM, 'Blog Martijn Snoep: Navigating the Online Platform Regulatory Revolution: Charting a New Course for Regulators' (*ACM*, 4 May 2023) <https://www.acm.nl/en/publications/blog-martijn-snoep-navigating-online-platform-regulatory-revolution-charting-new-course-regulators>.

18 ACM, 'ACM/22/180896 Uitvoerings- en handhavingstoets Digital Markets Act (DMA)' (29 March 2023) Letter to the Ministry of Economic Affairs and Climate <https://www.acm.nl/system/files/documents/brief-uitvoeringstoets-dma.pdf> accessed 11 July 2024.

19 Ministry of Economic Affairs and Climate, Digital Markets Implementation Act (2024) <https://www.internetconsultatie.nl/uitvoeringswetdma/b1> accessed 11 July 2024.

20 Proposal for a law to implement Regulation 2022/1925 of the European Parliament and of the Council of 14 September 2022 on contestable and fair markets in the digital sector and amending Directives 2019/1937 and 2020/1828 (DMA Implementation Act).

writing (2024), the proposal has been reviewed by the Dutch Legislative Advisory Body (see Section III.2 below). After consideration of this advice, the Parliament will vote on the adoption of the final version. Next, it will be put to vote before the Senate. Once the law has been adopted, it will enter into force by Royal Decree, but it is not yet known when entry into force will occur.

13. The relatively brief DMA Implementation Act consists of five substantive articles. It arranges the appointment of the ACM as the relevant authority to monitor the compliance with the obligations of Articles 5–7 DMA in the Netherlands. It also expands the scope of the law governing the powers of the ACM (*Instellingswet ACM*) to its monitoring of the DMA. Following Article 2 of the DMA Implementation Act, the ACM receives all investigative powers that it has for the enforcement of competition law so as to monitor compliance with the DMA, with the exception of the power to impose sanctions as laid down in Articles 12(h) (binding directions), 12(j) (restorative measures and periodic penalty payments) and 12(m) (fines). Article 3 of the DMA Implementation Act allows the ACM to provide assistance to the Commission in conducting inspections, and Article 4 of the Act lays down procedures in case of appeals by the investigated undertaking regarding these inspections.

14. Article 5 of the DMA Implementation Act amends Article 44(b) of the Dutch Civil Code so that the Commission can provide written and oral comments on decisional practices related to the DMA within the Member State in accordance with Article 39 DMA. Article 39 DMA provides rules for dialogue between the Commission and national courts. The Commission may provide information in its possession or its opinion to national courts where it pertains to the application of DMA rules, whether it be on request of the national court or on its own initiative.[21] For the purpose of preparing such statements, the Commission may request the courts to supply any documents necessary to assess the case.[22] The changes in Article 5 of the DMA Implementation Act organise the Commission's possibility to request and receive those documents and its ability to provide such statements procedurally. It will be up to the national courts to assess whether sharing the documents is necessary.

15. The Dutch Government elaborates on its position in a Memorandum appended to the DMA Implementation Act (*Memorie van Toelichting bij Uitvoeringswet Digitalemarktverordening*). Here, the government reiterates the importance of new rules to govern digital markets, their ambitions regarding regulating the digital realm, and the general content and scope of the DMA. Particularly relevant here are titles 3–4, where the government elaborates on how it views its role in monitoring the implementation of the DMA. The Dutch Government recognises that the role of Member States in enforcing the DMA is limited as the Commission reserves most rights of enforcement. However, the Dutch Government has aimed to maximise the use of their discretionary space by mandating the ACM to proactively monitor the implementation of the DMA in the Netherlands.[23] The Dutch

[21] DMA art 39(1) and 39(3), respectively.
[22] DMA art 39(4).
[23] Digital Markets Implementation Act 17–18.

Government provides several reasons why it uses this discretionary space. First, it believes that the threshold for business users to complain about possible anti-competitive behaviour to the ACM is much lower than for lodging a complaint with the Commission directly. Business users have the right to provide information regarding such complaints to the NCA either way under Article 27 DMA. Therefore, it would be sensible to allow the ACM to screen and investigate such complaints on behalf of the Commission. Second, the ACM has specific knowledge about possible competition issues related to the Dutch domain and society. This knowledge can be used to identify and effectively investigate notifications by complainants. This would likely create benefits for the efficiency of enforcement as coordination between the ACM and the Commission would lead to synergetic uses of resources.[24]

16. According to the Memorandum, the scope of the ACM's powers is limited to investigating designated gatekeepers' compliance with the substantive obligations imposed on them in Articles 5–7 DMA. The scope of the investigations themselves is limited to establishing possible non-compliance, without granting the ACM the ability to intervene in any way. The Memorandum argues that the idea of the Commission as the sole enforcer of the DMA is thus respected. In terms of powers, the ACM is granted the power to enter non-residential areas as foreseen by the Dutch General Administrative Act (Article 5:15 *Algemene Wet Bestuursrecht* – AwB); issuing binding requests for information (Article 5:16 AwB); seizing documents and information (Article 5:17 AwB); investigating (samples of) goods (Article 5:18 AwB) and the power to seal the entry of locations or to summon the police to a location following the ACM Establishment Act (*Instellingswet ACM*). The Memorandum also motivates the choice to grant the ACM the powers to enter private residences of natural persons in conducting investigations related to DMA compliance, noting that this power should be used as a measure of last resort. However, the Memorandum proposes that even with the use of such an intrusive measure, the duty of cooperation for investigations under administrative law (as laid down in Article 5:20 AwB) should still apply. Thus, it seems that the ACM has received all expansions of capacity and powers that it has requested in its 2023 letter to the Ministry.

17. The Memorandum also elaborates on the Dutch ambition for inter-institutional and interdisciplinary cooperation and enforcement. In this regard, it states that any information gathered in the procedure of establishing non-compliance with the DMA can also be used in other areas of enforcement with which the ACM is tasked. The Memorandum notes that this is permitted under Article 7 of the ACM Establishment Act, as this allows for information and documents gathered for one purpose to be shared and used throughout the entire organisation of the ACM.[25] The Memorandum also explicitly notes that if the ACM finds information that may be relevant for other public authorities, it is allowed to share this information. It may do so via the Digital Regulation Cooperation Platform (see further

---

24 Digital Markets Implementation Act 17–18.

25 Digital Markets Implementation Act 19.

Section III.3 below). The Memorandum does not seem to extend these rights with respect to international cooperation in the European Competition Network (ECN). It notes that different rules apply to international collaboration, and that here the standards should be set by the Commission.

18. The Memorandum also briefly discuss the other tasks imposed on the ACM through the DMA, such as the duty to cooperate with the Commission and the possibility that the Commission requests the ACM to engage in certain inspection and other activities as directed by the Commission. Here, the Memorandum emphasises the independence of the ACM and its discretion for fulfilling such tasks.

19. Finally, the Memorandum discusses the consequences of the DMA Implementation Act for business users and gatekeepers. For business users, the consequences are viewed as generally positive, as this implementation of the DMA helps them gain quick access to a relevant authority and grants that authority rights to investigate. For gatekeepers, the Memorandum recognises that the Act may raise their compliance costs. The Memorandum argues that there is no increase in direct compliance costs, as the Act does not add any new substantive rules to the DMA. It will however raise indirect compliance costs due to investigations, liaison time between the ACM and the gatekeeper and requests for information by the ACM. It is expected that the ACM will conduct one to three investigations yearly, and there will be somewhat significant costs for the investigation and on-site inspections. Most of these costs will be incurred by the ACM, while the costs of compliance for gatekeepers themselves remain small (estimated, without detailed calculation, at €1.085–3.850 per gatekeeper per three years for small-scale investigations and at €10.260–21.945 per gatekeeper per ten years).

2. Appraisal of the Proposed Role of the ACM by the Dutch Legislative Advisory Body

20. On 26 January 2024, the Dutch Legislative Advisory Body (*Afdeling Advisering van de Raad van State* – AARvS) issued its official advice on the proposed DMA Implementation Act.[26] In its advice, the AARvS warned of the risk of overlap between the activities and powers of the ACM and those of the Commission.[27] The AARvS started its observations by noting that following Article 38 DMA, any investigation by Member States related to the DMA should be stopped once the Commission starts its own investigation (similarly to the procedure under competition law, see Section IV below). As it is not always clear to which type of infringement an investigation relates when it is initiated, stopping such an investigation prematurely may have an impact on the enforcement of related laws. For instance, what starts as an investigation into compliance with the DMA may result in findings that there has been an infringement of competition law or the

---

26 Advice of the Council of State on the proposal for a law to implement Regulation 2022/1925 of the European Parliament and of the Council of 14 September 2022 on contestable and fair markets in the digital sector and amending Directives 2019/1937 and 2020/1828 ('Digital Markets Act' or DMA) [2022] OJ L265/1 (Digital Markets Regulation Implementation Act, Government Gazette 2024).

27 Advice of the Council of State on the proposal for a law to implement Regulation 2022/1925 3–7.

P2B Regulation.[28] If this is the case, the ACM will not merely have a supporting role but will have the ability to impose sanctions. This may mean that if the Commission takes over an ACM investigation related to the DMA, the ACM must stop investigating other types of infringements. The AARvS argues that a clarification is needed as to whether the ACM could then still pursue its own investigation on other grounds, or whether they must cease their investigation fully. The AARvS argues that if this is not clarified, there may be a risk of unintended side effects that hinder the ability of the ACM to investigate infringement of (competition) rules outside of the DMA.

21. The AARvS has also identified related concerns on competition law enforcement. As the DMA provides clear *ex ante* rules, such investigations may require significantly less resources than competition law investigations. Consequently, the ACM may not be inclined to pursue possible abuses of dominance if it can expect a decision by the Commission related to an infringement of the DMA. Alternatively, if the ACM does pursue a competition law infringement in parallel with DMA enforcement by the Commission, there may be a risk of infringing the *ne bis in idem* principle. The AARvS recognises, however, that risks of infringing this principle are mitigated by coordination through the ECN, correction of a possible infringement of *ne bis in idem* through judicial review or justifications of specific instances of double jeopardy (see further Section III.3 below).

22. The AARvS also looks into possible overlap between the DMA and the General Data Protection Regulation (GDPR).[29] Here, the AARvS observes that the Memorandum has touched upon collaboration between the ACM and the Dutch data protection authority (*Autoriteit Persoonsgegevens* – AP), as well as coordination within the ECN, but that it does not clarify what such cooperation looks like in practice. According to the AARvS, it remains unclear if and how consistency is safeguarded when both competition authorities and data protection authorities enforce rules related to the use of personal data. The Memorandum also does not explain how consistency is safeguarded, how it can be prevented that gatekeepers are subjected to unnecessary overlapping investigations, or whether there is the ambition to identify coherent norms that align obligations under the DMA and the GDPR. The AARvS sees no indication in the Memorandum that the AP has been consulted in preparing the DMA Implementation Act. The AARvS advises to elaborate on the collaboration between the ACM and the AP in the Memorandum to explain which mechanisms are used to ensure consistency. At the same time, the AARvS recognises that the ability of the ACM and AP to coordinate enforcement is very limited as the ACM is not tasked with enforcing the DMA but is limited to monitoring compliance. This would mean that the AP would have to cooperate with the Commission. It is likely that it will do so through the European

---

28 Regulation 2019/1150 of the European Parliament and of the Council of 20 June 2019 on promoting fairness and transparency for business users of online intermediation services (Platform-to-Business Regulation or P2B-Regulation) [2019] OJ L186/57.

29 Regulation 2016/679 of the European Parliament and of the Council of 27 April 2016 on the protection of natural persons with regard to the processing of personal data and on the free movement of such data, and repealing Directive 95/46 (General Data Protection Regulation) [2016] OJ L119/1.

Data Protection Board (EDBP) and the DMA High-level Group, but it is unlikely that there will be extensive collaboration between the Commission and the AP specifically when the former enforces the DMA.

23. In essence, the AARvS does not object to the proactive role of the ACM in monitoring non-compliance. However, it does stress the need for further clarifications as to how this role may impact the ACM's enforcement activities in other areas. It makes similar observations regarding the ambition to have more cooperation between regulatory authorities, highlighting the complex enforcement structure involving the Commission and national regulatory authorities with varying degrees of discretion and power to enforce certain rules. The advice to ensure coherence, coordination and consistency in the process of converging enforcement activities across legal domains and regulatory authorities is warranted, considering the possible impact on legal certainty and predictability for business users and gatekeepers.

3. Coordination between ACM and other Authorities

24. In its advice, the AARvS has highlighted the potential coordination problems that arise when the same (or overlapping) rules are enforced by multiple authorities. These concerns are legitimate and may have a significant impact on the enforcement of the DMA and related laws. The ACM, in preparing for the DMA and other (upcoming) legislation, has taken it upon itself to develop mechanisms and processes for cooperation with the Commission and other national regulators. These initiatives to ensure a high level of coordination in enforcement activities across different areas of law should mitigate possible coordination issues.

25. First, it is important to acknowledge that there are already many initiatives that allow for cooperation between authorities at the EU and Member State level. Participation in the ECN ensures that the Commission and NCAs exchange information and coordinate enforcement efforts in the area of competition law. The European Data Protection Board provides a forum for national data protection authorities to exchange information while involving EU institutions. Many other regulated sectors (e.g., energy and telecommunications) have similar bodies. In that sense, having to coordinate enforcement activities related to the DMA does not break new ground.

26. Second, in the area of competition law enforcement, the ACM has already demonstrated its willingness and ability to recalibrate investigations if the Commission initiates an investigation into the same conduct (see the discussion of the *Apple* case in Section IV below). When a risk of double jeopardy does arise, the judgment in *Nordzucker* has clarified its application when multiple NCAs impose penalties on the same infringement spanning multiple Member States.[30]

---

30 Case C-151/20 *Bundeswettbewerbsbehörde v Nordzucker AG and others* ECLI:EU:C:2022:203, see Francis Donnat, *Ne bis in idem: La Cour de justice de l'Union européenne précise sa jurisprudence sur le principe ne bis in idem au regard de l'articulation entre réglementation sectorielle et droit de la concurrence et au regard de l'utilisation dans deux États membres des mêmes faits (bpost) (Nordzucker)*, CONCURRENCES No. 2-2022, art. No. 106654.

27. Third, in DMA enforcement, the risk of coordination issues is low – or even non-existent – as the ACM is limited to monitoring compliance and informing the Commission of possible non-compliance. In transferring a case to the Commission, there will be an opportunity to coordinate enforcement actions between the competition authorities as to determining whether or not the ACM should proceed with an independent investigation. The risk of infringing *ne bis in idem* would be more pronounced if the ACM were to pursue an abuse of dominance case against a designated gatekeeper when the conduct considered by the ACM addresses the same facts as the DMA. The *bpost* judgment has clarified how to assess whether penalties infringe on the *ne bis in idem* principle where competition law and sector-specific regulation overlap.[31] And the coordination channels created in the DMA appear consistent with the *bpost* judgment, thereby avoiding the risk of double jeopardy.[32]

28. Fourth, the AARvS remarked on possible issues related to cooperation among national authorities, arguing that there is a need to clarify how the ACM and AP will cooperate to create a consistent set of rules relating to the data provisions in the DMA. Note that such problems are unlikely to arise as the ACM cannot say anything about the substance of the law, which is the exclusive domain of the Commission. Nevertheless, the ACM has taken a leading role in enhancing national cooperation between different bodies. In order to devise a multi-faceted strategy on implementing a growing body of digital laws – such as the DMA, Digital Services Act, Data Act, and AI Act – the Netherlands has established a Digital Regulation Cooperation Platform (*Samenwerking Digitale Toezichthouders* – SDT Platform). This platform consists of the ACM, the Financial Markets Authority, the AP, and the Media Authority. Through this platform, the parties assess potential problem areas and overlap and exchange knowledge to develop a coherent strategy to regulate developments within the digital economy.[33] These initiatives are also found elsewhere (e.g. in the UK) as regulators realise that in order to regulate digital markets effectively, it is important to have a holistic view of the various public interests that different regulators pursue. Knowledge-sharing allows for an alignment of views and better-informed enforcement.[34] This platform can still be expanded as the number of regulations and regulatory authorities grow and ensures that there is also knowledge exchange between authorities in different fields, whether for the purposes of monitoring the DMA, enforcing competition law or data protection rules, or beyond. The new cooperative arrangement should be seen as an extension of the activities that are already conducted to ensure coherent enforcement in the EU and the Netherlands, rather than a wholly new activity.

---

31 Case C-117/20 *bpost v Autorité belge de la concurrence* ECLI:EU:C:2022:202. For a discussion of its DMA implications, see Alessandra Fratini, 'Double Jeopardy Between Regulatory and Competition Proceedings: The *bpost* Judgment and the Digital Markets Act' in Pier Luigi Parcu and others (eds), *Postal Strategies: Logistics, Access, and the Environment* (Springer 2024).

32 DMA arts 1(6), 37 and 38.

33 ACM, 'The Digital Regulation Cooperation Platform (SDT)' (*ACM*, 2024) <https://www.acm.nl/en/about-acm/cooperation/national-cooperation/digital-regulation-cooperation-platform-sdt> accessed 11 July 2024.

34 See generally Giorgio Monti and Alexandre de Streel, 'Improving EU Institutional Design to Better Supervise Digital Platforms' (CERRE Report 2022) 40–42.

Existing activities, and a proactive approach to expanding cooperation across legislative regimes, is likely to minimise the already limited risks of coordination issues that could arise in co-monitoring DMA compliance with the Commission.

29. Finally, the ACM is also looking forward to coordination with other NCAs in the ECN. President Snoep has stated he considers such cooperation 'extremely important to ensure that there are neither overlaps nor gaps in the enforcement'.[35] The ACM organised the 'ECN–DMA Conference' on 24 June 2024, where it invited stakeholders to participate in workshops to highlight the potential positive impact of the DMA for business users and to further develop ideas on how NCAs can support the Commission.[36]

IV. National Enforcement Experience in Digital Markets

30. In this section, we discuss the Dutch enforcement experience in digital markets. We start by looking at public enforcement, in particular the ACM's competition law investigations of digital markets (Section IV.1) and its 'pre-enforcement' of the P2B Regulation (Section IV.2). Then, we turn to private enforcement (Section IV.3).

1. ACM's Competition Law Enforcement in Digital Markets

31. For an authority of its size, the ACM boasts significant experience enforcing competition law in digital markets. Its most notable enforcement action concerns Apple,[37] but it has also carried out several market studies, and it has meanwhile started scrutinising the conduct of another online marketplace. In this section, we discuss these developments, pointing out how they interact with the DMA.

32. The ACM started a market study into app stores in 2018, completing it in 2019.[38] It was the first study to take a comprehensive look at the competitive conditions and issues in app store markets. Other authorities followed suit with similar investigations.[39] Upon conclusion of the study, the ACM began an investigation into Apple, focussing on the App Store's treatment of Dutch news media apps.[40] One year later, in 2020, the Commission opened an investigation into the App Store, with a focus on music streaming and e-book apps.[41] This created a coordination issue, given

---

35 Stijn Huijts and Ruben Elkerbout, 'Interview with Martijn Snoep, Head of the Dutch Competition Authority' (*Platform Law Blog*, 13 March 2024) <https://theplatformlaw.blog/2024/03/13/interview-with-martijn-snoep-head-of-the-dutch-competition-authority/> accessed 11 July 2024.

36 See Martijn Snoep LinkedIn page (2024) <https://www.linkedin.com/posts/msnoep_call-for-an-expression-of-interest-the-european-activity-7169420255608434688-LPRR/> accessed 11 July 2024.

37 The section on app stores/Apple draws on Friso Bostoen, 'The ACM's Apple Decision: To Boldly Go Where No Enforcer Has Gone Before' (2022) 10 Journal of Antitrust Enforcement 583.

38 ACM, 'Market Study into Mobile App Stores' (ACM Report 2019). The study even featured in a popular late-night show, see 'Tech Monopolies: Last Week Tonight with John Oliver' (HBO, 2023) <https://www.youtube.com/watch?v=jXf04bhcjbg> accessed 11 July 2024.

39 See, e.g., CMA, 'Mobile Ecosystems Market Study' (ACM Final Report 2022).

40 ACM Press Release, 'ACM Launches Investigation into Abuse of Dominance by Apple in its App Store' (*ACM*, 11 April 2019) <https://www.acm.nl/en/publications/acm-launches-investigation-abuse-dominance-apple-its-app-store> accessed 11 July 2024.

41 European Commission Press Release, 'Commission Opens Investigations into Apple's App Store rules' (16 June 2020) <https://ec.europa.eu/commission/presscorner/detail/en/ip_20_1073> accessed 11 July 2024.

that NCAs are relieved of their competence when the Commission opens similar proceedings.[42] While the coordination process itself is shielded from public view, the authorities ended up with a solution whereby the ACM would pivot to dating apps (a category of apps Apple does not compete with), while the Commission would zoom in on music streaming (a category of apps Apple does compete with). This allowed the ACM to continue its investigation, albeit after a slight reorientation.[43]

33. The ACM's decision was shaped, in no small part, by this division of competences. As Apple did not compete with dating app developers, the theory of harm and corresponding form of abuse had to be one of exploitation. And indeed, when the ACM adopted a decision in 2021, it found that Apple had imposed unfair terms and conditions on developers.[44] The offending terms were twofold: first, Apple obliged developers to use its In-App Purchase system (IAP), through which it levied a 30% fee; second, it prohibited developers from informing users of cheaper purchasing options outside of the App Store (anti-steering). According to the ACM, and the Court of Rotterdam that provisionally confirmed its decision,[45] these terms disproportionately restrict the freedom of app developers, without being necessary for the App Store's business model.

34. The toughest part of the enforcement journey was the remedy stage. The remedy was for Apple to remove or adapt the offending terms so that app developers could refer to and make use of payment systems besides IAP. The ACM quickly established that Apple had not met the ACM's remedial requirements.[46] This led to a series of penalty payments that finally reached the maximum of €50m.[47] After a six-month process, the ACM was finally satisfied with Apple's implementation of the remedy.[48] Notably, under the new system, dating app developers still owed Apple a fee for purchases outside of IAP, though of 27% instead of the previous 30% (with the 3% difference compensating for the fee charged by payment processors other than Apple).[49]

35. The ACM's market study and investigation of app stores have influenced the DMA and hold lessons for its enforcement. Apple is prohibited from imposing its IAP and anti-steering obligations by, respectively, Article 5(7) and Article 5(4) and (5) of

---

42 Regulation 1/2003 of 16 December 2002 on the implementation of the rules on competition laid down in Articles 81 and 82 of the Treaty [2003] OJ L1/1, art 11(6).

43 ACM Press Release, 'ACM Can Continue its Investigation into the Apple App Store' (*ACM*, 22 June 2021) <https://www.acm.nl/en/publications/acm-can-continue-its-investigation-apple-app-store> accessed 11 July 2024.

44 Case ACM/19/035630 *Apple*, 24 August 2021 (ACM Summary of Decision) <https://www.acm.nl/sites/default/files/documents/summary-of-decision-on-abuse-of-dominant-position-by-apple.pdf> accessed 11 July 2024.

45 Court of Rotterdam, Cases ROT/21/4781–82 *Apple v ACM*, 24 December 2021, see Sander Timmerman and Rogier Meijer, *The Rotterdam District Court largely denies a Big Tech company's requests to block the Dutch Competition Authority's publication of a decision and fines in an abuse of dominance case against dating-app developers (Apple)*, E-COMPETITIONS December 2021, art. No. 105395.

46 ACM Press Release, 'Apple Fails to Satisfy Requirements Set by ACM' (*ACM*, 24 January 2022) <https://www.acm.nl/en/publications/apple-fails-satisfy-requirements-set-acm> accessed 11 July 2024.

47 For another episode of the back-and-forth, see ACM Press Release, 'Developing a New App is an Unnecessary and Unreasonable Condition that Apple Imposes on Dating-App Providers' (*ACM*, 14 February 2022) <https://www.acm.nl/en/publications/acm-developing-new-app-unnecessary-and-unreasonable-condition-apple-imposes-dating-app-providers> accessed 11 July 2024.

48 ACM Press Release, 'Apple Changes Unfair Conditions, Allows Alternative Payments Methods in Dating Apps' (*ACM*, 11 June 2022) <https://www.acm.nl/en/publications/acm-apple-changes-unfair-conditions-allows-alternative-payments-methods-dating-apps> accessed 11 July 2024.

49 See <https://developer.apple.com/support/storekit-external-entitlement/> accessed 11 July 2024.

the DMA. As the ACM's *Apple* case demonstrates, however, such prohibitions have little effect on the *level* of app store fees. In part, this may be an issue of compliance. Indeed, Commissioner Vestager has suggested that Apple's implementation of the ACM's remedy may be an example of circumvention under Article 13 of the DMA.[50] But it may also be an issue of case/remedy design: when enforcement does not specifically target the fee itself, that fee is unlikely to change markedly. The DMA does target the level of the fee, in Article 6(12), by requiring app stores to apply FRAND (fair, reasonable and non-discriminatory) conditions. Another issue concerns coordination. Given the existence of just two notable mobile ecosystems and embedded app stores, both of which have been designated under the DMA, app store cases are unlikely to require much coordination in the future.

36. In addition to its work on app stores, the ACM carried out a market study into cloud services, which it concluded in 2022.[51] It was, once more, a trendsetter, as the UK and French authorities concluded similar investigations in 2023.[52] The ACM's study surveyed the market, described the main providers and examined the various barriers to entry. It noted, in particular, the risk of user lock-in due to switching difficulties. The ACM specifically discussed the applicability of the DMA.[53] It expected the three largest cloud providers, i.e. Amazon, Microsoft and Google, to be designated as gatekeepers. That expectation remained unmet during the first round of designations, as the Commission did not designate any cloud provider.[54] The ACM pointed out how, after designation, Articles 6(6) (on end-user switching) and 6(9) (on data portability) may help resolve lock-in issues. However, it saw greater potential in the Data Act, which more specifically targets the barriers to customer switching between cloud providers.[55]

37. Most recently, in February 2024, the ACM announced it was investigating an unnamed online platform.[56] The platform, which quickly outed itself as the marketplace bol.com,[57] may be favouring itself (self-preferencing) and certain business users. In particular, several firms have complained that their offers are less visible, even if they provide the best price and/or quality. In addition, there are signals

---

50 Margrethe Vestager Speech, 'Shared Objectives for Framing the Tech Economy' (The Riesenfeld Award Ceremony – Berkeley California, 22 February 2022).

51 ACM, 'Market Study Cloud Services' (ACM Report 2022).

52 Autorité de la concurrence, 'Opinion 23-A-08 on Competition in the Cloud Sector' (29 June 2023); Ofcom, 'Cloud Services Market Study' (Final Report 2023).

53 Market Study Cloud Services (n 51) 69–70.

54 See European Commission Press Release, 'Digital Markets Act: Commission Designates Six Gatekeepers' (6 September 2023) <https://ec.europa.eu/commission/presscorner/detail/en/ip_23_4328> accessed 11 July 2024.

55 At the time of ACM's market study, the Data Act was only at the proposal stage, and the ACM made specific suggestions for improvement, see Market Study Cloud Services (n 51) 67–69 and ACM, 'Proposal to Enhance the Draft Data Act' <https://www.acm.nl/system/files/documents/proposal-to-enhance-the-draft-data-act.pdf> accessed 11 July 2024. The Act has meanwhile been adopted, see Regulation 2023/2854 of the European Parliament and of the Council of 13 December 2023 on harmonised rules on fair access to and use of data and amending Regulation 2017/2394 and Directive 2020/1828 (Data Act) [2023] OJ L1/71.

56 ACM Press Release, 'ACM Launches Investigation into Online Platform' (14 February 2024) <https://www.acm.nl/nl/publicaties/acm-start-onderzoek-naar-online-platform> accessed 12 July 2024.

57 'Bol Receives Questions from the ACM about Platform Structure for Sales Partners' (*Bol.Newroom*, 14 February 2024) <https://pers.bol.com/en/nieuws/bol-receives-questions-from-the-acm-about-platform-structure-for-sales-partners/> accessed 12 July 2024.

that bol.com uses its business users' data to strengthen its position. The case is not covered by the DMA as bol.com has not been designated as a gatekeeper. As the marketplace is mainly popular in the Netherlands and Belgium, it is unlikely to meet the DMA's thresholds in the future. If bol.com were designated, the alleged conduct could be covered by Articles 6(5) (self-preferencing in ranking) and 6(2) (reliance on business user data to compete with them). The case provides an illustration of the type of cases that NCAs may be particularly interested in post-DMA, i.e. cases involving platforms that are nationally significant but escape the DMA due to their more limited geographic scope.

2. ACM's 'Pre-Enforcement' of the P2B Regulation

38. The 2019 P2B Regulation in some sense paved the way for the DMA.[58] The Regulation did not prescribe specific changes to the conduct of a limited set of platforms. Instead, it obliged all platforms to be transparent about their terms and conditions, to communicate about changes clearly and early, to give reasons for termination, and to set up dispute settlement mechanisms. In contrast to the DMA, its enforcement fell to Member States, which could entrust authorities – including courts – with its enforcement.[59] The ACM is expected to be appointed as the competent enforcement authority, partially in view of the synergies with the enforcement of other laws such as the DMA.[60]

39. The ACM has been busy readying itself for this new role. In 2023, it commissioned a study that surveyed 400 business users about the way in which platforms were implementing the obligations of the P2B Regulation.[61] It emerged that most business users were not familiar with the P2B Regulation. When it came to the P2B Regulation's obligations, the compliance of platforms – as gauged by reactions from business users – varied. For example, about a quarter of respondents reported not receiving the reasons for their termination, suspension or limitation. In 2024, the ACM published its Guidance on the P2B Regulation.[62] The Guidance is meant to inform the platforms subject to the regulation of their obligations, and to specify them. To comply with the transparency requirements, it recommends platforms to make information clear and intelligible, specific and detailed, complete and easily available. Once the ACM is granted enforcement authority, the Guidance is likely to form the basis of investigations.

---

58 Regulation 2019/1150 of the European Parliament and of the Council of 20 June 2019 on promoting fairness and transparency for business users of online intermediation services (Platform-to-Business Regulation or P2B-Regulation) [2019] OJ L186/57.

59 Regulation 2019/1150 art 15 and recital 46.

60 See the proposed law appointing the ACM: Implementation of public oversight and enforcement of Regulation (EU) 2019/1150 of the European Parliament and of the Council of 20 June 2019 on promoting fairness and transparency for business users of online intermediation services (*Wet publiek toezicht en handhaving verordening bevordering billijkheid en transparantie voor zakelijke gebruikers van onlinetussenhandelsdiensten*).

61 ACM, 'Onderzoek naar ervaring van zakelijke gebruikers van onlineplatforms met algemene voorwaarden' (Research into the experience of business users of online platforms with general terms and conditions) (Study by Panteia) 2023.

62 ACM, 'Bevorderen van een transparante en eerlijke onlineplatformeconomie voor ondernemingen' (Fostering a transparent and fair online platform economy for businesses) (ACM Guidance 2024).

3. Private Enforcement

40. We can expect two kinds of private claimants: businesses might, individually or collectively, be aggrieved at the conduct of dominant firms. The DMA's principal beneficiaries, for example, are business users. These would be interested in injunctive relief to secure changes in the conduct of the dominant firm or the gatekeeper as well as damages for past harm. The Dutch courts are presently hearing an action for collective redress brought against Google by competitors offering comparison shopping services. This is a follow-on action based on the *Google Shopping* decision.[63] The plaintiffs sued Google Netherlands BV, a subsidiary of the addressee of the Commission's decision. The defendants contested the jurisdiction of the Dutch courts but, following the *Sumal* judgment,[64] the Amsterdam District Court held that it had jurisdiction in that the Dutch subsidiary could be jointly liable for the infringement if the case succeeds on the meris.[65] The second kind of claimants are consumers who experience economic losses as a result of an infringement of competition law or non-compliance with the DMA. In this section we focus on the opportunities made available in the Netherlands by the WAMCA.[66]

41. Collective redress has been a feature of modern Dutch law for some time, but the enactment of the WAMCA in 2020 placed this action on a much stronger footing. The legislator tried to balance two competing policies: to facilitate compensation on the one hand, and to avoid wasteful litigation on the other. This is achieved by a number of safeguards, including a soft law claims code to ensure that those who fund litigation do not secure excessive rewards thereby depleting the damages pot available to claimants; procedures by which only one collective action is available per wrongful act; encouraging settlement during the proceedings; identifying the group of claimants that are going to be bound by the WAMCA proceedings and establishing an opt out regime for Dutch class members,[67] thereby delimiting the class: this creates legal certainty about the size of the claim and can facilitate settlement. Settlement is also made attractive for claimants because it must be approved judicially. The court will assess the settlement package having regard

---

63 Case AT.39740 – *(Google Search (Shopping))* Decision of 27 June 2017 relating to a proceeding under Article 102 TFEU and Article 54 of the EEA Agreement C(2017) 4444 final <https://eur-lex.europa.eu/legal-content/EN/TXT/?uri=CELEX%3A52018XC0112%2801%29&qid=1720456993009> accessed 12 July 2024. See Frédéric Marty, *Anticompetitive leverage: EU Commission sanctions the dominant operator of the online search market on the basis of an anticompetitive leverage strategy oriented toward the online price compactors market (Google Shopping)*, CONCURRENCES No. 1-2018, art. No. 86088.

64 Case C-882/19 *Sumal SL v Mercedes Benz Trucks España SL* ECLI:EU:C:2021:800, see Miguel Verdeguer, *The EU Court of Justice issues a preliminary ruling clarifying the single economic unit doctrine in private enforcement providing an analysis that has far-reaching consequences on future damages claims across the EEA (Sumal/Mercedes Benz Trucks España)*, E-COMPETITIONS October 2021, art. No. 103583.

65 Rechtbank Amsterdam, *Wolfson Capital Ltd v Google Netherlands NV and others* NL:RBAMS:2023:3441, 31 May 2023, see Ruben Elkerbout, Eline Grondman and Simon Boersen, *The Dutch District Court of Amsterdam assumes jurisdiction over a private enforcement claim against a Big Tech company for abuse of dominance (Google Shopping)*, E-COMPETITIONS May 2023, art. No. 113715.

66 The applicable primary laws are found in arts 3:305a-d of the Dutch Civil Code and Title 14a of the Code of Civil Procedure. For an overview, see Dennis Horeman and Machteld de Monchy (eds), *Unlocking the WAMCA: A Practical Guide to the New Collective Action Regime in the Netherlands* (2nd edn, De Brauw Blackstone 2022).

67 Foreign class members must opt in, see Code of Civil Procedure art 1018(f)(5).

to a range of factors, including whether the compensation is reasonable, whether the claim organisations are sufficiently representative of the class and whether the group of persons who will benefit is large enough to warrant a settlement.[68] The system has led to US funders and law firms entering the Netherlands and the market for collective redress across a range of fields is growing.

V. Conclusion

42. The Netherlands appears ready for the implementation of the DMA. The ACM has involved itself early on as a partner in developing the DMA. As one of the self-identified 'Friends of an Effective DMA', the Netherlands has actively provided input on the role that NCAs could play in co-enforcing the DMA, on the relationship between national competition rules and the DMA and on ensuring the effectiveness of the rules laid down in the DMA itself. The Commission, the European Parliament and the Council have taken the ideas proposed by the Netherlands (together with those of France and Germany) into account when drafting the final version of the DMA, expanding the role that Member States can play in enforcing this regulatory regime. Now that the DMA has entered into force, the ACM has profiled itself as a proactive partner that will go beyond what is legally required to support the Commission in monitoring and enforcing the DMA. It does so with the support of the Dutch Government, which has provided it with the powers and resources to fulfil this role.

43. The ACM's views on competition in digital markets are shaped by its enforcement experience. Its most notable case concerns Apple, but it has also carried out market investigations and is now investigating bol.com. Hence, the ACM has conducted complex assessments of digital platform markets, including a number (such as app stores and cloud services) that are regulated under the DMA. This experience surely informed the DMA. Despite the new rules and enforcement structure, risks of clashing with the Commission are low. In its *Apple* case, the ACM has demonstrated that it is willing and able to recalibrate its investigation when the Commission starts its own case against the same undertaking. With regard to the DMA specifically, the ACM has signalled its preparedness to act in a supporting role and to defer to the judgement of the Commission in making substantive decisions related to the DMA. Therefore, while the ACM goes beyond the obligations imposed on it under the DMA, it does not exceed its legal mandate either.

44. Besides its role as an international cooperation partner, the Netherlands is also preparing for the increasing complexity of coordinating enforcement between its national regulators. A new Digital Regulation Cooperation Platform, where the ACM, the Financial Markets Authority, the AP, and the Media Authority collaborate, should help to exchange knowledge and develop consistent rules and standards for conduct in digital markets. When it comes to the DMA, the risk of intra-national inconsistency is in any case minimal, as any matters related to substantive law remain the exclusive domain of the Commission.

---

68 Dutch Civil Code art 7.907(3), listing all the relevant criteria.

45. Finally, the Dutch legal regime for private enforcement is conducive to private follow-up actions related to the DMA. The possibilities for collective redress in the Netherlands provide opportunities for private parties to complement enforcement activities by public authorities. This could further enhance the effectiveness of the DMA in promoting fairness and contestability.

46. In short, the Netherlands has been an active partner in developing and implementing the DMA, and the ACM shows every intention of becoming a proactive partner in monitoring DMA compliance. This, combined with Dutch experiences of public enforcement in digital markets and its collective redress mechanisms, may make the Netherlands a DMA enforcement paradise.

DMA Private Enforcement – Navigating Uncharted Waters

Portugal

MIGUEL SOUSA FERRO* AND NUNO PIRES SALPICO**

Sousa Ferro & Associados

Abstract

The Digital Markets Act represents a significant development in the regulation of the digital economy. Aiming to establish a balance between competition policy and economic regulation, various Member States are likely to face numerous challenges when cooperating in the application of the DMA. Portugal is seen as a jurisdiction where collective actions have a strong presence. The national legislator has already transposed Directive 2020/1828 via Decree-Law 114-A/2023. In this context, we discuss the relationship between the DMA and its private enforcement, and its potential application within the Portuguese jurisdiction.

---

* Miguel Sousa Ferro Professor at University of Lisbon Law School and Managing Partner at Sousa Ferro & Associados. For correspondence: miguelferro@fd.ulisboa.pt.

** Nuno Pires Salpico, Guest Lecturer at University of Lisbon Law School and Lawyer at Sousa Ferro & Associados. For correspondence: nunosalpico@fd.ulisboa.pt.

I. General Remarks

1. With the latest legal and empirical expansions of European Law's private enforcement, particularly in Competition Law, the emergence of the Regulation 2022/1925 Digital Markets Act (DMA), reignites the discussion.

2. The digital market has brought particularities that have hindered the effective pursuit of competition law's goals. In addition to various economic features present in these markets (e.g. multi-sided markets; strong network effects; low or zero 'prices'[1]), notable factors include their rapid growth,[2] extensive use of the data economy[3] and challenges in regulating economic activities.[4]

3. Drawing inspiration from Competition Law,[5] the DMA adopts a hybrid regulatory approach, aiming to ensure contestability and fairness (Article 1(1) of the DMA) by establishing a set of obligations such as those outlined in Articles 5 to 7 of the DMA. In this context, the DMA's public enforcement is, currently, highly centralised on the European Commission (EC), which retains all the decision-making powers (Articles 4, 18, 29–31 of the DMA) and dominates the investigative initiative (Articles 20–23 of the DMA).

---

1 OECD Handbook on Competition Policy in the Digital Age (OECD 2022) 13–14. For a study of the most impactful economic literature on the platform markets, see Jean-Charles Rochet and Jean Tirole, 'Platform Competition in Two-sided Markets' (2003) 1 Journal of the European Economic Association 990; Bernard Caillaud and Bruno Jullien, 'Chicken & Egg: Competition among Intermediation Service Providers' (2003) 34 RAND Journal of Economics 309; David S Evans and Richard Schmalensee, 'The Antitrust Analysis of Multisided Platform Businesses' (February 2013) NBER Working Paper No 18783; Marc Bourreau and Alexandre de Streel, 'Digital Conglomerates and EU Competition Policy' (11 March 2019) 17 <https://papers.ssrn.com/sol3/papers.cfm?abstract_id=3350512> accessed 12 July 2024; Justus Haucap, 'Competition and Competition Policy in a Data-Driven Economy' (2019) 54 Intereconomics 207–208; Regulation 2022/1925 of the European Parliament and of the Council of 14 September 2022 on contestable and fair markets in the digital sector and amending Directives 2019/1937 and 2020/1828 (Digital Markets Act or DMA) [2022] OJ L265/1 recitals 36, 59; Inge Graef, 'Differentiated Treatment in Platform-to-Business Relations: EU Competition Law and Economic Dependence' (2019) 38 Yearbook of European Law 453.

2 Analysing the growth of online platforms with an increase by more than 50% from 2013 to 2019, Hélia Costa and others, 'Welcome to the (Digital) Jungle: Measuring Online Platform Diffusion' (2021) OECD Economics Department Working Papers No 1683 14–16.

3 Guillaume Beaumier and others, 'Global Regulations for a Digital Economy: Between New and Old Challenges' (2020) 11 Global Policy 516, 518.

4 John Taladay and Paul Lugard, 'The Ten Principles of Ex Ante Competition Regulation' (OECD November 2022) 2–5; Matthias Bauer and others, 'The EU Digital Markets Act: Assessing the Quality of Regulation' (ECIPE Policy Brief February 2022) 5–20; Giuseppe Nicoletti, Cristiana Vitale and Carolina Abate, 'Competition, Regulation and Growth in a Digitized World: Dealing with Emerging Competition Issues in Digital Markets' (2023) OECD Economics Department Working Papers No 1752 5; Lisa Quest, Jo Ann Barefoot and Owain Service, 'The Digital Economy Cannot Be Managed With 18th-Century Regulation' (*BRINK*, July 28, 2021) <https://www.brinknews.com/the-digital-economy-cannot-be-managed-with-18th-century-regulation/> accessed 12 July 2024.

5 Bauer and others (n 4) 1, 20; Josef Drexl and others, 'Implementation of Digital Markets Act (DMA)' (2 May 2023) Max Planck Institute for Innovation & Competition Research Paper No 23-11 3–7; Friso Bostoen, 'Understanding the Digital Markets Act' (15 January 2023) 3–4 <https://papers.ssrn.com/sol3/papers.cfm?abstract_id=4440819> accessed 12 July 2024. Noting that the DMA is essentially a sector specific competition law, Nicolas Petit, 'The Proposed Digital Markets Act (DMA): A Legal and Policy Review' (11 May 2021) 2 <https://papers.ssrn.com/sol3/papers.cfm?abstract_id=3843497> accessed 12 July 2024; Natalia Moreno Belloso and Nicolas Petit, 'The EU Digital Markets Act (DMA): A Competition Hand in a Regulatory Glove' (5 April 2023) 4 <https://papers.ssrn.com/sol3/papers.cfm?abstract_id=4411743> accessed 12 July 2024.

4. Despite some discussions that have taken place,[6] it does not seem possible to argue that the DMA has closed the door to private enforcement. First, the DMA directly establishes that Directive 2020/1828[7] applies to collective actions brought against breaches of the provisions of this regulation committed by gatekeepers that harm or are likely to harm the collective interests of consumers (Article 42 of the DMA). If private enforcement were not possible, the provision of Article 42 of the DMA would be useless.

5. Second, the scope of the duties outlined in Articles 5 to 7 of the DMA serves to protect both end users and business users. Private enforcement is possible with regard to all provisions that are unconditional and that grant individuals actionable rights, provisions that benefit from 'direct effect', which is (apparently) the case for the prohibitions contained in Articles 5 and 6 of the DMA.[8] Due to the DMA's direct effect[9] (Article 288 TFEU), private individuals may bring actions for an injunction before national courts for the fulfilment of the obligations laid down in the DMA (e.g. in Article 5 of the DMA) and actions for damages for breach of the same obligations.

6. Before addressing any doubts and questions that may arise regarding the private enforcement of the DMA, it is pertinent to note two observations: one concerning general principles of private enforcement, and the other regarding private enforcement through public enforcement.

7. Any private enforcement regulation must aim to remove practical obstacles to compensation for all victims of infringements of EU antitrust law (principle of effectiveness) and ensure the interplay between: (i) private damages actions; and (ii) public enforcement of the EU rules by the Commission and national competition authorities.[10]

8. Following the European jurisprudence developed in the context of private enforcement of competition law, it follows that the grounds and constitutive conditions (or preconditions) of a right to injunctive relief or damages relating to the private enforcement of European rules are governed by European Union law. While the assumptions of the right are governed by European law, the procedures for exercising this right (or its details of application) are governed by the law of the Member States, while respecting the principle of effectiveness and equivalence.[11] Regarding these principles, it should be noted that:

---

6 On this context see Assimakis P Komninos, *The Digital Markets Act and Private Enforcement: Proposals for an Optimal System of Enforcement* in *Eleanor M. Fox Liber Amicorum, Antitrust Ambassador to the World*, Concurrences 2021.

7 Directive 2020/1828 of the European Parliament and of the Council of 25 November 2020 on representative actions for the protection of the collective interests of consumers and repealing Directive 2009/22 [2020] OJ L409/1.

8 Ana Rita Calmeiro Barroca and Nuno Pires Salpico, 'DMA: Private Enforcement Lurking?' (2023) unpublished manuscript.

9 Case 26-62 *NV Algemene Transport- en Expeditie Onderneming van Gend en Loos v Nederlandse Administratie der Belastingen* ECLI:EU:C:1963:1.

10 Barroca and Salpico (n 8).

11 Opinion of AG Kokott, C-557/12 *Kone AG v OBB-Infrastruktur AG* ECLI:EU:C:2014:45 paras 24 and 26; Opinion of AG Wahl, C-724/17 *Vantaan kaupunki v Skanska Industrial Solutions Oy* ECLI:EU:C:2019:100 paras 40–41; Case C-724/17 *Skanska Industrial Solutions Oy* ECLI:EU:C:2019:204 para 28, see Alexandre G Verheyden, Charlotte Breuvart and Henry de la Barre d'Erquelinnes, *The EU Court of Justice expands cartel*

> "[T]he Court's case-law, according to which the rules relating to actions for safeguarding rights which individuals derive from EU law must not be less favourable than those governing similar domestic actions (principle of equivalence) and must not make it in practice impossible or excessively difficult to exercise rights conferred by EU law (principle of effectiveness)."[12]

9. Given the limited development in this matter, it is necessary to make some remarks about the possible follow-on and stand-alone modalities in private enforcement. Some doubts have been raised regarding the feasibility of private enforcement in the stand-alone modality. Some authors firmly believe:

> "[T]hat the EU legislator would be well advised to introduce certain proportionate limitations on the private enforcement of the DMA rules or a 'rule of precedence' for public enforcement. Private enforcement should only be allowed in its 'follow-on' form, i.e. only after the Commission has taken a decision and has declared *erga omnes* that a particular gatekeeper has violated the DMA rules."[13]

10. While plausible concerns exist about the harmony of private enforcement, a balanced solution is desirable that does not drain the rights of those harmed by DMA infringements, making them purely hostage to the opportunity criteria followed in public enforcement.
11. One outstanding difficulty refers to the rules in Article 6 of the DMA, susceptible to further clarification or specification, either through an implementing act or regulatory dialogue. Until the needed clarification is provided, the harmed parties may struggle to identify harmful conduct.
12. In the follow-on modality, the possibility of invoking the well-known binding effect of the EC decision is already discussed (Articles 1(7) and 39(5) of the DMA). In addition, the relational schemes with national authorities with competencies related to the DMA, with national competition authorities (Articles 37 and 38 of the DMA) and with national courts (Article 39 of the DMA) have attracted special attention. This process mirrors Article 3(1) of Regulation 1/2003 on competition law.[14]
13. And what about *private enforcement through public enforcement*?

---

damages liability for corporate parents and successors (Vantaan Kaupunki / Skanska Industrial Solutions), E-COMPETITIONS March 2019, art. No. 96737. www.concurrences.com/96737; Opinion of AG Kokott, C-435/18 *Otis GmbH v Land Oberosterreich* ECLI:EU:C:2019:651 paras 44–45.

12 Case C-312/21 *Tráficos Manuel Ferrer SL v Daimler AG* ECLI:EU:C:2023:99 para 39. See Alexandre Lacresse, *Principle of effectiveness: The Court of Justice of the European Union confirms the competence of the judge to estimate the damage suffered in the context of an action for damages, without, however, being able to take the place of the claimant or make up for his or her failure to produce evidence (Tráficos Manuel Ferrer)*, CONCURRENCES No. 2-2023, art. No. 112564. www.concurrences.com/112564

13 Komninos (n 6) 438.

14 Regulation 1/2003 of 16 December 2002 on the implementation of the rules on competition laid down in arts 81 and 82 of the Treaty [2003] OJ L1/1.

14. Compensation for injured parties may occur in the context of public enforcement.[15] One of the aspects concerns the determination of the amount of the fine. Since the seriousness of the offence (Article 30(4) of the DMA) is a relevant factor, and since seriousness can be measured according to the consequences, a more damaging and harmful offence is, in principle, more serious than one that causes less damage.[16] First, this means that there can be a correlation between the amount of the fine and the degree of damage caused. In this way, the EC can incentivise agents to repair the damage caused by the infringement as a way of determining a lower fine.[17] Second, the EC's commitments decision could also prove to be a useful instrument (Article 25), since compensation for the damage caused by the infringement is a possible compromise.[18] The European Commission has the option to use these mechanisms to compensate for damage in a faster and potentially less expensive way.

15. On a final note, given that the 'regulatory' approach of the DMA draws inspiration from competition law, two major topics arise: (i) considering the evolution of private enforcement in competition law, what solutions can be applied to the private enforcement of the DMA (for instance, based on CJEU case law and Directive 2014/104, such as the presumption of harm and access to evidence rules); and (ii) What is the relationship between the DMA, competition law, and data protection law.[19]

II. Claims under National Law

1. Injunctions and Claims for Damages

16. Considering the set of obligations outlined in Articles 5 to 7 of the DMA as well as the reference to the applicability of Directive 2020/1828 (Article 42 of the DMA), and unless the CJEU excludes direct effect of these provisions,[20] there is the possibility for individuals (end users and business users) to bring private claims in national courts based on a breach of these DMA obligations.

17. Under national law individuals will have the possibility to bring: (i) injunctive actions; and (ii) actions for damages.

18. Injunctive actions will be 'declaratory condemnation actions' (*ação declarativa de condenação*, see Article 10(b) of the Portuguese Code of Civil Procedure,[21] (*Código de Processo Civil* – PCCP) in which individuals should request that DMA infringers take measures to comply with Articles 5 to 7 of the DMA. Claimants can also resort to injunctive measures of a conservatory or anticipatory nature

---

15 With the same thoughts, regarding the public enforcement of EC Competition Law, Miguel Sousa Ferro and Nuno Salpico, '*Indemnização dos consumidores como prioridade dos reguladores*/Consumer Redress as a Priority for Regulators' (2021) 63 Lisbon Law Review 407.

16 Barroca and Salpico (n 8).

17 *Ibid.*

18 *Ibid.*

19 Directive 2014/104 of the European Parliament and of the Council of 26 November 2014 on certain rules governing actions for damages under national law for infringements of the competition law provisions of the Member States and of the European Union [2014] OJ L349/1.

20 These provisions must be interpreted as unconditional and must grant individual's actionable rights.

21 The purpose of declaratory actions is '(b) condemnation actions, to demand the performance of a thing or a fact, presupposing or foreseeing the violation of a right;' (author translation).

specifically suitable to ensure the effective result and ensure the effectiveness of the threatened right (injuctive relief, *Providências Cautelares* as provided for in Articles 362(1) of the PCCP[22]). For the granting of an injunction relief, three prerequisites must be met: (i) *fumus boni juris*, meaning there must be an appearance or plausibility of the invoked right; (ii) *periculum in mora* (danger of delay), which consists of the idea of there being a well-founded fear of serious and hardly reparable harm to the right, preventing the damage resulting from the natural delay of the process; (iii) proportionality, meaning that the safeguarded right must outweigh, in a proportionality judgment, the 'sacrificed' right.

19. Actions for damages will also be declaratory condemnation actions under Article 10(b) of the PCCP. Despite the national tort law provided for in Article 483(1) of the Portuguese Civil Code[23] (*Código Civil* – PCC), the right to compensation for a violation under the DMA derives from European Law. Therefore, and following the CJEU private enforcement case law, the grounds and constitutive conditions (or pre-conditions) of the right to damages relating to the private enforcement of European rules are governed by European Union law. On the other hand, the procedures for exercising this right (or its details of application) are governed by the law of the Member States, while respecting the principle of effectiveness and equivalence.

20. Another interesting issue relates to quantifying damages. Estimating damages is often a technical and complex exercise, and quantifying damages for infringements of the DMA will certainly represent a challenge – for example for certain types of damage, such as:

- Loss of turnover or loss of business opportunities for business users;
- Overpricing paid by business users for access to certain platforms, goods or services useful for their activity;
- Losses for consumers arising from the abusive use of their personal data;
- Losses suffered as a result of the lower quality and higher price of the products or services offered to the consumer.

21. Adding to the complexity of these issues, on both injunctions and claims for damages, there is currently no specialised court to judge on DMA private enforcement matters. While public enforcement of competition law falls under the jurisdiction of the Competition, Regulation, and Supervision Court (Competition Court)

22 Portuguese Code of Civil Procedure: 'Whenever someone shows a well-founded fear that someone else will cause serious and difficult-to-repair damage to their right, they can request the conservatory or anticipatory measure that is concretely appropriate to ensure the effectiveness of the threatened right.' (author translation).

23 Portuguese Civil Code: 'Whoever, with intent or mere negligence, unlawfully violates the right of another or any legal provision intended to protect the interests of others is obliged to compensate the injured party for the damages resulting from the violation.' (author translation).

(Article 112(1)[24] and (2),[25] of Law No 62/2013), in private enforcement the same court is only competent to judge in actions whose cause of action is based exclusively on violations of competition law. This competence applies to both injunctive actions (Article 112(4))[26] and actions for damages (Article 112(3)[27] Law No 62/2013).

22. In this context, if the conduct constituting an infringement of the DMA also constitutes a violation of competition law, there is nothing preventing the harmed parties from bringing a claim under Portuguese private enforcement act (Law No 23/2018, which transposed Directive 2014/104). However, for the Competition Court to be competent, the claimant could only invoke Articles 101 and 102 of the TFEU and/or the national provisions of competition law.

2. Consumer Collective Redress

23. In Article 42, the DMA clarifies the applicability of Directive 2020/1828, which has already been transposed in Portugal by Decree-Law No 114-A/2023 (Collective Redress Act). As a result, consumers affected by DMA infringements will be able to file injunctions and actions for damages under the collective redress mechanism provided for in this law.

24. While Portugal has the well-known popular action (*opt out* collective action mechanism) provided for in Law No 83/95 (Popular Action Act), now collective consumer protection also includes the Collective Redress Act.

25. The Collective Redress Act applies to national and cross-border collective actions for the protection of consumers' rights and interests brought on the grounds of infringements committed by professionals, including where the infringement ceased before the collective action was brought or before its conclusion, to the

---

24 Law No 62/2013: 'The competition, regulatory and supervisory court is responsible for ruling on matters relating to the appeal, review and enforcement of decisions, orders and other measures in administrative offense proceedings that can legally be contested: (a) The Competition Authority (PCA); (b) The Mobility and Transport Authority (AMT); (c) The National Civil Aviation Authority (ANAC); (d) The National Communications Authority (ANACOM); (e) The Insurance and Pension Funds Supervisory Authority (ASF); (f) The Bank of Portugal (BP); (g) The Portuguese Securities Market Commission (CMVM); (h) The Media Regulatory Authority (ERC); (i) The Health Regulatory Authority (ERS); (j) The Water and Waste Services Regulatory Authority (ERSAR); (k) The Energy Services Regulatory Authority (ERSE).' (author translation).

25 Law No 62/2013: 'The Competition, Regulation and Supervision Court is also responsible for ruling on matters relating to appeal, review and enforcement: (a) PCA decisions handed down in administrative procedures referred to in the competition law regime, as well as the ministerial decision provided for in article 34 of Decree-Law no. 10/2003, of January 18; (b) Other decisions of the PCA that may be appealed, under the terms of the competition law regime.' (author translation).

26 Law No 62/2013: 'The court is also competent to rule on all other civil actions whose cause of action is based exclusively on infringements of competition law provided for in Articles 9, 11 and 12 of Law no. 19/2012, of May 8 (Portuguese Competition Act), in corresponding rules of other Member States and/or in Articles 101 and 102 of the Treaty on the Functioning of the European Union, as well as requests for access to evidence relating to such actions, under the terms provided for in Law no. 23/2018, of June 5 (Portuguese Private Enforcement Act)' (author translation).

27 Law No 62/2013: 'The court is responsible for ruling on actions for damages whose cause of action is based exclusively on infringements of competition law, actions aimed at exercising the right of recourse between co-infringers, as well as requests for access to evidence relating to such actions, under the terms of Law no. 23/2018, of June 5' (author translation).

provisions of national and European Union law referred to in Annex I of Directive 2020/1828, which harm or are likely to harm the collective interests of consumers (Article 2(1) of the Collective Redress Act). Naturally, the Collective Redress Act will have to be interpreted in accordance with Directive 2020/1828 and in accordance with European law.

26. Associations and foundations, regardless of whether or not they have a direct interest in the claim, and local authorities are entitled to represent consumers under the right of consumer collective action (Article 5(1) of the Collective Redress Act). On the other hand, qualified entities previously designated by other Member States are entitled to cross-border collective action, which may request injunctions or redress measures, in particular through the same collective action (Article 5(2) of the Collective Redress Act).

27. According to Article 6(1) of the Collective Redress Act, the following are requirements for the active legitimacy of associations and foundations:

> "(a) Legal personality;
>
> (b) The express inclusion, in their attributions or statutory objectives, of the defense of the interests in question in the type of action in question;
>
> (c) The non-exercise of any type of professional activity competing with companies or liberal professionals;
>
> (d) The independence and absence of influence from persons other than consumers, in particular professionals, who have an economic interest in bringing a collective action, particularly in the case of funding by third parties, and the adoption of procedures to prevent their influence, as well as to prevent conflicts of interest between themselves, their funders and the interests of consumers."[28]

28. An association or foundation is independent, 'namely if it is exclusively responsible for making the decisions to bring, withdraw or settle a collective action, with the guiding principle of defending the interests of consumers'.[29]

29. For a national entity to be designated as a qualified entity for the purposes of filing cross-border collective actions, there are additional requirements, such as:

> "(a) Being a legal person incorporated under Portuguese law and demonstrating that it has exercised twelve months of effective public activity in the protection of consumers' interests prior to its request for designation;
>
> (b) Its statutory purpose demonstrates the existence of a legitimate interest in the protection of consumers' interests, as provided for in the provisions of EU law referred to in Annex I to the Directive."[30]

---

[28] Collective Redress Act art 6(1) (author translation).
[29] Collective Redress Act art 6(2) (author translation).
[30] Collective Redress Act art 7(1).

30. While the Portuguese class action operates under an opt-out system, cross-border collective actions now follow an opt-in scheme for non-residents in Portugal.[31]

31. In the case of injunctions, prior consultation with a professional is now required, and only after that can legal action be filed.[32] And when the defendant loses a collective action for injunctive relief, they may be ordered to pay a penalty payment, which may not exceed the amount of €4,987.98 for each infringement if it fails to comply with the obligation established in a final judgment.[33] The amount of the penalty payment shall be allocated in equal parts to the claimant and to the Fund for the Promotion of Consumer Rights.[34]

32. Litigation funding has been a hot topic in Portuguese popular actions, with defendants contesting the plaintiff's active legitimacy and invoking abuse of right.[35] However, the Collective Redress Act clarifies the conditions under which funding can occur, as showed previously regarding Article 6(1)(d) of that Act.

33. First and in accordance with the Directive, there are obligations to disclose the Litigation Funding Agreement (LFA) to the court (Article 10(1) of the Collective Redress Act[36]). The LFA must ensure the independence of the claimant and the absence of conflicts of interest (Article 10(3) of the Collective Redress Act).

34. The plaintiff is independent of the third-party funder if the plaintiff is exclusively responsible for taking all decisions relating to the representative action, with the guiding principle being the defense of the interests at stake, including, in particular, the choice of legal representatives, the definition of the procedural strategy and also the decisions to bring, continue, withdraw, settle, appeal or not appeal and, in general, to perform or not to perform any procedural act within the scope of the representative action.[37].

---

31 Collective Redress Act art 12(1): 'Without prejudice to the provisions of articles 14 and 15 of Law no. 83/95, of August 31, in its current wording, consumers who are not habitually resident in Portugal at the time of the service of process on the holders of the interests in question in the collective action for redress measures are only represented by the plaintiff if they expressly state their wish to be represented in the collective action in question, in order to be bound by its outcome.' (author translation).

32 Collective Redress Act art 11: '1 - measures of injunction aimed at stopping or, where appropriate, identifying or prohibiting a practice considered to be an infringement, under the terms of the legislation for the protection of consumer rights and interests, can only be requested after a prior consultation process with the professional. 2 - Prior consultation takes place by means of communication to the professional, by registered letter with acknowledgement of receipt, and must include: (a) A description of the conduct or facts whose practice must cease or which may have caused damage to consumers; and (b) The rules of consumer protection legislation violated. 3 - If the professional does not put an end to the infringement within two weeks of receiving the communication referred to in the previous paragraph, the holder of the right of collective action that triggered the prior consultation procedure may request an injunction.' (author translation).

33 Collective Redress Act art 15(1).

34 Collective Redress Act art 15(3).

35 See Nuno Pires Salpico, 'Portugal: EC Law Private Enforcement's Holy Grail?' (2022) 6 CoRe 269–270.

36 Collective Redress Act: 'In the event that a funding agreement concerning the pursuit of a representative action is concluded with a third party, and so that compliance with the following paragraphs of this article can be assessed, the claimant of the representative action shall provide the court with a certified copy of the agreement, drafted in a clear and easily understandable manner and in Portuguese, and shall include the following elements: (a) A financial summary listing the sources of funding used to support the representative action; (b) The various costs and expenses that will be borne by the third-party funder' (author translation).

37 Collective Redress Act art 10(4) (author translation).

35. The LFA for a representative action cannot 'provide for remuneration for the funder that goes beyond a fair and proportionate amount, assessed in the light of the characteristics and risk factors of the representative action in question and the market price of such funding.'[38] A representative action brought by a plaintiff who has entered into a LFA is inadmissible when at least one of the defendants in the action is a competitor of the funder or is an entity on which the funder depends.[39].

36. With regard to the consequences of the violation of Articles 10(3), (5) and (7) of the Collective Redress Act, the court 'shall invite the claimant to, within a certain period of time, refuse or make changes to the third-party funding in order to ensure compliance with the provisions of the violated rule, and shall declare the claimant's legal standing if the necessary changes are not made within the established period of time.'[40] However, when the plaintiff's standing is rejected because the necessary changes were not made within the established period of time, this rejection 'does not affect the rights of the holders of the interests covered by the representative action in question, and the Public Prosecutor's Office may substitute itself for the plaintiff by pursuing the action.'[41]

37. Another relevant topic is that of access to evidence. According to Article 13(1) of the Collective Redress Act, a plaintiff who has produced evidence reasonably available and sufficient to support the collective action and has indicated other evidence in the possession of the defendant or a third party may, upon reasoned application, request the court to order the production of such evidence by the defendant or a third party.[42] The defendant may, upon justified request, ask the court to order the production of relevant evidence in the possession of the plaintiff or a third party. In assessing these requests, the court takes into account the principle of proportionality and the applicable legal rules on confidentiality (Article 13(3) of the Collective Redress Act). Failure to comply with a court order to present evidence and/or the destruction or concealment of evidence shall be punishable by a procedural fine.[43] A conviction for a procedural fine does not prevent the court from reversing the burden of proof when the defendant's conduct leads to the impossibility of proof[44] for the claimant.

38. We must now discuss the condemnatory judgment in an action for damages and the destination of the compensation. The condemnatory sentence handed down in a collective action that determines the civil liability of the defendants, establishes the criteria for identifying the injured consumers and for quantifying the damages

---

38 Collective Redress Act art 10(6) (author translation).

39 Collective Redress Act art 10(7) (author translation).

40 Collective Redress Act art 10(8) (author translation).

41 Collective Redress Act art 10(9) (author translation).

42 Collective Redress Act art 13(1) (author translation).

43 Collective Redress Act art 13(4): 'The following conduct shall be punishable by a procedural fine to be set by the court pursuant to Article 417(2) of the Code of Civil Procedure: (a) failure or refusal to comply with an order to produce evidence issued pursuant to paragraphs 1 and 2; (b) destroying, concealing or otherwise making impossible effective access to evidence ordered to be produced pursuant to paragraphs 1 and 2.' (author translation).

44 PCC art 344(2): 'There is also a reversal of the burden of proof, when the opposing party has culpably made it impossible for the burdened party to prove, without prejudice to the sanctions that procedural law specifically mandates for disobedience or false statements' (author translation).

suffered by each injured consumer who is individually identified (Article 16(1) of the Collective Redress Act). If not all the injured consumers are individually identified, a global amount of compensation is fixed (Article 16(2) of the Collective Redress Act), and if that amount is not sufficient to compensate for the damage suffered by the injured consumers who have been individually identified in the meantime, that amount shall be distributed, in proportion to the respective damage, to the individually identified injured consumers (Article 16(3) of the Collective Redress Act). The court will have to designate the entity responsible for receiving, managing and paying the compensation owed to injured consumers who are not individually identified. The plaintiff or one or more injured consumers identified in the action may be designated for this purpose.[45]

39. Compensation that is not claimed, in whole or in part, by the injured consumers within a reasonable period set by the judge of the case shall be allocated to the payment of all costs, fees and other expenses incurred by the plaintiff as a result of the action (Article 16(6) of the Collective Redress Act). In this case, the remuneration of a third-party funder of the collective action shall be deemed to be an expense incurred by the plaintiff by virtue of the action, including with regard to the fairness and proportionality of such remuneration, as assessed by the court, by order made after the expiry of the reasonable period provided for in the preceding paragraph, in an incident processed as an appendix to the collective action.[46]

---

45 Collective Redress Act art 16(4): 'The judgement shall indicate the entity responsible for receiving, managing and paying the compensation due to injured consumers who are not individually identified, and the claimant or one or more injured consumers identified in the action may be designated for this purpose' (author translation).
Collective Redress Act art 16(5): 'And the claim for this amount must be made in accordance with the criteria established in the judgment, with consumers being able to identify: (a) Direct payment by the defendant to represented consumers who are still its customers and are identifiable; (b) Direct information by the defendant to the represented consumers through the channels with which it normally communicates with its customers, provided that it is on a durable medium, including a notice on an invoice, post, email or written telephone message, repeating this information in more than one monthly billing cycle, if applicable; (c) The use of one or more electronic platforms for the dissemination and distribution of global compensation, whether private or public in nature; (d) Information to the media and social networks' (author translation).

46 Collective Redress Act art 16 (7).
Collective Redress Act art 16 (8): 'Any remaining compensation that is not paid as a result of the statute of limitations or the impossibility of identifying the respective owners and that has not been allocated to the payment of the claimant's costs, fees and expenses in accordance with paragraph 5 shall revert: (a) 60% /prct per year to the Fund for the Promotion of Consumer Rights; (b) 40% to the Instituto de Gestão Financeira e Equipamentos da Justiça, I. P' (author translation).

Pioneering EU and National Digital Policy and Enforcement – the Romanian Experience

Romania

BOGDAN MARIUS CHIRIŢOIU[*]
VLAD DAN ROMAN[**]
Romanian Competition Council
Directorate-General for Competition, European Commission

Abstract

Beginning with its initial exploration of the e-commerce sector in Romania and progressing to antitrust enforcement, the Competition Council has taken a leading role in addressing competition concerns within the rapidly evolving national platform economy landscape. The Agency's entry into the EU digital policy world coincided with Romania's EU Council Presidency and continued through the enactment of the Digital Markets Act. Now, the new EU regime on fairness and contestability feeds into a regulatory dynamic which already counted competition law, unfair trading practice instruments or market failure legislation.

---

* Bogdan Marius Chiriţoiu, PhD, President of the Romanian Competition Council and Vice-President of the Administrative Board of the Agency for the Cooperation of Energy Regulators.

** Vlad Dan Roman, Seconded National Expert in Directorate-General for Competition, European Commission. The views and opinions of authors expressed herein do not necessarily state or reflect those of the Romanian Competition Council, European Competition Network, Digital Markets Advisory Committee, the High-level group for the Digital Markets Act, the European Commission or other EU bodies or institutions. The co-authors would like to express their gratitude to Dr Michael König and Dr Gunnar Wolf for their thorough review and invaluable suggestions for this chapter.

I. Introduction

1. This chapter covers a timeframe of five years, starting with the final period of the Junker Commission, and concluding the analysis with the last months of the current one. The Romanian Competition Council (NCA, RCC or the Agency) has been providing policy contributions to the digital regimes introduced by the P2B Regulation[1] as well as the Digital Markets Act (DMA), venturing into the realm of platform economy regulation as early as 2017.[2]

2. The enactment and subsequent application of the Digital Markets Act occurs within the context of the RCC transitioning towards becoming a markets' authority. Looking back over the past years, the Agency received new powers in areas which took on normative significance. The transition from competition policy and enforcement to a broader regulatory mandate grants the RCC a larger foundation for intervention. On this matter, new sector-specific or horizontal regulations, based on principles of business fairness are now placed within the NCA's monitoring and enforcement remits. At the same time, security and public order mandates have extended the legacy attributes of control in antitrust, mergers, respectively state aid.[3]

3. Considering the Digital Markets Act, the authors have structured their contribution on several areas of interest. These are instances where the Agency can initiate Digital Markets Act investigations, or where parallel enforcement action can be undertaken. Here, attention is given to the interplay between the DMA and the applicable legal framework for antitrust, respectively for unfair trading practices, and other legislation addressing market failures. At the same time, another relevant aspect involves the practical application of the Digital Markets Act at the national level, and the assistance provided by the NCA to the Commission, as sole enforcer of the DMA.[4] Throughout this chapter, a special focus is being placed on the idea of an effective application of the Digital Markets Act and the legal mechanics allowing for this.

II. The Initial Digital Policy Iterations

1. From Antitrust Enforcement to Digital Regulation

4. The NCA's initial exposure to the platform economy occurred via the domestic e-commerce sector inquiry[5] and the parallel enforcement action taken against eMAG, an e-commerce platform and one of the largest online marketplaces in

---

1 Regulation 2019/1150 of the European Parliament and of the Council of 20 June 2019 on promoting fairness and transparency for business users of online intermediation services (Platform-to-Business Regulation or P2B-Regulation) [2019] OJ L186/57.

2 Regulation 2022/1925 of the European Parliament and of the Council of 14 September 2022 on contestable and fair markets in the digital sector and amending Directives 2019/1937 and 2020/1828 (Digital Markets Act or DMA) [2022] OJ L265/1.

3 For more details regarding the overall process of becoming a markets authority, please see Bogdan Marius Chiriţoiu and Vlad Dan Roman, "The Romanian Competition Council: Towards Becoming a Markets Authority" (2023) 7 CoRe 179–182.

4 In terms of limitations, this chapter does not address the interplay between the DMA and the mergers regime. At the same time, it does not discuss aspects related to private enforcement.

5 Consiliul Concurenţei, "Raport al investigaţiei privind sectorul comerţului electronic" (2018) <www.consiliulconcurentei.ro/wp-content/uploads/2019/12/raport_al_investigatiei_privind_sectorul_comertului_electronic.pdf > accessed 27 November 2024.

Central and Eastern Europe.[6] This track record positioned the RCC as well placed to deal with the uncharted realm of business-to-business platform regulation, a task received during the Romanian Presidency of the EU Council. Here, the P2B Regulation was one of the files for which the rotating Presidency had represented the EU Council in negotiations with the European Parliament.

5. Through its Proposal for a Regulation, the Commission introduced enhanced transparency (and to some extent fairness) with a view to platforms' terms and conditions, including ranking mechanisms, data policies, respectively in consideration of cases involving differentiated treatment or parity requirements.

6. Given the dynamics of the times (i.e. the Romanian Presidency concluded 90 legislative files in 100 days[7]), the relatively complex nature of the file and the resistance from important stakeholders acknowledging the issues in digital markets but considering that it was not the right time to regulate, or that EU was set to stifle innovation, the proposal needed a push forward. Considering the growing significance of the platform economy in the NCA's priorities[8] and the potential of the policy to complement competition law enforcement,[9] the RCC assigned resources and ensured the needed governmental coordination in Bucharest and Brussels[10] supporting its advancement during the Council Presidency, in strong liaison with the Commission.

7. Given that the Romanian Council Presidency benefited for only half of its presidency in terms of legislative negotiations, this required back-to-back Council meetings for revised mandates and follow-on political and technical trilogues.[11] The process benefited of the prompt support from Member States and the Commission, which lead to the conclusion of an agreement with the European Parliament in the morning of 14 February 2019. In the Commission's words from that time, "[…] these [were] the first rules of this kind anywhere in the world" which "create[d] a benchmark for transparency" and "outlaw[ed] some of the most unfair practices" from the platform economy.[12]

---

6 Consiliul Concurenţei, "Consiliul Concurenţei a sancţionat Dante International cu 6,7 milioane euro" (2020) <https://luba.ro/wp-content/uploads/2020/12/amenda-Emag-dec-2020.pdf> accessed 27 November 2024.

7 See "How Romania's EU Council Presidency Delivered on Europe's Common Future" (*Politico* 10 July 2019) <www.politico.eu/sponsored-content/how-romanias-eu-council-presidency-delivered-on-europes-common-future/> accessed 27 November 2024.

8 Besides the national digital investigations pursued by the RCC, digital economy has been part of the secondment/mission letter of the Permanent Representation competition attaché.

9 Commission, Staff Working Document Impact Assessment accompanying the document Proposal for a Regulation of the European Parliament and of the Council on promoting fairness and transparency for business users of online intermediation services, SWD(2018) 138 final <https://eur-lex.europa.eu/legal-content/EN/TXT/HTML/?uri=CELEX:52018SC0138> accessed 27 November 2024.

10 This included both leadership and working level colleagues from the Permanent Representation of Romania to the European Union and the Romanian Ministry of Economy.

11 The opportunity to conclude legislative files spanned approximately two months within the total of six months of the Rotating Presidency, given the European Parliament elections which followed in May 2019. There were more than twenty meetings, which took place at various levels and formats (e.g. from working groups to COREPER; technical and political trilogues), short of counting the various engagements with stakeholders. Related to stakeholders, this was the first time the Commission and the co-legislators entered the territories of business-to-business platform regulation and confronted parts of the industry which, on the one hand, aimed to ringfence the regulation exclusively to transparency standards and, on the other, sought to minimise the information obligations as much as possible.

12 See "Brussels Tech Regulation Aims to Strengthen Businesses' Rights" *Financial Times* London, (14 February 2019) <www.ft.com/content/d5d56dee-3041-11e9-8744-e7016697f225> accessed 27 November 2024.

8. In the context of the P2B enactment, the discussion revolved around the nature of the new "digital norms" and the harmonisation effect enabled by the new regulation, which specifies that it "shall be without prejudice to national rules which, [...], prohibit or sanction unilateral conduct or unfair commercial practices"[13] if the P2B regulation doesn't cover certain relevant aspects.[14] The Commission statement following its adoption further clarifies that the P2B Regulation unfair trading practices regime only extends "to the extent that the issue in question is specifically regulated" by the P2B Regulation.[15] In this regard, "where the provisions [...] set out a specific level of transparency or specific information obligations" Member States cannot prescribe different ones.[16] Thus, in addition to the few substantive unfair trading practices that are prohibited, it becomes clear that the co-legislators have provided for a new regulatory layer which is largely aimed at fostering instances of market transparency, as a standalone regime.[17]

9. After the enactment of the file, the RCC received the enforcement mandate[18] for the regulation. Romania has been one of the fifteen Member States placing the enforcement in the hands of a public authority.[19] With this, the NCA gained an additional role, that of a digital regulator at the national level. From an institutional perspective, the new mandate had to be framed in compliance with the ECN+ Directive requirements, which prioritises the allocation of resources[20] for antitrust duties, by only gradually growing the team allocated to the new task.

10. Besides the legislative negotiations, another important moment which took place during the Romanian Presidency of the EU Council, related to DG-Comp being invited by the Council Working Party on Competition[21] to present its takeaways from the report

---

13 Furthermore, according to the P2B Regulation art 1(5) it "shall be without prejudice to Union law, in particular Union law applicable in the areas of judicial cooperation in civil matters, competition, data protection, trade secrets protection, consumer protection, electronic commerce and financial services".

14 Proposal for a Regulation of the European Parliament and of the Council on promoting fairness and transparency for business users of online intermediation services COM(2018) 238 <https://eur-lex.europa.eu/procedure/EN/2018_112> accessed 27 November 2024. The declaration further complements with "[...] provided that the national law is applied in conformity with Union law and is compatible with the Regulation".

15 This makes it clear that the Regulation does not cover every aspect of commercial relationships in a digital business-to-business setting.

16 *Ibid.*

17 Even though framed on previous antitrust focal points such as ranking, access to data, self-preferencing or parity clauses.

18 This took place through the Romanian Government's approval via the Emergency Ordinance No 23 of 31 March 2021 regarding measures for the implementation of the P2B-Regulation, on promoting fairness and transparency for business users of online intermediation services, as well as for amending and supplementing Competition Law No 21/1996. This has been followed-up by the Draft Law No 188/2021 for the approval of the Government Emergency Ordinance No 23/2021, which is expected to keep consistency with the approach in the Emergency Ordinance No 23/2021.

19 European Commission, Report on the first preliminary review on the implementation of Regulation 2019/1150 on promoting fairness and transparency for business users of online intermediation services COM(2023) 525 final, SWD(2023) 300 final, 11.

20 According to the legal text, Member States need to ensure "a sufficient number of qualified staff and sufficient financial, technical and technological resources". Directive 2019/1 of the European Parliament and of the Council of 11 December 2018 to empower the competition authorities of the Member States to be more effective enforcers and to ensure the proper functioning of the internal market [2019] OJ L11/3.

21 European Council Meeting, "Working Party on Competition" (6 May 2019) <www.consilium.europa.eu/en/meetings/mpo/2019/5/working-party-on-competition-(279587)/> accessed 27 November 2024.

of the special advisors to Commissioner Vestager "Competition policy for the digital era". The report already pointed out that "regulation can bolster the role competition law in protecting competition in the platform economy", referring to the new transparency regime enabled by the P2B Regulation.[22] This further validated the policy stance proposed by the Commission and embraced by the co-legislators during negotiations, in not providing for hard (substantive) restrictions in the absence of market power.[23] The report further provided for instances of market behaviour which would be best addressed by regulation, limiting this to market power-dependency types of cases.[24] It suggested a model where competition law would be "specify[ing] the general preconditions and inform the possible regulatory regimes",[25] especially where "similar issues arise continuously and intervention may be needed on an ongoing basis".[26]

2. A Policy Narrative Extending Across Two EU Regulations

11. In less than two years after discussing the report in the EU Council, the Digital Services Package,[27] incorporating two regulatory proposals, namely the Digital Services Act and the Digital Markets Act,[28] was adopted by the Commission. The latter embeds the same fairness objective as the P2B Regulation, now enabled by substantive obligations, to which the twin aim of ensuring contestable markets was added. This approach shielded against previous false positive concerns, as it solely applies to platforms that have a gatekeeping position. In this context, the threshold-based approach provided the legislator with a broader scope to comprehensively substantiate the concept of fairness, well beyond a common denominator applicable to the multitude of existing digital platforms.

12. Both the P2B Regulation and the Digital Markets Act are based on Article 114 Treaty on the Functioning of the European Union (TFEU). However, in the case of the Digital Markets Act, the Commission has been authorised to enact implementing acts, aiming to establish a unified approach in addressing the systematic issues arising from gatekeepers' behaviour. It is worth nothing that this comes as a result of the centralised enforcement set-up, which equipped the Commission with the exclusive authority to enforce the DMA.

13. At the same time, both regulations are framed around the principle of technological neutrality.[29] Here, the level of innovation exemplified in the legislative

---

22 Jacques Crémer, Yves-Alexandre de Montjoye and Heike Schweitzer, "Report: Competition Policy for the Digital Era" (*Publications Office of the European Union*, 2019) 7 and 70 <https://data.europa.eu/doi/10.2763/407537> accessed 27 November 2024.

23 *Ibid* 69: "[…] given the risk of errors, we feel that imposing far-reaching conduct rules on all platforms, irrespective of market power, could be a dangerous path, given that many types of conduct – including potentially self-preferential conduct – may have pro-competitive effects".

24 *Ibid.*

25 *Ibid* 109.

26 *Ibid* 7 and 70. The report provides for the example to subject platforms to an interoperability regime. The authors continue by stating that they would not envision a new type of "public utility regulation" opposing risks associated with lack of flexibility (126).

27 European Commission, "The Digital Services Act package" <https://digital-strategy.ec.europa.eu/en/policies/digital-services-act-package> accessed 27 November 2024.

28 DMA [2022] OJ L265/1.

29 P2B Regulation recital 13 and DMA recital 14.

process varies in line with the pace of technological developments. In 2019, the then technologically neutral approach meant that the definition of online search engines would encompass, for example, voice requests. In 2024, we can see that the Digital Markets Act factors in further advancements such as Artificial Intelligence. Of relevance is the Digital Markets Act High Level Group joint statement acknowledging that "[t]o the extent that such AI systems are embedded into designated core platform services, the DMA obligations apply, and compliance has to be assessed taking into account how AI systems determine the behaviours that are covered by the Digital Market Act provisions".[30] Furthermore, the Digital Markets Act benefits from the P2B Regulation legal infrastructure in terms of its definitions, e.g. for online intermediation service and online search engines, building on what the co-legislators codified in 2019.

14. The overall policy narrative indicates that the general P2B regime has served as a precursor to the Digital Markets Act, *sine qua non* without which the later – special regime – would have been hard to imagine. A strong indicator for this is the design of the review clause in the P2B Regulation, which covers several practices for which the Digital Markets Act either prohibits or establishes positive obligations.[31] The review clause mandated the Commission to analyse issues, such as the systemic nature of problems caused by unfair commercial practices, the issue of fair competition in online intermediation, including the misuse of privileged data, or concerns linked to behaviour of operating systems providers. This was intended to be accomplished with a focus on fairness, particularly considering the option of reevaluating the enforcement mechanism.[32] Importantly, the prohibitions and obligations now outlined in the Digital Markets Act were preceded by discussions in which it was proposed to equip the P2B Regulation with a general fairness clause, or potentially transform many transparency obligations into substantive bans. However, these proposals did not find a majority among the co-legislators, because the P2B Regulation retained its horizontal nature.

15. Throughout the P2B Regulation and Digital Markets Act legislative process, the co-legislators have been preoccupied to equip the two legal instruments with mechanisms which would ensure their effective application. For example, during its last iterations, the P2B Regulation gained an increased level of detail or specificity in covering access via functionalities and interfaces, or entry points, thus substantiating the discussion on effective application. This was further observed by way of the European Parliament amendments aimed at the introduction of an anti-circumvention mechanism.[33]

16. While the co-legislators fell short of equipping the P2B Regulation with an anti-circumvention provision, they managed to complement the Digital Markets

---

30 European Commission, "High-Level Group on the Digital Markets Act: Public Statement on Artificial Intelligence" (22 May 2024) <https://digital-markets-act.ec.europa.eu/high-level-group-digital-markets-act-public-statement-artificial-intelligence-2024-05-22_en> accessed 27 November 2024.

31 P2B-Regulation art 18.

32 P2B-Regulation art 18.

33 European Parliament, "Report on a European Strategy on Cooperative Intelligent Transport Systems" (2018) <www.europarl.europa.eu/doceo/document/A-8-2018-0444_EN.html> accessed 27 November 2024.

Act set of obligations with such a mechanism, giving full magnitude to the idea of effective implementation of the law. Considering the *ex ante* nature of the DMA, it would be expected that its applications would imply looking more into the law itself. Yet, Article 13 (anti-circumvention), respectively, Article 8 (compliance with obligations for gatekeepers) of the Digital Markets Act help transitions from a "tick-box" style application to a truly effective implementation, where the legal interpretation fully embodies the two guiding principles, namely, contestability and fairness. This follows the legislative approach adopted by the co-legislators which, aware of the dynamics in digital markets, have purposively strengthened its scope and reach. The political choices backing the DMA allowed for such a provision, to appropriately address all forms of conduct that fall short of the broader delegation mandate outlined in Article 12 of the Digital Markets Act. Going into more detail, it can be observed that both the digital and competition communities have shared this concern. Taking a close look at two competition-inspired provisions of the Digital Markets Act i.e. Articles 5(3) – prohibition of parity, and 6(5) – ban on self-preferencing in ranking, the corresponding recitals[34] further incriminate behaviour amounting to an "equivalent effect" to the respective practices. This wording is very similar to that used in the *Google Shopping* decision, where the Commission ordered that the undertaking should refrain from any conduct "having the same or an equivalent object or effect" as the one at stake.[35]

17. Considering the *zeitgeist* of the Union's political cycle analysed by the authors, one could also add the Commission's initial thinking on the proposal of a new competition tool as feeding into the same policy narrative, of closing possible loopholes or gaps when equipping enforcers with the necessary set of tools.

18. It can thus be concluded that, across the broader policy cycle, commencing with the P2B Regulation and during the adoption process of the Digital Markets Act, there has been a constant focus from policymakers on ways to operationalise the principle of effectiveness (in contrast to a mood towards formalism and pronounced limiting principles) and also to develop strategies to combat circumvention.

19. Overall, there have been several initiatives, like the proposal for a so-called general fairness clause during the P2B Regulation co-decision process, the mechanisms to prevent circumvention (which only made it into the Digital Markets Act) or the idea of a new competition tool. These all are good examples of measures aimed at ensuring that illicit conduct does not "slip through the cracks" and that breaches with a higher level of complexity in probing would not receive a false negative label. In this regard, these EU-level preoccupations have been mirrored by national-level initiatives, which – from a policy perspective – triggered the necessity for a harmonised approach throughout the internal market.[36]

---

34 DMA recitals 39 and 52.

35 Case AT.39740 – *(Google Search (Shopping))* Decision of 27 June 2017 relating to a proceeding under Article 102 TFEU and Article 54 of the EEA Agreement C(2017) 4444 final, art 3 <https://eur-lex.europa.eu/legal-content/EN/TXT/?uri=CELEX%3A52018XC0112%2801%29&qid=1720456993009> accessed 27 November 2024.

36 From these examples, it is only the DMA anti-circumvention clause which received EU-level normative power, the rest remaining at the state of past policy proposals or amendments.

III. Regulatory Dynamics: Market Failures, Fragmented Regulation and Oversight

1. Policy Drivers Considered by the Digital Markets Act Impact Assessment

20. The Digital Markets Act impact assessment identifies market failures, fragmented regulation and oversight as the primary drivers that make the new policy necessary. Romania has been identified by the DMA's *travaux préparatoires* as one of the jurisdictions where some initiatives have already occurred, an overall fact which introduced the necessity for EU-level intervention.[37] Here, the Digital Markets Act impact assessment identified legislative initiatives (e.g. Germany, France and Romania) "correcting disparities in the relationships between digital platforms with economic power and their business users" or different instruments addressing market failures (e.g. Greece, Romania).

21. Considering that the scope of intervention for these tools is virtually limited to the national dimension, the Digital Markets Act impact assessment provides that individual intervention by Member States or NCAs would be inadequate for effectively addressing "gatekeeper related market failures across the Union".[38] At the same time, in order to avoid fragmented regulation and oversight where such instruments exist, the co-legislators (especially the EU Council) provided for specific cooperation and coordination mechanisms.

22. From the moment of the DMA's impact assessment, the domestic unfair trading practices regime has undergone amendments,[39] introducing the prohibition on leveraging a superior bargaining position, a policy similar to the one adopted by other Member States.[40] Here, the dependency criteria follows a horizontal logic, since the measures apply across the board rather than targeting specific sectors.[41] The level of intervention is not tied to dominance – as defined in competition law – but it is scoped by market features favouring significant imbalances between undertakings. This is to be assessed according to a set of cumulative criteria such as the existence of an imbalanced power relationship,[42] factors determining the importance of commercial relationships[43] and respectively the lack of an equivalent alternative trading option.

---

37 According to the impact assessment, "Member States have begun to take regulatory initiatives to address these [distortive] effects, potentially fragmenting the Internal Market". It further develops that this can lead to both fragmented regulation and oversight.

38 *Ibid* pts 1/2, 27–29.

39 Ministerul Justiţiei, Ordonanţă de urgenţă 84/2022 privind combaterea acţiunilor speculative şi pentru modificarea şi completarea unor acte normative <https://legislatie.just.ro/Public/DetaliiDocument/256569> accessed 27 November 2024.

40 Other EU Member States which adopted similar regimes are Germany, France, Belgium and Italy. The NCA already investigated a possible breach under the new regime. See Consiliul Concurenţei, "Raport privind Inspecţiile Oxigen" (June 2024) <www.consiliulconcurentei.ro/wp-content/uploads/2024/06/Inspectii-oxigen-iun-2024.pdf> accessed 27 November 2024.

41 Through contrast, the P2B Regulation imposes sector-specific measures, which – to a large extent – translate in an increased level of transparency or specific information obligations which are regarded as fully harmonised across the European Union.

42 Which can arise from factors like market share or brand recognition.

43 The significant sales or purchases, roles of key inputs, and sunk costs related to the investment.

23. At the same time, Romania is also mentioned as one of the very few Member States[44] which benefits from an instrument that enables the NCA to tackle market failures.[45] The market investigation tool, intended to correct market failures, drew inspiration from the model put in place by the United Kingdom.[46] The Romanian NCA is empowered to impose any remedial measures it deems appropriate – including of a structural nature – to solve market dysfunctions that impede market competition. Such remedies are subject to a suitability and proportionality test but do not require the finding of an individual infringement, in the sense of EU or national antitrust law.[47] However, the Agency has not tested this tool yet; it has rather served as a deterrence mechanism, especially when considering the imposition of last-resort remedies, such as divestitures.

24. Considering the broad powers for which the NCA has asked and received at the national level, there was no surprise during the Digital Markets Act legislative process that the RCC would support measures covering all foreseeable regulatory blind spots. The RCC has advocated for measures fit to ensure an effective application of the DMA, be it in terms of substance (e.g. the anti-circumvention mechanism) or procedure (e.g. monitoring via retention orders[48]).[49] The same level of support has been shown for the governance of the Digital Markets Act (e.g. centralised enforcement) as well as for the cooperation and coordination mechanisms.

2. The Prohibition on Leveraging a Superior Bargaining Position and the Market Investigation Tool

25. For both, (i) the prohibition of leveraging a superior bargaining position, and (ii) the market investigation tool, the national legislator has opted to give prominence to structural attributes i.e. "market features which favour the emergence of significant imbalances between undertakings" and "market dysfunctions that

---

44 Together with Greece. In the meantime, Denmark has operated relevant amendments to its regime. See Christian Bergqvist and Mark Gall, "Significant Amendments to the Danish Competition Act" (*Kluwer Competition Law Blog*, 5 June 2024) <https://competitionlawblog.kluwercompetitionlaw.com/2024/06/05/significant-amendments-to-the-danish-competition-act/> accessed 27 November 2024.

45 Romania was one of the few authorities that have a very similar tool to the so-called "new competition tool" which was under consideration by the European Commission during 2020. For more details regarding this instrument please see, European Commission, "Single Market – new complementary tool to strengthen competition enforcement" <https://ec.europa.eu/info/law/better-regulation/have-your-say/initiatives/12416-Single-Market-new-complementary-tool-to-strengthen-competition-enforcement_en> accessed 27 November 2024.

46 UK Competition and Markets Authority, "CMA Response to the Digital Services Act Package and New Competition Tool Consultations" <https://assets.publishing.service.gov.uk/media/5f5f4b36e90e076cd6c18186/CMA-response_to_DSA_and_NCT_consultations.pdf> accessed 27 November 2024.

47 Romanian Competition Law No 21/1996 art 25(5)(c).

48 The aim of the retention orders is to ensure that designated gatekeepers preserve relevant documents and information relevant to the Commission's monitoring of compliance as well as potential investigations. These only mandate for a preservation of documents obligation as the gatekeepers must hand over all relevant documents solely upon request.

49 Prior to supporting an update to the mechanisms of Regulation 1/2003 of 16 December 2002 on the implementation of the rules on competition laid down in Articles 81 and 82 of the Treaty [2003] OJ L1/1, via the DMA, the RCC's work related to digital inspections has been presented to the European Commission and other NCAs.

disrupt the competitive process", respectively. With respect to the leveraging of a superior bargaining position, the legal text requires the existence of an explicit behavioural limb. The abuse (exploitation) needs to be demonstrated via actions or inactions. It must also arise in commercial dealings which can possibly cause significant harm to the undertaking, and respectively impact market competition.[50]

26. As a general framework, the interplay between the Digital Markets Act and national laws is set out in Article 1, paragraphs (5) to (7) of the DMA Regulation and the corresponding recitals.[51] While all these paragraphs serve a harmonisation purpose, the co-legislators have provided for caveats, enabling the parallel application of other EU or national regimes.[52]

27. Article 1(5) DMA provides that "in order to avoid the fragmentation of the internal market, Member States shall not impose further obligations on gatekeepers by way of laws, regulations or administrative measures" for the purpose of the objectives protected by the Digital Markets Act. Thus, Member States are prohibited from introducing national legislation that would impose fairness and contestability obligations on gatekeepers. However, Member States can still regulate issues lying beyond the Digital Markets Act scope and objectives. In such cases, these obligations need to meet the compatibility criteria with Union law and not result from the fact that the relevant undertakings have the status of a gatekeeper.

28. When assessing the scope of domestic intervention, it must be mentioned that Article 1(5) of the Digital Markets Act is complemented by two other provisions which enrich its contours. Article 8(1) DMA provides that gatekeepers cannot use the Digital Markets Act to escape other regulatory obligations and need to also factor in compliance with other regulatory rules e.g. consumers protection, product safety, regimes which themselves can fall under the concept of "laws, regulations or administrative measures" to which Article 1(5) relates. Furthermore, Article 13(6) DMA provides for the prohibition of so-called "dark patterns", elements which can also fall under an existing part of the acquis (e.g. consumer protection).[53] By importing elements from other regimes in the compliance standards of the Digital Markets Act, this broad "vacuum effect" of Article 1(5) functions to ensure both effectiveness and to shield against circumvention, neutralising

---

50 For completeness, it is worth noting that after the COVID-19 outbreak, Romania further added an anti-gouging tool to its unfair trading practices regime, which addresses instances of speculative exposures occurring in very specific circumstances. Regardless of the business model, undertakings are banned from engaging in behaviour which would lead to unwarranted increases in prices or major disparities between supply and demand. The analysis factors in artificial cost hikes, unusual distribution chains, unjustified production limits, stockpiling, and compares past prices.

51 DMA recitals 8, 9, 10 and 11.

52 In terms of limiting principles, one should also not forget about Regulation 1/2003 [2003] OJ L1/1 art 3(2), which provides that the application of national competition law may not lead to the prohibition of behaviours "which may affect trade between Member States but which do not restrict competition within the meaning of Article 101(1) of the Treaty, or which fulfil the conditions of Article 101(3) of the Treaty or which are covered by a Regulation for the application of Article 101(3) of the Treaty".

53 For more details please see OECD, "Dark Commercial Patterns" (*OECD*, 2023) Working Paper No 336 <www.oecd.org/en/publications/dark-commercial-patterns_44f5e846-en.html> accessed 27 November 2024; Competition and Markets Authority, "Online Choice Architecture: How Digital Design Can Harm Competition and Consumers" (*CMA*, 7 April 2022) <www.gov.uk/government/publications/online-choice-architecture-how-digital-design-can-harm-competition-and-consumers> accessed 27 November 2024.

situations where there would be still room to game the system. Given the internal market objective of the Digital Markets Act an EU-wide approach is important and needs to be prioritised. However, in the theoretical case where the regime at stake would provide for a delta coming out from a possibly more extensive standard (than the one prescribed under the Digital Markets Act), parallel action should benefit of coherent outcomes.

29. At the same time, Article 1(6) DMA provides – *expressis verbis* – that the Digital Markets Act is without prejudice to the application of Articles 101 and 102 TFEU, respectively their national equivalents. Here, Article 1(6) paragraph (b) DMA limits the "without prejudice" to specific competition rules. In this regard, prohibitions on other forms of unilateral conduct are only allowed in cases where the conduct under scrutiny leads to "further obligations" on gatekeepers, that would not go against its harmonisation aspect. When scoping the relevant competition rules caught under this paragraph, reference is being made to "individualised assessment of market positions and behaviour".[54]

30. However, independent of the nature of the national norm and possible variations in terms of mandated assessment and subsequent legal test, Article 1(7) DMA provides for the general obligation for any national authorities to consider. The ban on taking national decisions going against a decision adopted by the Commission under the Digital Markets Act is an overarching obligation, applicable across national administrations and bodies; thus, it is not circumscribed to the application of the relation between Digital Markets Act and competition law.[55]

31. The theoretical foundations for the parallel application of competition law and the Digital Markets Act, respectively the cooperation and coordination mechanisms are further described in the next section.

IV. The Parallel Application of Articles 101 and 102 TFEU and the Digital Markets Act

1. Exploring the Theoretical Foundations

32. The relationship between the Digital Markets Act and competition law is determined by Article 1(6) and (7) and Recitals 10 and 11 DMA. The general principles of EU law also play a role in this regard.[56] Furthermore, other rules on cooperation between the Commission with national authorities can be found in Articles 37 and 38 DMA and the corresponding recitals,[57] being introduced by the co-legislators

---

54 According to DMA recital 10, this includes the precise scope of the illegal practice, its actual or eventual effects and the option to provide for efficiency and objective justifications for the behaviour at stake. For more details please see Dr Gunnar Wolf and Dr Niklas Brüggemann, "AGENDA 2025: The Digital Markets Act And Section 19a Gwb" (*D'Kart*, 19 July 2022) <www.d-kart.de/en/blog/2022/07/19/agenda-2025-der-digital-markets-act-und-%C2%A719a-gwb/> accessed 27 November 2024.

55 Case C-344/98 *Masterfoods Ltd (t/a Mars Ireland) v HB Ice Cream Ltd* ECLI:EU:C:2000:689.

56 In particular the principle of sincere cooperation. See, Consolidated Version of the Treaty on European Union [2012] OJ C326/13 art 4(3) <https://eur-lex.europa.eu/resource.html?uri=cellar:2bf140bf-a3f8-4ab2-b506-fd71826e6da6.0023.02/DOC_1&format=PDF> accessed 27 November 2024.

57 DMA recitals 90 and 91.

during co-decision, for the purpose of satisfying the aim for more predictability in terms of governance.

33. As provided in the above section, the Digital Markets Act and competition law are complementary instruments. This is the case as both safeguard distinct legal objectives and are operationalised via distinct mechanisms,[58] respectively they are accommodated by previous EU case law on the interaction of competition rules and other regulatory tools.[59] Here, the Digital Markets Act enables an *ex ante* regime based on Article 114 TFEU which only addresses situations of severe asymmetry i.e. important gateways for specific online services. This comes in contrast to anti-trust law, which applies to undertakings in general[60] and which addresses direct harm to consumers or indirect ones through effects on the competitive process. This is distinct from the Digital Markets Act, which provides for an exhaustive list of prohibitions and obligations that mandate intervention in cases of unfairness and lack of market contestability.

34. In practical terms, competition law may apply concurrently to the actions of a designated gatekeeper, whether entirely or in instances where the behaviour does not fall squarely within the scope of Digital Markets Act obligations. In terms of corporate scope, it can relate to other parts of the undertaking's structure where the gatekeeper may operate core platform services for which it has not been designated[61] or where the services do not qualify as such. Another perspective could be to view antitrust and Digital Markets Act enforcement as a continuous force, with antitrust measures taking precedence long before the designation of a gatekeeper,[62] while the DMA addresses the concerns that arise after designation.[63] In addition, antitrust future-proofs this overall enforcement system,[64] by tackling completely new anti-competitive strategies, not necessarily captured by the current text of the DMA.

2. A National Perspective on the Parallel Application

35. During the Digital Markets Act legislative negotiations, the RCC supported the view that the effective application of the DMA implies coordination with competition policy, to be best achieved by drawing inspiration from the legacy antitrust procedural framework, and possibly updating it. It also called on the Commission to ensure complementary antitrust and Digital Markets Act cases, whether at national or EU level, benefit from an unparalleled cooperation track, by accommodating the Digital Markets Act alongside the competition framework.

---

58 DMA recital 11.

59 In a manner akin to that of other regulated sectors such as telecom, energy or finance. For further details please see: Case C-117/20 *Bpost SA v Autorite Belge de la Concurrence* ECLI:EU:C:2022:202.

60 While only dominant undertakings are captured by the prohibition to abuse their position.

61 Or as provided by DMA art 5(8), which meet the thresholds in art 3(2), point (b) without necessarily being designated as gatekeepers.

62 The temporary dimension of antitrust investigations is scoped around past conduct.

63 DMA art 3(10) provides that compliance needs to be ensured in six months from designation.

64 Composed of competition law and the Digital Markets Act.

36. Here, by drawing inspiration from Article 11(3) and (4) of Regulation 1/2003,[65] the Digital Markets Act imports mechanisms which have been tested and perfected under the European Competition Network (ECN) framework. Furthermore, the NCA welcomed that the DMA mandates that the ECN be the relevant fora in which the Commission and NCAs should carry out their cooperation and coordination with a view to parallel enforcement actions. Here, the ECN offers a legacy framework which has been operationalised and developed by allowing NCAs "to pool their experience and identify best practices" both on policy, and respectively on case substance and procedure.[66]

37. The Digital Markets Act mandates for cooperation and coordination between the Commission and national authorities for the scope of achieving "effective, complementary and coherent enforcement of the available legal instruments".[67] Operationalisation of these principles should lead to the optimal utilisation or resources and actions that are mutually supportive.

38. Article 38 DMA provides for the legal framework steering the coordination and cooperation process, to take place at the outset and at the conclusion of national investigations. Here – in the second paragraph – it provides that an NCA needs to notify the Commission in writing before or immediately after taking a "first formal investigative measure".[68] At the same time, it requires – in the third paragraph – that if an NCA plans to impose obligations on gatekeepers under national competition laws, it must communicate the draft measure to the Commission at least 30 days before adoption. This notice needs to be accompanied by the justification for the measure.

39. The Romanian Competition Council aims at building on the best practices in terms of cooperation developed under the antitrust cooperation in Regulation 1/2003,[69] and – where it is the case – will continue to have timely exchanges with Commission services from the very incipient stages of an investigation. Furthermore, the NCA has a customary practice of engaging on the merits of a case from an early stage i.e. before sending the statement of objections to the undertaking, well before drafting a decision. Having this as a premise, the potential for enforcement actions to overlap will be safeguarded by timely exchanges.

40. Besides the matter of resources and avoidance redundancies, the NCA would also factor in the degree to which the available enforcement tools can address the extent of the conduct's reach, either in substance or geography. Given the *ex ante* nature of the Digital Markets Act, it enables quicker enforcement actions compared to competition law. Here, it is evident that one of the initial effects of DMA investigations is to broaden the scope of scrutiny from specific

---

65 Regulation 1/2003 [2003] OJ L1/1, that provide for similar requirements for investigations and decisions pursued by the NCAs under Articles 101 and/or 102 TFEU.

66 Referred in DMA art 38. More on the European Competition Network (ECN) can be found at <https://competition-policy.ec.europa.eu/antitrust-and-cartels/european-competition-network_en> accessed 27 November 2024.

67 DMA recital 90.

68 DMA art 38.

69 Regulation 1/2003 [2003] OJ L1/1.

markets – as in antitrust cases – to a more generalised level (e.g. from music streaming to the entire inventory of an app store or from one to a variety of vertical/specialised search services).[70] In addition to the scale argument, by implementing the Digital Markets Act there is no longer a need to define markets, determine effects or analyse possible efficiencies of the respective behaviour, or for permitting ambitious deadlines, such as the envisaged 12 months for closing investigations.[71]

41. With a view to determining the levels of fines and periodic penalty payments, the Digital Markets Act mandates for further coordination between the relevant national authorities and the Commission. This is aimed at ensuring that the principles of proportionality and *ne bis in idem* are respected. In this regard, Recital 86 DMA requires consideration of any fines and penalties imposed on the same undertaking for identical actions in national cases.[72]

42. When imagining possible investigations, consideration should be given beyond Article 102 TFEU. Article 101 TFEU which can also hold significance when it comes to the relationship between the undertakings scoped by the Digital Markets Act, be it in the process of complying with the Articles 5, 6 and 7 or in the larger dynamics of the fast-moving digital sector. Incentives to maintain the *status quo* (e.g. in terms of less qualitative compliance solutions) via collusion or to allow for coordination which would enable mutually beneficial industry standards – at the expense of effective compliance – could bring these practices within the remits of horizontal competition. At the same time, anti-poaching agreements are not uncommon in digital markets.[73] Article 101 TFEU investigations could complement Digital Markets Act lines of inquiry and broaden the level of intervention at lengths which are not necessarily covered by the DMA itself. Here, a potential outcome of rapid market intervention – be it via the DMA or antitrust – could lead to having designated gatekeepers also challenging the incumbent market status of other gatekeepers for specific core platform services. While this might not be the case in instances where gatekeepers protect their incumbency via commercial arrangements or technical measures – generating walled gardens – the DMA fosters incentives that keep markets contestable while driving innovation. Examples include the implementation and propagation of effective choice screens or easy default switching, which create new business opportunities for entering other markets where incumbents' positions are no longer shielded.[74]

---

70 European Commission. "Commission opens non-compliance investigations against Alphabet, Apple, and Meta under Digital Markets Act" (25 March 2024) <https://digital-markets-act.ec.europa.eu/commission-opens-non-compliance-investigations-against-alphabet-apple-and-meta-under-digital-markets-2024-03-25_en> accessed 27 November 2024.

71 DMA art 29(2).

72 Related to breaches of other Union or national regulations. This aligns the DMA with *Bpost SA* (n 59).

73 United States Department of Justice, "Justice Department requires six high tech companies to stop entering into anticompetitive employee solicitation agreements" (*Office of Public Affairs*, 24 September 2010) <www.justice.gov/opa/pr/justice-department-requires-six-high-tech-companies-stop-entering-anticompetitive-employee> accessed 27 November 2024.

74 See, "Big Tech's Competitive New Era: Clashes Ahead" (*Enders Analysis*, 7 July 2023) <www.endersanalysis.com/reports/big-techs-competitive-new-era-clashes-ahead> accessed 27 November 2024.

V. National Implementation of the Digital Markets Act: New Amendments to the Romanian Competition Law

1. The Amendments to the Romanian Competition Law

43. Besides the current antitrust investigation into Apple for a possible abuse of dominant position on the market of advertising through iOS mobile applications,[75] the RCC's digital portfolio is further extended by regulatory means. From a substantive perspective, Recital 91 of the Digital Markets Act acknowledges that it might not be clear from the outset if an infringement relates to the Digital Markets Act, competition law or both.[76] For this reason, the co-legislators have provided the possibility for Member States to empower their national competent authorities enforcing competition rules to investigate potential non-compliance by gatekeepers. Here, as the older policy covering undertakings in general, competition law benefits from more clarity. Its remits have already been set by national and EU-level administrative practice (including the issuance of guidelines) and further clarified by the courts' review. This is especially true when it comes to defining markets, the need to prove effects or to take into consideration possible efficiencies. At the same time, competition law benefits from a high degree of harmonisation in the substantive standard of infringements.[77] The Digital Markets Act will only build this precedent-based legal infrastructure as we move forward. However, going back to Articles 8 (effectiveness) and 13 (anti-circumvention) DMA, it is clear from the outset that the scope of the Digital Markets Act infringements will be further advanced by these two provisions, thus touching on the remits of antitrust investigations.

44. Accordingly and as provided by the Romanian Emergency Ordinance 108/2023,[78] the NCA has been mandated to carry out investigations regarding possible violation, on the territory of Romania, of Articles 5–7 of the Digital Markets Act, and to report to the Commission on the findings such investigations, to assist the Commission in its role of single authority empowered to ensure compliance with the DMA.[79] These new duties are to be carried out by competition inspectors[80] and decided upon by the Board of the RCC. Here, an investigation into possible infringements – affecting the national territory – can be launched *ex officio*, with prior notification of the Commission.[81] Eventual Digital Markets

---

75 Consiliul Concurenţei, "Consiliul Concurenţei investighează piaţa publicităţii prin aplicaţii instalate pe dispozitive mobile Apple (iOS)" (October 2023) <www.consiliulconcurentei.ro/wp-content/uploads/2023/10/Inv-App-oct-2023.pdf> accessed 27 November 2024.

76 Exemplifying, before evaluating all necessary information, a behaviour might seem not to fall – at least squarely – within the scope of DMA obligations or prohibitions.

77 This will be furthermore advanced also by the theoretical/conceptual framework fostered by the digital regulation and competition scholars and doctrine.

78 Emergency Ordinance No 108 of 29 November 2023, for amending and supplementing Competition Law No 21/1996, as well as other normative acts. This was complemented by Law No 231/2024 regarding the approval of the Government Emergency Ordinance No 108/2023 for amending and supplementing Competition Law No 21/1996, as well as other normative acts.

79 Legea concurenţei 21/1996 art 25(1), letter w).

80 *Ibid* art 32(1).

81 *Ibid* art 33(1), letter c).

Act investigations would benefit from the same procedural toolbox as used in antitrust, including requests of information,[82] dawn raids,[83] taking interviews[84] or statements.[85] According to the latest clarifications provided in the amendments to the competition law, the inspection activity is not limited to classical paper documents but can be checked and retrieve any information stored or archived in the electronic environment, regardless of the medium on which it is located. This provision now spells out the principle of technological neutrality in national procedural law. The provision further exemplifies devices such as: mobile phones, tablets, personal digital assistants or laptops. This includes personal devices used for work-related matters. Simultaneously, it does not depend on the location where the data is stored or archived (e.g. external server or cloud).[86]

45. On this point, the Digital Markets Act does not allow NCAs to issue a decision setting out its finding of substantive non-compliance with Articles 5, 6 or 7 DMA, but does not preclude it from imposing possible sanctions based on procedural grounds (e.g. for providing misleading information following a request of information from the NCA), on gatekeepers.

46. Once an investigation has concluded that that the behaviour at stake would be a Digital Markets Act infringement, the RCC submits a report to the Commission, which then has the discretion to decide what solution it will adopt under the DMA.[87] Given that the RCC would not take any substantive decision, other procedural steps would not be pursued at the national level e.g. engaging with the gatekeepers for possible comments on the investigation report, organising a hearing or providing access to the file.[88] At the same time, the opening of proceedings by the Commission under the Digital Markets Act ends an investigation, and where it is already ongoing relieves the NCAs of the possibility to conduct it under the DMA.

2. Supporting the Commission under the Digital Markets Act

47. The co-legislators have opted for a centralised enforcement system, granting the Commission the role of sole enforcer of the Digital Markets Act. This approach has been endorsed by the RCC in Romania's general position throughout the legislative process, for the purpose of ensuring the uniform application of the new instrument. In this regard, the powers to issue decisions reside with the Commission, while national agencies play a role in assisting and contributing to the effective enforcement of the law. This is different from the case where a NCA would investigate possible non-compliance by gatekeepers with Articles 5, 6 and 7 DMA in its jurisdiction.

---

82 *Ibid* art 34.
83 *Ibid* art 38.
84 *Ibid* art 37.
85 *Ibid* art 36.
86 *Ibid* art 38.
87 *Ibid* art 46(6).
88 *Ibid* arts 44(1) and 44(8), which allows the parties concerned to consult the file and obtain electronic copies and/or extracts of documents from the investigation procedure.

48. Regarding the assistance provided to the Commission, this relates to inspections, interviews, the collection and transfer of information and respectively support in regard to market investigations and the monitoring of compliance. With a view to dawn raids, the Commission may request – with adequate forewarning – the assistance of the national competent authority of the Member State, enforcing the rules referred to in Article 1(6) DMA in whose territory the inspection is to be conducted.[89] Linked to this, the NCA may also assist in the preparation of the inspection. This scenario may refer to obtaining judicial authorisation.[90] Linked to this, the NCA's case-handlers may assist the Commission officials in interview procedures carried out in Romania. This would not be something new for the NCA, as similar actions supporting the Commission have been carried out under Regulation 1/2003.

49. In addition, the Digital Markets Act provides that, based on a letter of appointment,[91] NCA officials may assist the Commission in monitoring the compliance of gatekeepers with the obligations, and respectively with measures imposed under the Digital Markets Act.[92] This may refer to the implementation and compliance by gatekeepers with the prohibitions and obligations laid down in Articles 5 to 7 DMA as well as with specification decisions,[93] i.e. decisions finding systematic non-compliance,[94] imposing interim measures,[95] making commitments binding[96] and non-compliance decisions.[97] Furthermore, the Commission may request one or more NCAs to assist or support its market investigations for designating gatekeepers (pursuant to Articles 17), into systematic non-compliance (pursuant to Article 18) or into new services and practices (pursuant to Article 19).[98] This would relate to gathering, providing and analysing information received from gatekeeper or any other source.

50. Even though the Digital Markets Act does not provide for a formal complaint mechanism, any third party[99] can contact the RCC in order to provide information about possible conduct of a core platform service for which a gatekeeper has been designated under the Digital Markets Act. Here, if the NCA concludes that – *prima facie* – there might be a possible breach of the DAM, it will transfer the information to the Commission,[100] which – subject to its discretion – may utilise the information as evidence in a possible inquiry.

51. The support for the Commission's work is also taking place via the Digital Markets Advisory Committee (DMAC),[101] and respectively the High-Level Group on the Digital

---

89 DMA art 23(3).

90 DMA arts 23(9) and 23(10).

91 To be issued following consultation between the Commission and the NCA in question.

92 DMA art 26(2) and recital 85.

93 DMA art 8.

94 DMA art 18.

95 DMA art 24.

96 DMA art 25.

97 DMA art 29.

98 DMA arts 16(5) and 38(6).

99 Including business users, competitors, or end-users

100 DMA art 27(3).

101 Classified as a committee under Regulation 182/2011 of the European Parliament and of the Council of 16 February 2011 laying down the rules and general principles concerning mechanisms for control by Member States of the Commission's exercise of implementing powers, as voted on 13 January 2023.

Markets Act (DMA HLG). Both are part of the DMA's governance mechanisms. However, while the DMAC provides that each Member State is to be considered as one member of the committee,[102] the DMA HLG[103] is composed of European regulatory bodies and networks,[104] represented by a part of their member authorities.[105]

52. The DMAC offers support to the Commission in its day-to-day enforcement practice. This relates to the adoption of implementing acts under the DMA, mainly through the advisory procedures. The RCC sits on behalf of the Romanian administration in the DMAC and has attended all meetings, supporting the Committee's work in matters such as the adoption of the opinions on the DMA Implementing Regulation,[106] and respectively on several draft decisions on market investigations pursued under Articles 3(5) and 17(3) DMA.

53. At the same time, the RCC supported the creation of the HLG during the legislative phase, and its operationalisation starting in November 2022. Currently, the RCC Chairman is one of the six representatives of the ECN in the HLG,[107] while the RCC case-handlers contribute to the technical-level work. Here, the exchanges in the HLG are of utmost importance in building synergies between the different regimes and having unified approaches across instruments. Besides going in the direction of the cooperation mandated by the CJEU,[108] the HLG is also very well placed to provide steering on general matters where gatekeepers might use one policy as an excuse for non-complicity with another, bringing a false sense of conflicting imperatives. At the same time, the HLG plays an essential role in making sure that resources are used wisely by avoiding enforcement redundancies. Within this framework, the aim is to benefit of the Digital Markets Act framework by applying it as much as possible and as clearly as possible. Last but not least, in the context of market investigations into new services and new practices, the high-level group may provide expertise to the Commission on the need to amend, add or remove rules in the Digital Markets Act. This mechanism provides a larger foundation for policy intervention and futureproofing the DMA.[109]

---

102 European Commission Rules of Procedure for the Digital Markets Advisory Committee art 5(1), adopted by the Digital Markets Advisory Committee, <https://ec.europa.eu/transparency/comitology-register/screen/documents/088325/1/consult?lang=en> accessed 27 November 2024.

103 Set up as a group of experts, in compliance with the Commission Decision of 30 May 2016 establishing horizontal rules on the creation and operation of Commission expert groups.

104 DMA art 40 provides that the HLG is composed of the following European bodies and networks: (a) Body of the European Regulators for Electronic Communications, (b) European Data Protection Supervisor and European Data Protection Board, (c) European Competition Network, (d) Consumer Protection Cooperation Network, and (e) European Regulatory Group of Audio-visual Media Regulators. The Commission both chairs and provides secretariat services to the high-level group.

105 Commission Decision of 23 March 2023 on setting up the High-Level Group for the Digital Markets Act art 3, <https://competition-policy.ec.europa.eu/system/files/2023-03/High_Level_Group_on_the_DMA_0.pdf> accessed 27 November 2024.

106 Implementing Regulation 2023/814 of 14 April 2023 on detailed arrangements for the conduct of certain proceedings by the Commission pursuant to Regulation 2022/1925 of the European Parliament and of the Council C(2023) 2530 final.

107 European Commission, Register of Commission Expert Groups Member of the High-Level Group for the Digital Markets Act <https://ec.europa.eu/transparency/expert-groups-register/screen/members/consult?memberId=111640&memberTypeId=5&lang=en&fromExpertGroups=3904> accessed 27 November 2024.

108 Case C-252/21 *Meta Platforms Inc v Bundeskartellamt* ECLI:EU:C:2023:537.

109 DMA art 40(7).

VI. Conclusion

54. This chapter spans a timeframe of five years, transitioning from the final phase of one EU political cycle (2014–2019) concluding in the current cycle (2019–2024). The current year (2024)is only the fifth year since the EU *acquis* has comprised of business-to-business digital regulation. Even so, it can be observed from the outset that, in terms of the platform economy agenda and its links to more market fairness, the progression has been rapid, one could even say belt-tighteningly so. Moving from political agreement on the P2B Regulation in February 2019 to the Digital Markets Act only three years later – in March 2022 – and the application of its rules began in March 2023, this was followed by the designation of seven gatekeepers for twenty-four core platform services. Furthermore, this phase led to the initiation of six non-compliance investigations by July 2024, as frontlines became entrenched. In the authors' view, this rapid progress can be defended as a good approach, especially as market intervention must keep pace with fast-moving digital markets. The future is here and but is not evenly distributed.

55. Additionally, the enforcement of the Digital Markets Act is as important as its outreach, as business users and end users need to benefit from the effects of the DMA and the Commission's further actions. The benefits for Union business users relate to opportunities such as enhanced interoperability, alternative app stores, access to search data or other types of data access for third parties. At the same time, greater consumer choice is promoted through choice screens or increased personalisation options, alternative in-app payment methods and by addressing self-preferencing practices. On this point, the ministries and government agencies in charge of digital affairs and competitiveness have an important role in presenting the benefits of the Digital Markets Act, with the scope of translating towards the markets the actual opportunities – for business users – introduced by the Regulation.

56. At the national level, the Digital Markets Act is followed by a suit of other digital regulations which come across in a time when the RCC is taking on other regulatory mandates. On top of the P2B Regulation and Digital Markets Act, the NCA is currently also discussing its mandate under the Data Act.[110] This will enhance the RCC's already extensive digital-specific toolkit, which includes measures ensuring transparency, antitrust and now the asymmetric obligations outlined in the Digital Markets Act. In this context, the culture of coordination and cooperation, established by the experiences with Regulation 1/2003 and furthered by the Digital Markets Act mechanisms (through the ECN and the HLG), will facilitate effective collaboration with the Commission concerning antitrust measures and other market intervention instruments.

57. Looking forward to the 3 May 2026, as the first evaluation of the DMA,[111] the authors anticipate the possibility of the enhancement of the mechanics of the

---

110 Regulation 2023/2854 of the European Parliament and of the Council of 13 December 2023 on harmonised rules on fair access to and use of data and amending Regulation 2017/2394 and Directive 2020/1828 (Data Act) [2023] OJ L1/71.

111 To be sent to the European Parliament, the Council and the European Economic and Social Committee.

Digital Markets Act to make it even more robust and futureproof. This will indeed be the subject to upcoming compliance and enforcement takeaways, as well as technological advancements. In any case, the work achieved during the first Digital Markets Act legislative cycle which, comprised only one and a half years, merits acknowledgement for making good use of the political momentum and creating a very solid and legally sound basis for potential future improvements, where new layers of policy ideas and ambition can refine and advance the instrument as we move forward.

Legal Framework and Enforcement in Digital Sector in Slovakia

Slovakia

MICHAELA NOSA*
Comenius University in Bratislava

Abstract

The Digital Markets Act (DMA) is fully in force and the companies and consumers should already experience first benefits of its application. Member States should have appointed relevant authorities as partners for cooperation with the European Commission. This contribution focuses on the process of adoption of changes in the Slovak legal framework with regard to the DMA and related EU legislation, changes adopted, division of powers between relevant authorities and also investigations in digital sector conducted by the National Competition Authority.

* Michaela Nosa, PhD, was part of the AMO for over twenty years. She led the Legal, Legislative and International Relations Department, where her main tasks included representation of the AMO before courts, drafting legal analysis and opinions, European Competition Network agenda as well as legislative and international relations activities. Her team was also responsible for drafting the amendment to the Act on Protection of Competition implementing DMA and she was involved in the legislative process. She also cooperates with the Faculty of Law, Comenius University in Bratislava, where she teaches seminars on competition law and the EU law. She joined the Legal Services Department at National Bank of Slovakia in 2024 as a head of Legal Section. The views in this contribution are those of the author and cannot be interpreted as binding for any of the institutions she represents.

I. Implementation of the Digital Markets Act (DMA) in the Slovak Republic

1. Draft Amendment Implementing the DMA

1. The DMA implementation in the Slovak Republic started early in 2023. The Antimonopoly Office of the Slovak Republic (AMO) was assigned a role as an authority responsible for the implementation of the DMA and to fulfil the tasks stemming therefrom. The amendment to the Act on Protection of Competition[1] implementing the DMA into the national law framework was submitted for the public consultation process in June 2023.[2] The amendment also implements the EU Foreign Subsidies Regulation[3] (FSR) which is another part of future competence of the AMO as competent authority cooperating with the European Commission pursuant to the FSR covering all the areas of the FSR except for the public procurement (which is the competence of the Office for Public Procurement). Therefore, some provisions of the amendment cover both areas, especially regarding the expected cooperation with the European Commission. The changes with regard to the FSR are not covered by this contribution.

2. Initially, the draft law was planned to be in force in February 2024, before the date when gatekeepers should comply with the obligations under the DMA.[4] However, the early parliamentary elections in September 2023 slowed down the legislative process. The amendment was adopted by National Council of the Slovak Republic in April. New provisions introduced by the amendment, Act no. 93/2024, entered into force on 15 May 2024.

3. The amendment to the Act on Protection of Competition assigns the AMO with the new role and powers. The DMA recognises the duties of national competent authorities (NCAs), competent authorities and Member States in enforcing the rules referred to in Article 1(6) of the DMA. However, the DMA does not assign all of the obligations and powers to concrete authorities but assigns some powers to 'competent authorities' and 'Member States', thus, leaving it to Member States to decide which authority will be responsible for specific duties and powers under the DMA. The AMO should fulfil the role of the national competition authority, competent authority in addition to the duties assigned generally to Member States by the DMA. Although, considering the wording of the DMA, sometimes competent authorities other than the national competition authority may be more competent to provide assistance to the European Commission for specific purposes. Still, it is desirable, that there is one authority that would be responsible to communicate and coordinate these requests within Slovakia.

---

1 Act No 187/2021 Coll., on the protection of economic competition and on the amendment and supplementation of certain laws.

2 See <https://www.slov-lex.sk/legislativne-procesy/SK/LP/2023/400>.

3 Regulation 2022/2560 of the European Parliament and of the Council of 14 December 2022 on foreign subsidies distorting the internal market (FSR) [2022] OJ L330/1.

4 (6 March 2024).

4. These obligations and powers include:
   - Assistance of the national competent authorities in European Commission market investigations (pursuant to Article 16(5) – investigations with a view to the possible adoption of decisions pursuant to Articles 17, 18 and 19 DMA).
   - Providing all the information that competent authorities have at their disposal to the European Commission (Article 21(5) DMA).
   - Assistance of the NCA in oral explanations (Article 22(2) DMA).
   - Assistance and active participation of the NCA/Member State in European Commission inspections (Article 23(3), (7) to (9) DMA).
   - Providing support in monitoring the obligations, measures and provision of specific expertise or knowledge of the competent authorities to the European Commission (Article 26(2) DMA).
   - Receiving information (NCA) about practice or behaviour by gatekeepers that falls within the scope of the DMA from third parties and submitting relevant information to the European Commission and transferring information on possible non-compliance of gatekeepers to the European Commission (Article 27(1) and (3) DMA).
   - Cooperation (European Commission and national authorities).
   - Exchange of information regarding the DMA or investigations under Articles 101 and 102 TFEU, cooperation and coordination (information of the NCA on first investigation measure, information on draft measures to be adopted before the decision is taken, support of market investigations, Article 38(1) to (3) and (6) DMA).
   - Requesting the European Commission[5] to open a market investigation pursuant to Article 17 DMA – investigation as to whether an undertaking should be designated as a gatekeeper (Article 41(1) DMA).
   - Requesting the European Commission[6] to open a market investigation pursuant to Article 18[7] DMA – breach of obligations of a gatekeeper (Article 41(2) DMA).
   - Requesting the European Commission to conduct a market investigation pursuant to Article 19 DMA – services added to the list or practices of gatekeeper are not effectively addressed (Article 41(3) DMA).[8]
   - Investigation under national law on non-compliance if the national law provides for such a power (Article 38(7) DMA).

5. Naturally, the purpose of the implementation of regulations is not to replicate the regulation in national law but to introduce changes into the national law that will ensure the smooth application of the regulation within the national legal framework. Thus, the changes at national level in Member States will depend on their existing legislation.

---

5 Three or more Member States may submit such a request.

6 One or more Member States may submit such a request.

7 If Member States consider that there are reasonable grounds to suspect that a gatekeeper has obligations and has maintained, strengthened or extended its gatekeeper position in relation to the requirements under Article 3(1).

8 Three or more Member States may submit such a request.

6. The Slovak draft amendment has only sixteen points that introduce changes to the Act on Protection of Competition. The first important change is the introduction of the explicit power of the AMO as the competent authority for the digital markets pursuant to the DMA (Article 16(1)(j)[9] of the Act on Protection of Competition) within the Slovak Republic.

7. The AMO has power pursuant to Article 16(1)(a) to conduct investigations in the individual economic sectors in order to obtain information on the state of competition in the sector (sector inquiries) and to conduct investigations in order to determine whether there is a reason to commence the proceedings regarding the infringements of competition law pursuant to the Article 16(1)(b).

8. With the amendment implementing the DMA, the AMO gained two new powers to conduct investigations. Specifically, AMO has now additional power to:
   - Conduct investigation into a case of possible non-compliance with Articles 5, 6 and 7 of the DMA on its territory (new Article 16(1)(c) of the Act on Protection of Competition) pursuant to Article 38(7) of the DMA.
   - Conduct investigation on whether there are grounds to submit a request to the European Commission to start market investigation under Article 41(1) to (3) of the DMA (new Article 16(1)(d) of the Act on Protection of Competition).

9. Since the requests submitted to the European Commission under Article 41(1) to (3) of the DMA should be supported by evidence, the AMO must have tools at its disposal to facilitate the evidence. The power to conduct investigation for that purpose is therefore a pre-condition.

10. Other draft amendment points of more technical nature secure identical powers for the investigations for the purpose of the DMA such as the powers of the AMO for the purpose of investigation of infringements of Articles 101 and 102 TFEU and their national counterparts (Article 4 – agreements restricting competition and Article 5 – abuse of dominant position).

11. This means that the AMO has now power to (within its territory):
    - Conduct inspections in business premises of undertakings as well as private premises with the same toolkit of powers during the inspections.
    - Assist the European Commission with inspections pursuant to the DMA.
    - Request information from natural and legal persons for the purpose of DMA.

12. The AMO also has a new role as a 'coordinator' with the power to request any information from public authorities for the purpose of fulfilling its duties and powers under DMA. This should also facilitate effective methods to gather information and ease communication with the European Commission.

13. The issue on *ne bis in idem* was discussed in the course of the legislative process. Although, it is not very likely that the AMO would have the resources to conduct Article 101 or 102 TFEU investigations against gatekeepers, considering the rules on case allocation within ECN, the European Commission is more likely to be better placed authority to deal with these cases; still a possibility of investigations

---

[9] Act on Protection of Competition art 16(1), stipulates powers of the AMO.

pursuant to the competition rules and in parallel with DMA rules exists. As we know, some NCAs started investigations against gatekeepers before the DMA rules entered into force. However, considering the CJEU case law on *ne bis in idem*, it was concluded that no reflection in the legislation is needed for that purpose. The Data Protection Authority in Slovakia also submitted a comment in the legislative process requesting a provision that would introduce an obligation on the AMO to notify the Data Protection Authority of any data-related issues that might be part of the investigation. After the consultation, specific provision on notification was not included but can be in practice applied on the basis of in general provisions on cooperation.

14. The draft law should also bring three new expert positions for the AMO, although the AMO initially requested six positions as the expertise in this field will also be crucial for effective enforcement of the new rules along with antitrust enforcement and merger control. The analyses, with a detailed calculation of activities, was prepared as part of an impact assessment which justified the request for six new positions regarding the DMA. The expertise in this field will also be essential for effective enforcement of the new rules.

15. Members of the parliament were in general supportive for the new powers of the AMO. There was no discussion on further changes to the competition law in Slovakia beyond the implementation towards latest trends discussed in EU such as. empowering NCAs with new tools like possibility to impose remedies on the basis of the sector inquiry or 'call in' concentrations that would allow the AMO to assess mergers that do not meet the thresholds but that may have a negative impact on competition. The AMO proposed a draft law regarding the "call in" mergers in 2020 but strong opposition from the business community and the Ministry of Economy did not allow the proposal to go further in the legislative process. However, there are from time-to-time indications that a 'problematic' concentration took place, but there are no tools in the law to tackle this problem if the concentrating parties do not meet the legal thresholds. It is worth noting, that these cases were mainly not in the digital sector.

2. Cooperation Among State Institutions

16. A more formal way of cooperation of public authorities should take place, when the amendment is in force. The cooperation between state institutions may in general take place on the legal basis of provisions of general law on the organisation of the ministries and other state authorities;[10] memorandum is also quite a frequent, more formalised way of circulating explicit rules on cooperation which would be also very suitable and was also indicated as a possible basis of further cooperation.

17. The coordination and exchange of information will be needed, considering the representation in the High-level Group for the DMA as well as overall knowledge of the market, its development and contact with its players and users and last, but not least, to create a basis for effective communication channels as suggested by

---

[10] Act No 575/2001 Coll.

the reasoning of the European Court of Justice in the *Meta* judgement.[11] Since we need to look at the platforms as ecosystems, it is crucial that the intervention of one public authority in one matter does not completely contradict the intervention of the other at national level. It does not mean the objectives of the competition policy may be changed, on contrary, it should ensure that the objectives of the competition policy are reflected.

18. There are three main authorities that are relevant in this regard, the Council for Media Services, Data Protection Authority and possibly the Regulatory Authority for Electronic Communications and Postal Services.[12] The Council for Media Services, a national media regulator, should fulfil the role of Digital Services Coordinator pursuant to the draft amendment implementing the Digital Services Act (DSA).[13] The draft amendment implementing the DSA was submitted for public consultation in February 2024.[14] Many stakeholders submitted their comments to the draft amendment. The Ministry of Culture of the Slovak Republic, as the institution responsible for the draft amendment, had to consider altogether 95 different comments to the draft law. The amendment entered into force on 24 July 2024.[15] However, the cabinet sent a much shorter draft law to the parliament compared to what was initially introduced into legislative process. Nevertheless, the competent authority for the DSA application with certain rules and sanctions for their breach are now part of the legal framework.

19. The Data Protection Authority (Office for the Protection of Personal Data of the Slovak Republic) is responsible for the enforcement of the GDPR[16] rules.

20. In both draft amendments, implementing DMA and DSA, there is a specific provision on cooperation and coordination among relevant ministries and public authorities. The AMO already has a memorandum of cooperation with the telecom regulator where cooperation takes place when necessary, including the exchange of information. Therefore, the basis and some experience on cooperation already exists. However, a more formal way of cooperation might be suitable in the form of memoranda/agreements on cooperation, which is less formal but still quite a common way to express further rules of cooperation between institutions in the Slovak Republic. In this way, the public and stakeholders can learn how the relevant authorities plan to proceed and possibly more information on their cooperation could be available to the public.

---

11 Case C-252/21 *Meta Platforms Inc v Bundeskartellamt* ECLI:EU:C:2023:537, see Ann-Christin Richter and Merlin Gömann, *The EU Court of Justice holds that National Competition Authorities may consider violations of data protection laws during abuse of dominance assessments (Meta)*, E-COMPETITIONS July 2023, art. No. 114093.

12 The Regulatory Authority for Electronic Communications and Postal Services.

13 Regulation 2022/2065 of the European Parliament and of the Council of 19 October 2022 on a Single Market for Digital Services and amending Directive 2000/31 (the Digital Services Act or DSA) [2022] OJ L277/1.

14 Draft law amending Act No 264/2022 Coll. on media services and amendments to certain laws (the Act on Media Services) <https://www.slov-lex.sk/legislativne-procesy/SK/LP/2024/24> accessed 12 July 2024.

15 Act. No 203/2024 Coll. amending Act No 264/2022 Coll. on media services and amendments to certain laws (the Act on Media Services). Some changes will enter into force much later than initial day.

16 Regulation 2016/679 of the European Parliament and of the Council of 27 April 2016 on the protection of natural persons with regard to the processing of personal data and on the free movement of such data, and repealing Directive 95/46 (General Data Protection Regulation) [2016] OJ L119/1.

21. It is also expected that the AMO should be an institution to which the relevant players within the Slovak territory could turn, should they feel that the gatekeepers do not play according to the rules of the DMA.

II. Enforcement of Competition Rules in Digital Markets

22. When it comes to digital markets, there are a few regional players that are 'waiting' for the gatekeepers to comply with their duties under the DMA, such as price comparison websites, especially, when it comes to self-preferencing practices.

23. However, there may be areas where national players have a significant role alongside the gatekeepers or outside of the platforms and services as defined by the DMA. This is the case for example in e-commerce in the Slovak jurisdiction, where there are national/regional players/platforms that are quite popular along with designated gatekeeper in this field.

24. Lately, the AMO has investigated two cases of abuse of dominant position with the dominant regional player. One of the cases was closed, the other is still pending.

1. Commitment Decision

25. The proceedings on the first closed case[17] started for possible abuse of dominant position of the undertaking Slevomat.cz, s.r.o., based in Czechia, which runs the platform *zlavomat.sk* through its Slovak branch/subdivision. Zlavomat.sk is a two-sided platform providing online intermediary services in the area of discount portals within the territory of the Slovak Republic. The discount portals[18] started their activities in Slovakia between 2010 and 2011 and experienced their boom in 2014 to 2015. Their concept is to serve as an intermediary for the supply of goods and services of independent entrepreneurs/companies in the form of vouchers, with discounts or bundles, or with additional benefits, sometimes in form of gift cards or vouchers to promote their own products and benefits. Zlavomat.sk started with offering various types of products and services, from ballet classes, dinners, massages to wellness stays and hotel accommodation. According to the decision, at their peak, there were around 200 discount portals. Continuously, their numbers shrank significantly to only a few players. Moreover, the extent of the products and services narrowed to offers concerning only travelling and tourism, with offers and promotions on hotels, wellness stays, which were outside the territory of the Slovak Republic.

26. The investigation showed, that zlavomat.sk applied exclusivity and parity clauses (most favourable nation – MFN clauses) to suppliers of the services. As the decision is a commitment decision, i.e. the decision does not state the infringement and a fine was not imposed on Slevomat.cz, s.r.o. The decision (38 pages) is rather short considering the abuse of dominant position decisions nowadays, but certain conclusions might be derived from it.

---

17 Decision No 2024/DOZ/UPZ/2/3, 29 January 2024.

18 Known in some countries as 'coupon portals'.

27. First, the AMO did not conclude its findings on the definition of the relevant market in this case stating that since it was a commitment decision it was not necessary to provide exact definition.

28. On the basis of replies to RFIs from the suppliers – the AMO found that the discount portals were of specific complementary significance to the general distribution channels of their products and services. The important aspect being mainly the promotion and visibility of the company and its products and services towards a broad spectrum of potential customers. The suppliers consider the use of the discount portal to promote their products a very effective way of advertisement/promotion specifically with the opportunity to connect with customers they would otherwise not be able to reach. It seems especially an effective way of promotion for smaller and new entrepreneurs to win future, stable clientele.[19] The suppliers do not pay any fees to the provider of the portal; the provider takes the commission once the product/service is ordered by the customer. Flexibility was named as another benefit of the use of portal for suppliers which is reflected in the possibility of promoting the service or product for a specific time or period and to decide on the start and end day of the promotion. This way the suppliers, especially those active in travel and tourism, could reach customer in quieter times of the year to increase their revenues.

29. For the purpose of the definition of relevant product market, the AMO reviewed the substitutability of the discount portals to:
    - Own offline and online distribution channels of the suppliers/producers;
    - Online shops and online markets;
    - Search engine platforms;
    - Services of travel agents and agencies and their own selling channels;
    - Booking platforms of short-term accommodation; and
    - Portals offering specific types of experiences (such balloon flight, paragliding, parachuting, motorcars, etc.).

30. The AMO preliminary concluded after the analyses of the information, that own offline and online distribution channels of the suppliers/producers, online shops and online markets, search engine platforms, services for travel agents and agencies and their own selling channels and booking platforms of short-term accommodation were non-substitutable. In the case of online selling channels for travel agents/agencies certain similarities were found but these portals were not considered as substitutes.

31. In the case of portals offering specific types of experiences more similarities were found, specifically in some kinds of services and short-term offers as well as the fact that the price parity clause was also applied by Slevomat.cz, s.r.o. to portals offering specific types of experiences. However, the AMO did not make a final conclusion on whether the latter were substitutes, as for the purpose of the commitment decision this was not considered as inevitable. Finally, the AMO provided the following definition of the product market – 'online intermediary services provided through online discount portals within the territory of the Slovak

---

[19] Decision No 2024/DOZ/UPZ/2/3 Point 69.

Republic for commercial partners and their customers'. The AMO considered also potential division of the definition of the relevant market for the two sides of the platform but concluded that this would not affect the preliminary assessment of the existence of the dominant position, thus making one preliminary definition for the two-sided online discount portal.

32. The AMO also did not make definite conclusions on the dominant position of the undertaking, the decision does not provide information on the market share, but refers to the website traffic and the responses to the RFIs of the market players which also point out that they used analytical tools such as Similarweb, Google Trends/Google Analytics regarding online traffic and the behaviour of the customers in the online environment.[20] Overall, the AMO analysed the position of the Slevomat.cz, s.r.o. on the basis of: (a) the development of its turnover; (b) development of the realised transactions; (c) development of the amount of costs for the marketing services of their partners/clients; (d) data on the traffic on its discount portals; (e) importance of the discount portal for its partners/clients; and (f) barriers for existing discount portals to expand their activities and barriers to entry for new rivals. After analysis, the AMO came to the preliminary conclusion that Slevomat.cz, s.r.o. has, through its Slovak branch, the dominant position on the defined relevant market.

33. The investigated practices of the Slevomat.cz, s.r.o. concerned exclusivity and price parity clauses which were part of the contract conditions with the partners/clients and were enforced in practice. The exclusivity conditions were considered as a barrier to expanding activities of existing portals, difficulties in maintaining important customers and winning new customers, etc. At the same time, the information from the investigation showed, that there was an interest on the side of suppliers/partners to promote their products and services on more than one discount portal.

34. The investigation also indicated that a wide price parity clause was applied in the form of prohibition for business partners to offer their products and services via other online portals at the same or lower price as that of zlavomat.sk. This condition was also part of the general terms and conditions of zlavomat.sk at the end 2018 at the latest.[21] The application of a wide parity clause could have potentially affected the intensity of competition on prices as the business partners (suppliers) could not offer the same or lower prices on other portals; since end users are sensitive on small differences in prices, as the decision states, there could have been restriction of effective competition on prices (as a problem that should be addressed). These practices could also have had a negative impact on new entrants to compete for customers on prices.

35. The investigation started in 2022 (the AMO received a claim at the beginning of February 2022), and the formal proceedings were open on 8 March 2023;[22] the first version of the proposed commitment was tested in October 2023. The draft of the commitments was published on the AMO website and directly addressed

---

20 *Ibid* Point 117.

21 *Ibid* Point 135.

22 Please note, that the Act on Protection of Competition differentiates between the investigation which is conducted to determine whether there is a reason to commence the proceedings and the formal proceedings. The investigation always precedes the proceedings. The AMO has all the investigative powers in all phases, however an

the request to submit opinions on the draft commitments to some of the market players. All major rivals of zlavomat.sk apparently submitted their position to the draft commitments.[23]

36. According to the commitment decision, Slevomat.cz, s.r.o. shall not apply exclusivity clauses and shall allow its business partners to promote their products and services on other portals. Additionally, the business partners shall be allowed to offer their products and services on other portals and their own offline channels for the same or lower prices compared to the prices offered via the zlavomat portal. After the testing the commitments, the changes were introduced. Initially, the commitments were proposed for three years, and the final decision requires Slevomat.cz, s.r.o. to abstain from both exclusivity and price parity clauses for the period of five years. Slevomat.cz, s.r.o. must publish press releases for a twelve-month period, informing about the proceedings of the AMO and the commitment not to apply exclusivity and parity clauses. In addition, it must adjust its general terms and conditions and also its practice in such a way that it is not favouring or discriminating against customers who decide to promote their products and services on other discount portals. Market players also suggested monitoring the commitments, however, the AMO stated in the decision that there was no need for specific commitment on monitoring. An interesting opinion within the testing raised the issue of the wording of the Slevomat.cz, s.r.o. press release which it said sounded like 'positive promotion of the discount portal www.zlavomat.sk and its activities towards its business partners'. The wording of the press release has since been changed and the text in the commitment decision omits certain initially published formulations, however, one could claim that it still possesses the 'positive character' regarding the position of the investigated undertaking on the market, where the Slevomat.cz, s.r.o. 'boasts' of being an important, almost 'dominant' player.

37. Commitment decisions are not very usual in AMO proceedings. There were about two decisions adopted before the latest one, although the possibility to adopt commitment decisions has been part of the Slovak competition law for many years.

2. Open Proceedings Regarding Real Estate Sales Platform

38. In February 2022, the AMO issued a press release on the initiation of proceedings for possible abuse of dominant position in the area of online real estate portals (platforms offering advertising of leases/rentals and purchase/sell of real estate). The AMO opened proceedings for possible abuse of dominant position in the form of unfair prices for online advertising, imposing conditions discriminating against certain undertakings in online advertising, restricting the possibility of choice of certain real estate portals for online advertising, tying the online advertising with other products, restricting the possibility of uploading advertisements and add-on services and functions of online real estate portals for online advertising.[24]

---

undertaking, party to the proceedings, has full procedural rights once the proceedings are open (for example, as of the moment of the commencement of proceedings, an undertaking has the right to access to file at any time).

23 Decision No 2024/DOZ/UPZ/2/3 Point 151.

24 No information regarding the case has been publicly available since 2022.

39. In terms of other areas of competition law, there have been no significant cases concerning the digital sector.

III. Activities Concerning Digital Agenda

40. The Slovak Republic has a ministry dedicated to the informatisation, which is the Ministry of Investments, Regional Development and Informatisation of the Slovak Republic. Several strategies and non-legislative materials were adopted within the digital transformation. A few interdepartmental working groups[25] were established which bring together representatives of different ministries, authorities and sometimes also external partners with regard to digital transformation, implementation of new EU regulations, etc. which should be positively acknowledged. Some of the working groups are more formal with official members and the official rules of procedure and adopting decisions, some are more informal. All EU legislation proposals should be discussed in these working groups. The AMO has a representative in one of the groups. It is essential that any legislation that is going to be adopted reflects other laws and rules in the drafting process. The Ministry has also commissioned an in-depth analysis on the implementation of EU legislation which among other issues should identify the areas and competences to effectively distribute the competences and duties among relevant authorities. It is also important that the information on upcoming EU legislation is communicated to all relevant partners.

IV. Conclusions

41. The legislative process on the implementation of the DMA was concluded and the provisions are expected to be effectively applied in practice. AMO has additional powers to lead its own investigations in digital sector and to be a relevant partner for the European Commission as well as stakeholders. Nevertheless, at the moment of adoption of new law, it seems there is not much interest among stakeholders on these topics. It is mostly the relevant national authorities and certain stakeholders that are involved in the discussions. There are plans and strategies for digital transition, however, after the Covid pandemic and the war on the eastern border of Slovakia, it is not the central focus.

42. The two AMO investigations suggest that there might be problems at regional/national levels with local dominant players in digital sector. Thus, *ex ante* regulation is very important, but there still might be cases at national level that need to be tackled by traditional antitrust powers. The AMO, as a national competition authority, will have an important role in both the DMA application as well as the *ex post* investigation of infringements of competition law and control of concentrations. The communication and coordination between relevant authorities will be crucial at national level as well as at EU level. It is necessary to work together for competition while not setting back innovation and growth. So far, it seems that relevant authorities are all aware of this fact.

---

25 Two main working groups are responsible for digital transformation and strategic priorities of informatisation.

The Digital Markets Act: The CNMC Perspective

Spain

CANI FERNÁNDEZ VICIÉN[*], ISABEL ÁLVAREZ FERNÁNDEZ DEL VALLADO[**] AND FRANCISCO RIPOLL VÁZQUEZ[***]

Spanish National Markets and Competition Commission (CNMC)

Abstract

The entry into force and application of the Digital Markets Act (DMA) has opened a new scenario for digital markets which poses novel challenges not only for the gatekeepers to which it is addressed, but also for the institutional bodies in charge of the surveillance of the digital markets it affects. The Spanish National Markets and Competition Commission (CNMC) has backed the adoption of the DMA since its very inception. At the same time, we have called for a greater involvement of National Competition Authorities (NCAs) in the application of the DMA in order to ensure a consistent and robust enforcement. It is of relevance that we have actually been empowered by our national Parliament to monitor possible non-compliance with the DMA within the Spanish territory. We are also participating in fora created to ensure a coordinated and coherent functioning of the DMA, notably as one of the European Competition Network (ECN) representatives in the High-level Group (HLG).

---

[*] President of the Spanish National Markets and Competition Commission (CNMC).

[**] Case Handler in the Information Society Unit of the Competition Directorate of the CNMC.

[***] Case Handler in the Information Society Unit of the Competition Directorate of the CNMC.

I. Introduction: A Short Description of the DMA

1. The entry into force and application of the Digital Markets Act (DMA), has opened a new scenario for the regulation of digital markets which poses novel challenges, not only for the gatekeepers to which it is addressed, but also for the institutional bodies in charge of the surveillance of the digital markets it affects.[1] In this regard, the Spanish National Markets and Competition Commission (CNMC) is only one among all the European authorities which need to adapt to this new reality; adaptation which becomes essential to take full advantage of the toolkit that the DMA provides to ensure fairness and contestability in the digital sector.

2. This regulation, which represents a significant milestone in the EU's regulatory framework, stands as an *ex ante* regulation of digital markets, although it is strongly influenced by competition policy in terms of its principles and the prescribed conducts. As we develop below, the DMA is a regulation that targets particular firms or gatekeepers, when providing certain core platform services (CPS) and carrying out specific conduct. The legal interest of the DMA is ensuring fairness and contestability in digital markets, thereby contributing to the proper functioning of the internal market. This is different from the legal interest of competition policy, which is protecting undistorted competition (on any given market).

3. Consequently, this means that the DMA is without prejudice to the enforcement of competition policy: Articles 101 and 102 of the Treaty on the Functioning of the European Union (TFEU) and their national equivalents, national competition rules prohibiting other forms of unilateral conduct and merger control. Competition policy will continue to be applicable in digital markets by the European Commission (EC) and the national competition authorities (NCAs) for all firms, including for designated gatekeepers when providing CPS and carrying out the conduct foreseen in the DMA. Indeed, recitals 10 and 11 of the DMA establish complementarity with competition law as one of the inspiring principles of this legislation.

4. In terms of its subjective scope, the DMA designates the 'gatekeepers', identified as entities wielding significant influence in the digital sphere and characterised by substantial revenue, market capitalisation, and user engagement, measured by quantitative and qualitative criteria. Such criteria encompass a proactive understanding of market dynamics, ensuring that only a few selected entities with considerable impact on the internal market come under regulatory scrutiny.

5. On the other hand, it establishes specific services known as CPS which are currently subject to its regulatory framework: online intermediation services (like marketplaces or app stores), search engines, social networking services, video-sharing platforms, interpersonal communications independent of numbering, operating systems, web browsers, virtual assistants cloud computing and advertising services.

6. Once the aforementioned gatekeepers have been designated as such in relation with one or more CPS, the DMA establishes a set of obligations and

---

[1] Regulation 2022/1925 of the European Parliament and of the Council of 14 September 2022 on contestable and fair markets in the digital sector and amending Directives 2019/1937 and 2020/1828 (Digital Markets Act or DMA) [2022] OJ L265/1.

prohibitions, whether immediately enforceable (Article 5 DMA) or subject to regulatory dialogue for compliance modulation (Articles 6 and 7 DMA). Some of these prescriptions include refraining from imposing most-favoured-nation clauses, avoiding the use of data in competition with commercial users, ensuring fair access to search and app store data, not restricting the pre-installation, installation or uninstallation of software, allowing interoperability, portability and access to data, and other conduct (such as no self-preferencing, no data combination, portability and access to data or no restriction on presentation of complaints, etc.). In addition to these obligations, there are also specific interoperability obligations for messaging applications (NI-ICS or number independent interpersonal communication services).

7. Regarding mergers and acquisitions, the DMA also provides for close scrutiny of gatekeepers' intended acquisitions by requiring them to notify any operation before its execution. This notification will allow the EC to inform the national competent authorities, which in turn could use the information provided to request case referrals to the EC in light of Article 22 of the EC Merger Regulation.[2]

8. One of the DMA's primary tools is in market investigations, which are mainly aimed at examining compliance with the obligations set up by the rule. Besides, this regulation also foresees other types of investigations, such as those aimed at designating gatekeepers or identifying new services and behaviour to include in its scope. Regarding the procedural instruments envisaged by its text for its implementation, these encompass inspections, information requests, interviews, or the reception of information from third parties, some of which may require the collaboration of NCAs.

9. In terms of situations of non-compliance with the DMA, the regulation foresees that the infringements may lead to fines of up to 10% of the global turnover of the gatekeepers, or even up to 20% in cases of recurrence, whereas procedural non-compliance findings may result in the application of fines of 1% of the undertaking's global turnover. In addition, where applicable, interim measures and cease-and-desist orders can be imposed, including a merger moratorium for systematic breaches occurring three times within a period of eight years.

II. Assessment of the DMA from the Perspective of the Spanish CNMC

10. The CNMC has backed the adoption of the DMA since its very inception. The CNMC has firmly supported this new tool in several statements, such as, among others, the CNMC's Position Paper for the public consultation on the Digital Services Act (DSA) and a New Competition Tool (NCT)[3] or the CNMC's market study on

---

2 Regulation 139/2004 of 20 January 2004 on the control of concentrations between undertakings (the EC Merger Regulation).

3 CNMC, Position Paper for public consultation on the Digital Services Act (DSA) (10 November 2020) <https://www.cnmc.es/sites/default/files/editor_contenidos/Notas%20de%20prensa/2020/CNMC%20position%20paper%20on%20DSA%20and%20NCT.pdf> accessed 14 July 2024.

competition conditions in the online advertising sector in Spain,[4] apart from the June 2021 joint paper from the European Competition Network (ECN) NCAs.[5]

11. From the point of view of the Spanish CNMC, we value especially two features of the final version of the DMA.

12. On the one hand, is the fact that the DMA is without prejudice to the application of competition policy, also to digital gatekeepers. This is key for the success of this new regulation. It is essential that competition policy goes on being applied vigorously to digital markets and gatekeepers, both by the EC and the NCAs. This is also the best way to ensure that the DMA is future proof. Competition policy offers a flexible framework to assess potentially problematic conduct or market contexts that could in the future be included in the scope of the DMA if warranted. In this respect, it is important to recall the messages conveyed by aforementioned ECN/NCAs' joint paper. Without the application of competition law to digital markets (both by the EC and the national authorities) the DMA would not exist, since we would not have grasped digital services from the perspective of market definition, theories of harm or remedies design. Therefore, the best way to make the DMA future proof is by ensuring that competition policy continues being applied to digital markets, both by the EC and the NCAs.

13. On the other hand, is the fact that NCAs are to play a role in the DMA's implementation, even if the EC is its 'sole enforcer'. The implementation of the DMA involves an intense and close coordination across EU institutions, as NCAs will now exchange more information with the EC when applying competition policy to gatekeepers. And the exchange of information will be bidirectional, also from the EC to the NCAs. Although we already have a strong and solid coordination framework thanks to the ECN, such cooperation should be strengthened in the post-DMA era.

III. Towards a Coherent, Effective and Complementary Approach in the Digital Sector

14. The DMA and its accompanying institutional settings open a whole new era of cooperation between the EC and the NCAs. The vast previous experience applying Articles 3, 11 and 12 of Regulation 1/2003 serves as an inspiration.[6] This cooperation, which has been upgraded in the specific realm of the digital markets, will be governed by the rules established by the DMA (notably its Articles 1(5), 1(6), 1(7) and 38).

15. Article 1(5) establishes that Member States shall not impose further obligations on gatekeepers for the purpose of ensuring contestable and fair markets. Other obligations can be imposed on gatekeepers nationally, but not with the same legal

[4] CNMC, 'Market Study' (7 July 2021) <https://www.cnmc.es/sites/default/files/3696007_0.pdf > accessed 14 July 2024.

[5] ECN, 'How National Competition Agencies Can Strengthen the DMA' (22 June 2021) <https://www.bundeskartellamt.de/SharedDocs/Publikation/EN/Others/DMA_ECN_Paper.pdf?__blob=publicationFile&v=2> accessed 14 July 2024.

[6] Regulation 1/2003 of 16 December 2002 on the implementation of the rules on competition laid down in Articles 81 and 82 of the Treaty [2003] OJ L1/1.

interest or objectives as those of the DMA. The aim of this article is averting the fragmentation of the internal market.

16. It follows then that if the legal interest of competition rules is different from that of the DMA, then the application of the DMA is without prejudice of the competition rules: Articles 101 and 102 of the TFEU and their national equivalents and merger control rules. It is also without prejudice to the application of national unilateral conduct rules (not equivalent to Article 102), although these can only be applied to gatekeepers insofar as they amount to the imposition of further obligations to those of the DMA. This is stated by Article 1(6).

17. And finally, Article 1(7) establishes that national authorities shall not take decisions contrary to a decision adopted by the EC under the DMA. Article 1(7) calls the EC and Member States to work in close cooperation and coordinate their enforcement actions (on the basis of Articles 37 and 38 DMA, as developed below).

18. Ensuring that these coordination mechanisms work smoothly is of utmost importance given the specificities of digital markets. The DMA offers a solution that is expected to cut through many of the market failures currently found in digital markets. Given the diagnosis that some of these issues in digital markets may have become too entrenched or systemic, the DMA may end up being a more efficient tool in addressing them. However, competition law enforcement will still play a main role in protecting undistorted competition side to side with this new regulation. For this reason, the respective enforcers of the DMA and of competition policy are due to cooperate in their respective tasks.

19. Article 37 DMA establishes general cooperation principles between the EC and Member States to coordinate their enforcement actions in order to ensure the coherence, effectiveness and complementarity of available legal instruments.

20. Article 38 DMA sets specific cooperation mechanisms between the EC and national authorities enforcing competition rules (like the CNMC, as the Spanish competition authority).

21. Article 38(1) establishes that the EC and the NCAs shall cooperate and inform each other regarding their respective enforcement actions through the ECN, including through the exchange of information (which can only be used for the purposes of the DMA and competition law enforcement).

22. In this regard, Articles 38(2) and 38(3) DMA state that NCAs, when applying national competition rules (other than merger control) on gatekeepers, must inform the EC when intending to launch an investigation (before or immediately after the start of the first formal investigative measure), when envisaging to adopt interim measures (as soon as possible, and at the latest, immediately after the adoption of such measures) and when planning to impose obligations (no later than 30 days before its adoption).

23. This framework has the objective of ensuring the maximum coherence, consistency and efficiency in the use of the respective instruments (the DMA and competition policy) and resources (of the EC and the NCAs).

24. And the efficiency in the use of resources is also achieved through other means. Articles 16(5) and 38(6) DMA include the possibility for the EC to ask the NCAs to support any of its market investigations pursuant to the DMA.

NCAs can also assist the EC in conducting inspections (Article 23), carrying out interviews and taking statements (Article 22), monitoring the obligations of gatekeepers (Article 26) and receiving information from third parties (Article 27). These mechanisms will allow the use of the resources of NCAs for the enforcement of the DMA, which may be useful to ensure that the expertise of NCAs in digital markets is leveraged to the maximum extent possible.

25. Finally, Member States may also request the EC to initiate a market investigation on non-compliance with the DMA or for the designation of new gatekeepers or CPS or considering new obligations or prohibitions (Article 41 DMA).

26. But perhaps the most relevant tool to ensure coherence, consistency and efficiency of the respective instruments is regulated in Article 38(7) DMA, which considers that NCAs (when empowered to do so by national law) may on their own initiative conduct an investigation into possible non-compliance with Articles 5, 6 and 7 of the DMA within its territory. The NCA, apart from informing the EC before its first formal investigative measure, must report on its findings to the EC, which is the sole enforcer of the DMA.

27. Recital 91 of the DMA states that this is especially relevant for cases where it cannot be determined from the outset whether a gatekeeper is infringing the DMA, competition law or both. This conveys two significant messages. First, a gatekeeper may be infringing both the DMA and competition rules, so given the complementarity of these two tools and given their different legal interest and objectives, NCAs can go on applying competition law in digital markets (including to gatekeepers providing CPS and in conduct that may be at the same time an infringement of the DMA). Second, an NCA can assist the EC in monitoring non-compliance with the DMA, hence contributing to the coherence, consistency and efficiency in the use of the respective instruments (the DMA and competition policy) and resources (of the EC and the NCAs).

28. It is worth mentioning that for the CNMC, as the Spanish competition authority, this empowerment has crystallised in Article 18(3) of the Spanish Competition Act,[7] which establishes that the CNMC may conduct investigations regarding cases of alleged infringements of Articles 5, 6 or 7 of the DMA in the Spanish national territory.

29. These investigations will follow the confidential procedure established under Article 49(2) of the Spanish Competition Act. For this purpose, the CNMC may send requests for information or conduct interviews or inspections as established in Articles 39, 39-*bis* and 40 of the Spanish Competition Act. In any case, the second paragraph of this Article 18(3) of the Spanish Competition Act mandates the Competition Directorate of the CNMC to inform the EC in writing before taking the first formal investigative measure (according to the mechanisms introduced in Article 38(7) of the DMA).

30. Article 18(3) of the Spanish Competition Act also foresees that the Competition Directorate of the CNMC may use any information received from third parties

---

[7] Law No 15/2007 in this version, in force from 30 June 2023 (after the reform implemented by Royal Decree-Law 8/2023).

under Article 27 of the DMA for the purpose of starting and conducting the aforementioned investigations. Besides, regarding the possible uses of information related to these investigations, this provision allows advantage to be taken of the information gathered under such DMA-related investigations for the enforcement of the antitrust rules foreseen in the Spanish Competition Act; and vice versa, the information gathered under the antitrust proceedings foreseen in the Spanish Competition Act may be used for the DMA investigations followed under Article 18(3) of the Spanish Competition Act.

31. Given the previously mentioned role of the EC as the sole enforcer of the DMA, Article 18(3) of the Spanish Competition Act foresees that the CNMC shall refrain from opening or continuing with an ongoing investigation when the EC opens formal proceedings under the DMA. The Competition Directorate of the CNMC will inform to the EC on the final findings of its investigation.

32. In the area of mergers and acquisitions a gatekeeper shall inform the EC of any intended concentration where the merging entities or the target of the concentration provide CPS or any other services in the digital sector or enable the collection of data. The EC, apart from publishing the list of acquisitions of which it has been informed by gatekeepers,[8] must provide this information to the NCAs, which in turn may request the EC to assess the operation in light of Article 22 of the EC Merger Regulation. Indeed, the so-called referral mechanism for transactions outlined in this article takes on particular relevance within the context of the DMA.

33. Finally, the DMA establishes several forms of coordination and cooperation with other authorities and institutions in addition to the ones described before (which are specifically addressed to NCAs).

34. First, as mentioned above, Article 37 DMA establishes for the EC and national authorities of the Member States to work in close cooperation and coordination regarding their enforcement actions to ensure coherent, effective and complementary enforcement of available legal instruments applied to gatekeepers. Article 37 also opens the way for the EC to consult national authorities where appropriate, on any matter relating to the application of the DMA.

35. These principles are enshrined in settled case-law of the Court of Justice of the European Union (CJEU).[9] The principle of sincere cooperation established in Article 4(3) TFEU implies that, in the regulatory fields covered by EU law, all Member States and their administrative authorities must not only assist each other in the performance and achievement of the EU's tasks, but also take all appropriate measures and refrain from measures which could jeopardise the EU's objectives. In this regard it is worth recalling that (as already mentioned) Article 1(7) establishes that National authorities shall not take measures contrary to a decision adopted by the EC under the DMA.

---

8 See, <https://digital-markets-act-cases.ec.europa.eu/acquisitions> accessed 14 July 2024.

9 Case C-518/11 *UPC Nederland BV v Gemeente Hilversum* ECLI:EU:C:2013:709 para 59, and Joined Cases C-14/21 and C-15/21 *Sea Watch eV v Ministero delle Infrastrutture e dei Trasporti* ECLI:EU:C:2022:604 parag 156, among others.

36. Recent rulings, such as recent case *Meta v Bundeskartellamt*[10] have pointed out the relevance of cooperation between authorities in other fields, such as competition law and data protection.

37. Second, Article 39 DMA also addresses the cooperation with national courts. In proceedings for the application of the DMA, national courts may ask the EC to transmit information or its opinion to them. Member States shall forward to the EC a copy of any written judgment of national courts deciding on the application of the DMA. The EC may submit written or oral observations to national courts where the coherent application of the DMA so requires, requesting the court to supply any necessary documents for the assessment of the case prior to its submission. National courts shall not give a decision which runs counter to a decision adopted by the Commission under the DMA (given also the abovementioned wording of Article 1(7) of the DMA). All this without prejudice to the possibility for national courts to request a preliminary ruling.

38. Third, Article 40 DMA has created a High-level Group for the DMA (HLG). The HLG is currently composed of 30 members distributed among the following European bodies and networks: the Body of the European Regulators for Electronic Communications (BEREC), the European Data Protection Supervisor (EDPS) and European Data Protection Board (EDPB), the ECN, the Consumer Protection Cooperation Network (CPCN), and the European Regulatory Group of Audiovisual Media Regulators (ERGA). The CNMC is currently one of the NCAs representing the ECN in the HLG, a task that is especially relevant at this initial stage of the DMA implementation.

39. The HLG, which was set up by the Commission Decision of 23 March 2023,[11] is aimed at providing the EC with advice and expertise for any general matter of implementation or enforcement of the DMA, and especially to promote a consistent approach across different regulatory instruments. In this sense, the HLG plays an advisory role.

40. For instance, the HLG is tasked with providing expertise in assessing the interaction between the DMA and sector-specific rules enforced by national authorities within European bodies and networks, submitting an annual report to the EC which should identify potential cross-regulatory issues, and which may also include recommendations. Such report is aimed to be communicated to both the European Parliament and the Council.[12]

41. The HLG is also encouraged to provide expertise to the EC on the need to amend the DMA in the context of market investigations into new services and practices.

---

[10] Case C-252/21, *Meta Platforms Inc v Bundeskartellamt* ECLI:EU:C:2023:537, see Marie Cartapanis and Claire Mongouachon, *Competence: The European Court of Justice accepts that the competition authorities have jurisdiction to penalise a breach of the General Data Protection Regulation on the grounds of abuse of a dominant position, and sets out the arrangements for cooperation with the authorities responsible for monitoring this regulation (Meta)*, Concurrences No. 4-2023, art. No. 115625.

[11] Commission Decision of 23 March 2023 on setting up the High-Level Group for the Digital Markets Act C(2023) 1833 final <https://competition-policy.ec.europa.eu/document/download/a46c9a1d-54c1-4025-aa45-f454f52790fc_en?filename=High_Level_Group_on_the_DMA_0.pdf> accessed 14 July 2024.

[12] Commission Decision C(2023) 1833 final art 2.

42. The HLG may also set up sub-groups in case the assessment of specific matters is required; sub-groups which shall be dissolved once its mandate is fulfilled.[13] Such sub-groups shall be composed of members of the HLG, although other representatives with expertise in the specific matters identified in the terms of references defined for its creation may also be nominated by these members of the HLG.[14] Both the HLG and the potential sub-groups are entitled to invite experts whenever this is needed.[15]

43. Finally, a Digital Markets Advisory Committee (DMAC) has been created (Article 50) with the representation of all the EU Member States. In addition to examining the implementing acts that develop the mechanisms for cooperation and coordination between the EC and national authorities, the Committee is established to issue an opinion on other implementing acts of the EC: acts specifying the measures that the gatekeeper concerned is to implement in order to effectively comply with the obligations laid down in Articles 6 and 7 DMA, acts suspending gatekeeper's obligations, acts excepting gatekeeper's obligations, acts designating gatekeepers after a market investigation, acts imposing behavioural or structural remedies to gatekeepers after a market investigation into systematic non-compliance with the obligations laid down in Articles 5, 6 or 7 DMA, acts ordering interim measures, acts making commitments binding on gatekeepers, acts setting out findings of gatekeeper's non-compliance, etc.

44. The CNMC participates in the DMAC together with the Ministry of Economic Affairs of Spain.

IV. Conclusion: the DMA as a Piece of a Wider Cosmos of EU and National Digital Transformation?

45. Competition policy will go on being relevant in digital markets for two reasons.

46. First, as we have mentioned, the DMA is without prejudice to the application of competition rules, including to gatekeepers providing CPS and when carrying out conduct included in the DMA. A gatekeeper may infringe both the DMA and competition law, so both tools may be applicable without giving rise to *ne bis in idem* issues, given that the legal interest of both tools is different. The post-DMA framework has introduced several mechanisms to ensure the maximum coherence, consistency and efficiency in the use of the respective instruments (the DMA and competition policy) and resources (of the EC and the NCAs).

47. Second, the DMA is not applicable to other contexts in digital markets such as firms which have not been designated as gatekeepers, gatekeepers providing other services than those defined as CPS and gatekeepers providing CPS but carrying out conduct not included in the DMA.

48. In the CNMC we are committed to continue enforcing competition policy in digital markets as a whole, including gatekeepers.

---

13 Commission Decision C(2023) 1833 final art 6.

14 Commission Decision C(2023) 1833 final art 6.

15 Commission Decision C(2023) 1833 final art 7.

49. In 2023 we issued a decision against Amazon and Apple for breaching Article 101 TFEU and its Spanish equivalent: Article 1 of the Spanish Competition Act.[16] In this case, the CNMC fined Amazon and Apple for entering into an agreement that restricted the number of resellers of Apple products on Amazon's website in Spain (what is often referred to as a brand-gating clause). Such agreement included two additional restrictions. On the one hand, it limited advertising space for Apple's competitors on amazon.es when searching for Apple's products. On the other, it restricted Amazon´s ability to target marketing campaigns to customers who had bought Apple products on amazon.es (when these campaigns are targeted to competing products from other brands).

50. Additionally, we currently have ongoing investigations against Google[17] and Booking[18] under Article 102 TFEU and its Spanish equivalent (Article 2 of the Spanish Competition Act) and Article 3 of the Spanish Competition Act.[19] They are still pending cases in which a final decision is due this year.

51. In the first case, the CNMC is looking into a possible abuse of Google's dominant position by imposing unfair commercial conditions on press publishers and news agencies regarding copyrighted content and possible acts of unfair competition that could affect the public interest by distorting free competition by infringing the Spanish intellectual property act and by exploiting the situation of economic dependence of press publishers.

52. In the second case, the CNMC is looking into a possible abuse of Booking in the provision of intermediation services to hotels by online travel agencies (OTAs) by imposing unfair trading conditions on hotels and through commercial policies that may have exclusionary effects on OTAs and other online sales channels, together with possible acts of unfair competition that could affect the public interest by distorting free competition by exploiting the situation of economic dependence of hotels.

53. In addition, over the last few years the CNMC has worked on other cases on digital markets (platforms rating mechanisms,[20] online bookings[21] and search services[22]), even if they have been closed without finding an infringement.

54. This intense activity shows that the CNMC, as stated in its action and strategic plans, has, as one of its top priorities the enforcement of competition policy in digital markets. Efforts will intensify in the post-DMA environment, with a wider toolkit to address the challenges of digital markets.

---

16 A summary of the case and all the public documents relating to it can be found on the CNMC's website <https://www.cnmc.es/expedientes/s001321> accessed 14 July 2024.

17 More information on this ongoing case can be found on the CNMC's website <https://www.cnmc.es/expedientes/s001322> accessed 14 July 2024.

18 More information on this ongoing case can be found on the CNMC's website <https://www.cnmc.es/expedientes/s000521> accessed 14 July 2024.

19 Ley 15/2007, de 3 de julio, de Defensa de la Competencia, art 3, which forbids unfair competition practices that affect the public interest by distorting free competition.

20 A decision involving Amazon, Booking and Tripadvisor can be found at: <https://www.cnmc.es/sites/default/files/4984480.pdf> accessed 14 July 2024.

21 A decision involving Trivago can be found at: <https://www.cnmc.es/expedientes/s004319> accessed 14 July 2024.

22 These decisions against Google Inc. (now named Alphabet Inc) and Google LLC can be found, respectively, at: <https://www.cnmc.es/expedientes/s000720> and <https://www.cnmc.es/expedientes/s002320> all accessed 14 July 2024.

Public Inquiry into New Competition Tools for Well-Functioning Markets

Sweden

KATHARINA VOSS*

Secretariat of the public inquiry into new competition tools for well-functioning markets

Abstract

This contribution presents legislation and case law on digital markets from Sweden. Sweden is known for its early digitalization and lively start up scene. However, in the European context, Sweden is a smaller EU member state and more recent action by the Swedish legislature reflects a measured and complimentary approach to EU legislation in the field. The cases that the Swedish Competition Authority and the Patent and Markets Courts have handled have primarily been of domestic significance. However, the Booking-cases as well as the damages case against Google show that Sweden has contributed significantly to the development of case law in EU competition law. In another complimentary action, the Swedish government has commissioned a public inquiry into a new competition tool. This tool is to compliment the DMA and other EU legislative initiatives, rather than duplicating these efforts. At the same time legislative action is underway to give the DMA proper effect.

---

* Katharina Voss is a secretary in the Swedish Government's public inquiry on new competition tools for well-functioning markets. She has previously been legal counsel at the Swedish Competition Authority and holds a Ph.D. in EU law from Stockholm University. All views expressed are the author's and should not be construed as representing the views of the Swedish government or that of the inquiry on new competition tools for well-functioning markets.

I. Introduction: General Views from Sweden

1. In the digital age, Sweden has been a frontrunner of societal digitalization. The European Commission's (the Commission) report on the state of the digital decade not only acknowledges Sweden's early and successful digital transformation but also anticipates its substantial contribution to the digital decade's ambitious targets. Nevertheless, the report also sheds light on recent impediments in Sweden's digital journey, notably in areas crucial for sustaining digital evolution, such as 5G connectivity and the development of human resources in digital industries.[1] This contrast of achievements and emerging challenges frame the backdrop against which Sweden's digital advancements and legislative interplays are to be examined.

2. Central to this chapter is the interplay between EU and Swedish competition law and the Digital Markets Act (DMA).[2] The DMA, along with other EU legislative acts such as the Digital Services Act and the Digital Governance Act, aims at harmonising the digital marketplace, ensuring robust competitiveness, and fostering innovation.[3] The Swedish legislative response to this EU legislation has been focussed on giving these rules effect in the national context. This response should also be viewed through the lens of Sweden being one of the EU's smaller Member States.

3. This chapter is structured to expose the dynamics between new legislative initiatives, case law in digital markets and giving effect to relevant EU legislation. The initial section delves into the national legislative initiatives and landmark case law as well as an exposition of the Swedish Government's public inquiry into a new competition tool for well-functioning markets. This is then followed by the ongoing legislative action to give the DMA effect in Sweden. The concluding segment reflects on Sweden's approach to legislation for the digital sector, especially in the context of giving effect to the DMA and ongoing enforcement of competition law.

1. Legislation for the Digital Sector

4. In Sweden, legislative activity for the digital sector has primarily been focussed on the implementation of the digital initiatives adopted at EU-level, such as the Digital Markets Act,[4] the Digital Services Act[5] and the Digital Governance Act.[6]

---

1 European Commission, '2023 Report on the State of the Digital Decade' (2023) <https://digital-strategy.ec.europa.eu/en/library/2023-report-state-digital-decade> accessed 12 January 2024.

2 Regulation 2022/1925 of the European Parliament and of the Council of 14 September 2022 on contestable and fair markets in the digital sector and amending Directives 2019/1937 and 2020/1828 (Digital Markets Act or DMA) [2022] OJ L265/1.

3 Regulation 2022/2065 of the European Parliament and of the Council of 19 October 2022 on a Single Market for Digital Services and amending Directive 2000/31 (Digital Services Act or DSA) [2022] OJ L277/1, and Regulation 2022/868 of the European Parliament and of the Council of 30 May 2022 on European data governance and amending Regulation 2018/1724 (Data Governance Act) [2022] OJ L152/1.

4 Memoranda from the Ministry of Climate and Enterprise, New rules adjacent to competition rules, KN2023/03687.

5 A common market for digital services – additions and changes to Swedish law, SOU 2023:39.

6 Implementation of the EU data governance act, Ds 2023:24.

This is natural given the international scope of many digital markets. However, the Swedish Government also has several ongoing initiatives that aim to facilitate and support digitalisation. As most of these initiatives are not directly competition-related, the following gives illustrations, primarily of ongoing initiatives.

5. Several initiatives aim for example at supporting incoming EU legislation or policy. An example for this is the recent public inquiry regarding interoperability in the context of data sharing between public authorities and from public authorities to third parties.[7] Further, the Swedish Government has commissioned a public inquiry that is tasked with identifying the need for and submission of proposals that promote a competitive, safe, and ethical AI development and AI use in Sweden. This inquiry shall also identify prioritised international initiatives and submit proposals on how Sweden can act proactively and in a coordinated manner when developing international policies and regulations for AI.[8]

6. There is also activity regarding infrastructures that support digitalisation. The Swedish Government has for example appointed a national coordinator for digital infrastructure in healthcare services.[9] Several Swedish initiatives have further been awarded EU funding to develop electronic communication infrastructure, both based on fibre-optic cable connections, via land and water and based on 5G networks.[10]

7. It is notable that the Swedish Government has not undertaken any specific legislative activity beyond the implementation of EU legislation concerning the functioning of digital markets. However, this is a reasonable approach given that Sweden is a smaller Member State. Giving the incoming EU legislation proper effect and thereby furthering the EU internal market before adding national legislation is a sensible approach. However, as will be described below, the Swedish Government has commissioned a public inquiry on new competition tools for well-functioning markets. This tool, if implemented, has the potential of filling holes potentially left once the DMA and related legislation for digital markets has been implemented.

2. Landmark National Cases

8. Competition law enforcement in Sweden is primarily carried out by the Swedish Competition Authority (SCA). Decisions taken by the SCA can be appealed to the Patent and Markets Court (PMD). From there, further appeal can be made to the Patent and Market Court of Appeal (PMÖD). These courts are specialised in, amongst other things, competition cases. Private litigation in competition cases, for example regarding damages, is heard by these courts as well.

---

7 A reform for data sharing, SOU 2023:96.

8 Ministry of Finance, 'Enhanced AI Capability in Sweden' (*Regeringen*, 8 December 2023) <https://regeringen.se/rattsliga-dokument/kommittedirektiv/2023/12/dir.-2023164> accessed 7 February 2024.

9 Ministry of Social Affairs, 'The Government Appoints a National Coordinator for Digital Infrastructure in Healthcare' (*Regeringen*, 18 December 2023) <https://www.regeringen.se/pressmeddelanden/2023/12/regeringen-tillsatter-en-nationell-samordnare-for-digital-infrastruktur-i-halso--och-sjukvarden/> accessed 7 February 2024.

10 Ministry of Finance, '14 Million Euros for Swedish Development of 5G and Underwater Infrastructure for Electronic Communication' (*Regeringen*, 21 December 2023) <https://www.regeringen.se/pressmeddelanden/2023/12/14-miljoner-euro-till-svensk-utveckling-av-5g-och-undervattensinfrastruktur-for-elektronisk-kommunikation/> accessed 7 February 2024.

9. The SCA has investigated several cases in digital markets. The emphasis has been on investigations of undertakings with a domestic significance, rather than large multinational undertakings. There are however a few notable exceptions, such as the cases regarding Booking and Expedia. This shows that there is plenty of leeway for cases with a primarily national significance, arguably even after the DMA and other related legislation has come into place. The PMD and PMÖD have so far seen relatively few cases in digital markets. The most important cases are summarised below.

A. *The SJ Booking Platform Case*

10. In 2018, the SCA received two complaints regarding SJ, one of the major players in the passenger train industry. These complaints centred on SJ's conduct in the online sale and mediation of train tickets, specifically concerning its interactions with MTR and Saga Rail. The complainants alleged that SJ's actions had a detrimental impact on the market for commercial train traffic. The core issue revolved around SJ's refusal to allow the sale of MTR and Saga Rail train tickets through its digital sales channels. SJ's argument was that these companies did not complement or promote SJ's own offerings. This stance was alleged to be a breach of competition laws.

11. The investigation conducted by the SCA showed that SJ's online channels possessed substantial network effects. These network effects essentially meant that customers using SJ's platform were potentially locked into it due to the platform's strong market position. This was exacerbated by the fact that SJ could withhold its services from competitors' booking platforms, further cementing its position. The result was an entry barrier for other commercial passenger train operators, stifling their incentives to innovate or enhance their own sales channels.

12. A critical finding was that SJ's online channel was far from neutral. Instead, it gave SJ a substantial level of influence over consumers' choices, putting other operators at a significant disadvantage. This prompted the SCA to propose an inquiry into potential legislation in the ticket sales segment of commercial passenger train services, with the aim of addressing these issues and restoring a fairer competitive landscape.[11]

13. Furthermore, in 2019, a government-appointed inquiry recognised the problems outlined by the SCA and recommended the introduction of a national, competition-neutral sales channel for all public transportation. This recommendation acknowledged the need for a government entity to manage this channel, taking into account SJ's extensive access to data due to its position in online ticket sales. The inquiry emphasised the importance of data and artificial intelligence in shaping future customer relationships and ensuring fair competition in the passenger train industry. In essence, the inquiry aimed to address the issues raised by the SCA and promote a more competitive and consumer-friendly environment in the public transportation sector.[12] However, the results of the inquiry have so far not led to further legislative action by the Swedish Government.

---

[11] SCA Decision in Case No 380/2018 *SJ AB*, 4 June 2019.

[12] A national ticketing system for all public transport, SOU 2020:25.

B. *The Training Aggregator Case*

14. In late 2019 and early 2020, the SCA investigated the practices of fitness aggregators Bruce, Classpass and Swiftr regarding the use of exclusivity clauses in their agreements with fitness facilities. The SCA examined whether these companies' application of exclusivity clauses could constitute violations of the prohibition against anti-competitive agreements.

15. Fitness aggregators are companies that bring together various types of fitness facilities under a single membership, allowing their members access to different fitness options at multiple locations. To enable the aggregation of fitness opportunities, fitness facilities provide an input facility to the fitness aggregator, which includes access to facilities and workout sessions. These sessions are carried out in-person, but members can search, compare fitness facilities and manage their memberships digitally through the fitness aggregator's mobile application.

16. The SCA's initial investigation revealed that the market was characterised by indirect network effects, meaning that the more popular fitness facilities were within the aggregator's service, the more attractive the service became to consumers. Therefore, the aggregators' fitness business model relied on their ability to enter agreements with numerous fitness facilities. Exclusivity agreements prevented fitness facilities from offering their services to the competitors of the investigated company, allowing the company to reserve a significant portion of the input commodity on which other fitness aggregators depended. This foreclosure of the input facility reduced the opportunities for competitors to provide an attractive and competitive service to consumers in the downstream market. If the actions of the investigated company led to the foreclosure of the input facility in the upstream markets, it could potentially exclude or marginalise competing fitness aggregators in the downstream markets, where aggregators competed for consumers. This could ultimately lead to consumer harm as fitness aggregator offerings, to some extent, are not interchangeable with individual fitness facilities or gym chain services due to the variety of fitness forms and concepts they offer.

17. The investigated market was relatively new, and the fitness aggregator phenomenon was still in its infancy, suggesting that the market structure was subject to rapid development. If the investigated company continued to reserve a significant share of the input facility from fitness facilities, potentially excluding other fitness aggregators from accessing it, the anti-competitive effects could be noticeable and enduring, given the market's developmental phase.

18. Due to the risk that exclusivity agreements could hinder other companies' opportunities to enter and grow in the market, potentially having lasting effects on new and immature markets, the SCA issued an interim decision. This decision prohibited the undertaking Bruce from using exclusivity agreements in certain geographical areas.[13] The decision was appealed to the PMD, which upheld the SCA's decision. The company's appeal to PMD was unsuccessful and was not granted leave to be heard by the PMÖD.[14]

---

13 SCA Decision in Case No 572/2019 *Im with Bruce*, 5 December 2019.

14 PMD Decision in Case No PMÄ 17901-19 *Im with Bruce*, 17 January 2020; PMÖD Decision in Case No PMÖÄ 1691-20 *Im with Bruce*, 20 February 2020.

19. The interim decision initially targeted Bruce, but during the investigation, it was discovered that Bruce's competitors also used exclusivity clauses in their agreements with fitness facilities. Therefore, the SCA expanded the investigation to include exclusivity agreements entered into by competitors Swiftr and Classpass with fitness facilities in Sweden. However, these investigations were closed without any further measures because of the undertakings' limited turnover and foreclosure effects respectively.[15]

20. In the continued investigation of Bruce, the SCA found that the exclusivity agreements the company had entered into could potentially constitute a violation of the prohibition against anti-competitive cooperation. After Bruce provided voluntary commitments that limited the application of exclusivity agreements, the SCA concluded that these commitments were sufficient to address the identified competition issues and accepted the voluntary commitments. The company committed, among other things, to refrain from applying the existing exclusivity clauses in the agreements covered by the SCA's interim decision and not to apply or enter into more than a certain number of new exclusivity agreements with existing or new partners in specific geographical areas for a period of 24 months.[16]

C. *The Booking Cases*

21. In 2013, the SCA initiated investigations into agreements between hotels and the two online travel agencies, Booking and Expedia. Both Booking and Expedia operated similar business models, providing online platforms where consumers could search, compare and book rooms at affiliated hotels. The compensation received by these online travel agencies from hotels consisted of commissions for each booking. Similar competition issues arose in most EU countries, leading to complaints filed with several national competition authorities. The Commission was informed early on about the parallel proceedings by some of these national competition authorities. The investigations by the SCA concerning online travel agencies were coordinated with the competition authorities in France and Italy, with the assistance of the Commission.

22. The competition issue revolved around online travel agencies, in their agreements with affiliated hotels, imposing conditions known as price parity, aimed at ensuring that the agencies received the same or better prices for the same rooms compared to the hotels' other sales and distribution channels. These parity conditions applied both horizontally, affecting the relationship between Booking and its competitors (also called broad parity clauses), and vertically (also called narrow parity clauses), affecting the relationship between Booking and the hotels.

23. The investigation found that the broad parity clauses, in combination with hotels being affiliated with multiple competing platforms, reduced Booking's incentive to compete with other platforms by offering low commissions compared to what would have been the case without the conditions. This posed a risk of higher

---

15 SCA Decision in Case No 749/2020 *Swiftr*, 7 July 2020; SCA Decision in Case No 750/2019 *Fitness collection/ Classpass*, 7 July 2020.

16 Case *Im with Bruce* (n 13).

commissions and, ultimately, higher room prices for consumers. However, the investigation did not find that the so-called narrow price parity conditions, where hotels were not allowed to offer better room prices through their own sales channels than via Booking, restricted competition between Booking and hotels.

24. In the case against Booking, the SCA reached the preliminary conclusion that the broad price parity clause in Booking's agreements, which ensured that Booking received the same or lower prices for hotel rooms compared to its competing platforms, constituted a restriction of competition in violation of Swedish and EU competition law. After being informed of this preliminary assessment, Booking proposed voluntary commitments to address the identified competition issues. This commitment involved Booking agreeing not to apply the clause on broad price parity in agreements with hotels. As for the narrow parity conditions, which significantly reduced the risk of hotels free riding on Booking's investments, the SCA concluded that they would allow Booking to receive compensation for the service provided to the benefit of consumers.[17]

25. During the SCA's investigation, Expedia unilaterally changed its behaviour in a manner similar to that of Booking. The SCA assessed that Expedia's changes were sufficient to eliminate the identified competition problems. Therefore, with reference to the SCA's prioritisation policy, the case was closed in October 2015.[18]

26. The follow-up on the effects of the modified contract terms carried out by the SCA, together with nine national competition authorities and the Commission in 2016, showed greater variation in hotel prices on different online travel agencies' sites after the intervention.[19]

27. In July 2020, Booking's commitment expired. However, Booking and Expedia announced their intention to voluntarily continue applying the changes to contract terms they introduced in 2015. According to Booking, these terms would remain in effect for an additional three years, but Expedia has not specified the duration of their continued application.[20]

28. The Swedish trade and employers' association for the Swedish hospitality industry, Visita, sued Booking in 2016 at the PMD with the support of the special right to act in competition cases provided for in competition law. Visita sought an injunction against Booking's application of narrow price parity. In July 2018, the PMD ordered Booking to remove the clause on narrow price parity from its agreements with hotels in Sweden. However, this decision was later appealed to the PMÖD which reversed the PMD's ruling, finding that Visita had not demonstrated that the narrow parity conditions constituted a prohibited competition restriction under competition law or the EU Treaty.

---

17 SCA Decision in Case No 596/2013 *Booking.com*, 15 April 2015.

18 SCA Decision in Case No 595/2013 *Expedia Inc*, 5 October 2013.

19 European Commission, 'Report on the Monitoring Exercise Carried Out in the Online Hotel Booking Sector by EU Competition Authorities in 2016' (2017) <https://competition-policy.ec.europa.eu/system/files/2021-07/hotel_monitoring_report_en.pdf> accessed 14 July 2024.

20 Konkurrensverket, 'Online Travel Agencies Continue to Apply Changed Contractual Terms for Hotels' (*Konkurrensverket*, 26 August 2020) <https://www.konkurrensverket.se/informationsmaterial/nyhetsarkiv/onlineresebyraer-fortsatter-tillampa-andrade-avtalsvillkor-for-hotell/> accessed 7 February 2024.

29. The compatibility of parity conditions with competition law and their detrimental impact on competition have been the subject of discussion with varying opinions.[21] The lack of guidance from previous practices and the absence of clear consensus regarding economic theory have led to differences in how authorities and courts in EU Member States have assessed and addressed parity conditions. In that context, it can be noted That Article 5(3) DMA specifically prohibits the use of both wide and narrow parity clauses. Booking has previously stated that it expects to be designated as a gatekeeper, meaning that it may have to adjust its practices regarding parity clauses further.[22]

D. *The Storytel Case*

30. The SCA investigated the digital book subscription service offered by Storytel. The investigation was initiated after Nextory, a provider of digital book subscriptions, filed a complaint with the SCA in December 2022. Nextory believed that the conditions set by Storytel to grant access to its catalogue of digital books were unreasonable and constituted an abuse of dominant position.

31. The SCA's investigation primarily focused on whether the delivery conditions set by Storytel to grant access to the catalogue were unreasonable and posed a risk of exclusionary effects in violation of competition rules. During the investigation, concerns were raised about exclusionary effects on both digital book subscription services and publishers in Sweden.

32. The SCA found that Storytel had adjusted its behaviour to reduce concerns regarding competition, and the company has resumed contract negotiations with other companies. As a result, the SCA concluded that there is no reason to continue investigating whether the conduct violates the prohibition of abuse of a dominant position under competition rules.[23]

E. *Pricerunner v Google*

33. The PMD has received a lawsuit from PriceRunner against Google. The lawsuit is a follow-on case to the Commission's finding that Google violated competition law by manipulating search results to favour its own product and price comparison service.[24] However, PriceRunner claims that the abuse is still ongoing, meaning that it will have to prove that Google's abuse continued beyond the date of the Commission's decision.

---

21 For a more recent update on this question, see, Adrian Deuschle, 'Good night, "Most Favoured Nation" Clauses!' (*D'Kart*, 10 May 2021). Adrian Deuschle, 'Good night, "Most Favoured Nation" Clauses' (*D'Kart*, 19 May 2021) <https://www.d-kart.de/en/blog/2021/05/19/good-night-bestpreisklauseln/> accessed 23 February 2024.

22 Booking Holdings Inc, 'Booking.com Updates Expected Timing for European Commission DMA Notification' (*Booking Holdings*, 4 July 2023) <https://ir.bookingholdings.com/news/news-details/2023/Booking.com-Updates-Expected-Timing-for-European-Commission-DMA-Notification/default.aspx> accessed 14 July 2024.

23 SCA Decision in Case No 817/2022 *Storytel*, 20 December 2023.

24 Commission Decision in Case AT.39740 – *(Google Search (Shopping))*, 27 June 2017, see Frédéric Marty, *Anticompetitive leverage: EU Commission sanctions the dominant operator of the online search market on the basis of an anticompetitive leverage strategy oriented toward the online price compactors market (Google Shopping)*, CONCURRENCES No. 1-2018, art. No. 86088.

34. The lawsuit focuses on Google's abuse of its dominant position and how it has harmed PriceRunner and other price comparison services. PriceRunner's claim for damages is a preliminary sum of 22bn Swedish crowns. If successful, PriceRunner expects that sum to be increased as it claims that Google's abuse is ongoing.[25]

35. The case is still pending, and there is thus no official assessment from the PMD as yet.

3. Overlapping Issues

36. As already mentioned, the cases above have mainly been of national significance, which shows that there is plenty of scope left for competition authorities' enforcement of competition rules, even given the impact of the DMA and related legislation. However, the cases above also show the use of competition rules to remedy competition problems in the cases that have been investigated by the SCA, has had mixed outcomes. In the SJ booking platform case, the suggested legislation has not (yet) been implemented. In the training aggregator cases and Booking cases, a decision was only issued against one of the investigated undertakings. One of the ongoing discussions, both among competition authorities and academics, has indeed been whether competition rules as they stand are fit for purpose in remedying competition problems that may arise.[26] Against this backdrop, the Swedish Government has commissioned the public inquiry which is presented below.

A. *The Swedish Government's Public Inquiry into New Competition Tools*

37. The Swedish Government, in a directive issued on 28 September 2023, commissioned a public inquiry into the need for new and supplementary rules within the field of competition.[27] The purpose is to reinforce and augment existing competition legislation, aiming to ensure more effective competition and well-functioning markets. This directive underscores the significance of efficient market competition as a cornerstone for productivity, economic growth and societal prosperity. It acknowledges the challenges posed by rapidly evolving markets, especially due to technological advancements and climate change adaptation, requiring innovative responses.

38. The existing competition legislation, primarily based on the EU framework, focuses on prohibiting specific anti-competitive practices, such as restrictive agreements, abuse of dominant positions and control of mergers. However, this framework can be criticised for its limited scope, as it primarily targets individual company behaviours and cannot address broader market-wide issues effectively. Reports

---

25 PriceRunner, 'PriceRunner is Suing Google for SEK 22 Billion' (*PriceRunner*, 7 February 2022) <https://nyhetsrum.pricerunner.se/posts/pressreleases/pricerunner-stammer-google-pa-22-miljarder-kr> accessed 26 January 2024.

26 See for example the European Commission, 'Inception Impact Assessment on a New Competition Tool' (4 June 2020) <https://ec.europa.eu/info/law/better-regulation/have-your-say/initiatives/12416-Single-Market-new-complementary-tool-to-strengthen-competition-enforcement_en> accessed 16 February 2024, and the new legislation recently introduced in Germany German Competition Act, § 32f.

27 Public inquiry into New Competition Tools for Well-Functioning Markets, KN 2023:03.

from the SCA highlight the necessity for a more flexible competition tool to address these broader market structural problems, especially in sectors characterised by high market concentration, low price transparency and limited competition.

4. New Competition Tool

39. The inquiry is first tasked with analysing and assessing the need for a broader competition tool that would complement the existing legislation. This tool is envisioned to address market-wide issues more effectively and efficiently than the current legislation allows. The investigator must consider how this new tool would interact with national and international legislation and authorities, and how it would function in relation to markets and companies both within and outside of Sweden.

40. The model for this broader tool can be seen in systems like the UK's market investigation tool, which makes it possible to intervene in market structures as a whole, not just in individual company practices.[28] Similarly, competition authorities in countries such as Greece, Iceland, Mexico and South Africa have tools for broader market interventions.[29] The Commission also contemplated a similar tool, although this has not yet led to a broader initiative at the EU level.[30]

5. Information Duty for Certain Mergers

41. The second part of the inquiry revolves around evaluating the necessity of an information duty for mergers that do not meet the thresholds for mandatory notification under the current legislation. While certain large-scale mergers require notification, there is a gap in oversight for smaller-scale mergers or acquisitions that might still have substantial effects on competition. The investigation will consider whether there should be a duty for companies to inform the SCA about such mergers.

42. This information duty is already present in certain jurisdictions. For example, in Norway, the SCA may require companies to inform about mergers that do not meet the notification thresholds. Such a duty is usually applied to sectors characterised by structures that warrant increased attention from a competition standpoint, like markets with dominant companies or oligopolistic structures.

6. Aim and Deadline for the Inquiry

43. The Swedish Government's directive represents a proactive step towards modernising the country's competition law framework. It acknowledges the complexities of contemporary markets, especially the digital economy and sectors undergoing rapid transformation due to technological innovation and climate change responses. The inquiry is set to balance the need for robust competition to drive innovation and

---

28 UK Enterprise Act 2002 pt 4.

29 For further detail see Richard Whish, 'Market Investigations in the UK and Beyond' in Motta and others (eds), *Market Investigations: A New Competition Tool for Europe?* (CUP 2022).

30 However, it should be noted that the European Parliament has called on the Commission to reconsider such a tool. See European Parliament, 'Report on Competition Policy – Annual Report 2023' (2023) para 7.

consumer benefits with the requirement for regulatory frameworks that effectively address market-wide issues beyond the scope of individual company behaviours.

44. The directive mandates the completion and presentation of the inquiry's findings by 28 February 2025.

II. Actions Undertaken by Sweden to Facilitate the Integration and to Enhance Synergies between EU and National Legislation for the Digital Sector

45. Following the adoption of the DMA, the Swedish Government commissioned an inquiry to assess what additional rules would be needed to give full effect to the DMA. The inquiry's results were subsequently published in a report.[31]

46. The report scrutinises the roles of national authorities, particularly the SCA, in regulating digital markets, discussing coordination with the Commission and evaluating the practicality of designating competent authorities. The report provides key recommendations, suggesting new legislation and thereby potentially shaping Sweden's approach to giving effect to the DMA. The report has been subject to a public consultation[32] and subsequently to a legislative proposal by the Swedish Government.[33] The government proposal makes several changes as compared to the inquiry report. The proposal is further processed within the Swedish parliament at the time of writing.

47. Below, the report's key recommendations as well as the content of the government proposal are recounted and discussed.

1. The Role of Public Authorities

48. Regarding the role of public authorities, the report notes that the DMA refers to:
   - National competent authority of the Member State that is enforcing the rules referred to in Article 1(6) (DMA);
   - National competent authorities; and
   - National authorities.

49. However, the DMA does not include an obligation on Member States to designate any authorities in accordance with the abovementioned terms.[34]

50. With regard to Article 1(6) DMA, the report specifically identifies the SCA as the national competent authority entrusted with enforcing the rules specified in this provision. Interestingly, while the DMA envisages the active involvement of national competition authorities, it does not explicitly mandate the establishment of such authorities. This nuanced approach potentially allows for flexibility and

---

31 Memoranda from the Ministry of Climate and Enterprise, New rules adjacent to competition rules, KN2023/03687.

32 Ministry of Climate and Business, 'Referral of the Memorandum New Regulations in Connection with the Competition Regulations' (*Regeringen*, 18 August 2023) <https://www.regeringen.se/remisser/2023/08/remiss-av-promemorian-nya-bestammelser-i-anslutning-till-konkurrensregelverket/> accessed 16 February 2024.

33 Government proposition 2023/24:154, Supplementary rules to new Union regulations in the field of competition.

34 *Ibid* 32.

adaptation to the unique administrative and legal structures of each Member State, while ensuring that the objectives of the DMA can be fulfilled across the Union.

51. In the practical application and enforcement of the DMA regulation, the cooperation between the Commission and national competent authorities assumes a central role. The report therefore proposes that the SCA should not only fulfil its designated supervisory role but should also function as the primary contact point for the Commission, especially in scenarios where the Commission might lack clarity about the appropriate authority to contact concerning certain DMA articles.[35]

52. It can be noted that public authorities in Sweden cooperate in various ways to ensure the smooth functioning of the government and the welfare of its citizens. The cooperation between public authorities is governed by the Public Administration Act. The Act outlines the principles of cooperation, such as the obligation of authorities to provide each other with information and assistance, and the requirement to coordinate their activities to achieve common goals.[36]

53. National competent authorities are referred to several times in the DMA, for example with regard to assistance in market investigations.[37] However, the report asserts that this terminology should not be interpreted as meaning that Member States are required to designate competent authorities.[38] Authorities that could be considered as competent authorities within the scope of the DMA are likely those that are part of the High-level Group appointed by the Commission that is the Swedish Post and Telecom Authority, the Swedish Authority for Privacy Protection, the Swedish Consumer Agency and the Swedish Agency for the Media.[39]

54. Moreover, the report also presents a critical assessment of the practicality of appointing national authorities as competent authorities. It argues that the term 'national authorities' as used in the DMA, encompasses all Swedish authorities, thereby removing the need for explicit legislative action to designate specific competent authorities. This interpretation could simplify the enforcement mechanism, ensuring that the regulatory responsibilities mandated by the DMA can be efficiently distributed and managed within the existing framework of Swedish authorities.[40]

55. The concluding assessment reiterates the centrality of the SCA in overseeing DMA compliance. Yet, it also cautions against the expansive designation of national authorities as competent authorities, suggesting a more measured approach. This caution is likely to stem from considerations of administrative efficacy, resource optimisation, and the need to maintain a focused and specialised enforcement framework that can adeptly navigate the complex and evolving landscape of digital markets.

---

35 *Ibid* 35.

36 Public Administration Act (*Förvaltningslagen* 2017:900) 8 §.

37 DMA art 16(5).

38 Referral of the Memorandum (n 32).

39 *Ibid* 34.

40 *Ibid* 35.

56. The legislative proposal by the government is by nature more concise text, focussing on the purpose of introducing legislation rather than discussing different options. With regard to competent authorities, it simply concludes that it follows from the Swedish Competition Act that the SCA is the competent authority according to article 1(6) DMA. This means that it follows directly from the text of the DMA that the SCA is the competent authority referred to in article 1(6) DMA for the part of Sweden. There is no further discussion as regards a role for the SCA as a contact point or the like in the government proposal. Regarding other authorities that may be concerned by the DMA, the government proposal agrees with the memorandum that these are likely to be the Swedish Post and Telecom Authority, the Swedish Authority for Privacy Protection, the Swedish Consumer Agency and the Swedish Agency for the Media[41]

2. Coordination between the Commission and the SCA and Enforcement at the National Level

57. Article 38(7) DMA plays a critical role in delineating the relationship and procedural interplay between national competition authorities and the Commission, particularly in the context of investigations into potential non-compliance with the DMA's provisions. The primary purpose of this provision is to consolidate the oversight of compliance with the DMA under the leadership of the Commission, especially when it initiates a formal investigation procedure under Article 20 of the DMA. This consolidation is crucial for avoiding duplicative efforts, potential conflicts of jurisdiction and the fragmentation of enforcement actions across different Member States. It ensures that the DMA's enforcement remains streamlined, coherent and efficient, reflecting the regulation's overarching objectives to create a fair and competitive digital market environment.

58. The report formulates detailed recommendations with respect to Article 38(7) DMA and its ramifications for Swedish legislation. The document underscores the need to furnish the SCA with the requisite investigative powers to ensure the DMA's effective enforcement within the Member States. It specifically advocates for the empowerment of the SCA to independently conduct investigations into violations of Articles 5, 6 and 7 of the DMA.[42]

59. The rationale for such empowerment is manifold. Primarily, the authority to perform investigations under Article 38(7) DMA positions the SCA to bolster the Commission in supervising and securing compliance with the DMA regulations. This capability is instrumental in enabling the SCA to rapidly detect and rectify instances of non-compliance, thus protecting users of platform services, encompassing both businesses and consumers, from potential infractions by gatekeepers.[43]

60. The report acknowledges an existing overlap between the obligations addressed by the DMA and those under national competition laws, as well as Articles 101 and 102 of the Treaty on the Functioning of the European Union (TFEU). Despite this overlap and the stipulation in Article 1(6) DMA that its application should

[41] Government proposition 2023/24:154 (n 33), 29–30.
[42] *Ibid* 40–41.
[43] *Ibid* 40.

not impact the enforcement of Articles 101 or 102 or national competition rules prohibiting the abuse of a dominant position, the report accentuates the inherent complexities in distinguishing between DMA violations and dominance abuses, especially in the preliminary stages of an investigation. It asserts that the SCA should be endowed with investigative powers equivalent to those required for probing infractions under the diverse regulatory frameworks.[44]

61. Furthermore, the report cautions that the absence of investigative powers as delineated in Article 38(7) DMA could potentially result in DMA regulation violations not being thoroughly investigated in Sweden. This deficiency may engender an enforcement inconsistency vis-à-vis other EU countries where national competition authorities are vested with such powers. The limitation of these powers might also curtail the SCA's capacity to actively engage in the collective enforcement efforts within the EU concerning the DMA's application. The report notes that other Member States, such as Hungary have decided to confer similar investigative powers upon their national competition authorities, with analogous resolutions anticipated from France, Germany and Italy, and deliberations underway in Denmark.[45]

62. Given these considerations, the report advocates for the provision of authority and investigative powers to the SCA to independently investigate violations pursuant to Article 38(7) of the DMA. Such empowerment would facilitate the SCA's initiation of investigations either autonomously upon detecting an infraction of the DMA's stipulations in Articles 5, 6, and 7 or through information furnished by third parties as per Article 27 DMA. However, the report underlines that should the Commission initiate proceedings under Article 20 of the DMA, the SCA is obliged to halt or refrain from initiating its own investigations, thus adhering to the DMA's centralised enforcement strategy.[46]

63. The government proposal nevertheless does not propose legislation to give the SCA investigatory powers regarding violations of the DMA. The reason given for this is that the DMA is a new regulation and that it remains to be seen to what extent investigations by the SCA will be needed in compliment to the Commissions investigations. However, the proposal does not entirely exclude the possibility of introducing investigatory powers for the SCA at a later point.[47]

3. Legislative Mechanisms Provided at National Level to Ensure Coordination with EU Regulations

64. The report commissioned by the Swedish Government, the consultation that followed it and the legislative proposal by the government signify the first steps in adapting Swedish national legislation so that the DMA can have its desired effect. The proposal has been submitted to parliament where it is handled in the competent committee. After examination and potential amendment, the proposed bill is debated in the plenary of the parliament and eventually voted upon.

---

44 *Ibid* 40.

45 *Ibid* 40–41.

46 *Ibid* 41.

47 Government proposition 2023/24:154 (n 33), 27–28.

65. Notwithstanding the comprehensive nature of the Swedish legislative process, it reconciles the aims of ensuring the prompt and accurate effect of EU legislation with the aim of following national legislative traditions.

66. This means that the Swedish legislator has some steps ahead of it before additional rules necessary to give full effect to the DMA are still to be taken. This contribution can therefore only present a preliminary picture of the Swedish rules regarding the DMA, as amendments may still be made, as outlined above.

III. Conclusion: the DMA as a Piece of a Wider Cosmos of EU and national Legislative Initiatives for Digital Transformation?

67. This chapter has presented an overview of the Swedish jurisdiction in issues related to the DMA, ongoing legislative initiatives, case law and legislation to give effect to the DMA. The picture that emerges is that the Swedish approach to these issues is one of complimenting EU legislation rather than parallel mirroring of such legislation. This is visible in the overview of legislative initiatives. More particularly regarding the DMA, the inquiry on new competition tools can be viewed as the first step in adopting new competition rules that could be used to remedy competition problems both in digital markets where the DMA and other competition rules do not apply.

68. The same pattern is visible in case law. There are several competition cases that have touched digital markets however, these have mainly concerned domestic circumstances. At the same time, it is obvious from the Booking and PriceRunner cases that Sweden and the SCA are not insular from the rest of the EU and will successfully coordinate and cooperate with other EU organs if necessary.

69. Thus, the DMA can be seen as one puzzle piece in the efforts to ensure the functioning of digital markets within the EU and more particularly in Sweden. It must in this context be remembered that while the gatekeepers that are designated in accordance with the DMA have a huge impact on undertakings and citizens in the EU, in Sweden, the DMA is particularly important for undertakings that are business customers to gatekeepers, such as the many start up in Sweden's tech scene. At the same time, there are plenty of circumstances that remain relatively untouched by the DMA, as the reported case law shows.

70. In this context, it is important to take all necessary measures to ensure that the DMA and related EU legislation is given full effect. At the same time, it is important not to overregulate undertakings, especially when the full effect of legislation is yet to be seen.[48] The Swedish approach is therefore nuanced, balancing the need for clear rules in digital markets with the need for a predictable climate for undertakings within which to work.

---

48 In this regard, see the recent report from the Swedish National Board of Trade, Karin Atthoff, 'The EU Single Market in the Digital Era – from Legislative Complexity to Clarity' (*Kommerskollegium*, 2024) <https://www.kommerskollegium.se/globalassets/publikationer/rapporter/2024/the-eu-single-market-in-the-digital-era.pdf> accessed 14 July 2024

EPILOGUE

ALBERTO BACCHIEGA*
European Commission

Sectoral regulation is the norm for strategic and sensitive industries in developed economies: the financial, telecoms, energy, and pharmaceutical sectors are just a few examples of regulated industries. Equally common is the interplay between sectoral regulation and competition enforcement as mutually reinforcing instruments to ensure a level playing field in instances where market forces alone could lead to suboptimal outcomes for society.

From this perspective, there is nothing particularly surprising or novel in the decision of the European legislator to regulate large digital platforms under the Digital Markets Act (DMA), given the pervasive and strategic role these platforms play in the lives of European businesses and citizens.

At the same time, the DMA marks a turning point in the digital sector: for the first time, large digital platforms become regulated subjects for their business practices and their relationship with businesses and end users that interact with them. The European Union has taken the lead in this project, with several other jurisdictions following or considering similar regimes.

The DMA is also innovative in unequivocally identifying the European Commission as the sole enforcer of its provisions and departing from a longstanding tradition of national enforcement coordinated at European level or shared European/national enforcement.

Although there is a clear element of centralisation in the DMA, it would be a mistake to conclude that, as the Commission is the sole enforcer, it is alone in enforcing. Quite to the contrary, the DMA sets out the principles of close coordination and cooperation between the Commission and national competition authorities (NCAs) to make full use of their respective capabilities and strengths in ensuring fairness and contestability in the digital sector.

The DMA sets out a simple yet efficient structure to bring together NCAs and the Commission for the implementation of its provisions. According to Article 1(7) DMA, '[t]he Commission and Member States shall work in close cooperation and coordinate their enforcement actions'.

Article 1(6) DMA clarifies that the DMA is without prejudice to the application of Articles 101 and 102 of the Treaty on the Functioning of the European Union (TFEU), their national equivalents, competition rules that apply to non-gatekeepers or gatekeepers insofar as they impose 'further obligations', as well as merger control. Beyond these

---

* Director, Directorate-General for Competition (DG COMP) – European Commission

well-defined instances, national authorities cannot intervene in instances covered by the DMA.

Article 38, in turn, stresses the role of the European Competition Network (ECN) as the body through which the cooperation and information exchanges between the Commission and the competent national authorities (identified in the NCAs) take place. In doing so, the DMA leverages a longstanding and fruitful collaboration between European and Member State authorities in the enforcement of antitrust rules under Regulation 1/2003. The ECN is providing a precious platform to exchange information and coordinate actions.

However, the ongoing collaboration with NCAs is not limited to the formal exchanges mandated by Article 38. It extends to informal exchanges of views and intelligence, leveraging the experience and knowledge of all actors.

As the contributions in this volume well illustrate, there has been, and there is, a differentiated approach to the enforcement of competition rules in the digital sector at national level, explained by specificities in the economic context in which NCAs operate, and also by their size and capacity to mobilise resources to investigate a fast-moving and complex sector.

It is, however, beyond doubt that competition enforcement, both at national and European level, and regulation under the DMA go hand in hand.

First of all, the DMA exists thanks to at least twenty years of experience accumulated in enforcing competition rules in the digital sector in Europe. Without that experience, we would not have a targeted, largely self-enforcing regulatory tool. We would have an uninformed attempt at regulation, which would most likely cast the net too wide or too narrow and give no certainty to gatekeepers about what they must do and no certainty to other companies about what they can expect.

Perhaps more importantly, competition enforcement and regulation under the DMA will have to work together for the foreseeable future. It is not just about the 'division of labour' in Articles 1(6) and 38 DMA, and the formal aspects of which authority pursues which conduct. It is about how to leverage both regulation and antitrust enforcement to strive for a fair, competitive and contestable digital sector for the benefit of European citizens and businesses.

The DMA alone will never be able to achieve that goal. To start with, the DMA covers only a subset of practices that could be caught by competition law. First, it applies to core platform services, not all digital services. Second, it applies to gatekeepers, not all providers of digital services. And third, it has a specific list of obligations and prohibitions that address specific behaviours of gatekeepers, but not all the possible anticompetitive conduct. This means that there is ample room for competition law enforcement outside of the DMA. This may, for example, concern practices by non-gatekeepers. But it may also concern designated gatekeepers, for example when some of their services have not been designated or if they engage in conduct not covered by the obligations and prohibitions in the DMA.

Similarly, merger control in the digital sector continues unabated. Merger control has the capacity to prevent the creation of a dysfunctional market structure, and the problems that the DMA is trying to address. Again, complementarity is the keyword.

Looking ahead, for genuinely new conduct and new services that affect competition in digital markets, competition law will remain our best intervention tool. Conversely, the DMA will be the most effective tool to tackle *ex ante* specific and identified conducts that are more systemic in nature and whose harmful effects are well known.

In the longer term, the relationship between competition law and the DMA can create a virtuous dynamic relationship between the two tools. On the one hand, competition law will benefit from the fact that the DMA will tackle systemic issues from a sectoral perspective. On the other hand, the DMA will continue to be inspired by competition law, as was the case for many of the DMA's obligations.

Due to the complementary nature of regulation and competition law, it is of the utmost importance to ensure close, proactive and sustained coordination between the Commission and NCAs through the ECN and to work together to reinforce this collaboration.

So far, NCAs' involvement with the implementation of the DMA has taken various forms, in some instances going beyond a narrow reading of the requirements set out in Article 38 of the Regulation.

For example, the Commission has concluded memoranda of understanding (MoUs) with the NCAs of the Netherlands, Italy, Spain, Belgium and Luxembourg to allow for the formation of joint investigative teams on DMA issues. Under these MoUs, NCAs have seconded officials to the Commission to work on DMA cases, bringing their expertise and contributing to ongoing investigations. This experience has also been extremely valuable from the perspective of NCAs carrying out investigations on possible non-compliance cases under Article 38(7) DMA.

In conclusion, the collaboration between the Commission and NCAs is a central building block of the DMA construction. In the first instances of its application, the authorities involved have demonstrated their capacity and will to make the best use possible of this collaboration. There is no doubt this trend will continue and will be reinforced in the future.

Appendix

Table of DMA Regulation Transposition in National Legislations

COUNTRY	DMA REGULATION TRANSPOSED	TRANSPOSITION LAW	COMPETENT AUTHORITY	INTERINSTITUTIONAL STEERING COMMITTEE	INVESTIGATIVE POWERS ARTICLE 38(7) DMA	NEW ANTITRUST INSTRUMENTS	NEW DIGITAL LEGISLATIONS
BELGIUM	Yes	Act of 28 March 2024 – Bill 55K3813, which amended Books I and IV of the Code of Economic Law (CEL)	**Belgian Competition Authority (BCA)**	**Informal Platform for Digital Governance** formed by: 1. Belgian Competition Authority (BCA), responsible for enforcing the DMA. 2. Centre for Cybersecurity Belgium (CCB). 3. Federale Overheidsdienst Economie (FOE), also known as the Service public fédéral Économie (SPF Économie), responsible for enforcing the DSA and the P2B Regulation. 4. Directorate-General for Simplification and Digital Transformation of the FOD/SPF Policy and Support. 5. Financial Services and Markets Authority (FSMA). 6. Belgian Data Protection Authority (APD, Autorité de protection des données in French or GBA, Gegevensbeschermingsautoriteit in Dutch). 7. Belgian Institute for Postal Services and Telecommunications (IBPT/BIPT).	**Conducting investigations:** The BCA can investigate breaches of Articles 5, 6 and 7 DMA after notifying the Commission, provided no proceedings have been initiated (Act of 28 March 2024 arts 50–53, new art IV.96 CEL). The BCA has the power, under Articles IV.40 to IV.40/5 CEL, to gather information essential for investigations, including: – making information requests; – investigating potential infringements; – conducting inspections (dawn raids); – appointing experts.	**New competition tool (NCT)** that would allow the BCA to address market distortions without needing to prove a specific infringement of competition rules.	**Bill (no 55K3799)** was introduced to align Belgian laws with the DSA. Key measures include designating the IBPT/BIPT as the federal authority for DSA supervision, issuing decrees to designate competent authorities in federated entities, and establishing a cooperation agreement between the federal and community levels.

COUNTRY	DMA REGULATION TRANSPOSED	TRANSPOSITION LAW	COMPETENT AUTHORITY	INTERINSTITUTIONAL STEERING COMMITTEE	INVESTIGATIVE POWERS ARTICLE 38(7) DMA	NEW ANTITRUST INSTRUMENTS	NEW DIGITAL LEGISLATIONS
BULGARIA	No	No	No	No	No	**The latest amendment to the Law on Protection of Competition (LPC)**, effective February 2021, implements the ECN+ Directive of 11 December 2018. This amendment aims to strengthen the enforcement capabilities of Member States' competition authorities and ensure the proper functioning of the EU internal market.	**The Act on the Supply of Digital Content and Digital Services and on the Sale of Goods, promulgated on 19 March 2021 and effective from 1 January 2022**, aligns Bulgarian law with Directives 2019/770 and 2019/771. It updates the consumer protection framework, particularly regarding consumer rights for non-conformity of goods, digital content, and digital services. **On 15 December 2023, the Bulgarian Council of Ministers published a draft proposal to amend the Electronic Communications Act** to implement the DSA. The proposal underwent public consultation until 15 January 2024. The proposal designates the Communications Regulation Commission (CRC) as Bulgaria's Digital Services Coordinator (DSC), responsible for non-video-sharing intermediary service providers, while the Council for Electronic Media (CEM) oversees video-sharing platforms under the Radio and Television Act. Personal data processing related to online advertisements and minors' protection (arts 26 and 28 DSA) is monitored by the Commission for Personal Data Protection.

COUNTRY	DMA REGULATION TRANSPOSED	TRANSPOSITION LAW	COMPETENT AUTHORITY	INTERINSTITUTIONAL STEERING COMMITTEE	INVESTIGATIVE POWERS ARTICLE 38(7) DMA	NEW ANTITRUST INSTRUMENTS	NEW DIGITAL LEGISLATIONS
CROATIA	Yes	Decree, Official Gazette 131/2023 of 2 November 2023	**Croatian Competition Agency (CCA)**	No	**Conducting investigations:** The CCA can investigate breaches of Articles 5, 6 and 7 DMA after notifying the Commission, provided no proceedings have been initiated. To do so, it must inform the Commission in writing about its intention to initiate a procedure against access controls under competition regulations, either before or immediately after the action begins.	The Act on the Amendments to the Competition Act was published in Official Gazette 41/2021 on 16 April 2021. **The Revised Competition Act** 2021 introduced new legal tools, including 'interviews,' 'periodic penalty payments,' 'uniform instruments', and 'settlement in cartel cases'. It also clarifies the process for 'access to leniency statements and settlement submissions'. Additionally, the Act specifies the imposition of fines when an infringement is committed by an association of undertakings.	The Croatian Parliament's Committee on Information, Computerisation, and Media has approved a **bill to implement the DSA**. The DSA, effective since 17 February 2024, aims to prevent illegal online activities and the spread of disinformation. It applies to all online platforms that act as intermediaries for goods, services, or content. The Croatian Regulatory Authority for Network Industries (HAKOM) will coordinate digital services with other bodies responsible for enforcement. **Smart Specialisation Strategy (S3)** is a strategic framework designed to guide investments in research, innovation, and economic development by focusing on the country's unique strengths and competitive advantages.

COUNTRY	DMA REGULATION TRANSPOSED	TRANSPOSITION LAW	COMPETENT AUTHORITY	INTERINSTITUTIONAL STEERING COMMITTEE	INVESTIGATIVE POWERS ARTICLE 38(7) DMA	NEW ANTITRUST INSTRUMENTS	NEW DIGITAL LEGISLATIONS
CZECH REPUBLIC	Yes	Act no 226/2023 Coll., amending the Act on the Protection of Competition art 20a(3)(i)	**Office for the Protection of Competition (OPC)**	N/A	No	The Czech government is proposing **amendments to the Act on the Protection of Competition** to enhance the powers of the Office for the Protction of Competition (OPC). Key changes include: 1. **New remedies for uncompetitive markets:** The OPC could impose remedies on markets found to be significantly distorted, even without proof of anticompetitive conduct. 2. **Call-in model for merger control:** The OPC could request merger notifications for deals that do not meet current thresholds but may still harm competition, particularly with high-revenue competitors. 3. **Administrative sanctions for executives:** The proposal shifts the responsibility for sanctioning executives involved in cartels to administrative liability, allowing fines and activity bans.	The Czech Chamber of Deputies discussed the **draft Digital Finance Act on 13 June 2024**, aimed at implementing the EU's Digital Operational Resilience Act (DORA) and Markets in Crypto-Assets Regulation (MiCAR). The draft law revises offence categorisation and grants the Czech National Bank authority to license and oversee crypto service providers. It included provisions for asset reserves for issuers of asset-referenced tokens (ARTs) and electronic money tokens (EMTs) to ensure smooth MiCAR application. The Czech government approved the **Digital Economy Bill to align with the EU's DSA and DGA**, aiming to protect internet users, ensure fair competition, and support a secure digital environment. The DSA focuses on user rights, content moderation, and preventing illegal content online, while the DGA promotes trusted data sharing and innovation. The Czech Telecommunications Office will oversee compliance, with penalties for violations reflecting EU standards.

COUNTRY	DMA REGULATION TRANSPOSED	TRANSPOSITION LAW	COMPETENT AUTHORITY	INTERINSTITUTIONAL STEERING COMMITTEE	INVESTIGATIVE POWERS ARTICLE 38(7) DMA	NEW ANTITRUST INSTRUMENTS	NEW DIGITAL LEGISLATIONS
DENMARK	Yes	Act no 1533 of 12 December 2023 (effective from 1 January 2024)	**Danish Competition and Consumer Authority (DCCA)** The DCCA is also responsible for enforcing the DSA and the P2B Regulation.	No	**Conducting investigations:** The DCCA has the power to investigate possible non-compliance with Articles 5, 6, and 7 DMA, either on its own initiative or based on a complaint (Act no 1533 of 12 December 2023 s 3(1)) The DCCA can demand all necessary information, including access to algorithms and information about tests, and request explanations when deemed necessary. The DCCA can also conduct interviews with any legal or natural person who consents, provided they are believed to possess relevant information (Act no 1533 of 12 December 2023 s 5, equivalent to art 22(1) DMA).	**Bill amending the Competition Act of 21 May 2024**, which expanded the DCCA's powers horizontally. The Bill introduces three key amendments: 1. It allows the DCCA to require certain mergers to be notified, even if turnover thresholds are not exceeded (the 'call-in option'). 2. It grants the DCCA a market investigation tool to examine structures or behaviours that harm competition, with the power to issue behavioural orders. 3. It revises the principles for imposing civil fines, aligning them with EU standards and increasing the fining level.	**Government proposal 'Tech giants: Fairer competition and better consumer protection'**, which created, among other things, an expert support group tasked with helping the government through interim reports.

COUNTRY	DMA REGULATION TRANSPOSED	TRANSPOSITION LAW	COMPETENT AUTHORITY	INTERINSTITUTIONAL STEERING COMMITTEE	INVESTIGATIVE POWERS ARTICLE 38(7) DMA	NEW ANTITRUST INSTRUMENTS	NEW DIGITAL LEGISLATIONS
DENMARK					**Imposing fines for non-compliance:** The DCCA can impose daily or weekly fines if a company fails to provide complete and correct information within the established timeframe (Act no 1533 of 12 December 2023 s 8(1)). **Autonomous decision-making:** The DCCA can decide whether to initiate or discontinue an investigation. It also has the power to refuse to handle a complaint. **Confidentiality of information:** The DCCA is empowered to maintain the confidentiality of the information gathered during investigations, except when the information relates to documents that require third-party comments or are of significant economic importance.		

Country	DMA Regulation Transposed	Transposition Law	Competent Authority	Interinstitutional Steering Committee	Investigative Powers Article 38(7) DMA	New Antitrust Instruments	New Digital Legislations
Estonia	No (but the Ministry of Justice is planning to amend the Estonian Competition Act)	No	No	N/A	No	N/A	N/A
France	Yes	Security and Regulation of the Digital Space (SREN) Act (Law no 2024-449 of 21 May 2024)	**Autorité de la concurrence (Aut. Conc.)** and **General Directorate for Competition Policy, Consumer Affairs and Fraud Control (DGCCRF)**	**National coordination network for the regulation of digital services** formed by: 1. Audiovisual and digital communication regulator (ARCOM) for the DSA. 2. General Directorate for Competition Policy, Consumer Affairs and Fraud Control (DGCCRF) for monitoring compliance with the obligations of marketplace providers. 3. Data privacy regulator (CNIL) for monitoring platforms' compliance with restrictions on advertising profiling. 4. Telecom regulator (ARCEP) for regulating cloud services. 5. Autorité de la concurrence for the DMA. 6. National agency for information systems security. 7. Authority for employment platforms labour relations. 8. Other relevant government departments.	**Conducting investigations**: According to Article L 450-12 of the French Commercial Code, the Autorité de la concurrence and the DGCCRF, in performing their functions under the DMA, enjoy the same investigation powers and can impose the same sanctions provided by the national antitrust law.	**The Security and Regulation of Digital Space (SREN) Act (Law no 2024-449 of 21 May 2024)** grants new powers to the Autorité de la concurrence regarding self-preferencing practices. Under the Act, the practice of 'self-preferencing' may be sanctioned. Specifically, if a cloud computing service provider that also supplies software offers unjustifiably different pricing and functional conditions depending on whether or not the customer subscribes to its cloud computing service, this could be subject to sanctions.	**Security and Regulation of the Digital Space SREN Act (Law no 2024-449 of 21 May 2024)** enhances digital security and regulation in France. It mandates strict cybersecurity standards for companies, requires online platforms to quickly remove illegal content, and enforces age verification to protect minors. Large digital platforms must disclose their algorithms and ensure data protection. The law enhances user rights over personal data, regulates online advertising for transparency and privacy, and addresses 'play-to-earn' games to prevent fraud. Cloud providers must comply with security standards and data transparency.

COUNTRY	DMA REGULATION TRANSPOSED	TRANSPOSITION LAW	COMPETENT AUTHORITY	INTERINSTITUTIONAL STEERING COMMITTEE	INVESTIGATIVE POWERS ARTICLE 38(7) DMA	NEW ANTITRUST INSTRUMENTS	NEW DIGITAL LEGISLATIONS
GERMANY	Yes	11th amendment to the German Competition Act (GWB), effective from 7 November 2023	**Bundeskartellamt (BKartA)**	N/A	**Conducting investigations:** According to the transposition law, the BKartA is empowered as the national competent authority to conduct non-compliance investigations with Articles 5, 6, and 7 DMA. For the purpose of such investigations, the BKartA may make use of the investigative powers conferred on it by the GWB for the enforcement of competition law, including the issuance of requests for information and the execution of searches of premises (s 32g(1) and (2) GWB). In case the non-compliance investigation concerns Article 7 DMA (related to the interoperability of number-independent interpersonal communications services), the BKartA must also give the German Federal Network Agency a chance to express its opinion on the matter (s 32g(2) GWB).	**The 10th amendment to the 'GWB Digitalisation Act':** The new Section 19a GWB targets companies with 'paramount significance for competition across markets', especially in digital ecosystems. The BKartA can restrict these companies from favouring their own offers, unfairly expanding, using anti-competitive strategies like tying or bundling, exploiting data-driven power, or hindering market entry and interoperability. The **11th amendment to the GWB** introduced significant changes: 1. **New competition tools:** The BKartA gains powers to address problematic market conditions without needing proof of competition law violations, using tools like the UK and proposed EU competition measures. These include both behavioural and structural remedies.	**The German Digital Services Act (DDG)**, proclaimed on 13 May 2024, came into effect on 14 May 2024. It establishes a national framework for implementing the EU's DSA in Germany, including adjustments to jurisdictions and information duties. The EU's DSA, in force since November 2022, aims to ensure a safe online environment and effective consumer protection across digital intermediary services. The DDG adapts Germany's legal framework to the DSA's requirements and entered into force alongside other related provisions.

Country	DMA Regulation Transposed	Transposition Law	Competent Authority	Interinstitutional Steering Committee	Investigative Powers Article 38(7) DMA	New Antitrust Instruments	New Digital Legislations
Germany						2. **Sector inquiries:** The BKartA can now require merger notifications even below usual thresholds, based on the significant impediment to competition standards. It can also enforce remedies like data access, preventing harmful information sharing, and oblige firms to separate accounts, with divestitures as a last resort.	
Ireland	Yes	Statutory Instrument no 117 of 27 March 2024	**Competition and Consumer Protection Commission (CCPC)** The CCPC is also responsible for enforcing Articles 30, 31 and 32 DSA and for the P2B Regulation.	**Digital Regulators Group (DRG)** formed by: 1. Competition and Consumer Protection Commission (CCPC) for the DMA, the P2B Regulation and part of the DSA. 2. Commission for Communications Regulations (ComReg) for the regulation of the electronic communications sector and the postal sector. 3. Data Protection Commission (DPC) for the GDPR. 4. Coimisiún na Meán (CNAM) for the DSA.	No	The CCPC has published a **draft procedure for settling investigations** into suspected competition law breaches. This procedure, part of the CCPC's new civil enforcement powers under the Competition (Amendment) Act 2022, allows for voluntary and discretionary discussions with undertakings under investigation to enter formal 'settlement discussions'.	**Digital Services Act 2024 (the 'Irish Act')** was signed into law on 11 February 2024 and came into force on 17 February 2024. The act integrates DSA enforcement into Ireland's Broadcasting Act, designating CNAM as the Digital Services Coordinator (DSC) and the primary regulator, alongside the CCPC, which oversees specific marketplace-related articles (arts 30–32).

Country	DMA Regulation Transposed	Transposition Law	Competent Authority	Interinstitutional Steering Committee	Investigative Powers Article 38(7) DMA	New Antitrust Instruments	New Digital Legislations
Ireland						A successful settlement will involve financial sanctions and potentially other remedies, with the undertaking acknowledging the breach. The settlement process aims to offer efficiency and resource savings for the CCPC, while providing a reduction in penalties for cooperating companies.	
Italy	Yes	Law no 214/2023 (Annual Law on Competition and Market 2022)	**Italian Competition Authority (ICA) – (Autorità Garante della Concorrenza e del Mercato - AGCM)**	N/A	**Conducting investigations:** The AGCM has the power to conduct investigations within the national legal system to identify potential DMA violations. The AGCM, in performing its functions under the DMA, enjoys the same investigation powers and can impose the same sanctions provided by the national antitrust law, using the support of the Italian Financial Police.	**Law no 118/2022 (Annual Market and Competition Law 2021),** which amended the new Article 9 of Law no 192/1998 on abuse of economic dependence for digital platforms. **New merger control powers** Law no 118/2022 amended Law no 287/1990, resulting in: 1. Expanded powers for the AGCM regarding mergers. 2. A revised substantive test for evaluating mergers. 3. Broader investigative powers for the AGCM.	**Legislative Decree no 26/2023**, which brings additions and modifications to the Italian Consumer Code, such as updating general conditions in light of the digital context and new information obligations for contracts concluded in online markets (art 49-bis of the Italian Consumer Code). **Draft law no 908/2023, titled 'Provisions on the Annual Digital Law'**, proposes an annual review of the digital sector in Italy. Its goals include assessing policy progress, removing barriers to digital innovation, strengthening protections for users and workers, and updating regulations to ensure equitable access to a rights-protecting digital ecosystem for businesses, consumers, and workers.

Country	DMA Regulation Transposed	Transposition Law	Competent Authority	Interinstitutional Steering Committee	Investigative Powers Article 38(7) DMA	New Antitrust Instruments	New Digital Legislations
Italy					**Information sharing power:** The AGCM can use information collected during DMA investigations for broader purposes, including enforcing rules on anti-competitive agreements, abuse of dominance, economic dependence, and merger control, provided it aligns with EU legislation.	Under Article 16(1-bis) of Law no 287/1990, the AGCM can exercise its 'call-in' power to require the notification of a concentration (within 30 days) if: 1. Any of the two cumulative turnover thresholds in Article 16 of the antitrust law is exceeded. 2. The total global turnover of the companies involved exceeds EUR 5 billion. 3. There are significant risks to competition in the national market or part of it, and the merger has been completed within the last six months.	**Draft law titled 'Measures on the Transparency of Content Generated by Artificial Intelligence'**, presented to the Italian Parliament on 19 October 2023, aims to enhance transparency in AI-generated content. It requires content creators to label or watermark AI-generated material at the start and end to ensure users can easily recognise it. The law entrusts the Italian Communications Regulatory Authority (AGCOM) with the task of defining implementation methods and overseeing compliance. It also outlines processes for reporting and removing non-compliant content, along with sanctions for violations.

COUNTRY	DMA REGULATION TRANSPOSED	TRANSPOSITION LAW	COMPETENT AUTHORITY	INTERINSTITUTIONAL STEERING COMMITTEE	INVESTIGATIVE POWERS ARTICLE 38(7) DMA	NEW ANTITRUST INSTRUMENTS	NEW DIGITAL LEGISLATIONS
ITALY						In the summer of 2023, **Italy's 'Asset Decree'** granted the AGCM new powers to impose remedies in all economic sectors to address market distortions, even in the absence of anti-competitive conduct or wrongdoing. These measures, based on findings from market studies, aim to eliminate obstacles harming competition and consumers. The tool aligns with similar mechanisms in the UK and Germany, allowing the AGCM to address market failures and restrictive state measures.	
LITHUANIA	Yes	Law on Competition Amendments of 2023 (Law no XIV-2035)	**Konkurencijos taryba (KT) (Lithuanian Competition Authority)** The KT is also responsible for enforcing the P2B Regulation	N/A	No	N/A	**Lithuania's updated Cybersecurity Law, effective 18 October 2024**, aligns with EU legislation, including the NIS2 Directive, the Cybersecurity Act, and the regulation establishing a European Cybersecurity Centre. It introduces comprehensive requirements for cybersecurity governance, including risk management, incident reporting, supply chain security, and the appointment of cybersecurity officers.

COUNTRY	DMA REGULATION TRANSPOSED	TRANSPOSITION LAW	COMPETENT AUTHORITY	INTERINSTITUTIONAL STEERING COMMITTEE	INVESTIGATIVE POWERS ARTICLE 38(7) DMA	NEW ANTITRUST INSTRUMENTS	NEW DIGITAL LEGISLATIONS
NETHERLANDS	Not yet	DMA Implementation Act (Proposal)	**Dutch Authority for Consumers and Markets (ACM)** The ACM is also responsible for enforcing the P2B Regulation.	**Digital Regulation Cooperation Platform** formed by: – Authority for Consumers and Markets (ACM) responsible for the enforcement of the DMA and the P2B Regulation. – Dutch Authority for the Financial Markets (AFM). – Dutch Data Protection Authority (Autoriteit Persoonsgegevens – AP), responsible for the GDPR. – Dutch Media Authority, which monitors compliance with DSA obligations.	**Conducting investigations:** The ACM is granted all its competition law investigative powers to monitor compliance with the DMA, except for the authority to impose sanctions such as binding directions, restorative measures with periodic penalty payments, and fines, as specified in Article 12(h), (j), and (m) of the DMA. This power is limited to establishing possible non-compliance, without granting the ACM the ability to intervene in any way. The ACM is granted powers under the Dutch General Administrative Act, including: – entering non-residential areas; – issuing binding; – information requests; – seizing documents; – investigating goods; – sealing locations; – summoning police.	**The ACM has proposed two competition law amendments:** 1. The first introduces a call-in power to address gaps in merger oversight by allowing scrutiny of below-threshold transactions, such as 'roll-up' or 'killer' acquisitions, that may harm competition. This would raise the turnover threshold to reduce administrative burdens while enabling targeted reviews. A supporting motion has been passed, and the Minister of Economic Affairs is set to act. 2. The second amendment proposes a new competition tool (NCT) to empower the ACM to tackle insufficient competition by removing barriers to market entry and improving consumer outcomes. The Minister supports the NCT and expects to introduce legislation by early 2025 after stakeholder consultations.	**Digital Government Act** , which came into force on 1 July 2023, is a Dutch law designed to establish a regulatory framework for the secure and reliable use of digital technologies in government services and interactions between citizens, businesses, and public authorities.

COUNTRY	DMA REGULATION TRANSPOSED	TRANSPOSITION LAW	COMPETENT AUTHORITY	INTERINSTITUTIONAL STEERING COMMITTEE	INVESTIGATIVE POWERS ARTICLE 38(7) DMA	NEW ANTITRUST INSTRUMENTS	NEW DIGITAL LEGISLATIONS
NETHERLANDS					**Information sharing power:** Under Article 7 of the ACM Establishment Act, the ACM can share and use information gathered for one purpose across its organisation and may also share relevant information with other public authorities.		
PORTUGAL	No	N/A	N/A	N/A	N/A	N/A	On 29 January 2022, Portugal implemented **Law no 82/2021**, introducing unique rules for the national online content market. Unlike standard EU transpositions, this law establishes procedures to monitor, control, remove, and block access to content protected by copyright and related rights in the digital environment. It also imposes new obligations on intermediary networking service providers to uphold these protections.

COUNTRY	DMA REGULATION TRANSPOSED	TRANSPOSITION LAW	COMPETENT AUTHORITY	INTERINSTITUTIONAL STEERING COMMITTEE	INVESTIGATIVE POWERS ARTICLE 38(7) DMA	NEW ANTITRUST INSTRUMENTS	NEW DIGITAL LEGISLATIONS
ROMANIA	Yes	Emergency Ordinance no 108 of 29 November 2023 for amending and supplementing Competition Law	**Romanian Competition Authority (RCA)** The RCA is also responsible for enforcing the P2B Regulation.	N/A	**Conducting investigations:** The RCA has the power to investigate possible violations of Articles 5, 6, and 7 DMA, *ex officio*, with prior notification to the Commission, and to report to the Commission on the findings of such investigations, to assist the Commission in its role of single authority empowered to ensure compliance with the DMA. Investigations under the DMA would benefit from utilising procedural tools similar to those in antitrust enforcement, such as: – requests for information; – dawn raids; – conducting interviews; – taking statements. When an investigation concludes that certain behaviour constitutes a DMA infringement, the RCA submits a report to the Commission, which has the discretion to determine the appropriate solution under the DMA, since the RCA is not allowed to take decisions in those cases.	**Romanian Competition Law no 21/1996 art 25(5)(c)** Romania is among the few EU Member States with a market investigation tool – the so-called new competition tool (NCT) – empowering its national competition authority (NCA) to address market failures. Inspired by the UK model, this tool allows the NCA to impose suitable and proportional remedies, including structural measures, to resolve competition issues without requiring proof of individual infringements under EU or national antitrust law. While the tool has not yet been tested, it has acted as a deterrent, particularly regarding severe remedies like divestitures.	In July 2024, Romania's government approved a **national artificial intelligence (AI) strategy for 2024–2027**, aligning with EU goals to lead globally in AI. The strategy emphasises the use of EU funding for advanced technologies, aiming to modernise digital public administration, economy, education, cybersecurity, and future technologies like AI.

Country	DMA Regulation Transposed	Transposition Law	Competent Authority	Interinstitutional Steering Committee	Investigative Powers Article 38(7) DMA	New Antitrust Instruments	New Digital Legislations
Slovakia	Yes	Act no 93/2024 Coll., on the Protection of Economic Competition and on the Amendment and Supplementation of Certain Laws	**Antimonopoly Office of the Slovak Republic (AMO)** The AMO is also responsible for enforcing the FSR except for public procurement	Slovakia is planning to build an **inter-institutional coordinating body that** would be composed of the following four main authorities: 1. Antimonopoly Office of the Slovak Republic (AMO): Responsible for the DMA. 2. Council for Media Services: The national media regulator, which should fulfil the role of Digital Services Coordinator (DSC) according to the draft amendment implementing the DSA. 3. Data Protection Authority (Office for the Protection of Personal Data of the Slovak Republic): Responsible for enforcing GDPR rules. 4. Regulatory Authority for Electronic Communications and Postal Services (potentially): The authority for electronic communications and postal services, which could be involved in the coordination, depending on the circumstances.	**Conducting investigations:** the AMO can investigate possible violations of Articles 5, 6, and 7 DMA within its jurisdiction (Act on Protection of Competition new art 16(1)(c)), as per Article 38(7) DMA. The AMO has identical powers for investigations under the DMA as it does for breaches of Articles 101 and 102 TFEU, and their national counterparts: – conduct inspections at business and private premises with the same set of powers; – assist the Commission with DMA-related inspections; – request information from natural and legal persons for DMA purposes.	Slovakia's **Competition Act, effective 1 June 2021**, modernises legislation to align with EU standards and implement the ECN+ Directive. It broadens the definition of an undertaking to include company groups, allows liability to transfer to successors, and exempts irrelevant joint ventures from merger notifications. The Act expands the competition authority's powers to impose interim measures and remedies for market abuses and introduces procedural changes like stricter notification requirements and extended sanction periods.	**Amendment to Act no 264/2022 – Media Services Act** The Media Services Council was established on 1 August 2022 to address online hate speech and illegal content. Citizens can file complaints if digital platforms like Facebook or YouTube fail to remove reported content. Complaints must include justification, the posting date, and the platform's name. The Council monitors hate speech, including subtle content that targets groups indirectly, and requires platforms to act, especially in cases that incite violence. Large platforms, however, often fail to address reported content effectively.

COUNTRY	DMA REGULATION TRANSPOSED	TRANSPOSITION LAW	COMPETENT AUTHORITY	INTERINSTITUTIONAL STEERING COMMITTEE	INVESTIGATIVE POWERS ARTICLE 38(7) DMA	NEW ANTITRUST INSTRUMENTS	NEW DIGITAL LEGISLATIONS
SPAIN	Yes	Royal Decree-Law 8/2023	**Spanish National Markets and Competition Commission (CNMC)** The CNMC will act as the national Digital Services Coordinator (DSC) and oversee the implementation of the DSA in Spain.	N/A	**Investigation of DMA non-compliance:** The CNMC has the power to investigate possible violations of Articles 5, 6, and 7 DMA within its jurisdiction (Spanish Competition Act new art 18(3)), as per Article 38(7) DMA. Before initiating formal investigative actions, the CNMC must inform the Commission in writing (according to the mechanisms introduced in art 38(7) DMA). The CNMC may use any information received from third parties under Article 27 DMA for the purpose of starting and conducting those investigations. **Information sharing power:** Article 18(3) allows information collected during DMA-related investigations to be used for enforcing antitrust rules under the Spanish Competition Act, and vice versa, information from antitrust proceedings under the Spanish Competition Act can be used in DMA investigations under Article 18(3).	**Royal Decree-Law 8/2023: Reforms to the Spanish Competition Act** Published on 29 June 2023, the reform introduced significant changes. In merger control, the simplified procedure review was reduced from one month to 15 working days, provided there was prior pre-notification. The consultation on notifiability was shortened from three months to one month, and the in-depth review period was extended from two to three months. For infringement proceedings, the time to respond to the statement of objections was extended from 15 days to one month, and the overall investigation duration was increased from 18 to 24 months.	On 8 November 2023, the Spanish government passed **Royal Decree 817/2023** to launch a pilot programme for testing the upcoming EU Regulation on Artificial Intelligence, creating a unique sandbox initiative. This initiative allows authorities and companies to collaborate and develop guidelines for implementing the regulation. The CNMC raised three main concerns: – potential competitive advantages for participants; – the need for safeguards to prevent sensitive information exchanges; – ensuring the guidelines remain neutral.

COUNTRY	DMA REGULATION TRANSPOSED	TRANSPOSITION LAW	COMPETENT AUTHORITY	INTERINSTITUTIONAL STEERING COMMITTEE	INVESTIGATIVE POWERS ARTICLE 38(7) DMA	NEW ANTITRUST INSTRUMENTS	NEW DIGITAL LEGISLATIONS
SWEDEN	Not yet	Government proposition 2023/24:154 – Supplementary rules to new Union regulations in the field of competition	**Swedish Competition Authority (SCA)**	N/A	No, but the proposal does not entirely exclude the possibility of introducing investigatory powers for the SCA.	The **Swedish Government's Public Inquiry** examines the potential need for an information duty for smaller mergers that fall below the mandatory notification thresholds but could still significantly impact competition. While large mergers are subject to notification, smaller ones currently lack oversight. The investigation will explore whether companies should be required to inform the SCA about such mergers. This approach is already used in some jurisdictions, such as Norway, where companies must report certain mergers in markets with dominant players or oligopolistic structures, ensuring greater scrutiny in sectors prone to competition concerns.	In December 2023, the Swedish Government appointed **an AI commission** led by Carl-Henric Svanberg to boost Sweden's AI competitiveness. The commission's task is to propose policies that ensure the ethical, secure, and competitive development of AI in both the public and private sectors. This initiative also presents opportunities for increased collaboration and business between the US and Sweden in the AI field.

Regulation 2022/1925 of the European Parliament and the Council – Contestable and fair markers in the digital sector

Digital Markets Act (DMA)

- **Regulation (EU) 2022/1925 of the European Parliament and of the Council of 14 September 2022 on contestable and fair markets in the digital sector and amending Directives (EU) 2019/1937 and (EU) 2020/1828 (Digital Markets Act)**

(Text with EEA relevance)

THE EUROPEAN PARLIAMENT AND THE COUNCIL OF THE EUROPEAN UNION,

Having regard to the Treaty on the Functioning of the European Union, and in particular Article 114 thereof,

Having regard to the proposal from the European Commission,

After transmission of the draft legislative act to the national parliaments,

Having regard to the opinion of the European Economic and Social Committee[1],

Having regard to the opinion of the Committee of the Regions[2],

Acting in accordance with the ordinary legislative procedure[3],

Whereas:

1. Digital services in general and online platforms in particular play an increasingly important role in the economy, in particular in the internal market, by enabling businesses to reach users throughout the Union, by facilitating cross-border trade and by opening entirely new business opportunities to a large number of companies in the Union to the benefit of consumers in the Union.
2. At the same time, among those digital services, core platform services feature a number of characteristics that can be exploited by the undertakings providing them. An example of such characteristics of core platform services is extreme scale economies, which often result from nearly zero marginal costs to add business users or end users. Other such characteristics of core platform services are very strong network effects, an ability to connect many business users with many end users through the multisidedness of these services, a significant degree of dependence of both business users and end users, lock-in effects, a lack of multi-homing for the same purpose by end users, vertical integration, and data driven-advantages. All these characteristics, combined with unfair practices by undertakings providing the core platform services, can have the effect of substantially undermining the contestability of the core platform services, as well as impacting the fairness of the commercial relationship between undertakings providing such services and their business users and end users. In practice, this leads to rapid and potentially far-reaching decreases in business users' and end users' choice, and therefore can confer on the provider of those services the position of a so-called gatekeeper. At the same time, it should be recognised that services which act in a non-commercial purpose capacity such as collaborative projects should not be considered as core platform services for the purpose of this Regulation.

---

1 OJ C 286, 16.7.2021, p. 64.

2 OJ C 440, 29.10.2021, p. 67.

3 Position of the European Parliament of 5 July 2022 (not yet published in the Official Journal) and decision of the Council of 18 July 2022.

3. A small number of large undertakings providing core platform services have emerged with considerable economic power that could qualify them to be designated as gatekeepers pursuant to this Regulation. Typically, they feature an ability to connect many business users with many end users through their services, which, in turn, enables them to leverage their advantages, such as their access to large amounts of data, from one area of activity to another. Some of those undertakings exercise control over whole platform ecosystems in the digital economy and are structurally extremely difficult to challenge or contest by existing or new market operators, irrespective of how innovative and efficient those market operators may be. Contestability is reduced in particular due to the existence of very high barriers to entry or exit, including high investment costs, which cannot, or not easily, be recuperated in case of exit, and the absence of, or reduced access to, some key inputs in the digital economy, such as data. As a result, the likelihood increases that the underlying markets do not function well, or will soon fail to function well.
4. The combination of those features of gatekeeper is likely to lead, in many cases, to serious imbalances in bargaining power and, consequently, to unfair practices and conditions for business users, as well as for end users of core platform services provided by gatekeepers, to the detriment of prices, quality, fair competition, choice and innovation in the digital sector.
5. It follows that the market processes are often incapable of ensuring fair economic outcomes with regard to core platform services. Although Articles 101 and 102 of the Treaty on the Functioning of the European Union (TFEU) apply to the conduct of gatekeepers, the scope of those provisions is limited to certain instances of market power, for example dominance on specific markets and of anti-competitive behaviour, and enforcement occurs *ex post* and requires an extensive investigation of often very complex facts on a case by case basis. Moreover, existing Union law does not address, or does not address effectively, the challenges to the effective functioning of the internal market posed by the conduct of gatekeepers that are not necessarily dominant in competition-law terms.
6. Gatekeepers have a significant impact on the internal market, providing gateways for a large number of business users to reach end users everywhere in the Union and on different markets. The adverse impact of unfair practices on the internal market and the particularly weak contestability of core platform services, including the negative societal and economic implications of such unfair practices, have led national legislators and sectoral regulators to act. A number of regulatory solutions have already been adopted at national level or proposed to address unfair practices and the contestability of digital services or at least with regard to some of them. This has created divergent regulatory solutions which results in the fragmentation of the internal market, thus raising the risk of increased compliance costs due to different sets of national regulatory requirements.
7. Therefore, the purpose of this Regulation is to contribute to the proper functioning of the internal market by laying down rules to ensure contestability and fairness for the markets in the digital sector in general, and for business users and end users of core platform services provided by gatekeepers in particular. Business users and end users of core platform services provided by gatekeepers should be afforded appropriate regulatory safeguards throughout the Union against the unfair practices of gatekeepers, in order to facilitate cross-border business within the Union and thereby improve the proper functioning of the internal market, and to eliminate existing or likely emerging fragmentation in the specific areas covered by this Regulation. Moreover, while gatekeepers tend to adopt global or at least pan-European business models and algorithmic structures, they can adopt, and in some cases have adopted, different business conditions and practices in different Member States, which is liable to create disparities between the competitive conditions for the users of core platform services provided by gatekeepers, to the detriment of integration of the internal market.
8. By approximating diverging national laws, it is possible to eliminate obstacles to the freedom to provide and receive services, including retail services, within the internal market. A targeted set of harmonised legal obligations should therefore be established at Union level to ensure contestable and fair digital markets featuring the presence of gatekeepers within the internal market to the benefit of the Union's economy as a whole and ultimately of the Union's consumers.
9. Fragmentation of the internal market can only effectively be averted if Member States are prevented from applying national rules which are within the scope of and pursue the same objectives as this Regulation. That does not preclude the possibility of applying to gatekeepers within the meaning of this Regulation other national rules which pursue other legitimate public interest objectives as set out in the TFEU or which pursue overriding reasons of public interest as recognised by the case law of the Court of Justice of the European Union ('the Court of Justice').

10. At the same time, since this Regulation aims to complement the enforcement of competition law, it should apply without prejudice to Articles 101 and 102 TFEU, to the corresponding national competition rules and to other national competition rules regarding unilateral conduct that are based on an individualised assessment of market positions and behaviour, including its actual or potential effects and the precise scope of the prohibited behaviour, and which provide for the possibility of undertakings to make efficiency and objective justification arguments for the behaviour in question, and to national rules concerning merger control. However, the application of those rules should not affect the obligations imposed on gatekeepers under this Regulation and their uniform and effective application in the internal market.
11. Articles 101 and 102 TFEU and the corresponding national competition rules concerning anticompetitive multilateral and unilateral conduct as well as merger control have as their objective the protection of undistorted competition on the market. This Regulation pursues an objective that is complementary to, but different from that of protecting undistorted competition on any given market, as defined in competition-law terms, which is to ensure that markets where gatekeepers are present are and remain contestable and fair, independently from the actual, potential or presumed effects of the conduct of a given gatekeeper covered by this Regulation on competition on a given market. This Regulation therefore aims to protect a different legal interest from that protected by those rules and it should apply without prejudice to their application.
12. This Regulation should also apply without prejudice to the rules resulting from other acts of Union law regulating certain aspects of the provision of services covered by this Regulation, in particular Regulations (EU) 2016/679[4] and (EU) 2019/1150[5] of the European Parliament and of the Council and a Regulation on a single market for digital services, and Directives 2002/58/EC[6], 2005/29/EC[7], 2010/13/EU[8], (EU) 2015/2366[9], (EU) 2019/790[10] and (EU) 2019/882[11] of the European Parliament and of the Council, and Council Directive 93/13/EEC[12], as well as national rules aimed at enforcing or implementing those Union legal acts.
13. Weak contestability and unfair practices in the digital sector are more frequent and pronounced for certain digital services than for others. This is the case in particular for widespread and commonly used digital services that mostly directly intermediate between business users and end users and where features such as extreme scale economies, very strong network effects, an ability to connect many

---

4 Regulation (EU) 2016/679 of the European Parliament and of the Council of 27 April 2016 on the protection of natural persons with regard to the processing of personal data and on the free movement of such data, and repealing Directive 95/46/EC (General Data Protection Regulation) (OJ L 119, 4.5.2016, p. 1).

5 Regulation (EU) 2019/1150 of the European Parliament and of the Council of 20 June 2019 on promoting fairness and transparency for business users of online intermediation services (OJ L 186, 11.7.2019, p. 57).

6 Directive 2002/58/EC of the European Parliament and of the Council of 12 July 2002 concerning the processing of personal data and the protection of privacy in the electronic communications sector (OJ L 201, 31.7.2002, p. 37).

7 Directive 2005/29/EC of the European Parliament and of the Council of 11 May 2005 concerning unfair business-to-consumer commercial practices in the internal market and amending Council Directive 84/450/EEC, Directives 97/7/EC, 98/27/EC and 2002/65/EC of the European Parliament and of the Council and Regulation (EC) No2006/2004 of the European Parliament and of the Council ('Unfair Commercial Practices Directive') (OJ L 149, 11.6.2005, p. 22).

8 Directive 2010/13/EU of the European Parliament and of the Council of 10 March 2010 on the coordination of certain provisions laid down by law, regulation or administrative action in Member States concerning the provision of audiovisual media services (Audiovisual Media Services Directive) (OJ L 95, 15.4.2010, p. 1).

9 Directive (EU) 2015/2366 of the European Parliament and of the Council of 25 November 2015 on payment services in the internal market, amending Directives 2002/65/EC, 2009/110/EC and 2013/36/EU and Regulation (EU) No1093/2010, and repealing Directive 2007/64/EC (OJ L 337, 23.12.2015, p. 35).

10 Directive (EU) 2019/790 of the European Parliament and of the Council of 17 April 2019 on copyright and related rights in the Digital Single Market and amending Directives 96/9/EC and 2001/29/EC (OJ L 130, 17.5.2019, p. 92).

11 Directive (EU) 2019/882 of the European Parliament and of the Council of 17 April 2019 on the accessibility requirements for products and services (OJ L 151, 7.6.2019, p. 70).

12 Council Directive 93/13/EEC of 5 April 1993 on unfair terms in consumer contracts (OJ L 95, 21.4.1993, p. 29).

business users with many end users through the multisidedness of these services, lock-in effects, a lack of multi-homing or vertical integration are the most prevalent. Often, there is only one or very few large undertakings providing those digital services. Those undertakings have emerged most frequently as gatekeepers for business users and end users, with far-reaching impacts. In particular, they have gained the ability to easily set commercial conditions and terms in a unilateral and detrimental manner for their business users and end users. Accordingly, it is necessary to focus only on those digital services that are most broadly used by business users and end users and where concerns about weak contestability and unfair practices by gatekeepers are more apparent and pressing from an internal market perspective.

14. In particular, online intermediation services, online search engines, operating systems, online social networking, video sharing platform services, number-independent interpersonal communication services, cloud computing services, virtual assistants, web browsers and online advertising services, including advertising intermediation services, all have the capacity to affect a large number of end users and businesses, which entails a risk of unfair business practices. Therefore, they should be included in the definition of core platform services and fall into the scope of this Regulation. Online intermediation services can also be active in the field of financial services, and they can intermediate or be used to provide such services as listed non-exhaustively in Annex II to Directive (EU) 2015/1535 of the European Parliament and of the Council[13]. For the purposes of this Regulation, the definition of core platform services should be technology neutral and should be understood to encompass those provided on or through various means or devices, such as connected TV or embedded digital services in vehicles. In certain circumstances, the notion of end users should encompass users that are traditionally considered business users, but in a given situation do not use the core platform services to provide goods or services to other end users, such as for example businesses relying on cloud computing services for their own purposes.
15. The fact that a digital service qualifies as a core platform service does not in itself give rise to sufficiently serious concerns of contestability or unfair practices. It is only when a core platform service constitutes an important gateway and is operated by an undertaking with a significant impact in the internal market and an entrenched and durable position, or by an undertaking that will foreseeably enjoy such a position in the near future, that such concerns arise. Accordingly, the targeted set of harmonised rules in this Regulation should apply only to undertakings designated on the basis of those three objective criteria, and they should only apply to those of their core platform services that individually constitute an important gateway for business users to reach end users. The fact that it is possible that an undertaking providing core platform services not only intermediates between business users and end users, but also between end users and end users, for example in the case of number-independent interpersonal communications services, should not preclude the conclusion that such an undertaking is or could be an important gateway for business users to reach end users.
16. In order to ensure the effective application of this Regulation to undertakings providing core platform services which are most likely to satisfy those objective requirements, and where unfair practices weakening contestability are most prevalent and have the most impact, the Commission should be able to directly designate as gatekeepers those undertakings providing core platform services which meet certain quantitative thresholds. Such undertakings should in any event be subject to a fast designation process which should start once this Regulation becomes applicable.
17. The fact that an undertaking has a very significant turnover in the Union and provides a core platform service in at least three Member States constitutes compelling indication that that undertaking has a significant impact on the internal market. This is equally true where an undertaking providing a core platform service in at least three Member States has a very significant market capitalisation or equivalent fair market value. Therefore, an undertaking providing a core platform service should be presumed to have a significant impact on the internal market where it provides a core platform service in at least three Member States and where either its group turnover realised in the Union is equal to or exceeds a specific, high threshold, or the market capitalisation of the group is equal to or exceeds a certain high absolute value. For undertakings providing core platform services that

---

13 Directive (EU) 2015/1535 of the European Parliament and of the Council of 9 September 2015 laying down a procedure for the provision of information in the field of technical regulations and of rules on Information Society services (OJ L 241, 17.9.2015, p. 1).

belong to undertakings that are not publicly listed, the equivalent fair market value should be used as the reference. It should be possible for the Commission to use its power to adopt delegated acts to develop an objective methodology to calculate that value.

A high group turnover realised in the Union in conjunction with the threshold number of users in the Union of core platform services reflects a relatively strong ability to monetise those users. A high market capitalisation relative to the same threshold number of users in the Union reflects a relatively significant potential to monetise those users in the near future. This monetisation potential in turn reflects, in principle, the gateway position of the undertakings concerned. Both indicators, in addition, reflect the financial capacity of the undertakings concerned, including their ability to leverage their access to financial markets to reinforce their position. This can, for example, happen where this superior access is used to acquire other undertakings, an ability which has in turn been shown to have potential negative effects on innovation. Market capitalisation can also reflect the expected future position and effect on the internal market of the undertakings concerned, despite a potentially relatively low current turnover. The market capitalisation value should be based on a level that reflects the average market capitalisation of the largest publicly listed undertakings in the Union over an appropriate period.

18. Whereas a market capitalisation at or above the threshold in the last financial year should give rise to a presumption that an undertaking providing core platform services has a significant impact on the internal market, a sustained market capitalisation of the undertaking providing core platform services at or above the threshold over three or more years should be considered as further strengthening that presumption.

19. By contrast, there could be a number of factors concerning market capitalisation that would require an in-depth assessment in determining whether an undertaking providing core platform services should be deemed to have a significant impact on the internal market. This could be the case where the market capitalisation of the undertaking providing core platform services in preceding financial years was significantly lower than the threshold and the volatility of its market capitalisation over the observed period was disproportionate to overall equity market volatility or its market capitalisation trajectory relative to market trends was inconsistent with a rapid and unidirectional growth.

20. Having a very high number of business users that depend on a core platform service to reach a very high number of monthly active end users enables the undertaking providing that service to influence the operations of a substantial part of business users to its advantage and indicate, in principle, that that undertaking is an important gateway. The respective relevant levels for those numbers should be set representing a substantive percentage of the entire population of the Union when it comes to end users and of the entire population of businesses using core platform services to determine the threshold for business users. Active end users and business users should be identified and calculated in such a way as to adequately represent the role and reach of the specific core platform service in question. In order to provide legal certainty for gatekeepers, the elements to determine the number of active end users and business users per core platform service should be set out in an Annex to this Regulation. Such elements can be affected by technological and other developments. The Commission should therefore be empowered to adopt delegated acts to amend this Regulation by updating the methodology and the list of indicators used to determine the number of active end users and active business users.

21. An entrenched and durable position in its operations or the foreseeability of enjoying such a position in the future occurs notably where the contestability of the position of the undertaking providing the core platform service is limited. This is likely to be the case where that undertaking has provided a core platform service in at least three Member States to a very high number of business users and end users over a period of at least 3 years.

22. Such thresholds can be affected by market and technical developments. The Commission should therefore be empowered to adopt delegated acts to specify the methodology for determining whether the quantitative thresholds are met, and to regularly adjust it to market and technological developments where necessary. Such delegated acts should not amend the quantitative thresholds set out in this Regulation.

23. An undertaking providing core platform services should be able, in exceptional circumstances, to rebut the presumption that the undertaking has a significant impact on the internal market by demonstrating that, although it meets the quantitative thresholds set out in this Regulation, it does not fulfil the requirements for designation as a gatekeeper. The burden of adducing evidence that the presumption deriving from

the fulfilment of the quantitative thresholds should not apply should be borne by that undertaking. In its assessment of the evidence and arguments produced, the Commission should take into account only those elements which directly relate to the quantitative criteria, namely the impact of the undertaking providing core platform services on the internal market beyond revenue or market cap, such as its size in absolute terms, and the number of Member States in which it is present; by how much the actual business user and end user numbers exceed the thresholds and the importance of the undertaking's core platform service considering the overall scale of activities of the respective core platform service; and the number of years for which the thresholds have been met.

Any justification on economic grounds seeking to enter into market definition or to demonstrate efficiencies deriving from a specific type of behaviour by the undertaking providing core platform services should be discarded, as it is not relevant to the designation as a gatekeeper. If the arguments submitted are not sufficiently substantiated because they do not manifestly put into question the presumption, it should be possible for the Commission to reject the arguments within the timeframe of 45 working days provided for the designation. The Commission should be able to take a decision by relying on information available on the quantitative thresholds where the undertaking providing core platform services obstructs the investigation by failing to comply with the investigative measures taken by the Commission.

24. Provision should also be made for the assessment of the gatekeeper role of undertakings providing core platform services which do not satisfy all of the quantitative thresholds, in light of the overall objective requirements that they have a significant impact on the internal market, act as an important gateway for business users to reach end users and benefit from an entrenched and durable position in their operations or it is foreseeable that they will do so in the near future. When the undertaking providing core platform services is a medium-sized, small or micro enterprise, the assessment should carefully take into account whether such an undertaking would be able to substantially undermine the contestability of the core platform services, since this Regulation primarily targets large undertakings with considerable economic power rather than medium-sized, small or micro enterprises.

25. Such an assessment can only be done in light of a market investigation, while taking into account the quantitative thresholds. In its assessment the Commission should pursue the objectives of preserving and fostering innovation and the quality of digital products and services, the degree to which prices are fair and competitive, and the degree to which quality or choice for business users and for end users is or remains high. Elements can be taken into account that are specific to the undertakings providing core platform services concerned, such as extreme scale or scope economies, very strong network effects, data-driven advantages, an ability to connect many business users with many end users through the multisidedness of those services, lock-in effects, lack of multi-homing, conglomerate corporate structure or vertical integration. In addition, a very high market capitalisation, a very high ratio of equity value over profit or a very high turnover derived from end users of a single core platform service can be used as indicators of the leveraging potential of such undertakings and of the tipping of the market in their favour. Together with market capitalisation, high relative growth rates are examples of dynamic parameters that are particularly relevant to identifying such undertakings providing core platform services for which it is foreseeable that they will become entrenched and durable. The Commission should be able to take a decision by drawing adverse inferences from facts available where the undertaking providing core platform services significantly obstructs the investigation by failing to comply with the investigative measures taken by the Commission.

26. A particular subset of rules should apply to those undertakings providing core platform services for which it is foreseeable that they will enjoy an entrenched and durable position in the near future. The same specific features of core platform services make them prone to tipping: once an undertaking providing the core platform service has obtained a certain advantage over rivals or potential challengers in terms of scale or intermediation power, its position could become unassailable and the situation could evolve to the point that it is likely to become entrenched and durable in the near future. Undertakings can try to induce this tipping and emerge as gatekeeper by using some of the unfair conditions and practices regulated under this Regulation. In such a situation, it appears appropriate to intervene before the market tips irreversibly.

27. However, such early intervention should be limited to imposing only those obligations that are necessary and appropriate to ensure that the services in question remain contestable and enable the qualified risk of unfair conditions and practices to be avoided. Obligations that prevent the undertaking providing core platform services concerned from enjoying an entrenched and durable position in its

operations, such as those preventing leveraging, and those that facilitate switching and multi-homing are more directly geared towards this purpose. To ensure proportionality, the Commission should moreover apply from that subset of obligations only those that are necessary and proportionate to achieve the objectives of this Regulation and should regularly review whether such obligations should be maintained, suppressed or adapted.

28. Applying only those obligations that are necessary and proportionate to achieve the objectives of this Regulation should allow the Commission to intervene in time and effectively, while fully respecting the proportionality of the measures considered. It should also reassure actual or potential market participants about the contestability and fairness of the services concerned.
29. Gatekeepers should comply with the obligations laid down in this Regulation in respect of each of the core platform services listed in the relevant designation decision. The obligations should apply taking into account the conglomerate position of gatekeepers, where applicable. Furthermore, it should be possible for the Commission to impose implementing measures on the gatekeeper by decision. Those implementing measures should be designed in an effective manner, having regard to the features of core platform services and the possible circumvention risks, and in compliance with the principle of proportionality and the fundamental rights of the undertakings concerned, as well as those of third parties.
30. The very rapidly changing and complex technological nature of core platform services requires a regular review of the status of gatekeepers, including those that it is foreseen will enjoy an entrenched and durable position in their operations in the near future. To provide all of the market participants, including the gatekeepers, with the required certainty as to the applicable legal obligations, a time limit for such regular reviews is necessary. It is also important to conduct such reviews on a regular basis and at least every 3 years. Furthermore, it is important to clarify that not every change in the facts on the basis of which an undertaking providing core platform services was designated as a gatekeeper should require amendment of the designation decision. Amendment will only be necessary if the change in the facts also leads to a change in the assessment. Whether or not that is the case should be based on a case-by-case assessment of the facts and circumstances.
31. To safeguard the contestability and fairness of core platform services provided by gatekeepers, it is necessary to provide in a clear and unambiguous manner for a set of harmonised rules with regard to those services. Such rules are needed to address the risk of harmful effects of practices by gatekeepers, to the benefit of the business environment in the services concerned, of users and ultimately of society as a whole. The obligations correspond to those practices that are considered as undermining contestability or as being unfair, or both, when taking into account the features of the digital sector and which have a particularly negative direct impact on business users and end users. It should be possible for the obligations laid down by this Regulation to specifically take into account the nature of the core platform services provided. The obligations in this Regulation should not only ensure contestability and fairness with respect to core platform services listed in the designation decision, but also with respect to other digital products and services into which gatekeepers leverage their gateway position, which are often provided together with, or in support of, the core platform services.
32. For the purpose of this Regulation, contestability should relate to the ability of undertakings to effectively overcome barriers to entry and expansion and challenge the gatekeeper on the merits of their products and services. The features of core platform services in the digital sector, such as network effects, strong economies of scale, and benefits from data have limited the contestability of those services and the related ecosystems. Such a weak contestability reduces the incentives to innovate and improve products and services for the gatekeeper, its business users, its challengers and customers and thus negatively affects the innovation potential of the wider online platform economy. Contestability of the services in the digital sector can also be limited if there is more than one gatekeeper for a core platform service. This Regulation should therefore ban certain practices by gatekeepers that are liable to increase barriers to entry or expansion, and impose certain obligations on gatekeepers that tend to lower those barriers. The obligations should also address situations where the position of the gatekeeper may be entrenched to such an extent that inter-platform competition is not effective in the short term, meaning that intra-platform competition needs to be created or increased.
33. For the purpose of this Regulation, unfairness should relate to an imbalance between the rights and obligations of business users where the gatekeeper obtains a disproportionate advantage. Market participants, including business users of core platform services and alternative providers of services

provided together with, or in support of, such core platform services, should have the ability to adequately capture the benefits resulting from their innovative or other efforts. Due to their gateway position and superior bargaining power, it is possible that gatekeepers engage in behaviour that does not allow others to capture fully the benefits of their own contributions, and unilaterally set unbalanced conditions for the use of their core platform services or services provided together with, or in support of, their core platform services. Such imbalance is not excluded by the fact that the gatekeeper offers a particular service free of charge to a specific group of users, and may also consist in excluding or discriminating against business users, in particular if the latter compete with the services provided by the gatekeeper. This Regulation should therefore impose obligations on gatekeepers addressing such behaviour.

34. Contestability and fairness are intertwined. The lack of, or weak, contestability for a certain service can enable a gatekeeper to engage in unfair practices. Similarly, unfair practices by a gatekeeper can reduce the possibility of business users or others to contest the gatekeeper's position. A particular obligation in this Regulation may, therefore, address both elements.

35. The obligations laid down in this Regulation are therefore necessary to address identified public policy concerns, there being no alternative and less restrictive measures that would effectively achieve the same result, having regard to the need to safeguard public order, protect privacy and fight fraudulent and deceptive commercial practices.

36. Gatekeepers often directly collect personal data of end users for the purpose of providing online advertising services when end users use third-party websites and software applications. Third parties also provide gatekeepers with personal data of their end users in order to make use of certain services provided by the gatekeepers in the context of their core platform services, such as custom audiences. The processing, for the purpose of providing online advertising services, of personal data from third parties using core platform services gives gatekeepers potential advantages in terms of accumulation of data, thereby raising barriers to entry. This is because gatekeepers process personal data from a significantly larger number of third parties than other undertakings. Similar advantages result from the conduct of (i) combining end user personal data collected from a core platform service with data collected from other services; (ii) cross-using personal data from a core platform service in other services provided separately by the gatekeeper, notably services which are not provided together with, or in support of, the relevant core platform service, and vice versa; or (iii) signing-in end users to different services of gatekeepers in order to combine personal data. To ensure that gatekeepers do not unfairly undermine the contestability of core platform services, gatekeepers should enable end users to freely choose to opt-in to such data processing and sign-in practices by offering a less personalised but equivalent alternative, and without making the use of the core platform service or certain functionalities thereof conditional upon the end user's consent. This should be without prejudice to the gatekeeper processing personal data or signing in end users to a service, relying on the legal basis under Article 6(1), points (c), (d) and (e), of Regulation (EU) 2016/679, but not on Article 6(1), points (b) and (f) of that Regulation.

37. The less personalised alternative should not be different or of degraded quality compared to the service provided to the end users who provide consent, unless a degradation of quality is a direct consequence of the gatekeeper not being able to process such personal data or signing in end users to a service. Not giving consent should not be more difficult than giving consent. When the gatekeeper requests consent, it should proactively present a user-friendly solution to the end user to provide, modify or withdraw consent in an explicit, clear and straightforward manner. In particular, consent should be given by a clear affirmative action or statement establishing a freely given, specific, informed and unambiguous indication of agreement by the end user, as defined in Regulation (EU) 2016/679. At the time of giving consent, and only where applicable, the end user should be informed that not giving consent can lead to a less personalised offer, but that otherwise the core platform service will remain unchanged and that no functionalities will be suppressed. Exceptionally, if consent cannot be given directly to the gatekeeper's core platform service, end users should be able to give consent through each third-party service that makes use of that core platform service, to allow the gatekeeper to process personal data for the purposes of providing online advertising services.

Lastly, it should be as easy to withdraw consent as to give it. Gatekeepers should not design, organise or operate their online interfaces in a way that deceives, manipulates or otherwise materially distorts or impairs the ability of end users to freely give consent. In particular, gatekeepers should not be allowed to prompt end users more than once a year to give consent for the same processing purpose in respect of which they initially did not give consent or withdrew their consent. This Regulation is without prejudice to Regulation (EU) 2016/679, including its enforcement framework, which remains fully applicable with respect to any claims by data subjects relating to an infringement of their rights under that Regulation.

38. Children merit specific protection with regard to their personal data, in particular as regards the use of their personal data for the purposes of commercial communication or creating user profiles. The protection of children online is an important objective of the Union and should be reflected in the relevant Union law. In this context, due regard should be given to a Regulation on a single market for digital services. Nothing in this Regulation exempts gatekeepers from the obligation to protect children laid down in applicable Union law.

39. In certain cases, for instance through the imposition of contractual terms and conditions, gatekeepers can restrict the ability of business users of their online intermediation services to offer products or services to end users under more favourable conditions, including price, through other online intermediation services or through direct online sales channels. Where such restrictions relate to third-party online intermediation services, they limit inter-platform contestability, which in turn limits choice of alternative online intermediation services for end users. Where such restrictions relate to direct online sales channels, they unfairly limit the freedom of business users to use such channels. To ensure that business users of online intermediation services of gatekeepers can freely choose alternative online intermediation services or direct online sales channels and differentiate the conditions under which they offer their products or services to end users, it should not be accepted that gatekeepers limit business users from choosing to differentiate commercial conditions, including price. Such a restriction should apply to any measure with equivalent effect, such as increased commission rates or de-listing of the offers of business users.

40. To prevent further reinforcing their dependence on the core platform services of gatekeepers, and in order to promote multi-homing, the business users of those gatekeepers should be free to promote and choose the distribution channel that they consider most appropriate for the purpose of interacting with any end users that those business users have already acquired through core platform services provided by the gatekeeper or through other channels. This should apply to the promotion of offers, including through a software application of the business user, and any form of communication and conclusion of contracts between business users and end users. An acquired end user is an end user who has already entered into a commercial relationship with the business user and, where applicable, the gatekeeper has been directly or indirectly remunerated by the business user for facilitating the initial acquisition of the end user by the business user. Such commercial relationships can be on either a paid or a free basis, such as free trials or free service tiers, and can have been entered into either on the core platform service of the gatekeeper or through any other channel. Conversely, end users should also be free to choose offers of such business users and to enter into contracts with them either through core platform services of the gatekeeper, if applicable, or from a direct distribution channel of the business user or another indirect channel that such business user uses.

41. The ability of end users to acquire content, subscriptions, features or other items outside the core platform services of the gatekeeper should not be undermined or restricted. In particular, a situation should be avoided whereby gatekeepers restrict end users from access to, and use of, such services via a software application running on their core platform service. For example, subscribers to online content purchased outside a software application, software application store or virtual assistant should not be prevented from accessing such online content on a software application on the core platform service of the gatekeeper simply because it was purchased outside such software application, software application store or virtual assistant.

42. To safeguard a fair commercial environment and protect the contestability of the digital sector it is important to safeguard the right of business users and end users, including whistleblowers, to raise concerns about unfair practices by gatekeepers raising any issue of non-compliance with the relevant Union or national law with any relevant administrative or other public authorities, including national courts. For example, it is possible that business users or end users will want to complain about different types of unfair practices, such as discriminatory access conditions, unjustified closing of business user accounts or unclear grounds for product de-listings. Any practice that would in any way inhibit or hinder those users in raising their concerns or in seeking available redress, for instance by means of confidentiality clauses in agreements or other written terms, should therefore be prohibited. This prohibition should be without prejudice to the right of business users and gatekeepers to lay down

in their agreements the terms of use including the use of lawful complaints-handling mechanisms, including any use of alternative dispute resolution mechanisms or of the jurisdiction of specific courts in compliance with respective Union and national law. This should also be without prejudice to the role gatekeepers play in the fight against illegal content online.

43. Certain services provided together with, or in support of, relevant core platform services of the gatekeeper, such as identification services, web browser engines, payment services or technical services that support the provision of payment services, such as payment systems for in-app purchases, are crucial for business users to conduct their business and allow them to optimise services. In particular, each browser is built on a web browser engine, which is responsible for key browser functionality such as speed, reliability and web compatibility. When gatekeepers operate and impose web browser engines, they are in a position to determine the functionality and standards that will apply not only to their own web browsers, but also to competing web browsers and, in turn, to web software applications. Gatekeepers should therefore not use their position to require their dependent business users to use any of the services provided together with, or in support of, core platform services by the gatekeeper itself as part of the provision of services or products by those business users. In order to avoid a situation in which gatekeepers indirectly impose on business users their own services provided together with, or in support of, core platform services, gatekeepers should also be prohibited from requiring end users to use such services, when that requirement would be imposed in the context of the service provided to end users by the business user using the core platform service of the gatekeeper. That prohibition aims to protect the freedom of the business user to choose alternative services to the ones of the gatekeeper, but should not be construed as obliging the business user to offer such alternatives to its end users.

44. The conduct of requiring business users or end users to subscribe to, or register with, any other core platform services of gatekeepers listed in the designation decision or which meet the thresholds of active end users and business users set out in this Regulation, as a condition for using, accessing, signing up for or registering with a core platform service gives the gatekeepers a means of capturing and locking-in new business users and end users for their core platform services by ensuring that business users cannot access one core platform service without also at least registering or creating an account for the purposes of receiving a second core platform service. That conduct also gives gatekeepers a potential advantage in terms of accumulation of data. As such, this conduct is liable to raise barriers to entry and should be prohibited.

45. The conditions under which gatekeepers provide online advertising services to business users, including both advertisers and publishers, are often non-transparent and opaque. This opacity is partly linked to the practices of a few platforms, but is also due to the sheer complexity of modern day programmatic advertising. That sector is considered to have become less transparent after the introduction of new privacy legislation. This often leads to a lack of information and knowledge for advertisers and publishers about the conditions of the online advertising services they purchase and undermines their ability to switch between undertakings providing online advertising services. Furthermore, the costs of online advertising services under these conditions are likely to be higher than they would be in a fairer, more transparent and contestable platform environment. Those higher costs are likely to be reflected in the prices that end users pay for many daily products and services relying on the use of online advertising services. Transparency obligations should therefore require gatekeepers to provide advertisers and publishers to whom they supply online advertising services, when requested, with free of charge information that allows both sides to understand the price paid for each of the different online advertising services provided as part of the relevant advertising value chain.

This information should be provided, upon request, to an advertiser at the level of an individual advertisement in relation to the price and fees charged to that advertiser and, subject to an agreement by the publisher owning the inventory where the advertisement is displayed, the remuneration received by that consenting publisher. The provision of this information on a daily basis will allow advertisers to receive information that has a sufficient level of granularity necessary to compare the costs of using the online advertising services of gatekeepers with the costs of using online advertising services of alternative undertakings. Where some publishers do not provide their consent to the sharing of the relevant information with the advertiser, the gatekeeper should provide the advertiser with the information about the daily average remuneration received by those publishers for the relevant advertisements. The same obligation and principles of sharing the relevant information concerning the provision of online advertising services should apply in respect of requests by publishers. Since gatekeepers can use different pricing models for the provision of online advertising services to advertisers and publishers, for instance a price per impression, per view or any other criterion, gatekeepers should also provide the method with which each of the prices and remunerations are calculated.

46. In certain circumstances, a gatekeeper has a dual role as an undertaking providing core platform services, whereby it provides a core platform service, and possibly other services provided together with, or in support of, that core platform service to its business users, while also competing or intending to compete with those same business users in the provision of the same or similar services or products to the same end users. In those circumstances, a gatekeeper can take advantage of its dual role to use data, generated or provided by its business users in the context of activities by those business users when using the core platform services or the services provided together with, or in support of, those core platform services, for the purpose of its own services or products. The data of the business user can also include any data generated by or provided during the activities of its end users. This can be the case, for instance, where a gatekeeper provides an online marketplace or a software application store to business users, and at the same time provides services as an undertaking providing online retail services or software applications. To prevent gatekeepers from unfairly benefitting from their dual role, it is necessary to ensure that they do not use any aggregated or non-aggregated data, which could include anonymised and personal data that is not publicly available to provide similar services to those of their business users. That obligation should apply to the gatekeeper as a whole, including but not limited to its business unit that competes with the business users of a core platform service.
47. Business users can also purchase online advertising services from an undertaking providing core platform services for the purpose of providing goods and services to end users. In this case, it can happen that the data are not generated on the core platform service, but are provided to the core platform service by the business user or are generated based on its operations through the core platform service concerned. In certain instances, that core platform service providing advertising can have a dual role as both an undertaking providing online advertising services and an undertaking providing services competing with business users. Accordingly, the obligation prohibiting a dual role gatekeeper from using data of business users should apply also with respect to the data that a core platform service has received from businesses for the purpose of providing online advertising services related to that core platform service.
48. In relation to cloud computing services, the obligation not to use the data of business users should extend to data provided or generated by business users of the gatekeeper in the context of their use of the cloud computing service of the gatekeeper, or through its software application store that allows end users of cloud computing services access to software applications. That obligation should not affect the right of the gatekeeper to use aggregated data for providing other services provided together with, or in support of, its core platform service, such as data analytics services, subject to compliance with Regulation (EU) 2016/679 and Directive 2002/58/EC, as well as with the relevant obligations in this Regulation concerning such services.
49. A gatekeeper can use different means to favour its own or third-party services or products on its operating system, virtual assistant or web browser, to the detriment of the same or similar services that end users could obtain through other third parties. This can for instance happen where certain software applications or services are pre-installed by a gatekeeper. To enable end user choice, gatekeepers should not prevent end users from un-installing any software applications on their operating system. It should be possible for the gatekeeper to restrict such un-installation only when such software applications are essential to the functioning of the operating system or the device. Gatekeepers should also allow end users to easily change the default settings on the operating system, virtual assistant and web browser when those default settings favour their own software applications and services. This includes prompting a choice screen, at the moment of the users' first use of an online search engine, virtual assistant or web browser of the gatekeeper listed in the designation decision, allowing end users to select an alternative default service when the operating system of the gatekeeper directs end users to those online search engine, virtual assistant or web browser and when the virtual assistant or the web browser of the gatekeeper direct the user to the online search engine listed in the designation decision.
50. The rules that a gatekeeper sets for the distribution of software applications can, in certain circumstances, restrict the ability of end users to install and effectively use third-party software applications or software application stores on hardware or operating systems of that gatekeeper and restrict the ability of end users to access such software applications or software application stores outside

the core platform services of that gatekeeper. Such restrictions can limit the ability of developers of software applications to use alternative distribution channels and the ability of end users to choose between different software applications from different distribution channels and should be prohibited as unfair and liable to weaken the contestability of core platform services. To ensure contestability, the gatekeeper should furthermore allow the third-party software applications or software application stores to prompt the end user to decide whether that service should become the default and enable that change to be carried out easily.

In order to ensure that third-party software applications or software application stores do not endanger the integrity of the hardware or operating system provided by the gatekeeper, it should be possible for the gatekeeper concerned to implement proportionate technical or contractual measures to achieve that goal if the gatekeeper demonstrates that such measures are necessary and justified and that there are no less-restrictive means to safeguard the integrity of the hardware or operating system. The integrity of the hardware or the operating system should include any design options that need to be implemented and maintained in order for the hardware or the operating system to be protected against unauthorised access, by ensuring that security controls specified for the hardware or the operating system concerned cannot be compromised. Furthermore, in order to ensure that third-party software applications or software application stores do not undermine end users' security, it should be possible for the gatekeeper to implement strictly necessary and proportionate measures and settings, other than default settings, enabling end users to effectively protect security in relation to third-party software applications or software application stores if the gatekeeper demonstrates that such measures and settings are strictly necessary and justified and that there are no less-restrictive means to achieve that goal. The gatekeeper should be prevented from implementing such measures as a default setting or as pre-installation.

51. Gatekeepers are often vertically integrated and offer certain products or services to end users through their own core platform services, or through a business user over which they exercise control which frequently leads to conflicts of interest. This can include the situation whereby a gatekeeper provides its own online intermediation services through an online search engine. When offering those products or services on the core platform service, gatekeepers can reserve a better position, in terms of ranking, and related indexing and crawling, for their own offering than that of the products or services of third parties also operating on that core platform service. This can occur for instance with products or services, including other core platform services, which are ranked in the results communicated by online search engines, or which are partly or entirely embedded in online search engines results, groups of results specialised in a certain topic, displayed along with the results of an online search engine, which are considered or used by certain end users as a service distinct or additional to the online search engine.

Other instances are those of software applications which are distributed through software application stores, or videos distributed through a video-sharing platform, or products or services that are given prominence and display in the newsfeed of an online social networking service, or products or services ranked in search results or displayed on an online marketplace, or products or services offered through a virtual assistant. Such reserving of a better position of gatekeeper's own offering can take place even before ranking following a query, such as during crawling and indexing. For example, already during crawling, as a discovery process by which new and updated content is being found, as well as indexing, which entails storing and organising of the content found during the crawling process, the gatekeeper can favour its own content over that of third parties. In those circumstances, the gatekeeper is in a dual-role position as intermediary for third-party undertakings and as undertaking directly providing products or services. Consequently, such gatekeepers have the ability to undermine directly the contestability for those products or services on those core platform services, to the detriment of business users which are not controlled by the gatekeeper.

52. In such situations, the gatekeeper should not engage in any form of differentiated or preferential treatment in ranking on the core platform service, and related indexing and crawling, whether through legal, commercial or technical means, in favour of products or services it offers itself or through a business user which it controls. To ensure that this obligation is effective, the conditions that apply to such ranking should also be generally fair and transparent. Ranking should in this context cover all forms of relative prominence, including display, rating, linking or voice results and should also include instances where a core platform service presents or communicates only one result to the end user. To ensure that this obligation is effective and cannot be circumvented, it should also apply to any measure that has an equivalent effect to the differentiated or preferential treatment in ranking.

The guidelines adopted pursuant to Article 5 of Regulation (EU) 2019/1150 should also facilitate the implementation and enforcement of this obligation.

53. Gatekeepers should not restrict or prevent the free choice of end users by technically or otherwise preventing switching between or subscription to different software applications and services. This would allow more undertakings to offer their services, thereby ultimately providing greater choice to the end users. Gatekeepers should ensure a free choice irrespective of whether they are the manufacturer of any hardware by means of which such software applications or services are accessed and should not raise artificial technical or other barriers so as to make switching impossible or ineffective. The mere offering of a given product or service to consumers, including by means of pre-installation, as well as the improvement of the offering to end users, such as price reductions or increased quality, should not be construed as constituting a prohibited barrier to switching.
54. Gatekeepers can hamper the ability of end users to access online content and services, including software applications. Therefore, rules should be established to ensure that the rights of end users to access an open internet are not compromised by the conduct of gatekeepers. Gatekeepers can also technically limit the ability of end users to effectively switch between different undertakings providing internet access service, in particular through their control over hardware or operating systems. This distorts the level playing field for internet access services and ultimately harms end users. It should therefore be ensured that gatekeepers do not unduly restrict end users in choosing the undertaking providing their internet access service.
55. A gatekeeper can provide services or hardware, such as wearable devices, that access hardware or software features of a device accessed or controlled via an operating system or virtual assistant in order to offer specific functionalities to end users. In that case, competing service or hardware providers, such as providers of wearable devices, require equally effective interoperability with, and access for the purposes of interoperability to, the same hardware or software features to be able to provide a competitive offering to end users.
56. Gatekeepers can also have a dual role as developers of operating systems and device manufacturers, including any technical functionality that such a device may have. For example, a gatekeeper that is a manufacturer of a device can restrict access to some of the functionalities in that device, such as near-field-communication technology, secure elements and processors, authentication mechanisms and the software used to operate those technologies, which can be required for the effective provision of a service provided together with, or in support of, the core platform service by the gatekeeper as well as by any potential third-party undertaking providing such service.
57. If dual roles are used in a manner that prevents alternative service and hardware providers from having access under equal conditions to the same operating system, hardware or software features that are available or used by the gatekeeper in the provision of its own complementary or supporting services or hardware, this could significantly undermine innovation by such alternative providers, as well as choice for end users. The gatekeepers should, therefore, be required to ensure, free of charge, effective interoperability with, and access for the purposes of interoperability to, the same operating system, hardware or software features that are available or used in the provision of its own complementary and supporting services and hardware. Such access can equally be required by software applications related to the relevant services provided together with, or in support of, the core platform service in order to effectively develop and provide functionalities interoperable with those provided by gatekeepers. The aim of the obligations is to allow competing third parties to interconnect through interfaces or similar solutions to the respective features as effectively as the gatekeeper's own services or hardware.
58. The conditions under which gatekeepers provide online advertising services to business users, including both advertisers and publishers, are often non-transparent and opaque. This often leads to a lack of information for advertisers and publishers about the effect of a given advertisement. To further enhance fairness, transparency and contestability of online advertising services listed in the designation decision, as well as those that are fully integrated with other core platform services of the same undertaking, gatekeepers should provide advertisers and publishers, and third parties authorised by advertisers and publishers, when requested, with free of charge access to the gatekeepers' performance measuring tools and the data, including aggregated and non-aggregated data, necessary for advertisers, authorised third parties such as advertising agencies acting on behalf of a company placing advertising, as well as for publishers to carry out their own independent verification of the provision of the relevant online advertising services.

59. Gatekeepers benefit from access to vast amounts of data that they collect while providing the core platform services, as well as other digital services. To ensure that gatekeepers do not undermine the contestability of core platform services, or the innovation potential of the dynamic digital sector, by restricting switching or multi-homing, end users, as well as third parties authorised by an end user, should be granted effective and immediate access to the data they provided or that was generated through their activity on the relevant core platform services of the gatekeeper. The data should be received in a format that can be immediately and effectively accessed and used by the end user or the relevant third party authorised by the end user to which the data is ported. Gatekeepers should also ensure, by means of appropriate and high quality technical measures, such as application programming interfaces, that end users or third parties authorised by end users can freely port the data continuously and in real time. This should apply also to any other data at different levels of aggregation necessary to effectively enable such portability. For the avoidance of doubt, the obligation on the gatekeeper to ensure effective portability of data under this Regulation complements the right to data portability under the Regulation (EU) 2016/679. Facilitating switching or multi-homing should lead, in turn, to an increased choice for end users and acts as an incentive for gatekeepers and business users to innovate.
60. Business users that use core platform services provided by gatekeepers, and end users of such business users provide and generate a vast amount of data. In order to ensure that business users have access to the relevant data thus generated, the gatekeeper should, upon their request, provide effective access, free of charge, to such data. Such access should also be given to third parties contracted by the business user, who are acting as processors of this data for the business user. The access should include access to data provided or generated by the same business users and the same end users of those business users in the context of other services provided by the same gatekeeper, including services provided together with or in support of core platform services, where this is inextricably linked to the relevant request. To this end, a gatekeeper should not use any contractual or other restrictions to prevent business users from accessing relevant data and should enable business users to obtain consent of their end users for such data access and retrieval, where such consent is required under Regulation (EU) 2016/679 and Directive 2002/58/EC. Gatekeepers should also ensure the continuous and real time access to such data by means of appropriate technical measures, for example by putting in place high quality application programming interfaces or integrated tools for small volume business users.
61. The value of online search engines to their respective business users and end users increases as the total number of such users increases. Undertakings providing online search engines collect and store aggregated datasets containing information about what users searched for, and how they interacted with, the results with which they were provided. Undertakings providing online search engines collect these data from searches undertaken on their own online search engine and, where applicable, searches undertaken on the platforms of their downstream commercial partners. Access by gatekeepers to such ranking, query, click and view data constitutes an important barrier to entry and expansion, which undermines the contestability of online search engines. Gatekeepers should therefore be required to provide access, on fair, reasonable and non-discriminatory terms, to those ranking, query, click and view data in relation to free and paid search generated by consumers on online search engines to other undertakings providing such services, so that those third-party undertakings can optimise their services and contest the relevant core platform services. Such access should also be given to third parties contracted by a provider of an online search engine, who are acting as processors of this data for that online search engine. When providing access to its search data, a gatekeeper should ensure the protection of the personal data of end users, including against possible re-identification risks, by appropriate means, such as anonymisation of such personal data, without substantially degrading the quality or usefulness of the data. The relevant data is anonymised if personal data is irreversibly altered in such a way that information does not relate to an identified or identifiable natural person or where personal data is rendered anonymous in such a manner that the data subject is not or is no longer identifiable.
62. For software application stores, online search engines and online social networking services listed in the designation decision, gatekeepers should publish and apply general conditions of access that should be fair, reasonable and non-discriminatory. Those general conditions should provide for a Union based alternative dispute settlement mechanism that is easily accessible, impartial, independent and free of charge for the business user, without prejudice to the business user's own cost and proportionate measures aimed at preventing the abuse of the dispute settlement mechanism by business

users. The dispute settlement mechanism should be without prejudice to the right of business users to seek redress before judicial authorities in accordance with Union and national law. In particular, gatekeepers which provide access to software application stores are an important gateway for business users that seek to reach end users. In view of the imbalance in bargaining power between those gatekeepers and business users of their software application stores, those gatekeepers should not be allowed to impose general conditions, including pricing conditions, that would be unfair or lead to unjustified differentiation.

Pricing or other general access conditions should be considered unfair if they lead to an imbalance of rights and obligations imposed on business users or confer an advantage on the gatekeeper which is disproportionate to the service provided by the gatekeeper to business users or lead to a disadvantage for business users in providing the same or similar services as the gatekeeper. The following benchmarks can serve as a yardstick to determine the fairness of general access conditions: prices charged or conditions imposed for the same or similar services by other providers of software application stores; prices charged or conditions imposed by the provider of the software application store for different related or similar services or to different types of end users; prices charged or conditions imposed by the provider of the software application store for the same service in different geographic regions; prices charged or conditions imposed by the provider of the software application store for the same service the gatekeeper provides to itself. This obligation should not establish an access right and it should be without prejudice to the ability of providers of software application stores, online search engines and online social networking services to take the required responsibility in the fight against illegal and unwanted content as set out in a Regulation on a single market for digital services.

63. Gatekeepers can hamper the ability of business users and end users to unsubscribe from a core platform service that they have previously subscribed to. Therefore, rules should be established to avoid a situation in which gatekeepers undermine the rights of business users and end users to freely choose which core platform service they use. To safeguard free choice of business users and end users, a gatekeeper should not be allowed to make it unnecessarily difficult or complicated for business users or end users to unsubscribe from a core platform service. Closing an account or un-subscribing should not be made be more complicated than opening an account or subscribing to the same service. Gatekeepers should not demand additional fees when terminating contracts with their end users or business users. Gatekeepers should ensure that the conditions for terminating contracts are always proportionate and can be exercised without undue difficulty by end users, such as, for example, in relation to the reasons for termination, the notice period, or the form of such termination. This is without prejudice to national legislation applicable in accordance with the Union law laying down rights and obligations concerning conditions of termination of provision of core platform services by end users.

64. The lack of interoperability allows gatekeepers that provide number-independent interpersonal communications services to benefit from strong network effects, which contributes to the weakening of contestability. Furthermore, regardless of whether end users 'multi-home', gatekeepers often provide number-independent interpersonal communications services as part of their platform ecosystem, and this further exacerbates entry barriers for alternative providers of such services and increases costs for end users to switch. Without prejudice to Directive (EU) 2018/1972 of the European Parliament and of the Council[14] and, in particular, the conditions and procedures laid down in Article 61 thereof, gatekeepers should therefore ensure, free of charge and upon request, interoperability with certain basic functionalities of their number-independent interpersonal communications services that they provide to their own end users, to third-party providers of such services.

Gatekeepers should ensure interoperability for third-party providers of number-independent interpersonal communications services that offer or intend to offer their number-independent interpersonal communications services to end users and business users in the Union. To facilitate the practical implementation of such interoperability, the gatekeeper concerned should be required to publish a reference offer laying down the technical details and general terms and conditions of interoperability with its number-independent interpersonal communications services. It should be possible for the Commission, if applicable, to consult the Body of European Regulators for Electronic Communications,

[14] Directive (EU) 2018/1972 of the European Parliament and of the Council of 11 December 2018 establishing the European Electronic Communications Code (OJ L 321, 17.12.2018, p. 36).

in order to determine whether the technical details and the general terms and conditions published in the reference offer that the gatekeeper intends to implement or has implemented ensures compliance with this obligation.

In all cases, the gatekeeper and the requesting provider should ensure that interoperability does not undermine a high level of security and data protection in line with their obligations laid down in this Regulation and applicable Union law, in particular Regulation (EU) 2016/679 and Directive 2002/58/EC. The obligation related to interoperability should be without prejudice to the information and choices to be made available to end users of the number-independent interpersonal communication services of the gatekeeper and the requesting provider under this Regulation and other Union law, in particular Regulation (EU) 2016/679.

65. To ensure the effectiveness of the obligations laid down by this Regulation, while also making certain that those obligations are limited to what is necessary to ensure contestability and tackling the harmful effects of the unfair practices by gatekeepers, it is important to clearly define and circumscribe them so as to allow the gatekeeper to fully comply with them, whilst fully complying with applicable law, and in particular Regulation (EU) 2016/679 and Directive 2002/58/EC and legislation on consumer protection, cyber security, product safety and accessibility requirements, including Directive (EU) 2019/882 and Directive (EU) 2016/2102 of the European Parliament and of the Council[15]. The gatekeepers should ensure the compliance with this Regulation by design. Therefore, the necessary measures should be integrated as much as possible into the technological design used by the gatekeepers.

    It may in certain cases be appropriate for the Commission, following a dialogue with the gatekeeper concerned and after enabling third parties to make comments, to further specify some of the measures that the gatekeeper concerned should adopt in order to effectively comply with obligations that are susceptible of being further specified or, in the event of circumvention, with all obligations. In particular, such further specification should be possible where the implementation of an obligation susceptible to being further specified can be affected by variations of services within a single category of core platform services. For this purpose, it should be possible for the gatekeeper to request the Commission to engage in a process whereby the Commission can further specify some of the measures that the gatekeeper concerned should adopt in order to effectively comply with those obligations.

    The Commission should have discretion as to whether and when such further specification should be provided, while respecting the principles of equal treatment, proportionality, and good administration. In this respect, the Commission should provide the main reasons underlying its assessment, including any enforcement priorities. This process should not be used to undermine the effectiveness of this Regulation. Furthermore, this process is without prejudice to the powers of the Commission to adopt a decision establishing non-compliance with any of the obligations laid down in this Regulation by a gatekeeper, including the possibility to impose fines or periodic penalty payments. The Commission should be able to reopen proceedings, including where the specified measures turn out not to be effective. A reopening due to an ineffective specification adopted by decision should enable the Commission to amend the specification prospectively. The Commission should also be able to set a reasonable time period within which the proceedings can be reopened if the specified measures turn out not to be effective.

66. As an additional element to ensure proportionality, gatekeepers should be given an opportunity to request the suspension, to the extent necessary, of a specific obligation in exceptional circumstances that lie beyond the control of the gatekeeper, such as an unforeseen external shock that has temporarily eliminated a significant part of end user demand for the relevant core platform service, where compliance with a specific obligation is shown by the gatekeeper to endanger the economic viability of the Union operations of the gatekeeper concerned. The Commission should identify the exceptional circumstances justifying the suspension and review it on a regular basis in order to assess whether the conditions for granting it are still viable.

67. In exceptional circumstances, justified on the limited grounds of public health or public security laid down in Union law and interpreted by the Court of Justice, the Commission should be able to decide that a specific obligation does not apply to a specific core platform service. If harm is caused

---

[15] Directive (EU) 2016/2102 of the European Parliament and of the Council of 26 October 2016 on the accessibility of the websites and mobile applications of public sector bodies (OJ L 327, 2.12.2016, p. 1).

to such public interests that could indicate that the cost to society as a whole of enforcing a certain obligation is, in a specific exceptional case, too high and thus disproportionate. Where appropriate, the Commission should be able to facilitate compliance by assessing whether a limited and duly justified suspension or exemption is justified. This should ensure the proportionality of the obligations in this Regulation without undermining the intended *ex ante* effects on fairness and contestability. Where such an exemption is granted, the Commission should review its decision every year.

68. Within the timeframe for complying with their obligations under this Regulation, gatekeepers should inform the Commission, through mandatory reporting, about the measures they intend to implement or have implemented in order to ensure effective compliance with those obligations, including those measures concerning compliance with Regulation (EU) 2016/679, to the extent they are relevant for compliance with the obligations provided under this Regulation, which should allow the Commission to fulfil its duties under this Regulation. In addition, a clear and comprehensible non-confidential summary of such information should be made publicly available while taking into account the legitimate interest of gatekeepers in the protection of their business secrets and other confidential information. This non-confidential publication should enable third parties to assess whether the gatekeepers comply with the obligations laid down in this Regulation. Such reporting should be without prejudice to any enforcement action by the Commission at any time following the reporting. The Commission should publish online a link to the non-confidential summary of the report, as well as all other public information based on information obligations under this Regulation, in order to ensure accessibility of such information in a usable and comprehensive manner, in particular for small and medium enterprises (SMEs).

69. The obligations of gatekeepers should only be updated after a thorough investigation into the nature and impact of specific practices that may be newly identified, following an in-depth investigation, as unfair or limiting contestability in the same manner as the unfair practices laid down in this Regulation while potentially escaping the scope of the current set of obligations. The Commission should be able to launch an investigation with a view to determining whether the existing obligations need to be updated, either on its own initiative or following a justified request of at least three Member States. When presenting such justified requests, it should be possible for Member States to include information on newly introduced offers of products, services, software or features which raise concerns of contestability or fairness, whether implemented in the context of existing core platform services or otherwise. Where, following a market investigation, the Commission deems it necessary to modify essential elements of this Regulation, such as the inclusion of new obligations that depart from the same contestability or fairness issues addressed by this Regulation, the Commission should advance a proposal to amend this Regulation.

70. Given the substantial economic power of gatekeepers, it is important that the obligations are applied effectively and are not circumvented. To that end, the rules in question should apply to any practice by a gatekeeper, irrespective of its form and irrespective of whether it is of a contractual, commercial, technical or any other nature, insofar as the practice corresponds to the type of practice that is the subject of one of the obligations laid down by this Regulation. Gatekeepers should not engage in behaviour that would undermine the effectiveness of the prohibitions and obligations laid down in this Regulation. Such behaviour includes the design used by the gatekeeper, the presentation of end-user choices in a non-neutral manner, or using the structure, function or manner of operation of a user interface or a part thereof to subvert or impair user autonomy, decision-making, or choice. Furthermore, the gatekeeper should not be allowed to engage in any behaviour undermining interoperability as required under this Regulation, such as for example by using unjustified technical protection measures, discriminatory terms of service, unlawfully claiming a copyright on application programming interfaces or providing misleading information. Gatekeepers should not be allowed to circumvent their designation by artificially segmenting, dividing, subdividing, fragmenting or splitting their core platform services to circumvent the quantitative thresholds laid down in this Regulation.

71. To ensure the effectiveness of the review of gatekeeper status, as well as the possibility to adjust the list of core platform services provided by a gatekeeper, the gatekeepers should inform the Commission of all of their intended acquisitions, prior to their implementation, of other undertakings providing core platform services or any other services provided within the digital sector or other services that enable the collection of data. Such information should not only serve the review process regarding the status of individual gatekeepers, but will also provide information that is crucial to monitoring broader

contestability trends in the digital sector and can therefore be a useful factor for consideration in the context of the market investigations provided for by this Regulation. Furthermore, the Commission should inform Member States of such information, given the possibility of using the information for national merger control purposes and as, under certain circumstances, it is possible for the national competent authority to refer those acquisitions to the Commission for the purposes of merger control. The Commission should also publish annually a list of acquisitions of which it has been informed by the gatekeeper. To ensure the necessary transparency and usefulness of such information for different purposes provided for by this Regulation, gatekeepers should provide at least information about the undertakings concerned by the concentration, their Union and worldwide annual turnover, their field of activity, including activities directly related to the concentration, the transaction value or an estimation thereof, a summary of the concentration, including its nature and rationale, as well as a list of the Member States concerned by the operation.

72. The data protection and privacy interests of end users are relevant to any assessment of potential negative effects of the observed practice of gatekeepers to collect and accumulate large amounts of data from end users. Ensuring an adequate level of transparency of profiling practices employed by gatekeepers, including, but not limited to, profiling within the meaning of Article 4, point (4), of Regulation (EU) 2016/679, facilitates contestability of core platform services. Transparency puts external pressure on gatekeepers not to make deep consumer profiling the industry standard, given that potential entrants or start-ups cannot access data to the same extent and depth, and at a similar scale. Enhanced transparency should allow other undertakings providing core platform services to differentiate themselves better through the use of superior privacy guarantees.

    To ensure a minimum level of effectiveness of this transparency obligation, gatekeepers should at least provide an independently audited description of the basis upon which profiling is performed, including whether personal data and data derived from user activity in line with Regulation (EU) 2016/679 is relied on, the processing applied, the purpose for which the profile is prepared and eventually used, the duration of the profiling, the impact of such profiling on the gatekeeper's services, and the steps taken to effectively enable end users to be aware of the relevant use of such profiling, as well as steps to seek their consent or provide them with the possibility of denying or withdrawing consent. The Commission should transfer the audited description to the European Data Protection Board to inform the enforcement of Union data protection rules. The Commission should be empowered to develop the methodology and procedure for the audited description, in consultation with the European Data Protection Supervisor, the European Data Protection Board, civil society and experts, in line with Regulations (EU) N°182/2011[16] and (EU) 2018/1725[17] of the European Parliament and of the Council.

73. In order to ensure the full and lasting achievement of the objectives of this Regulation, the Commission should be able to assess whether an undertaking providing core platform services should be designated as a gatekeeper without meeting the quantitative thresholds laid down in this Regulation; whether systematic non-compliance by a gatekeeper warrants imposing additional remedies; whether more services within the digital sector should be added to the list of core platform services; and whether additional practices that are similarly unfair and limiting the contestability of digital markets need to be investigated. Such assessment should be based on market investigations to be carried out in an appropriate timeframe, by using clear procedures and deadlines, in order to support the *ex ante* effect of this Regulation on contestability and fairness in the digital sector, and to provide the requisite degree of legal certainty.

74. The Commission should be able to find, following a market investigation, that an undertaking providing a core platform service fulfils all of the overarching qualitative criteria for being identified as a gatekeeper. That undertaking should then, in principle, comply with all of the relevant obligations laid down by this Regulation. However, for gatekeepers that have been designated by the Commission

---

16 Regulation (EU) No182/2011 of the European Parliament and of the Council of 16 February 2011 laying down the rules and general principles concerning mechanisms for control by the Member States of the Commission's exercise of implementing powers (OJ L 55, 28.2.2011, p. 13).

17 Regulation (EU) 2018/1725 of the European Parliament and of the Council of 23 October 2018 on the protection of natural persons with regard to the processing of personal data by the Union institutions, bodies, offices and agencies and on the free movement of such data, and repealing Regulation (EC) No45/2001 and Decision No1247/2002/EC (OJ L 295, 21.11.2018, p. 39).

because it is foreseeable that they will enjoy an entrenched and durable position in the near future, the Commission should only impose those obligations that are necessary and appropriate to prevent that the gatekeeper concerned achieves an entrenched and durable position in its operations. With respect to such emerging gatekeepers, the Commission should take into account that this status is in principle of a temporary nature, and it should therefore be decided at a given moment whether such an undertaking providing core platform services should be subjected to the full set of gatekeeper obligations because it has acquired an entrenched and durable position, or the conditions for designation are ultimately not met and therefore all previously imposed obligations should be waived.

75. The Commission should investigate and assess whether additional behavioural, or, where appropriate, structural remedies are justified, in order to ensure that the gatekeeper cannot frustrate the objectives of this Regulation by systematic non-compliance with one or several of the obligations laid down in this Regulation. This is the case where the Commission has issued against a gatekeeper at least three non-compliance decisions within the period of 8 years, which can concern different core platform services and different obligations laid down in this Regulation, and if the gatekeeper has maintained, extended or further strengthened its impact in the internal market, the economic dependency of its business users and end users on the gatekeeper's core platform services or the entrenchment of its position. A gatekeeper should be deemed to have maintained, extended or strengthened its gatekeeper position where, despite the enforcement actions taken by the Commission, that gatekeeper still holds or has further consolidated or entrenched its importance as a gateway for business users to reach end users.

The Commission should in such cases have the power to impose any remedy, whether behavioural or structural, having due regard to the principle of proportionality. In this context, the Commission should have the power to prohibit, to the extent that such remedy is proportionate and necessary in order to maintain or restore fairness and contestability as affected by the systematic non-compliance, during a limited time-period, the gatekeeper from entering into a concentration regarding those core platform services or the other services provided in the digital sector or services enabling the collection of data that are affected by the systematic non-compliance. In order to enable effective involvement of third parties and the possibility to test remedies before its application, the Commission should publish a detailed non-confidential summary of the case and the measures to be taken. The Commission should be able to reopen proceedings, including where the specified remedies turn out not to be effective. A reopening due to ineffective remedies adopted by decision should enable the Commission to amend the remedies prospectively. The Commission should also be able to set a reasonable time period within which it should be possible to reopen the proceedings if the remedies prove not to be effective.

76. Where, in the course of an investigation into systematic non-compliance, a gatekeeper offers commitments to the Commission, the latter should be able to adopt a decision making these commitments binding on the gatekeeper concerned, where it finds that the commitments ensure effective compliance with the obligations set out in this Regulation. That decision should also find that there are no longer grounds for action by the Commission as regards the systematic non-compliance under investigation. In assessing whether the commitments offered by the gatekeeper are sufficient to ensure effective compliance with the obligations under this Regulation, the Commission should be allowed to take into account tests undertaken by the gatekeeper to demonstrate the effectiveness of the offered commitments in practice. The Commission should verify that the commitments decision is fully respected and reaches its objectives, and should be entitled to reopen the decision if it finds that the commitments are not effective.

77. The services in the digital sector and the types of practices relating to these services can change quickly and to a significant extent. To ensure that this Regulation remains up to date and constitutes an effective and holistic regulatory response to the problems posed by gatekeepers, it is important to provide for a regular review of the lists of core platform services, as well as of the obligations provided for in this Regulation. This is particularly important to ensure that a practice that is likely to limit the contestability of core platform services or is unfair is identified. While it is important to conduct a review on a regular basis, given the dynamically changing nature of the digital sector, in order to ensure legal certainty as to the regulatory conditions, any reviews should be conducted within a reasonable and appropriate timeframe. Market investigations should also ensure that the Commission has a solid evidentiary basis on which it can assess whether it should propose to amend this Regulation in order to review, expand, or further detail, the lists of core platform services. They should

equally ensure that the Commission has a solid evidentiary basis on which it can assess whether it should propose to amend the obligations laid down in this Regulation or whether it should adopt a delegated act updating such obligations.

78. With regard to conduct by gatekeepers that is not covered by the obligations set out in this Regulation, the Commission should have the possibility to open a market investigation into new services and new practices for the purposes of identifying whether the obligations set out in this Regulation are to be supplemented by means of a delegated act falling within the scope of the empowerment set out for such delegated acts in this Regulation, or by presenting a proposal to amend this Regulation. This is without prejudice to the possibility for the Commission to, in appropriate cases, open proceedings under Article 101 or 102 TFEU. Such proceedings should be conducted in accordance with Council Regulation (EC) N°1/2003[18]. In cases of urgency due to the risk of serious and irreparable damage to competition, the Commission should consider adopting interim measures in accordance with Article 8 of Regulation (EC) N°1/2003.

79. In the event that gatekeepers engage in a practice that is unfair or that limits the contestability of the core platform services that are already designated under this Regulation but without such practices being explicitly covered by the obligations laid down by this Regulation, the Commission should be able to update this Regulation through delegated acts. Such updates by way of delegated act should be subject to the same investigatory standard and therefore should be preceded by a market investigation. The Commission should also apply a predefined standard in identifying such types of practices. This legal standard should ensure that the type of obligations that gatekeepers could at any time face under this Regulation are sufficiently predictable.

80. In order to ensure effective implementation and compliance with this Regulation, the Commission should have strong investigative and enforcement powers, to allow it to investigate, enforce and monitor the rules laid down in this Regulation, while at the same time ensuring the respect for the fundamental right to be heard and to have access to the file in the context of the enforcement proceedings. The Commission should dispose of these investigative powers also for the purpose of carrying out market investigations, including for the purpose of updating and reviewing this Regulation.

81. The Commission should be empowered to request information necessary for the purpose of this Regulation. In particular, the Commission should have access to any relevant documents, data, database, algorithm and information necessary to open and conduct investigations and to monitor the compliance with the obligations laid down in this Regulation, irrespective of who possesses such information, and regardless of their form or format, their storage medium, or the place where they are stored.

82. The Commission should be able to directly request that undertakings or associations of undertakings provide any relevant evidence, data and information. In addition, the Commission should be able to request any relevant information from competent authorities within the Member State, or from any natural person or legal person for the purpose of this Regulation. When complying with a decision of the Commission, undertakings are obliged to answer factual questions and to provide documents.

83. The Commission should also be empowered to conduct inspections of any undertaking or association of undertakings and to interview any persons who could be in possession of useful information and to record the statements made.

84. Interim measures can be an important tool to ensure that, while an investigation is ongoing, the infringement being investigated does not lead to serious and irreparable damage for business users or end users of gatekeepers. This tool is important to avoid developments that could be very difficult to reverse by a decision taken by the Commission at the end of the proceedings. The Commission should therefore have the power to order interim measures in the context of proceedings opened in view of the possible adoption of a non-compliance decision. This power should apply in cases where the Commission has made a *prima facie* finding of infringement of obligations by gatekeepers and where there is a risk of serious and irreparable damage for business users or end users of gatekeepers. Interim measures should only apply for a specified period, either one ending with the conclusion

---

18 Council Regulation (EC) No1/2003 of 16 December 2002 on the implementation of the rules on competition laid down in Articles 81 and 82 of the Treaty (OJ L 1, 4.1.2003, p. 1).

of the proceedings by the Commission, or for a fixed period which can be renewed insofar as it is necessary and appropriate.

85. The Commission should be able to take the necessary actions to monitor the effective implementation of and compliance with the obligations laid down in this Regulation. Such actions should include the ability of the Commission to appoint independent external experts and auditors to assist the Commission in this process, including, where applicable, from competent authorities of the Member States, such as data or consumer protection authorities. When appointing auditors, the Commission should ensure sufficient rotation.
86. Compliance with the obligations imposed by this Regulation should be enforceable by means of fines and periodic penalty payments. To that end, appropriate levels of fines and periodic penalty payments should also be laid down for non-compliance with the obligations and breach of the procedural rules subject to appropriate limitation periods, in accordance with the principles of proportionality and *ne bis in idem*. The Commission and the relevant national authorities should coordinate their enforcement efforts in order to ensure that those principles are respected. In particular, the Commission should take into account any fines and penalties imposed on the same legal person for the same facts through a final decision in proceedings relating to an infringement of other Union or national rules, so as to ensure that the overall fines and penalties imposed correspond to the seriousness of the infringements committed.
87. In order to ensure effective recovery of fines imposed on associations of undertakings for infringements that they have committed, it is necessary to lay down the conditions on which it should be possible for the Commission to require payment of the fine from the members of that association of undertakings where it is not solvent.
88. In the context of proceedings carried out under this Regulation, the undertaking concerned should be accorded the right to be heard by the Commission and the decisions taken should be widely publicised. While ensuring the rights to good administration, the right of access to the file and the right to be heard, it is essential to protect confidential information. Furthermore, while respecting the confidentiality of the information, the Commission should ensure that any information on which the decision is based is disclosed to an extent that allows the addressee of the decision to understand the facts and considerations that led to the decision. It is also necessary to ensure that the Commission only uses information collected pursuant to this Regulation for the purposes of this Regulation, except where specifically envisaged otherwise. Finally, it should be possible, under certain conditions, for certain business records, such as communication between lawyers and their clients, to be considered confidential if the relevant conditions are met.
89. When preparing non-confidential summaries for publication in order to effectively enable interested third parties to provide comments, the Commission should give due regard to the legitimate interest of undertakings in the protection of their business secrets and other confidential information.
90. The coherent, effective and complementary enforcement of available legal instruments applied to gatekeepers requires cooperation and coordination between the Commission and national authorities within the remit of their competences. The Commission and national authorities should cooperate and coordinate their actions necessary for the enforcement of the available legal instruments applied to gatekeepers within the meaning of this Regulation and respect the principle of sincere cooperation laid down in Article 4 of the Treaty on European Union (TEU). It should be possible for the support from national authorities to the Commission to include providing the Commission with all necessary information in their possession or assisting the Commission, at its request, with the exercise of its powers so that the Commission is better able to carry out its duties under this Regulation.
91. The Commission is the sole authority empowered to enforce this Regulation. In order to support the Commission, it should be possible for Member States to empower their national competent authorities enforcing competition rules to conduct investigations into possible non-compliance by gatekeepers with certain obligations under this Regulation. This could in particular be relevant for cases where it cannot be determined from the outset whether a gatekeeper's behaviour is capable of infringing this Regulation, the competition rules which the national competent authority is empowered to enforce, or both. The national competent authority enforcing competition rules should report on its findings on possible non-compliance by gatekeepers with certain obligations under this Regulation to the Commission in view of the Commission opening proceedings to investigate any non-compliance as the sole enforcer of the provisions laid down by this Regulation.

The Commission should have full discretion to decide whether to open such proceedings. In order to avoid overlapping investigations under this Regulation, the national competent authority concerned should inform the Commission before taking its first investigative measure into a possible non-compliance by gatekeepers with certain obligations under this Regulation. The national competent authorities should also closely cooperate and coordinate with the Commission when enforcing national competition rules against gatekeepers, including with regard to the setting of fines. To that end, they should inform the Commission when initiating proceedings based on national competition rules against gatekeepers, as well as prior to imposing obligations on gatekeepers in such proceedings. In order to avoid duplication, it should be possible for information of the draft decision pursuant to Article 11 of Regulation (EC) N°1/2003, where applicable, to serve as notification under this Regulation.

92. In order to safeguard the harmonised application and enforcement of this Regulation, it is important to ensure that national authorities, including national courts, have all necessary information to ensure that their decisions do not run counter to a decision adopted by the Commission under this Regulation. National courts should be allowed to ask the Commission to send them information or opinions on questions concerning the application of this Regulation. At the same time, the Commission should be able to submit oral or written observations to national courts. This is without prejudice to the ability of national courts to request a preliminary ruling under Article 267 TFEU.
93. In order to ensure coherence and effective complementarity in the implementation of this Regulation and of other sectoral regulations applicable to gatekeepers, the Commission should benefit from the expertise of a dedicated high-level group. It should be possible for that high-level group to also assist the Commission by means of advice, expertise and recommendations, when relevant, in general matters relating to the implementation or enforcement of this Regulation. The high-level group should be composed of the relevant European bodies and networks, and its composition should ensure a high level of expertise and a geographical balance. The members of the high-level group should regularly report to the bodies and networks they represent regarding the tasks performed in the context of the group, and consult them in that regard.
94. Since the decisions taken by the Commission under this Regulation are subject to review by the Court of Justice in accordance with the TFEU, in accordance with Article 261 TFEU, the Court of Justice should have unlimited jurisdiction in respect of fines and penalty payments.
95. It should be possible for the Commission to develop guidelines to provide further guidance on different aspects of this Regulation or to assist undertakings providing core platform services in the implementation of the obligations under this Regulation. It should be possible for such guidance to be based in particular on the experience that the Commission obtains through the monitoring of compliance with this Regulation. The issuing of any guidelines under this Regulation is a prerogative and at the sole discretion of the Commission and should not be considered to be a constitutive element in ensuring that the undertakings or associations of undertakings concerned comply with the obligations under this Regulation.
96. The implementation of some of the gatekeepers' obligations, such as those related to data access, data portability or interoperability could be facilitated by the use of technical standards. In this respect, it should be possible for the Commission, where appropriate and necessary, to request European standardisation bodies to develop them.
97. In order to ensure contestable and fair markets in the digital sector across the Union where gatekeepers are present, the power to adopt acts in accordance with Article 290 TFEU should be delegated to the Commission in respect of amending the methodology for determining whether the quantitative thresholds regarding active end users and active business users for the designation of gatekeepers are met, which is contained in an Annex to this Regulation, in respect of further specifying the additional elements of the methodology not falling in that Annex for determining whether the quantitative thresholds regarding the designation of gatekeepers are met, and in respect of supplementing the existing obligations laid down in this Regulation where, based on a market investigation, the Commission has identified the need for updating the obligations addressing practices that limit the contestability of core platform services or are unfair, and the update considered falls within the scope of the empowerment set out for such delegated acts in this Regulation.
98. When adopting delegated acts under this Regulation, it is of particular importance that the Commission carries out appropriate consultations during its preparatory work, including at expert

level, and that those consultations be conducted in accordance with the principles laid down in the Interinstitutional Agreement of 13 April 2016 on Better Law-Making[19]. In particular, to ensure equal participation in the preparation of delegated acts, the European Parliament and the Council should receive all documents at the same time as Member States' experts, and their experts systematically have access to meetings of Commission expert groups dealing with the preparation of delegated acts.

99. In order to ensure uniform conditions for the implementation of this Regulation, implementing powers should be conferred on the Commission to specify measures to be implemented by gatekeepers in order to effectively comply with the obligations under this Regulation; to suspend, in whole or in part, a specific obligation imposed on a gatekeeper; to exempt a gatekeeper, in whole or in part, from a specific obligation; to specify the measures to be implemented by a gatekeeper when it circumvents the obligations under this Regulation; to conclude a market investigation for designating gatekeepers; to impose remedies in the case of systematic non-compliance; to order interim measures against a gatekeeper; to make commitments binding on a gatekeeper; to set out its finding of a non-compliance; to set the definitive amount of the periodic penalty payment; to determine the form, content and other details of notifications, submissions of information, reasoned requests and regulatory reports transmitted by gatekeepers; to lay down operational and technical arrangements in view of implementing interoperability and the methodology and procedure for the audited description of techniques used for profiling consumers; to provide for practical arrangements for proceedings, extensions of deadlines, exercising rights during proceedings, terms of disclosure, as well as for the cooperation and coordination between the Commission and national authorities. Those powers should be exercised in accordance with Regulation (EU) N°182/2011.

100. The examination procedure should be used for the adoption of an implementing act on the practical arrangements for the cooperation and coordination between the Commission and Member States. The advisory procedure should be used for the remaining implementing acts envisaged by this Regulation. This is justified by the fact that those remaining implementing acts relate to practical aspects of the procedures laid down in this Regulation, such as form, content and other details of various procedural steps, to practical arrangements of different procedural steps, such as, for example, extension of procedural deadlines or right to be heard, as well as to individual implementing decisions addressed to a gatekeeper.

101. In accordance with Regulation (EU) N°182/2011, each Member State should be represented in the advisory committee and decide on the composition of its delegation. Such delegation can include, *inter alia*, experts from the competent authorities within the Member States, which hold the relevant expertise for a specific issue presented to the advisory committee.

102. Whistleblowers can bring new information to the attention of competent authorities which can help the competent authorities detect infringements of this Regulation and enable them to impose penalties. It should be ensured that adequate arrangements are in place to enable whistleblowers to alert the competent authorities to actual or potential infringements of this Regulation and to protect the whistleblowers from retaliation. For that purpose, it should be provided in this Regulation that Directive (EU) 2019/1937 of the European Parliament and of the Council[20] is applicable to the reporting of breaches of this Regulation and to the protection of persons reporting such breaches.

103. To enhance legal certainty, the applicability, pursuant to this Regulation, of Directive (EU) 2019/1937 to reports of breaches of this Regulation and to the protection of persons reporting such breaches should be reflected in that Directive. The Annex to Directive (EU) 2019/1937 should therefore be amended accordingly. It is for the Member States to ensure that that amendment is reflected in their transposition measures adopted in accordance with Directive (EU) 2019/1937, although the adoption of national transposition measures is not a condition for the applicability of that Directive to the reporting of breaches of this Regulation and to the protection of reporting persons from the date of application of this Regulation.

---

19 OJ L 123, 12.5.2016, p. 1.

20 Directive (EU) 2019/1937 of the European Parliament and of the Council of 23 October 2019 on the protection of persons who report breaches of Union law (OJ L 305, 26.11.2019, p. 17).

104. Consumers should be entitled to enforce their rights in relation to the obligations imposed on gatekeepers under this Regulation through representative actions in accordance with Directive (EU) 2020/1828 of the European Parliament and of the Council[21]. For that purpose, this Regulation should provide that Directive (EU) 2020/1828 is applicable to the representative actions brought against infringements by gatekeepers of provisions of this Regulation that harm or can harm the collective interests of consumers. The Annex to that Directive should therefore be amended accordingly. It is for the Member States to ensure that that amendment is reflected in their transposition measures adopted in accordance with Directive (EU) 2020/1828, although the adoption of national transposition measures in this regard is not a condition for the applicability of that Directive to those representative actions. The applicability of Directive (EU) 2020/1828 to the representative actions brought against infringements by gatekeepers of provisions of this Regulation that harm or can harm the collective interests of consumers should start from the date of application of Member States' laws, regulations and administrative provisions necessary to transpose that Directive, or from the date of application of this Regulation, whichever is the later.

105. The Commission should periodically evaluate this Regulation and closely monitor its effects on the contestability and fairness of commercial relationships in the online platform economy, in particular with a view to determining the need for amendments in light of relevant technological or commercial developments. That evaluation should include the regular review of the list of core platform services and the obligations addressed to gatekeepers, as well as their enforcement, in view of ensuring that digital markets across the Union are contestable and fair. In that context, the Commission should also evaluate the scope of the obligation concerning the interoperability of number-independent electronic communications services. In order to obtain a broad view of developments in the digital sector, the evaluation should take into account the experiences of Member States and relevant stakeholders. It should be possible for the Commission in this regard also to consider the opinions and reports presented to it by the Observatory on the Online Platform Economy that was first established by Commission Decision C(2018)2393 of 26 April 2018. Following the evaluation, the Commission should take appropriate measures. The Commission should maintain a high level of protection and respect for the common rights and values, particularly equality and non-discrimination, as an objective when conducting the assessments and reviews of the practices and obligations provided in this Regulation.

106. Without prejudice to the budgetary procedure and through existing financial instruments, adequate human, financial and technical resources should be allocated to the Commission to ensure that it can effectively perform its duties and exercise its powers in respect of the enforcement of this Regulation.

107. Since the objective of this Regulation, namely to ensure a contestable and fair digital sector in general and core platform services in particular, with a view to promoting innovation, high quality of digital products and services, fair and competitive prices, as well as a high quality and choice for end users in the digital sector, cannot be sufficiently achieved by the Member States, but can rather, by reason of the business model and operations of the gatekeepers and the scale and effects of their operations, be better achieved at Union level, the Union may adopt measures, in accordance with the principle of subsidiarity as set out in Article 5 TEU. In accordance with the principle of proportionality, as set out in that Article, this Regulation does not go beyond what is necessary in order to achieve that objective.

108. The European Data Protection Supervisor was consulted in accordance with Article 42 of Regulation (EU) 2018/1725 and delivered an opinion on 10 February 2021[22].

109. This Regulation respects the fundamental rights and observes the principles recognised by the Charter of Fundamental Rights of the European Union, in particular Articles 16, 47 and 50 thereof. Accordingly, the interpretation and application of this Regulation should respect those rights and principles,

HAVE ADOPTED THIS REGULATION:

---

[21] Directive (EU) 2020/1828 of the European Parliament and of the Council of 25 November 2020 on representative actions for the protection of the collective interests of consumers and repealing Directive 2009/22/EC (OJ L 409, 4.12.2020, p. 1).

[22] OJ C 147, 26.4.2021, p. 4.

CHAPTER I
SUBJECT MATTER,
SCOPE AND DEFINITIONS

Article 1 Subject matter and scope

1. The purpose of this Regulation is to contribute to the proper functioning of the internal market by laying down harmonised rules ensuring for all businesses, contestable and fair markets in the digital sector across the Union where gatekeepers are present, to the benefit of business users and end users.
2. This Regulation shall apply to core platform services provided or offered by gatekeepers to business users established in the Union or end users established or located in the Union, irrespective of the place of establishment or residence of the gatekeepers and irrespective of the law otherwise applicable to the provision of service.
3. This Regulation shall not apply to markets related to:
   (a) electronic communications networks as defined in Article 2, point (1), of Directive (EU) 2018/1972;
   (b) electronic communications services as defined in Article 2, point (4), of Directive (EU) 2018/1972, other than those related to number-independent interpersonal communications services.
4. With regard to interpersonal communications services as defined in Article 2, point (5) of Directive (EU) 2018/1972, this Regulation is without prejudice to the powers and responsibilities granted to the national regulatory and other competent authorities by virtue of Article 61 of that Directive.
5. In order to avoid the fragmentation of the internal market, Member States shall not impose further obligations on gatekeepers by way of laws, regulations or administrative measures for the purpose of ensuring contestable and fair markets. Nothing in this Regulation precludes Member States from imposing obligations on undertakings, including undertakings providing core platform services, for matters falling outside the scope of this Regulation, provided that those obligations are compatible with Union law and do not result from the fact that the relevant undertakings have the status of a gatekeeper within the meaning of this Regulation.
6. This Regulation is without prejudice to the application of Articles 101 and 102 TFEU. It is also without prejudice to the application of:
   (a) national competition rules prohibiting anti-competitive agreements, decisions by associations of undertakings, concerted practices and abuses of dominant positions;
   (b) national competition rules prohibiting other forms of unilateral conduct insofar as they are applied to undertakings other than gatekeepers or amount to the imposition of further obligations on gatekeepers; and
   (c) Council Regulation (EC) N°139/2004[23] and national rules concerning merger control.
7. National authorities shall not take decisions which run counter to a decision adopted by the Commission under this Regulation. The Commission and Member States shall work in close cooperation and coordinate their enforcement actions on the basis of the principles established in Articles 37 and 38.

Article 2 Definitions

For the purposes of this Regulation, the following definitions apply:

(1) 'gatekeeper' means an undertaking providing core platform services, designated pursuant to Article 3;
(2) 'core platform service' means any of the following:
   (a) online intermediation services;
   (b) online search engines;
   (c) online social networking services;
   (d) video-sharing platform services;
   (e) number-independent interpersonal communications services;
   (f) operating systems;

---

23 Council Regulation (EC) No139/2004 of 20 January 2004 on the control of concentrations between undertakings (the EC Merger Regulation) (OJ L 24, 29.1.2004, p. 1).

(g) web browsers;

(h) virtual assistants;

(i) cloud computing services;

(j) online advertising services, including any advertising networks, advertising exchanges and any other advertising intermediation services, provided by an undertaking that provides any of the core platform services listed in points (a) to (i);

(3) 'information society service' means any service as defined in Article 1(1), point (b), of Directive (EU) 2015/1535;

(4) 'digital sector' means the sector of products and services provided by means of, or through, information society services;

(5) 'online intermediation services' means online intermediation services as defined in Article 2, point (2), of Regulation (EU) 2019/1150;

(6) 'online search engine' means an online search engine as defined in Article 2, point (5), of Regulation (EU) 2019/1150;

(7) 'online social networking service' means a platform that enables end users to connect and communicate with each other, share content and discover other users and content across multiple devices and, in particular, via chats, posts, videos and recommendations;

(8) 'video-sharing platform service' means a video-sharing platform service as defined in Article 1(1), point (aa), of Directive 2010/13/EU;

(9) 'number-independent interpersonal communications service' means a number-independent interpersonal communications service as defined in Article 2, point (7), of Directive (EU) 2018/1972;

(10) 'operating system' means a system software that controls the basic functions of the hardware or software and enables software applications to run on it;

(11) 'web browser' means a software application that enables end users to access and interact with web content hosted on servers that are connected to networks such as the Internet, including standalone web browsers as well as web browsers integrated or embedded in software or similar;

(12) 'virtual assistant' means a software that can process demands, tasks or questions, including those based on audio, visual, written input, gestures or motions, and that, based on those demands, tasks or questions, provides access to other services or controls connected physical devices;

(13) 'cloud computing service' means a cloud computing service as defined in Article 4, point (19), of Directive (EU) 2016/1148 of the European Parliament and of the Council[24];

(14) 'software application stores' means a type of online intermediation services, which is focused on software applications as the intermediated product or service;

(15) 'software application' means any digital product or service that runs on an operating system;

(16) 'payment service' means a payment service as defined in Article 4, point (3) of Directive (EU) 2015/2366;

(17) 'technical service supporting payment service' means a service within the meaning of Article 3, point (j), of Directive (EU) 2015/2366;

(18) 'payment system for in-app purchases' means a software application, service or user interface which facilitates purchases of digital content or digital services within a software application, including content, subscriptions, features or functionality, and the payments for such purchases;

(19) 'identification service' means a type of service provided together with or in support of core platform services that enables any type of verification of the identity of end users or business users, regardless of the technology used;

(20) 'end user' means any natural or legal person using core platform services other than as a business user;

(21) 'business user' means any natural or legal person acting in a commercial or professional capacity using core platform services for the purpose of or in the course of providing goods or services to end users;

---

24 Directive (EU) 2016/1148 of the European Parliament and of the Council of 6 July 2016 concerning measures for a high common level of security of network and information systems across the Union (OJ L 194, 19.7.2016, p. 1).

(22) 'ranking' means the relative prominence given to goods or services offered through online intermediation services, online social networking services, video-sharing platform services or virtual assistants, or the relevance given to search results by online search engines, as presented, organised or communicated by the undertakings providing online intermediation services, online social networking services, video-sharing platform services, virtual assistants or online search engines, irrespective of the technological means used for such presentation, organisation or communication and irrespective of whether only one result is presented or communicated;

(23) 'search results' means any information in any format, including textual, graphic, vocal or other outputs, returned in response to, and related to, a search query, irrespective of whether the information returned is a paid or an unpaid result, a direct answer or any product, service or information offered in connection with the organic results, or displayed along with or partly or entirely embedded in them;

(24) 'data' means any digital representation of acts, facts or information and any compilation of such acts, facts or information, including in the form of sound, visual or audiovisual recording;

(25) 'personal data' means personal data as defined in Article 4, point (1), of Regulation (EU) 2016/679;

(26) 'non-personal data' means data other than personal data;

(27) 'undertaking' means an entity engaged in an economic activity, regardless of its legal status and the way in which it is financed, including all linked enterprises or connected undertakings that form a group through the direct or indirect control of an enterprise or undertaking by another;

(28) 'control' means the possibility of exercising decisive influence on an undertaking, within the meaning of Article 3(2) of Regulation (EC) N°139/2004;

(29) 'interoperability' means the ability to exchange information and mutually use the information which has been exchanged through interfaces or other solutions, so that all elements of hardware or software work with other hardware and software and with users in all the ways in which they are intended to function;

(30) 'turnover' means the amount derived by an undertaking within the meaning of Article 5(1) of Regulation (EC) N°139/2004;

(31) 'profiling' means profiling as defined in Article 4, point (4), of Regulation (EU) 2016/679;

(32) 'consent' means consent as defined in Article 4, point (11), of Regulation (EU) 2016/679;

(33) 'national court' means a court or tribunal of a Member State within the meaning of Article 267 TFEU.

CHAPTER II
GATEKEEPERS

Article 3 Designation of gatekeepers

1. An undertaking shall be designated as a gatekeeper if:
   (a) it has a significant impact on the internal market;
   (b) it provides a core platform service which is an important gateway for business users to reach end users; and
   (c) it enjoys an entrenched and durable position, in its operations, or it is foreseeable that it will enjoy such a position in the near future.
2. An undertaking shall be presumed to satisfy the respective requirements in paragraph 1:
   (a) as regards paragraph 1, point (a), where it achieves an annual Union turnover equal to or above EUR 7,5 billion in each of the last three financial years, or where its average market capitalisation or its equivalent fair market value amounted to at least EUR 75 billion in the last financial year, and it provides the same core platform service in at least three Member States;
   (b) as regards paragraph 1, point (b), where it provides a core platform service that in the last financial year has at least 45 million monthly active end users established or located in the Union and at least 10 000 yearly active business users established in the Union, identified and calculated in accordance with the methodology and indicators set out in the Annex;
   (c) as regards paragraph 1, point (c), where the thresholds in point (b) of this paragraph were met in each of the last three financial years.
3. Where an undertaking providing core platform services meets all of the thresholds in paragraph 2, it shall notify the Commission thereof without delay and in any event within 2 months after those

thresholds are met and provide it with the relevant information identified in paragraph 2. That notification shall include the relevant information identified in paragraph 2 for each of the core platform services of the undertaking that meets the thresholds in paragraph 2, point (b). Whenever a further core platform service provided by the undertaking that has previously been designated as a gatekeeper meets the thresholds in paragraph 2, points (b) and (c), such undertaking shall notify the Commission thereof within 2 months after those thresholds are satisfied.

Where the undertaking providing the core platform service fails to notify the Commission pursuant to the first subparagraph of this paragraph and fails to provide within the deadline set by the Commission in the request for information pursuant to Article 21 all the relevant information that is required for the Commission to designate the undertaking concerned as gatekeeper pursuant to paragraph 4 of this Article, the Commission shall still be entitled to designate that undertaking as a gatekeeper, based on information available to the Commission.

Where the undertaking providing core platform services complies with the request for information pursuant to the second subparagraph of this paragraph or where the information is provided after the expiration of the deadline referred to in that subparagraph, the Commission shall apply the procedure set out in paragraph 4.

4. The Commission shall designate as a gatekeeper, without undue delay and at the latest within 45 working days after receiving the complete information referred to in paragraph 3, an undertaking providing core platform services that meets all the thresholds in paragraph 2.

5. The undertaking providing core platform services may present, with its notification, sufficiently substantiated arguments to demonstrate that, exceptionally, although it meets all the thresholds in paragraph 2, due to the circumstances in which the relevant core platform service operates, it does not satisfy the requirements listed in paragraph 1.

Where the Commission considers that the arguments submitted pursuant to the first subparagraph by the undertaking providing core platform services are not sufficiently substantiated because they do not manifestly call into question the presumptions set out in paragraph 2 of this Article, it may reject those arguments within the time limit referred to in paragraph 4, without applying the procedure laid down in Article 17(3).

Where the undertaking providing core platform services does present such sufficiently substantiated arguments manifestly calling into question the presumptions in paragraph 2 of this Article, the Commission may, notwithstanding the first subparagraph of this paragraph, within the time limit referred to in paragraph 4 of this Article, open the procedure laid down in Article 17(3).

If the Commission concludes that the undertaking providing core platform services was not able to demonstrate that the relevant core platform services that it provides do not satisfy the requirements of paragraph 1 of this Article, it shall designate that undertaking as a gatekeeper in accordance with the procedure laid down in Article 17(3).

6. The Commission is empowered to adopt delegated acts in accordance with Article 49 to supplement this Regulation by specifying the methodology for determining whether the quantitative thresholds laid down in paragraph 2 of this Article are met, and to regularly adjust that methodology to market and technological developments, where necessary.

7. The Commission is empowered to adopt delegated acts in accordance with Article 49 to amend this Regulation by updating the methodology and the list of indicators set out in the Annex.

8. The Commission shall designate as a gatekeeper, in accordance with the procedure laid down in Article 17, any undertaking providing core platform services that meets each of the requirements of paragraph 1 of this Article, but does not satisfy each of the thresholds in paragraph 2 of this Article.

For that purpose, the Commission shall take into account some or all of the following elements, insofar as they are relevant for the undertaking providing core platform services under consideration:

(a) the size, including turnover and market capitalisation, operations and position of that undertaking;

(b) the number of business users using the core platform service to reach end users and the number of end users;

(c) network effects and data driven advantages, in particular in relation to that undertaking's access to, and collection of, personal data and non-personal data or analytics capabilities;

(d) any scale and scope effects from which the undertaking benefits, including with regard to data, and, where relevant, to its activities outside the Union;

(e) business user or end user lock-in, including switching costs and behavioural bias reducing the ability of business users and end users to switch or multi-home;

(f) a conglomerate corporate structure or vertical integration of that undertaking, for instance enabling that undertaking to cross subsidise, to combine data from different sources or to leverage its position; or

(g) other structural business or service characteristics.

In carrying out its assessment under this paragraph, the Commission shall take into account foreseeable developments in relation to the elements listed in the second subparagraph, including any planned concentrations involving another undertaking providing core platform services or providing any other services in the digital sector or enabling the collection of data.

Where an undertaking providing a core platform service that does not satisfy the quantitative thresholds of paragraph 2 fails to comply with the investigative measures ordered by the Commission in a significant manner, and that failure persists after that undertaking has been invited to comply within a reasonable time limit and to submit observations, the Commission may designate that undertaking as a gatekeeper on the basis of the facts available to the Commission.

9. For each undertaking designated as a gatekeeper pursuant to paragraph 4 or 8, the Commission shall list in the designation decision the relevant core platform services that are provided within that undertaking and which individually are an important gateway for business users to reach end users as referred to in paragraph 1, point (b).

10. shall comply with the obligations laid down in Articles 5, 6 and 7 within 6 months after a core platform service has been listed in the designation decision pursuant to paragraph 9 of this Article.

Article 4 Review of the status of gatekeeper

1. The Commission may, upon request or on its own initiative, reconsider, amend or repeal at any moment a designation decision adopted pursuant to Article 3 for one of the following reasons:

   (a) there has been a substantial change in any of the facts on which the designation decision was based;

   (b) the designation decision was based on incomplete, incorrect or misleading information.

2. The Commission shall regularly, and at least every 3 years, review whether the gatekeepers continue to satisfy the requirements laid down in Article 3(1). That review shall also examine whether the list of core platform services of the gatekeeper which are individually an important gateway for business users to reach end users, as referred to in Article 3(1), point (b), needs to be amended. Those reviews shall have no suspending effect on the gatekeeper's obligations.

   The Commission shall also examine at least every year whether new undertakings providing core platform services satisfy those requirements.

   Where the Commission, on the basis of the reviews pursuant to the first subparagraph, finds that the facts on which the designation of the undertakings providing core platform services as gatekeepers was based, have changed, it shall adopt a decision confirming, amending or repealing the designation decision.

3. The Commission shall publish and update a list of gatekeepers and the list of the core platform services for which they need to comply with the obligations laid down in Chapter III on an on-going basis.

CHAPTER III
PRACTICES OF GATEKEEPERS THAT LIMIT CONTESTABILITY OR ARE UNFAIR

Article 5 Obligations for gatekeepers

1. The gatekeeper shall comply with all obligations set out in this Article with respect to each of its core platform services listed in the designation decision pursuant to Article 3(9).

2. The gatekeeper shall not do any of the following:

   (a) process, for the purpose of providing online advertising services, personal data of end users using services of third parties that make use of core platform services of the gatekeeper;

   (b) combine personal data from the relevant core platform service with personal data from any further core platform services or from any other services provided by the gatekeeper or with personal data from third-party services;

(c) cross-use personal data from the relevant core platform service in other services provided separately by the gatekeeper, including other core platform services, and vice versa; and

(d) sign in end users to other services of the gatekeeper in order to combine personal data,

unless the end user has been presented with the specific choice and has given consent within the meaning of Article 4, point (11), and Article 7 of Regulation (EU) 2016/679.

Where the consent given for the purposes of the first subparagraph has been refused or withdrawn by the end user, the gatekeeper shall not repeat its request for consent for the same purpose more than once within a period of one year.

This paragraph is without prejudice to the possibility for the gatekeeper to rely on Article 6(1), points (c), (d) and (e) of Regulation (EU) 2016/679, where applicable.

3. The gatekeeper shall not prevent business users from offering the same products or services to end users through third-party online intermediation services or through their own direct online sales channel at prices or conditions that are different from those offered through the online intermediation services of the gatekeeper.

4. The gatekeeper shall allow business users, free of charge, to communicate and promote offers, including under different conditions, to end users acquired via its core platform service or through other channels, and to conclude contracts with those end users, regardless of whether, for that purpose, they use the core platform services of the gatekeeper.

5. The gatekeeper shall allow end users to access and use, through its core platform services, content, subscriptions, features or other items, by using the software application of a business user, including where those end users acquired such items from the relevant business user without using the core platform services of the gatekeeper.

6. The gatekeeper shall not directly or indirectly prevent or restrict business users or end users from raising any issue of non-compliance with the relevant Union or national law by the gatekeeper with any relevant public authority, including national courts, related to any practice of the gatekeeper. This is without prejudice to the right of business users and gatekeepers to lay down in their agreements the terms of use of lawful complaints-handling mechanisms.

7. The gatekeeper shall not require end users to use, or business users to use, to offer, or to interoperate with, an identification service, a web browser engine or a payment service, or technical services that support the provision of payment services, such as payment systems for in-app purchases, of that gatekeeper in the context of services provided by the business users using that gatekeeper's core platform services.

8. The gatekeeper shall not require business users or end users to subscribe to, or register with, any further core platform services listed in the designation decision pursuant to Article 3(9) or which meet the thresholds in Article 3(2), point (b), as a condition for being able to use, access, sign up for or registering with any of that gatekeeper's core platform services listed pursuant to that Article.

9. The gatekeeper shall provide each advertiser to which it supplies online advertising services, or third parties authorised by advertisers, upon the advertiser's request, with information on a daily basis free of charge, concerning each advertisement placed by the advertiser, regarding:

(a) the price and fees paid by that advertiser, including any deductions and surcharges, for each of the relevant online advertising services provided by the gatekeeper,

(b) the remuneration received by the publisher, including any deductions and surcharges, subject to the publisher's consent; and

(c) the metrics on which each of the prices, fees and remunerations are calculated.

In the event that a publisher does not consent to the sharing of information regarding the remuneration received, as referred to in point (b) of the first subparagraph, the gatekeeper shall provide each advertiser free of charge with information concerning the daily average remuneration received by that publisher, including any deductions and surcharges, for the relevant advertisements.

10. The gatekeeper shall provide each publisher to which it supplies online advertising services, or third parties authorised by publishers, upon the publisher's request, with free of charge information on a daily basis, concerning each advertisement displayed on the publisher's inventory, regarding:

(a) the remuneration received and the fees paid by that publisher, including any deductions and surcharges, for each of the relevant online advertising services provided by the gatekeeper;

(b) the price paid by the advertiser, including any deductions and surcharges, subject to the advertiser's consent; and

(c) the metrics on which each of the prices and remunerations are calculated.

In the event an advertiser does not consent to the sharing of information, the gatekeeper shall provide each publisher free of charge with information concerning the daily average price paid by that advertiser, including any deductions and surcharges, for the relevant advertisements.

Article 6 Obligations for gatekeepers susceptible of being further specified under Article 8

1. The Gatekeeper shall comply with all obligations set out in this Article with respect to each of its core platform services listed in the designation decision pursuant to Article 3(9).
2. The gatekeeper shall not use, in competition with business users, any data that is not publicly available that is generated or provided by those business users in the context of their use of the relevant core platform services or of the services provided together with, or in support of, the relevant core platform services, including data generated or provided by the customers of those business users.

   For the purposes of the first subparagraph, the data that is not publicly available shall include any aggregated and non-aggregated data generated by business users that can be inferred from, or collected through, the commercial activities of business users or their customers, including click, search, view and voice data, on the relevant core platform services or on services provided together with, or in support of, the relevant core platform services of the gatekeeper.
3. The gatekeeper shall allow and technically enable end users to easily un-install any software applications on the operating system of the gatekeeper, without prejudice to the possibility for that gatekeeper to restrict such un-installation in relation to software applications that are essential for the functioning of the operating system or of the device and which cannot technically be offered on a standalone basis by third parties.

   The gatekeeper shall allow and technically enable end users to easily change default settings on the operating system, virtual assistant and web browser of the gatekeeper that direct or steer end users to products or services provided by the gatekeeper. That includes prompting end users, at the moment of the end users' first use of an online search engine, virtual assistant or web browser of the gatekeeper listed in the designation decision pursuant to Article 3(9), to choose, from a list of the main available service providers, the online search engine, virtual assistant or web browser to which the operating system of the gatekeeper directs or steers users by default, and the online search engine to which the virtual assistant and the web browser of the gatekeeper directs or steers users by default.
4. The gatekeeper shall allow and technically enable the installation and effective use of third-party software applications or software application stores using, or interoperating with, its operating system and allow those software applications or software application stores to be accessed by means other than the relevant core platform services of that gatekeeper. The gatekeeper shall, where applicable, not prevent the downloaded third-party software applications or software application stores from prompting end users to decide whether they want to set that downloaded software application or software application store as their default. The gatekeeper shall technically enable end users who decide to set that downloaded software application or software application store as their default to carry out that change easily.

   The gatekeeper shall not be prevented from taking, to the extent that they are strictly necessary and proportionate, measures to ensure that third-party software applications or software application stores do not endanger the integrity of the hardware or operating system provided by the gatekeeper, provided that such measures are duly justified by the gatekeeper.

   Furthermore, the gatekeeper shall not be prevented from applying, to the extent that they are strictly necessary and proportionate, measures and settings other than default settings, enabling end users to effectively protect security in relation to third-party software applications or software application stores, provided that such measures and settings other than default settings are duly justified by the gatekeeper.
5. The gatekeeper shall not treat more favourably, in ranking and related indexing and crawling, services and products offered by the gatekeeper itself than similar services or products of a third party. The gatekeeper shall apply transparent, fair and non-discriminatory conditions to such ranking.
6. The gatekeeper shall not restrict technically or otherwise the ability of end users to switch between, and subscribe to, different software applications and services that are accessed using the core platform services of the gatekeeper, including as regards the choice of Internet access services for end users.

7. The gatekeeper shall allow providers of services and providers of hardware, free of charge, effective interoperability with, and access for the purposes of interoperability to, the same hardware and software features accessed or controlled via the operating system or virtual assistant listed in the designation decision pursuant to Article 3(9) as are available to services or hardware provided by the gatekeeper. Furthermore, the gatekeeper shall allow business users and alternative providers of services provided together with, or in support of, core platform services, free of charge, effective interoperability with, and access for the purposes of interoperability to, the same operating system, hardware or software features, regardless of whether those features are part of the operating system, as are available to, or used by, that gatekeeper when providing such services.

   The gatekeeper shall not be prevented from taking strictly necessary and proportionate measures to ensure that interoperability does not compromise the integrity of the operating system, virtual assistant, hardware or software features provided by the gatekeeper, provided that such measures are duly justified by the gatekeeper.
8. The gatekeeper shall provide advertisers and publishers, as well as third parties authorised by advertisers and publishers, upon their request and free of charge, with access to the performance measuring tools of the gatekeeper and the data necessary for advertisers and publishers to carry out their own independent verification of the advertisements inventory, including aggregated and non-aggregated data. Such data shall be provided in a manner that enables advertisers and publishers to run their own verification and measurement tools to assess the performance of the core platform services provided for by the gatekeepers.
9. The gatekeeper shall provide end users and third parties authorised by an end user, at their request and free of charge, with effective portability of data provided by the end user or generated through the activity of the end user in the context of the use of the relevant core platform service, including by providing, free of charge, tools to facilitate the effective exercise of such data portability, and including by the provision of continuous and real-time access to such data.
10. The gatekeeper shall provide business users and third parties authorised by a business user, at their request, free of charge, with effective, high-quality, continuous and real-time access to, and use of, aggregated and non-aggregated data, including personal data, that is provided for or generated in the context of the use of the relevant core platform services or services provided together with, or in support of, the relevant core platform services by those business users and the end users engaging with the products or services provided by those business users. With regard to personal data, the gatekeeper shall provide for such access to, and use of, personal data only where the data are directly connected with the use effectuated by the end users in respect of the products or services offered by the relevant business user through the relevant core platform service, and when the end users opt in to such sharing by giving their consent.
11. The gatekeeper shall provide to any third-party undertaking providing online search engines, at its request, with access on fair, reasonable and non-discriminatory terms to ranking, query, click and view data in relation to free and paid search generated by end users on its online search engines. Any such query, click and view data that constitutes personal data shall be anonymised.
12. The gatekeeper shall apply fair, reasonable, and non-discriminatory general conditions of access for business users to its software application stores, online search engines and online social networking services listed in the designation decision pursuant to Article 3(9).

    For that purpose, the gatekeeper shall publish general conditions of access, including an alternative dispute settlement mechanism.

    The Commission shall assess whether the published general conditions of access comply with this paragraph.
13. The gatekeeper shall not have general conditions for terminating the provision of a core platform service that are disproportionate. The gatekeeper shall ensure that the conditions of termination can be exercised without undue difficulty.

Article 7 Obligation for gatekeepers on interoperability of number-independent interpersonal communications services

1. Where a gatekeeper provides number-independent interpersonal communications services that are listed in the designation decision pursuant to Article 3(9), it shall make the basic functionalities of its number-independent interpersonal communications services interoperable with the number-independent

interpersonal communications services of another provider offering or intending to offer such services in the Union, by providing the necessary technical interfaces or similar solutions that facilitate interoperability, upon request, and free of charge.

2. The gatekeeper shall make at least the following basic functionalities referred to in paragraph 1 interoperable where the gatekeeper itself provides those functionalities to its own end users:
   (a) following the listing in the designation decision pursuant to Article 3(9):
   (i) end-to-end text messaging between two individual end users;
   (ii) sharing of images, voice messages, videos and other attached files in end to end communication between two individual end users;
   (b) within 2 years from the designation:
      (i) end-to-end text messaging within groups of individual end users;
      (ii) sharing of images, voice messages, videos and other attached files in end-to-end communication between a group chat and an individual end user;
      (c) within 4 years from the designation:
      (i) end-to-end voice calls between two individual end users;
      (ii) end-to-end video calls between two individual end users;
      (iii) end-to-end voice calls between a group chat and an individual end user;
      (iv) end-to-end video calls between a group chat and an individual end user.
3. The level of security, including the end-to-end encryption, where applicable, that the gatekeeper provides to its own end users shall be preserved across the interoperable services.
4. The gatekeeper shall publish a reference offer laying down the technical details and general terms and conditions of interoperability with its number-independent interpersonal communications services, including the necessary details on the level of security and end-to-end encryption. The gatekeeper shall publish that reference offer within the period laid down in Article 3(10) and update it where necessary.
5. Following the publication of the reference offer pursuant to paragraph 4, any provider of number-independent interpersonal communications services offering or intending to offer such services in the Union may request interoperability with the number-independent interpersonal communications services provided by the gatekeeper. Such a request may cover some or all of the basic functionalities listed in paragraph 2. The gatekeeper shall comply with any reasonable request for interoperability within 3 months after receiving that request by rendering the requested basic functionalities operational.
6. The Commission may, exceptionally, upon a reasoned request by the gatekeeper, extend the time limits for compliance under paragraph 2 or 5 where the gatekeeper demonstrates that this is necessary to ensure effective interoperability and to maintain the necessary level of security, including end-to-end encryption, where applicable.
7. The end users of the number-independent interpersonal communications services of the gatekeeper and of the requesting provider of number-independent interpersonal communications services shall remain free to decide whether to make use of the interoperable basic functionalities that may be provided by the gatekeeper pursuant to paragraph 1.
8. The gatekeeper shall collect and exchange with the provider of number-independent interpersonal communications services that makes a request for interoperability only the personal data of end users that is strictly necessary to provide effective interoperability. Any such collection and exchange of the personal data of end users shall fully comply with Regulation (EU) 2016/679 and Directive 2002/58/EC.
9. The gatekeeper shall not be prevented from taking measures to ensure that third-party providers of number-independent interpersonal communications services requesting interoperability do not endanger the integrity, security and privacy of its services, provided that such measures are strictly necessary and proportionate and are duly justified by the gatekeeper.

Article 8 Compliance with obligations for gatekeepers

1. The gatekeeper shall ensure and demonstrate compliance with the obligations laid down in Articles 5, 6 and 7 of this Regulation. The measures implemented by the gatekeeper to ensure compliance with those Articles shall be effective in achieving the objectives of this Regulation and of the relevant obligation. The gatekeeper shall ensure that the implementation of those measures complies with

applicable law, in particular Regulation (EU) 2016/679, Directive 2002/58/EC, legislation on cyber security, consumer protection, product safety, as well as with the accessibility requirements.

2. The Commission may, on its own initiative or at the request of a gatekeeper pursuant to paragraph 3 of this Article, open proceedings pursuant to Article 20.

   The Commission may adopt an implementing act, specifying the measures that the gatekeeper concerned is to implement in order to effectively comply with the obligations laid down in Articles 6 and 7. That implementing act shall be adopted within 6 months from the opening of proceedings pursuant to Article 20 in accordance with the advisory procedure referred to in Article 50(2).

   When opening proceedings on its own initiative for circumvention pursuant to Article 13, such measures may concern the obligations laid down in Articles 5, 6 and 7.

3. A gatekeeper may request the Commission to engage in a process to determine whether the measures that that gatekeeper intends to implement or has implemented to ensure compliance with Articles 6 and 7 are effective in achieving the objective of the relevant obligation in the specific circumstances of the gatekeeper. The Commission shall have discretion in deciding whether to engage in such a process, respecting the principles of equal treatment, proportionality and good administration.

   In its request, the gatekeeper shall provide a reasoned submission to explain the measures that it intends to implement or has implemented. The gatekeeper shall furthermore provide a non-confidential version of its reasoned submission that may be shared with third parties pursuant to paragraph 6.

4. Paragraphs 2 and 3 of this Article are without prejudice to the powers of the Commission under Articles 29, 30 and 31.

5. With a view of adopting the decision under paragraph 2, the Commission shall communicate its preliminary findings to the gatekeeper within 3 months from the opening of the proceedings under Article 20. In the preliminary findings, the Commission shall explain the measures that it is considering taking or that it considers the gatekeeper concerned should take in order to effectively address the preliminary findings.

6. In order to effectively enable interested third parties to provide comments, the Commission shall, when communicating its preliminary findings to the gatekeeper pursuant to paragraph 5 or as soon as possible thereafter, publish a non-confidential summary of the case and the measures that it is considering taking or that it considers the gatekeeper concerned should take. The Commission shall specify a reasonable timeframe within which such comments are to be provided.

7. In specifying the measures under paragraph 2, the Commission shall ensure that the measures are effective in achieving the objectives of this Regulation and the relevant obligation, and proportionate in the specific circumstances of the gatekeeper and the relevant service.

8. For the purposes of specifying the obligations under Article 6(11) and (12), the Commission shall also assess whether the intended or implemented measures ensure that there is no remaining imbalance of rights and obligations on business users and that the measures do not themselves confer an advantage on the gatekeeper which is disproportionate to the service provided by the gatekeeper to business users.

9. In respect of proceedings pursuant to paragraph 2, the Commission may, upon request or on its own initiative, decide to reopen them where:

   (a) there has been a material change in any of the facts on which the decision was based; or

   (b) the decision was based on incomplete, incorrect or misleading information; or

   (c) the measures as specified in the decision are not effective.

Article 9 Suspension

1. Where the gatekeeper demonstrates in a reasoned request that compliance with a specific obligation laid down in Article 5, 6 or 7 for a core platform service listed in the designation decision pursuant to Article 3(9) would endanger, due to exceptional circumstances beyond the gatekeeper's control, the economic viability of its operation in the Union, the Commission may adopt an implementing act setting out its decision to exceptionally suspend, in whole or in part, the specific obligation referred to in that reasoned request ('the suspension decision'). In that implementing act, the Commission shall substantiate its suspension decision by identifying the exceptional circumstances justifying the suspension. That implementing act shall be limited to the extent and the duration necessary to address such threat to the gatekeeper's viability. The Commission shall aim to adopt

that implementing act without delay and at the latest 3 months following receipt of a complete reasoned request. That implementing act shall be adopted in accordance with the advisory procedure referred to in Article 50(2).

2. Where suspension is granted pursuant to paragraph 1, the Commission shall review its suspension decision every year, unless a shorter interval is specified in that decision. Following such a review the Commission shall either wholly or partly lift the suspension, or decide that the conditions in paragraph 1 continue to be met.
3. In cases of urgency, the Commission may, acting on a reasoned request by a gatekeeper, provisionally suspend the application of a specific obligation referred to in paragraph 1 to one or more individual core platform services already prior to the decision pursuant to that paragraph. Such a request may be made and granted at any time pending the assessment of the Commission pursuant to paragraph 1.
4. In assessing the request referred to in paragraphs 1 and 3, the Commission shall take into account, in particular, the impact of the compliance with the specific obligation on the economic viability of the operation of the gatekeeper in the Union as well as on third parties, in particular SMEs and consumers. The suspension may be made subject to conditions and obligations to be defined by the Commission in order to ensure a fair balance between those interests and the objectives of this Regulation.

Article 10 Exemption for grounds of public health and public security

1. The Commission may, acting on a reasoned request by a gatekeeper or on its own initiative, adopt an implementing act setting out its decision, to exempt that gatekeeper, in whole or in part, from a specific obligation laid down in Article 5, 6 or 7 in relation to a core platform service listed in the designation decision pursuant to Article 3(9), where such exemption is justified on the grounds set out in paragraph 3 of this Article ('the exemption decision'). The Commission shall adopt the exemption decision within 3 months after receiving a complete reasoned request and shall provide a reasoned statement explaining the grounds for the exemption. That implementing act shall be adopted in accordance with the advisory procedure referred to in Article 50(2).
2. Where an exemption is granted pursuant to paragraph 1, the Commission shall review its exemption decision if the ground for the exemption no longer exists or at least every year. Following such a review, the Commission shall either wholly or partially lift the exemption, or decide that the conditions of paragraph 1 continue to be met.
3. An exemption pursuant to paragraph 1 may only be granted on grounds of public health or public security.
4. In cases of urgency, the Commission may, acting on a reasoned request by a gatekeeper or on its own initiative, provisionally suspend the application of a specific obligation referred to in paragraph 1 to one or more individual core platform services already prior to the decision pursuant to that paragraph. Such a request may be made and granted at any time pending the assessment of the Commission pursuant to paragraph 1.
5. In assessing the request referred to in paragraphs 1 and 4, the Commission shall take into account, in particular, the impact of the compliance with the specific obligation on the grounds in paragraph 3, as well as the effects on the gatekeeper concerned and on third parties. The Commission may subject the suspension to conditions and obligations in order to ensure a fair balance between the goals pursued by the grounds in paragraph 3 and the objectives of this Regulation.

Article 11 Reporting

1. Within 6 months after its designation pursuant to Article 3, and in accordance with Article 3(10), the gatekeeper shall provide the Commission with a report describing in a detailed and transparent manner the measures it has implemented to ensure compliance with the obligations laid down in Articles 5, 6 and 7.
2. Within the deadline referred to in paragraph 1, the gatekeeper shall publish and provide the Commission with a non-confidential summary of that report.

   The gatekeeper shall update that report and that non-confidential summary at least annually.

   The Commission shall make a link to that non-confidential summary available on its website.

Article 12 Updating obligations for gatekeepers

1. The Commission is empowered to adopt delegated acts in accordance with Article 49 to supplement this Regulation with regard to the obligations laid down in Articles 5 and 6. Those delegated acts shall be based on a market investigation pursuant to Article 19 that has identified the need to keep those obligations up to date in order to address practices that limit the contestability of core platform services or that are unfair in the same way as the practices addressed by the obligations laid down in Articles 5 and 6.
2. The scope of a delegated act adopted in accordance with paragraph 1 shall be limited to:
   (a) extending an obligation that applies only in relation to certain core platform services, to other core platform services listed in Article 2, point (2);
   (b) extending an obligation that benefits certain business users or end users so that it benefits other business users or end users;
   (c) specifying the manner in which the obligations laid down in Articles 5 and 6 are to be performed by gatekeepers in order to ensure effective compliance with those obligations;
   (d) extending an obligation that applies only in relation to certain services provided together with, or in support of, core platform services to other services provided together with, or in support of, core platform services;
   (e) extending an obligation that applies only in relation to certain types of data to apply in relation to other types of data;
   (f) adding further conditions where an obligation imposes certain conditions on the behaviour of a gatekeeper; or
   (g) applying an obligation that governs the relationship between several core platform services of the gatekeeper to the relationship between a core platform service and other services of the gatekeeper.
3. The Commission is empowered to adopt delegated acts in accordance with Article 49 to amend this Regulation with regard to the list of basic functionalities identified in Article 7(2), by adding or removing functionalities of number-independent interpersonal communications services.

   Those delegated acts shall be based on a market investigation pursuant to Article 19 that has identified the need to keep those obligations up to date in order to address practices that limit the contestability of core platform services or that are unfair in the same way as the practices addressed by the obligations laid down in Article 7.
4. The Commission is empowered to adopt delegated acts in accordance with Article 49 to supplement this Regulation in respect of the obligations in Article 7 by specifying the manner in which those obligations are to be performed in order to ensure effective compliance with those obligations. Those delegated acts shall be based on a market investigation pursuant to Article 19, which has identified the need to keep those obligations up to date in order to address practices that limit the contestability of core platform services or that are unfair in the same way as the practices addressed by the obligations laid down in Article 7.
5. A practice as referred to in paragraphs 1, 3 and 4 shall be considered to limit the contestability of core platform services or to be unfair where:
   (a) that practice is engaged in by gatekeepers and is capable of impeding innovation and limiting choice for business users and end users because it:
      (i) affects or risks affecting the contestability of a core platform service or other services in the digital sector on a lasting basis due to the creation or strengthening of barriers to entry for other undertakings or to expand as providers of a core platform service or other services in the digital sector; or
      (ii) prevents other operators from having the same access to a key input as the gatekeeper; or
   (b) there is an imbalance between the rights and obligations of business users and the gatekeeper obtains an advantage from business users that is disproportionate to the service provided by that gatekeeper to those business users.

Article 13 Anti-circumvention

1. An undertaking providing core platform services shall not segment, divide, subdivide, fragment or split those services through contractual, commercial, technical or any other means in order to circumvent the quantitative thresholds laid down in Article 3(2). No such practice of an undertaking shall prevent the Commission from designating it as a gatekeeper pursuant to Article 3(4).

2. The Commission may, when it suspects that an undertaking providing core platform services is engaged in a practice laid down in paragraph 1, require from that undertaking any information that it deems necessary to determine whether that undertaking has engaged in such a practice.
3. The gatekeeper shall ensure that the obligations of Articles 5, 6 and 7 are fully and effectively complied with.
4. The gatekeeper shall not engage in any behaviour that undermines effective compliance with the obligations of Articles 5, 6 and 7 regardless of whether that behaviour is of a contractual, commercial or technical nature, or of any other nature, or consists in the use of behavioural techniques or interface design.
5. Where consent for collecting, processing, cross-using and sharing of personal data is required to ensure compliance with this Regulation, a gatekeeper shall take the necessary steps either to enable business users to directly obtain the required consent to their processing, where that consent is required under Regulation (EU) 2016/679 or Directive 2002/58/EC, or to comply with Union data protection and privacy rules and principles in other ways, including by providing business users with duly anonymised data where appropriate. The gatekeeper shall not make the obtaining of that consent by the business user more burdensome than for its own services.
6. The gatekeeper shall not degrade the conditions or quality of any of the core platform services provided to business users or end users who avail themselves of the rights or choices laid down in Articles 5, 6 and 7, or make the exercise of those rights or choices unduly difficult, including by offering choices to the end-user in a non-neutral manner, or by subverting end users' or business users' autonomy, decision-making, or free choice via the structure, design, function or manner of operation of a user interface or a part thereof.
7. Where the gatekeeper circumvents or attempts to circumvent any of the obligations in Article 5, 6, or 7 in a manner described in paragraphs 4, 5 and 6 of this Article, the Commission may open proceedings pursuant to Article 20 and adopt an implementing act referred to in Article 8(2) in order to specify the measures that the gatekeeper is to implement.
8. Paragraph 6 of this Article is without prejudice to the powers of the Commission under Articles 29, 30 and 31.

Article 14 Obligation to inform about concentrations

1. A gatekeeper shall inform the Commission of any intended concentration within the meaning of Article 3 of Regulation (EC) N°139/2004, where the merging entities or the target of concentration provide core platform services or any other services in the digital sector or enable the collection of data, irrespective of whether it is notifiable to the Commission under that Regulation or to a competent national competition authority under national merger rules.

   A gatekeeper shall inform the Commission of such a concentration prior to its implementation and following the conclusion of the agreement, the announcement of the public bid, or the acquisition of a controlling interest.
2. The information provided by the gatekeeper pursuant to paragraph 1 shall at least describe the undertakings concerned by the concentration, their Union and worldwide annual turnovers, their fields of activity, including activities directly related to the concentration, and the transaction value of the agreement or an estimation thereof, along with a summary of the concentration, including its nature and rationale and a list of the Member States concerned by the concentration.

   The information provided by the gatekeeper shall also describe, for any relevant core platform services, their Union annual turnovers, their numbers of yearly active business users and their numbers of monthly active end users, respectively.
3. If, following any concentration referred to in paragraph 1 of this Article, additional core platform services individually meet the thresholds in Article 3(2), point (b), the gatekeeper concerned shall inform the Commission thereof within 2 months from the implementation of the concentration and provide the Commission with the information referred to in Article 3(2).
4. The Commission shall inform the competent authorities of the Member States of any information received pursuant to paragraph 1 and publish annually the list of acquisitions of which it has been informed by gatekeepers pursuant to that paragraph.

   The Commission shall take account of the legitimate interest of undertakings in the protection of their business secrets.

5. The competent authorities of the Member States may use the information received under paragraph 1 of this Article to request the Commission to examine the concentration pursuant to Article 22 of Regulation (EC) N°139/2004.

Article 15 Obligation of an audit

1. Within 6 months after its designation pursuant to Article 3, a gatekeeper shall submit to the Commission an independently audited description of any techniques for profiling of consumers that the gatekeeper applies to or across its core platform services listed in the designation decision pursuant to Article 3(9). The Commission shall transmit that audited description to the European Data Protection Board.
2. The Commission may adopt an implementing act referred to in Article 46(1), point (g), to develop the methodology and procedure of the audit.
3. The gatekeeper shall make publicly available an overview of the audited description referred to in paragraph 1. In doing so, the gatekeeper shall be entitled to take account of the need to respect its business secrets. The gatekeeper shall update that description and that overview at least annually.

CHAPTER IV

MARKET INVESTIGATION

Article 16 Opening of a market investigation

1. When the Commission intends to carry out a market investigation with a view to the possible adoption of decisions pursuant to Articles 17, 18 and 19 it shall adopt a decision opening a market investigation.
2. Notwithstanding paragraph 1, the Commission may exercise its investigative powers under this Regulation before opening a market investigation pursuant to that paragraph.
3. The decision referred to in paragraph 1 shall specify:
   (a) the date of opening of the market investigation;
   (b) the description of the issue to which the market investigation relates to;
   (c) the purpose of the market investigation.
4. The Commission may reopen a market investigation that it has closed where:
   (a) there has been a material change in any of the facts on which a decision adopted pursuant to Article 17, 18 or 19 was based; or
   (b) the decision adopted pursuant to Article 17, 18 or 19 was based on incomplete, incorrect or misleading information.
5. The Commission may ask one or more national competent authorities to assist it in its market investigation.

Article 17 Market investigation for designating gatekeepers

1. The Commission may conduct a market investigation for the purpose of examining whether an undertaking providing core platform services should be designated as a gatekeeper pursuant to Article 3(8), or in order to identify the core platform services to be listed in the designation decision pursuant to Article 3(9). The Commission shall endeavour to conclude its market investigation within 12 months from the date referred to in Article 16(3), point (a), In order to conclude its market investigation, the Commission shall adopt an implementing act setting out its decision. That implementing act shall be adopted in accordance with the advisory procedure referred to in Article 50(2).
2. In the course of a market investigation pursuant to paragraph 1 of this Article, the Commission shall endeavour to communicate its preliminary findings to the undertaking providing core platform services concerned within 6 months from the date referred to in Article 16(3), point (a). In the preliminary findings, the Commission shall explain whether it considers, on a provisional basis, that it is appropriate for that undertaking to be designated as a gatekeeper pursuant to Article 3(8), and for the relevant core platform services to be listed pursuant to Article 3(9).
3. Where the undertaking providing core platform services satisfies the thresholds set out in Article 3(2), but has presented sufficiently substantiated arguments in accordance with Article 3(5) that have manifestly called into question the presumption in Article 3(2), the Commission shall endeavour to conclude the market investigation within 5 months from the date referred to in Article 16(3), point (a).

In such a case, the Commission shall endeavour to communicate its preliminary findings pursuant to paragraph 2 of this Article to the undertaking concerned within 3 months from the date referred to in Article 16(3), point (a).

4. When the Commission, pursuant to Article 3(8), designates as a gatekeeper an undertaking providing core platform services that does not yet enjoy an entrenched and durable position in its operations, but which will foreseeably enjoy such a position in the near future, it may declare applicable to that gatekeeper only one or more of the obligations laid down in Article 5(3) to (6) and Article 6(4), (7), (9), (10) and (13), as specified in the designation decision. The Commission shall only declare applicable those obligations that are appropriate and necessary to prevent the gatekeeper concerned from achieving, by unfair means, an entrenched and durable position in its operations. The Commission shall review such a designation in accordance with the procedure laid down in Article 4.

Article 18 Market investigation into systematic non-compliance

1. The Commission may conduct a market investigation for the purpose of examining whether a gatekeeper has engaged in systematic non-compliance. The Commission shall conclude that market investigation within 12 months from the date referred to in Article 16(3), point (a). Where the market investigation shows that a gatekeeper has systematically infringed one or more of the obligations laid down in Article 5, 6 or 7 and has maintained, strengthened or extended its gatekeeper position in relation to the requirements set out in Article 3(1), the Commission may adopt an implementing act imposing on such gatekeeper any behavioural or structural remedies which are proportionate and necessary to ensure effective compliance with this Regulation. That implementing act shall be adopted in accordance with the advisory procedure referred to in Article 50(2).
2. The remedy imposed in accordance with paragraph 1 of this Article may include, to the extent that such remedy is proportionate and necessary in order to maintain or restore fairness and contestability as affected by the systematic non-compliance, the prohibition, during a limited period, for the gatekeeper to enter into a concentration within the meaning of Article 3 of Regulation (EC) N°139/2004 regarding the core platform services or the other services provided in the digital sector or enabling the collection of data that are affected by the systematic non-compliance.
3. A gatekeeper shall be deemed to have engaged in systematic non-compliance with the obligations laid down in Articles 5, 6 and 7, where the Commission has issued at least three non-compliance decisions pursuant to Article 29 against a gatekeeper in relation to any of its core platform services within a period of 8 years prior to the adoption of the decision opening a market investigation in view of the possible adoption of a decision pursuant to this Article.
4. The Commission shall communicate its preliminary findings to the gatekeeper concerned within 6 months from the date referred to in Article 16(3), point (a). In its preliminary findings, the Commission shall explain whether it preliminarily considers that the conditions of paragraph 1 of this Article are met and which remedy or remedies it preliminarily considers necessary and proportionate.
5. In order to enable interested third parties to effectively provide comments, the Commission shall, at the same time as communicating its preliminary findings to the gatekeeper pursuant to paragraph 4 or as soon as possible thereafter, publish a non-confidential summary of the case and the remedies that it is considering imposing. The Commission shall specify a reasonable timeframe within which such comments are to be provided.
6. Where the Commission intends to adopt a decision pursuant to paragraph 1 of this Article by making commitments offered by the gatekeeper pursuant to Article 25 binding, it shall publish a non-confidential summary of the case and the main content of the commitments. Interested third parties may submit their comments within a reasonable timeframe which shall be set by the Commission.
7. In the course of the market investigation, the Commission may extend its duration where such extension is justified on objective grounds and proportionate. The extension may apply to the deadline by which the Commission has to issue its preliminary findings, or to the deadline for adoption of the final decision. The total duration of any extension or extensions pursuant to this paragraph shall not exceed 6 months.
8. In order to ensure effective compliance by the gatekeeper with its obligations laid down in Articles 5, 6 and 7, the Commission shall regularly review the remedies that it imposes in accordance with paragraphs 1 and 2 of this Article. The Commission shall be entitled to modify those remedies if, following a new market investigation, it finds that they are not effective.

Article 19 Market investigation into new services and new practices

1. The Commission may conduct a market investigation for the purpose of examining whether one or more services within the digital sector should be added to the list of core platform services laid down in Article 2, point (2) or for the purpose of detecting practices that limit the contestability of core platform services or that are unfair and which are not effectively addressed by this Regulation. In its assessment, the Commission shall take into account any relevant findings of proceedings under Articles 101 and 102 TFEU concerning digital markets as well as any other relevant developments.
2. The Commission may, when conducting a market investigation pursuant to paragraph 1, consult third parties, including business users and end users of services within the digital sector that are being investigated and business users and end users who are subject to practices under investigation.
3. The Commission shall publish its findings in a report within 18 months from the date referred to in Article 16(3), point (a).

   That report shall be submitted to the European Parliament and to the Council and, where appropriate, shall be accompanied by:

   (a) a legislative proposal to amend this Regulation in order to include additional services within the digital sector in the list of core platform services laid down in Article 2, point (2), or to include new obligations in Chapter III; or

   (b) a draft delegated act supplementing this Regulation with regard to the obligations laid down in Articles 5 and 6, or a draft delegated act amending or supplementing this Regulation with regard to the obligations laid down in Article 7, as provided for in Article 12.

   Where appropriate, the legislative proposal to amend this Regulation under point (a) of the second subparagraph may also propose to remove existing services from the list of core platform services laid down in Article 2, point (2), or to remove existing obligations from Article 5, 6 or 7.

CHAPTER V
INVESTIGATIVE, ENFORCEMENT AND MONITORING POWERS

Article 20 Opening of proceedings

1. Where the Commission intends to open proceedings with a view to the possible adoption of decisions pursuant to Articles 8, 29 and 30, it shall adopt a decision opening a proceeding.
2. Notwithstanding paragraph 1, the Commission may exercise its investigative powers under this Regulation before opening proceedings pursuant to that paragraph.

Article 21 Requests for information

1. In order to carry out its duties under this Regulation, the Commission may, by simple request or by decision, require from undertakings and associations of undertakings to provide all necessary information. The Commission may also, by simple request or by decision, require access to any data and algorithms of undertakings and information about testing, as well as requesting explanations of them.
2. When sending a simple request for information to an undertaking or association of undertakings, the Commission shall state the legal basis and purpose of the request, specify what information is required and fix the time limit within which the information is to be provided, as well as the fines provided for in Article 30 applicable for supplying incomplete, incorrect or misleading information or explanations.
3. Where the Commission requires undertakings and associations of undertakings to supply information by decision, it shall state the legal basis and purpose of the request, specify what information is required and fix the time limit within which the information is to be provided. Where the Commission requires undertakings to provide access to any data, algorithms and information about testing, it shall state the purpose of the request and fix the time – limit within which it is to be provided. It shall also indicate the fines provided for in Article 30 and indicate or impose the periodic penalty payments provided for in Article 31. It shall further indicate the right to have the decision reviewed by the Court of Justice.
4. The undertakings or associations of undertakings or their representatives shall supply the information requested on behalf of the undertaking or the association of undertakings concerned. Lawyers duly

authorised to act may supply the information on behalf of their clients. The latter shall remain fully responsible if the information supplied is incomplete, incorrect or misleading.

5. At the request of the Commission, the competent authorities of the Member States shall provide the Commission with all necessary information in their possession to carry out the duties assigned to it by this Regulation.

Article 22 Power to carry out interviews and take statements

1. In order to carry out its duties under this Regulation, the Commission may interview any natural or legal person which consents to being interviewed, for the purpose of collecting information, relating to the subject-matter of an investigation. The Commission shall be entitled to record such interviews by any technical means.
2. Where an interview pursuant to paragraph 1 of this Article is conducted on the premises of an undertaking, the Commission shall inform the national competent authority of the Member State that is enforcing the rules referred to in Article 1(6) and in whose territory the interview takes place thereof. If that authority so requests, its officials may assist the officials and other accompanying persons authorised by the Commission to conduct the interview.

Article 23 Powers to conduct inspections

1. In order to carry out its duties under this Regulation, the Commission may conduct all necessary inspections of an undertaking or association of undertakings.
2. The officials and other accompanying persons authorised by the Commission to conduct an inspection are empowered to:
   (a) enter any premises, land and means of transport of undertakings and associations of undertakings;
   (b) examine the books and other records related to the business, irrespective of the medium on which they are stored;
   (c) take or obtain in any form copies of or extracts from such books or records;
   (d) require the undertaking or association of undertakings to provide access to and explanations on its organisation, functioning, IT system, algorithms, data-handling and business practices and to record or document the explanations given by any technical means;
   (e) seal any business premises and books or records for the duration of, and to the extent necessary for, the inspection;
   (f) ask any representative or member of staff of the undertaking or association of undertakings for explanations of facts or documents relating to the subject-matter and purpose of the inspection, and to record the answers by any technical means.
3. To carry out inspections, the Commission may request the assistance of auditors or experts appointed by the Commission pursuant to Article 26(2), as well as the assistance of the national competent authority of the Member State, enforcing the rules referred to in Article 1(6) in whose territory the inspection is to be conducted.
4. During inspections the Commission, auditors or experts appointed by it and the national competent authority of the Member State, enforcing the rules referred to in Article 1(6) in whose territory the inspection is to be conducted may require the undertaking or association of undertakings to provide access to and explanations on its organisation, functioning, IT system, algorithms, data-handling and business conducts. The Commission and auditors or experts appointed by it and the national competent authority of the Member State, enforcing the rules referred to in Article 1(6) in whose territory the inspection is to be conducted may address questions to any representative or member of staff.
5. The officials and other accompanying persons authorised by the Commission to conduct an inspection shall exercise their powers upon production of a written authorisation specifying the subject matter and purpose of the inspection and the fines provided for in Article 30 applicable in the event that the production of the required books or other records related to the business is incomplete or where the answers to questions asked under paragraphs 2 and 4 of this Article are incorrect or misleading. In good time before the inspection, the Commission shall give notice of the inspection to the national competent authority of the Member State enforcing the rules referred to in Article 1(6) in whose territory it is to be conducted.

6. Undertakings or associations of undertakings are required to submit to an inspection ordered by a Commission decision. That decision shall specify the subject matter and purpose of the inspection, set the date on which it is to begin and indicate the fines and periodic penalty payments provided for in Articles 30 and 31 respectively, and the right to have that decision reviewed by the Court of Justice.
7. Officials of, and the persons authorised or appointed by, the national competent authority of the Member State enforcing the rules referred to in Article 1(6) in whose territory the inspection is to be conducted shall, at the request of that authority or of the Commission, actively assist the officials and other accompanying persons authorised by the Commission. To this end, they shall enjoy the powers set out in paragraphs 2 and 4 of this Article.
8. Where the officials and other accompanying persons authorised by the Commission find that an undertaking or association of undertakings opposes an inspection ordered pursuant to this Article, the Member State concerned shall afford them the necessary assistance, requesting, where appropriate, the assistance of the police or of an equivalent enforcement authority, so as to enable them to conduct their inspection.
9. If, according to national rules, the assistance provided for in paragraph 8 of this Article requires authorisation from a judicial authority, the Commission or the national competent authority of the Member State enforcing the rules referred to in Article 1(6) or officials authorised by those authorities shall apply for it. Such authorisation may also be applied for as a precautionary measure.
10. Where authorisation referred to in paragraph 9 of this Article is applied for, the national judicial authority shall verify that the Commission decision is authentic and that the coercive measures envisaged are neither arbitrary nor excessive having regard to the subject matter of the inspection. In its control of the proportionality of the coercive measures, the national judicial authority may ask the Commission, directly or through the national competent authority of the Member State, enforcing the rules referred to in Article 1(6), for detailed explanations in particular on the grounds the Commission has for suspecting infringement of this Regulation, as well as on the seriousness of the suspected infringement and on the nature of the involvement of the undertaking concerned. However, the national judicial authority may not call into question the necessity of the inspection nor demand that it be provided with the information in the file of the Commission. The lawfulness of the Commission decision shall be subject to review only by the Court of Justice.

Article 24 Interim measures

In case of urgency due to the risk of serious and irreparable damage for business users or end users of gatekeepers, the Commission may adopt an implementing act ordering interim measures against a gatekeeper on the basis of a *prima facie* finding of an infringement of Article 5, 6 or 7. That implementing act shall be adopted only in the context of proceedings opened with a view to the possible adoption of a non-compliance decision pursuant to Article 29(1). It shall apply only for a specified period of time and may be renewed in so far this is necessary and appropriate. That implementing act shall be adopted in accordance with the advisory procedure referred to in Article 50(2).

Article 25 Commitments

1. If, during proceedings under Article 18, the gatekeeper concerned offers commitments for the relevant core platform services to ensure compliance with the obligations laid down in Articles 5, 6 and 7 the Commission may adopt an implementing act making those commitments binding on that gatekeeper and declare that there are no further grounds for action. That implementing act shall be adopted in accordance with the advisory procedure referred to in Article 50(2).
2. The Commission may, upon request or on its own initiative, reopen by decision the relevant proceedings, where:

   (a) there has been a material change in any of the facts on which the decision was based;

   (b) the gatekeeper concerned acts contrary to its commitments;

   (c) the decision was based on incomplete, incorrect or misleading information provided by the parties;

   (d) the commitments are not effective.
3. If the Commission considers that the commitments submitted by the gatekeeper concerned cannot ensure effective compliance with the obligations laid down in Articles 5, 6 and 7, it shall explain the reasons for not making those commitments binding in the decision concluding the relevant proceedings.

Article 26 Monitoring of obligations and measures

1. The Commission shall take the necessary actions to monitor the effective implementation and compliance with the obligations laid down in Articles 5, 6 and 7 and the decisions taken pursuant to Articles 8, 18, 24, 25 and 29. Those actions may include, in particular, the imposition of an obligation on the gatekeeper to retain all documents deemed to be relevant to assess the implementation of, and compliance with, those obligations and decisions.
2. The actions pursuant to paragraph 1 may include the appointment of independent external experts and auditors, as well as the appointment of officials from national competent authorities of the Member States, to assist the Commission to monitor the obligations and measures and to provide specific expertise or knowledge to the Commission.

Article 27 Information by third parties

1. Any third party, including business users, competitors or end-users of the core platform services listed in the designation decision pursuant to Article 3(9), as well as their representatives, may inform the national competent authority of the Member State, enforcing the rules referred to in Article 1(6), or the Commission directly, about any practice or behaviour by gatekeepers that falls within the scope of this Regulation.
2. The national competent authority of the Member State, enforcing the rules referred to in Article 1(6), and the Commission shall have full discretion as regards the appropriate measures and are under no obligation to follow-up on the information received.
3. Where the national competent authority of the Member State, enforcing the rules referred to in Article 1(6), determines, based on the information received pursuant to paragraph 1 of this Article, that there may be an issue of non-compliance with this Regulation, it shall transfer that information to the Commission.

Article 28 Compliance function

1. Gatekeepers shall introduce a compliance function, which is independent from the operational functions of the gatekeeper and composed of one or more compliance officers, including the head of the compliance function.
2. The gatekeeper shall ensure that the compliance function referred to in paragraph 1 has sufficient authority, stature and resources, as well as access to the management body of the gatekeeper to monitor the compliance of the gatekeeper with this Regulation.
3. The management body of the gatekeeper shall ensure that compliance officers appointed pursuant to paragraph 1 have the professional qualifications, knowledge, experience and ability necessary to fulfil the tasks referred to in paragraph 5.

   The management body of the gatekeeper shall also ensure that such head of the compliance function is an independent senior manager with distinct responsibility for the compliance function.
4. The head of the compliance function shall report directly to the management body of the gatekeeper and may raise concerns and warn that body where risks of non-compliance with this Regulation arise, without prejudice to the responsibilities of the management body in its supervisory and managerial functions.

   The head of the compliance function shall not be removed without prior approval of the management body of the gatekeeper.
5. Compliance officers appointed by the gatekeeper pursuant to paragraph 1 shall have the following tasks:
   (a) organising, monitoring and supervising the measures and activities of the gatekeepers that aim to ensure compliance with this Regulation;
   (b) informing and advising the management and employees of the gatekeeper on compliance with this Regulation;
   (c) where applicable, monitoring compliance with commitments made binding pursuant to Article 25, without prejudice to the Commission being able to appoint independent external experts pursuant to Article 26(2);
   (d) cooperating with the Commission for the purpose of this Regulation.

6. Gatekeepers shall communicate the name and contact details of the head of the compliance function to the Commission.
7. The management body of the gatekeeper shall define, oversee and be accountable for the implementation of the governance arrangements of the gatekeeper that ensure the independence of the compliance function, including the division of responsibilities in the organisation of the gatekeeper and the prevention of conflicts of interest.
8. The management body shall approve and review periodically, at least once a year, the strategies and policies for taking up, managing and monitoring the compliance with this Regulation.
9. The management body shall devote sufficient time to the management and monitoring of compliance with this Regulation. It shall actively participate in decisions relating to the management and enforcement of this Regulation and ensure that adequate resources are allocated to it.

Article 29 Non-compliance

1. The Commission shall adopt an implementing act setting out its finding of non-compliance ('the non-compliance decision') where it finds that a gatekeeper does not comply with one or more of the following:
   (a) any of the obligations laid down in Article 5, 6 or 7;
   (b) measures specified by the Commission in a decision adopted pursuant to Article 8(2);
   (c) remedies imposed pursuant to Article 18(1);
   (d) interim measures ordered pursuant to Article 24; or
   (e) commitments made legally binding pursuant to Article 25.
   That implementing act shall be adopted in accordance with the advisory procedure referred to in Article 50(2).
2. The Commission shall endeavour to adopt its non-compliance decision within 12 months from the opening of proceedings pursuant to Article 20.
3. Before adopting the non-compliance decision, the Commission shall communicate its preliminary findings to the gatekeeper concerned. In those preliminary findings, the Commission shall explain the measures it is considering taking or that it considers that the gatekeeper should take in order to effectively address the preliminary findings.
4. Where it intends to adopt a non-compliance decision, the Commission may consult third parties.
5. In the non-compliance decision, the Commission shall order the gatekeeper to cease and desist with the non-compliance within an appropriate deadline and to provide explanations on how it plans to comply with that decision.
6. The gatekeeper shall provide the Commission with the description of the measures that it has taken to ensure compliance with the non-compliance decision.
7. Where the Commission decides not to adopt a non-compliance decision, it shall close the proceedings by a decision.

Article 30 Fines

1. In the non-compliance decision, the Commission may impose on a gatekeeper fines not exceeding 10 % of its total worldwide turnover in the preceding financial year where it finds that the gatekeeper, intentionally or negligently, fails to comply with:
   (a) any of the obligations laid down in Articles 5, 6 and 7;
   (b) measures specified by the Commission in a decision adopted pursuant to Article 8(2);
   (c) remedies imposed pursuant to Article 18(1);
   (d) interim measures ordered pursuant to Article 24; or
   (e) commitments made legally binding pursuant to Article 25.
2. Notwithstanding paragraph 1 of this Article, in the non-compliance decision the Commission may impose on a gatekeeper fines up to 20 % of its total worldwide turnover in the preceding financial year where it finds that a gatekeeper has committed the same or a similar infringement of an obligation laid down in Article 5, 6 or 7 in relation to the same core platform service as it was found to have committed in a non-compliance decision adopted in the 8 preceding years.

3. The Commission may adopt a decision, imposing on undertakings, including gatekeepers where applicable, and associations of undertakings, fines not exceeding 1 % of their total worldwide turnover in the preceding financial year where they intentionally or negligently:
   (a) fail to provide within the time limit information that is required for assessing their designation as gatekeepers pursuant to Article 3 or supply incorrect, incomplete or misleading information;
   (b) fail to comply with the obligation to notify the Commission according to Article 3(3);
   (c) fail to notify information or supply incorrect, incomplete or misleading information that is required pursuant to Article 14;
   (d) fail to submit the description or supply incorrect, incomplete or misleading information that is required pursuant to Article 15;
   (e) fail to provide access to data, algorithms or information about testing in response to a request made pursuant to Article 21(3);
   (f) fail to supply the information requested within the time limit fixed pursuant to Article 21(3) or supply incorrect, incomplete or misleading information or explanations that are requested pursuant to Article 21 or given in an interview pursuant to Article 22;
   (g) fail to rectify within a time limit set by the Commission, incorrect, incomplete or misleading information given by a representative or a member of staff, or fail or refuse to provide complete information on facts relating to the subject-matter and purpose of an inspection, pursuant to Article 23;
   (h) refuse to submit to an inspection pursuant to Article 23;
   (i) fail to comply with the obligations imposed by the Commission pursuant to Article 26;
   (j) fail to introduce a compliance function in accordance with Article 28; or
   (k) fail to comply with the conditions for access to the Commission's file pursuant to Article 34(4).
4. In fixing the amount of a fine, the Commission shall take into account the gravity, duration, recurrence, and, for fines imposed pursuant to paragraph 3, delay caused to the proceedings.
5. When a fine is imposed on an association of undertakings taking account of the worldwide turnover of its members and that association is not solvent, it shall be obliged to call for contributions from its members to cover the amount of the fine.

   Where such contributions have not been made to the association of undertakings within a time limit set by the Commission, the Commission may require payment of the fine directly by any of the undertakings whose representatives were members of the decision-making bodies concerned of that association.

   After having required payment in accordance with the second subparagraph, the Commission may require payment of the balance by any of the members of the association of undertakings, where necessary to ensure full payment of the fine.

   However, the Commission shall not require payment pursuant to the second or the third subparagraph from undertakings which show that they have not implemented the decision of the association of undertakings that infringed this Regulation, and either were not aware of its existence, or have actively distanced themselves from it before the Commission opened proceedings under Article 20.

   The financial liability of each undertaking in respect of the payment of the fine shall not exceed 20 % of its total worldwide turnover in the preceding financial year.

Article 31 Periodic penalty payments

1. The Commission may adopt a decision imposing on undertakings, including gatekeepers where applicable, and associations of undertakings periodic penalty payments not exceeding 5 % of the average daily worldwide turnover in the preceding financial year per day, calculated from the date set by that decision, in order to compel them:
   (a) to comply with the measures specified by the Commission in a decision adopted pursuant to Article 8(2);
   (b) to comply with the decision pursuant to Article 18(1);
   (c) to supply correct and complete information within the time limit required by a request for information made by decision pursuant to Article 21;
   (d) to ensure access to data, algorithms and information about testing in response to a request made pursuant to Article 21(3) and to supply explanations on those as required by a decision pursuant to Article 21;

(e) to submit to an inspection which was ordered by a decision taken pursuant to Article 23;

(f) to comply with a decision ordering interim measures taken pursuant to Article 24;

(g) to comply with commitments made legally binding by a decision pursuant to Article 25(1);

(h) to comply with a decision pursuant to Article 29(1).

2. Where the undertakings, or associations of undertakings, have satisfied the obligation which the periodic penalty payment was intended to enforce, the Commission may adopt an implementing act, setting the definitive amount of the periodic penalty payment at a figure lower than that which would arise under the original decision. That implementing act shall be adopted in accordance with the advisory procedure referred to in Article 50(2).

Article 32 Limitation periods for the imposition of penalties

1. The powers conferred on the Commission by Articles 30 and 31 shall be subject to a 5 year limitation period.
2. Time shall begin to run on the day on which the infringement is committed. However, in the case of continuing or repeated infringements, time shall begin to run on the day on which the infringement ceases.
3. Any action taken by the Commission for the purpose of a market investigation or proceedings in respect of an infringement shall interrupt the limitation period for the imposition of fines or periodic penalty payments. The limitation period shall be interrupted with effect from the date on which the action is notified to at least one undertaking or association of undertakings which has participated in the infringement. Actions which interrupt the running of the period shall include in particular the following:
   (a) requests for information by the Commission;
   (b) written authorisations to conduct inspections issued to its officials by the Commission;
   (c) the opening of a proceeding by the Commission pursuant to Article 20.
4. Each interruption shall start time running afresh. However, the limitation period shall expire at the latest on the day on which a period equal to twice the limitation period has elapsed without the Commission having imposed a fine or a periodic penalty payment. That period shall be extended by the time during which limitation is suspended pursuant to paragraph 5.
5. The limitation period for the imposition of fines or periodic penalty payments shall be suspended for as long as the decision of the Commission is the subject of proceedings pending before the Court of Justice.

Article 33 Limitation periods for the enforcement of penalties

1. The power of the Commission to enforce decisions taken pursuant to Articles 30 and 31 shall be subject to a limitation period of 5 years.
2. Time shall begin to run from the day on which the decision becomes final.
3. The limitation period for the enforcement of penalties shall be interrupted:
   (a) by notification of a decision varying the original amount of the fine or periodic penalty payment or refusing an application for variation; or
   (b) by any action of the Commission or of a Member State, acting at the request of the Commission, designed to enforce payment of the fine or periodic penalty payment.
4. Each interruption shall start time running afresh.
5. The limitation period for the enforcement of penalties shall be suspended for so long as:
   (a) time to pay is allowed; or
   (b) enforcement of payment is suspended pursuant to a decision of the Court of Justice or to a decision by a national court.

Article 34 Right to be heard and access to the file

1. Before adopting a decision pursuant to Article 8, Article 9(1), Article 10(1), Articles 17, 18, 24, 25, 29 and 30 and Article 31(2), the Commission shall give the gatekeeper or undertaking or association of undertakings concerned the opportunity of being heard on:
   (a) preliminary findings of the Commission, including any matter to which the Commission has taken objection; and
   (b) measures that the Commission may intend to take in view of the preliminary findings pursuant to point (a) of this paragraph.

2. Gatekeepers, undertakings and associations of undertakings concerned may submit their observations to the Commission concerning the Commission's preliminary findings within a time limit set by the Commission in its preliminary findings which may not be less than 14 days.
3. The Commission shall base its decisions only on preliminary findings, including any matter to which the Commission has taken objection, on which gatekeepers, undertakings and associations of undertakings concerned have been able to comment.
4. The rights of defence of the gatekeeper, undertaking or association of undertakings concerned shall be fully respected in any proceedings. The gatekeeper, undertaking or association of undertakings concerned shall be entitled to have access to the Commission's file under terms of disclosure, subject to the legitimate interest of undertakings in the protection of their business secrets. In the case of disagreement between the parties, the Commission may adopt decisions setting out those terms of disclosure. The right of access to the file of the Commission shall not extend to confidential information and internal documents of the Commission or the competent authorities of the Member States. In particular, the right of access shall not extend to correspondence between the Commission and the competent authorities of the Member States. Nothing in this paragraph shall prevent the Commission from disclosing and using information necessary to prove an infringement.

Article 35 Annual reporting

1. The Commission shall submit to the European Parliament and to the Council an annual report on the implementation of this Regulation and the progress made towards achieving its objectives.
2. The report referred to in paragraph 1 shall include:
   (a) a summary of the Commission's activities including any adopted measures or decisions and ongoing market investigations in connection with this Regulation;
   (b) the findings resulting from the monitoring of the implementation by the gatekeepers of the obligations under this Regulation;
   (c) an assessment of the audited description referred to in Article 15;
   (d) an overview of the cooperation between the Commission and national authorities in connection with this Regulation;
   (e) an overview of the activities and tasks performed by the High Level Group of Digital Regulators, including how its recommendations as regards the enforcement of this Regulation are to be implemented.
3. The Commission shall publish the report on its website.

Article 36 Professional secrecy

1. The information collected pursuant to this Regulation shall be used for the purposes of this Regulation.
2. The information collected pursuant to Article 14 shall be used for the purposes of this Regulation, Regulation (EC) N°139/2004 and national merger rules.
3. The information collected pursuant to Article 15 shall be used for the purposes of this Regulation and Regulation (EU) 2016/679.
4. Without prejudice to the exchange and to the use of information provided for the purpose of use pursuant to Articles 38, 39, 41 and 43, the Commission, the competent authorities of the Member States, their officials, servants and other persons working under the supervision of those authorities and any natural or legal person, including auditors and experts appointed pursuant to Article 26(2), shall not disclose information acquired or exchanged by them pursuant to this Regulation and of the kind covered by the obligation of professional secrecy.

Article 37 Cooperation with national authorities

1. The Commission and Member States shall work in close cooperation and coordinate their enforcement actions to ensure coherent, effective and complementary enforcement of available legal instruments applied to gatekeepers within the meaning of this Regulation.
2. The Commission may consult national authorities where appropriate, on any matter relating to the application of this Regulation.

Article 38 Cooperation and coordination with national competent authorities enforcing competition rules

1. The Commission and the national competent authorities of the Member States enforcing the rules referred to in Article 1(6) shall cooperate with each other and inform each other about their respective enforcement actions through the European Competition Network (ECN). They shall have the power to provide one another with any information regarding a matter of fact or of law, including confidential information. Where the competent authority is not a member of the ECN, the Commission shall make the necessary arrangements for cooperation and exchange of information on cases concerning the enforcement of this Regulation and the enforcement of cases referred to in Article 1(6) of such authorities. The Commission may lay down such arrangements in an implementing act as referred to in Article 46(1), point (l).
2. Where a national competent authority of the Member States enforcing the rules referred to in Article 1(6) intends to launch an investigation on gatekeepers based on national laws referred to in Article 1(6), it shall inform the Commission in writing of the first formal investigative measure, before or immediately after the start of such measure. This information may also be made available to the national competent authorities enforcing the rules referred to in Article 1(6) of the other Member States.
3. Where a national competent authority of the Member States enforcing the rules referred to in Article 1(6) intends to impose obligations on gatekeepers based on national laws referred to in Article 1(6), it shall, no later than 30 days before its adoption, communicate the draft measure to the Commission stating the reasons for the measure. In the case of interim measures, the national competent authority of the Member States enforcing the rules referred to in Article 1(6) shall communicate to the Commission the draft measures envisaged as soon as possible, and at the latest immediately after the adoption of such measures. This information may also be made available to the national competent authorities enforcing the rules referred to in Article 1(6) of the other Member States.
4. The information mechanisms provided for in paragraphs 2 and 3 shall not apply to decisions envisaged pursuant to national merger rules.
5. Information exchanged pursuant to paragraphs 1 to 3 of this Article shall only be exchanged and used for the purpose of coordination of the enforcement of this Regulation and the rules referred to in Article 1(6).
6. The Commission may ask national competent authorities of the Member States enforcing the rules referred to in Article 1(6) to support any of its market investigations pursuant to this Regulation.
7. Where it has the competence and investigative powers to do so under national law, a national competent authority of the Member States enforcing the rules referred to in Article 1(6) may, on its own initiative, conduct an investigation into a case of possible non-compliance with Articles 5, 6 and 7 of this Regulation on its territory. Before taking a first formal investigative measure, that authority shall inform the Commission in writing.

   The opening of proceedings by the Commission pursuant to Article 20 shall relieve the national competent authorities of the Member States enforcing the rules referred to in Article 1(6) of the possibility to conduct such an investigation or end it where it is already ongoing. Those authorities shall report to the Commission on the findings of such investigation in order to support the Commission in its role as sole enforcer of this Regulation.

Article 39 Cooperation with national courts

1. In proceedings for the application of this Regulation, national courts may ask the Commission to transmit to them information in its possession or its opinion on questions concerning the application of this Regulation.
2. Member States shall forward to the Commission a copy of any written judgment of national courts deciding on the application of this Regulation. Such copy shall be forwarded without delay after the full written judgment is notified to the parties.
3. Where the coherent application of this Regulation so requires, the Commission, acting on its own initiative, may submit written observations to national courts. With the permission of the court in question, it may also make oral observations.
4. For the purpose of the preparation of their observations only, the Commission may request the relevant national court to transmit or ensure the transmission to the Commission of any documents necessary for the assessment of the case.

5. National courts shall not give a decision which runs counter to a decision adopted by the Commission under this Regulation. They shall also avoid giving decisions which would conflict with a decision contemplated by the Commission in proceedings it has initiated under this Regulation. To that effect, the national court may assess whether it is necessary to stay its proceedings. This is without prejudice to the possibility for national courts to request a preliminary ruling under Article 267 TFEU.

Article 40 The high-level group

6. The Commission shall establish a high-level group for the Digital Markets Act ('the high-level group').
7. The high-level group shall be composed of the following European bodies and networks:
   (a) Body of the European Regulators for Electronic Communications;
   (b) European Data Protection Supervisor and European Data Protection Board;
   (c) European Competition Network;
   (d) Consumer Protection Cooperation Network; and
   (e) European Regulatory Group of Audiovisual Media Regulators.
8. The European bodies and networks referred to in paragraph 2 shall each have an equal number of representatives in the high-level group. The maximum number of members of the high-level group shall not exceed 30.
9. The Commission shall provide secretariat services to the high-level group in order to facilitate its work. The high-level group shall be chaired by the Commission, which shall participate in its meetings. The high-level group shall meet upon request of the Commission at least once per calendar year. The Commission shall also convene a meeting of the group when so requested by the majority of the members composing the group in order to address a specific issue.
10. The high-level group may provide the Commission with advice and expertise in the areas falling within the competences of its members, including:
    (a) advice and recommendations within their expertise relevant for any general matter of implementation or enforcement of this Regulation; or
    (b) advice and expertise promoting a consistent regulatory approach across different regulatory instruments.
11. The high-level group may, in particular, identify and assess the current and potential interactions between this Regulation and the sector-specific rules applied by the national authorities composing the European bodies and networks referred to in paragraph 2 and submit an annual report to the Commission presenting such assessment and identifying potential trans-regulatory issues. Such report may be accompanied by recommendations aiming at converging towards consistent transdisciplinary approaches and synergies between the implementation of this Regulation and other sectoral regulations. The report shall be communicated to the European Parliament and to the Council.
12. In the context of market investigations into new services and new practices, the high-level group may provide expertise to the Commission on the need to amend, add or remove rules in this Regulation, to ensure that digital markets across the Union are contestable and fair.

Article 41 Request for a market investigation

13. Three or more Member States may request the Commission to open a market investigation pursuant to Article 17 because they consider that there are reasonable grounds to suspect that an undertaking should be designated as a gatekeeper.
14. One or more Member States may request the Commission to open a market investigation pursuant to Article 18 because they consider that there are reasonable grounds to suspect that a gatekeeper has systematically infringed one or more of the obligations laid down in Articles 5, 6 and 7 and has maintained, strengthened or extended its gatekeeper position in relation to the requirements under Article 3(1).
15. Three or more Member States may request the Commission to conduct a market investigation pursuant to Article 19 because they consider that there are reasonable grounds to suspect that:
    (a) one or more services within the digital sector should be added to the list of core platform services laid down in Article 2, point (2), or
    (b) one or more practices are not effectively addressed by this Regulation and might limit the contestability of core platform services or be unfair.

16. Member States shall submit evidence in support of their requests pursuant to paragraphs 1, 2 and 3. For requests pursuant to paragraph 3, such evidence may include information on newly introduced offers of products, services, software or features which raise concerns of contestability or fairness, whether implemented in the context of existing core platform services or otherwise.
17. Within 4 months of receiving a request pursuant to this Article, the Commission shall examine whether there are reasonable grounds to open a market investigation pursuant to paragraph 1, 2 or 3. The Commission shall publish the results of its assessment.

Article 42 Representative actions

Directive (EU) 2020/1828 shall apply to the representative actions brought against infringements by gatekeepers of provisions of this Regulation that harm or may harm the collective interests of consumers.

Article 43 Reporting of breaches and protection of reporting persons

Directive (EU) 2019/1937 shall apply to the reporting of all breaches of this Regulation and the protection of persons reporting such breaches.

CHAPTER VI
FINAL PROVISIONS

Article 44 Publication of decisions

1. The Commission shall publish the decisions which it takes pursuant to Articles 3 and 4, Article 8(2), Articles 9, 10, 16 to 20 and 24, Article 25(1), Articles 29, 30 and 31. Such publication shall state the names of the parties and the main content of the decision, including any penalties imposed.
2. The publication shall have regard to the legitimate interest of gatekeepers or third parties in the protection of their confidential information.

Article 45 Review by the Court of Justice

In accordance with Article 261 TFEU, the Court of Justice has unlimited jurisdiction to review decisions by which the Commission has imposed fines or periodic penalty payments. It may cancel, reduce or increase the fine or periodic penalty payment imposed.

Article 46 Implementing provisions

1. The Commission may adopt implementing acts laying down detailed arrangements for the application of the following:
   (a) the form, content and other details of notifications and submissions pursuant to Article 3;
   (b) the form, content and other details of the technical measures that gatekeepers shall implement in order to ensure compliance with Article 5, 6 or 7;
   (c) operational and technical arrangements in view of implementing interoperability of number-independent interpersonal communications services pursuant to Article 7;
   (d) the form, content and other details of the reasoned request pursuant to Article 8(3);
   (e) the form, content and other details of the reasoned requests pursuant to Articles 9 and 10;
   (f) the form, content and other details of the regulatory reports delivered pursuant to Article 11;
   (g) the methodology and procedure for the audited description of techniques used for profiling of consumers provided for in Article 15(1); when developing a draft implementing act for this purpose, the Commission shall consult the European Data Protection Supervisor and may consult the European Data Protection Board, civil society and other relevant experts;
   (h) the form, content and other details of notifications and submissions made pursuant to Articles 14 and 15;
   (i) the practical arrangements of the proceedings concerning the market investigations pursuant to Articles 17, 18 and 19, and proceedings pursuant to Articles 24, 25 and 29;
   (j) the practical arrangements for exercising rights to be heard provided for in Article 34;

(k) the practical arrangements for the terms of disclosure provided for in Article 34;

(l) the practical arrangements for the cooperation and coordination between the Commission and national authorities provided for in Articles 37 and 38; and

(m) the practical arrangements for the calculation and extension of deadlines.

2. The implementing acts referred to in paragraph 1, points (a) to (k), and point (m) of this Article shall be adopted in accordance with the advisory procedure referred to in Article 50(2).

   The implementing act referred to in paragraph 1, point (l), of this Article shall be adopted in accordance with the examination procedure referred to in Article 50(3).

3. Before the adoption of any implementing act pursuant to paragraph 1, the Commission shall publish a draft thereof and invite all interested parties to submit their comments within a time limit, which may not be less than one month.

Article 47 Guidelines

The Commission may adopt guidelines on any of the aspects of this Regulation in order to facilitate its effective implementation and enforcement.

Article 48 Standardisation

Where appropriate and necessary, the Commission may mandate European standardisation bodies to facilitate the implementation of the obligations set out in this Regulation by developing appropriate standards.

Article 49 Exercise of the delegation

1. The power to adopt delegated acts is conferred on the Commission subject to the conditions laid down in this Article.
2. The power to adopt delegated acts referred to in Article 3(6) and (7) and Article 12(1), (3) and (4) shall be conferred on the Commission for a period of 5 years from 1 November 2022. The Commission shall draw up a report in respect of the delegation of power not later than 9 months before the end of the five-year period. The delegation of power shall be tacitly extended for periods of an identical duration, unless the European Parliament or the Council opposes such extension not later than 3 months before the end of each period.
3. The delegation of power referred to in Article 3(6) and (7), and Article 12(1), (3) and (4) may be revoked at any time by the European Parliament or by the Council. A decision to revoke shall put an end to the delegation of the power specified in that decision. It shall take effect the day following the publication of the decision in the *Official Journal of the European Union* or at a later date specified therein. It shall not affect the validity of any delegated acts already in force.
4. Before adopting a delegated act, the Commission shall consult experts designated by each Member State in accordance with the principles laid down in the Interinstitutional Agreement of 13 April 2016 on Better Law-Making.
5. As soon as it adopts a delegated act, the Commission shall notify it simultaneously to the European Parliament and to the Council.
6. A delegated act adopted pursuant to Article 3(6) and (7), and Article 12(1), (3) and (4) shall enter into force only if no objection has been expressed either by the European Parliament or by the Council within a period of 2 months of notification of that act to the European Parliament and to the Council or if, before the expiry of that period, the European Parliament and the Council have both informed the Commission that they will not object. That period shall be extended by 2 months at the initiative of the European Parliament or of the Council.

Article 50 Committee procedure

1. Where reference is made to this paragraph, Article 4 of Regulation (EU) N°182/2011 shall apply.
2. Where the opinion of the committee is to be obtained by written procedure, that procedure shall be terminated without result when, within the time limit for delivery of the opinion, the chair of the committee so decides or a simple majority of committee members so request.
3. Where reference is made to this paragraph, Article 5 of Regulation (EU) N°182/2011 shall apply.

4. The Commission shall communicate the opinion of the committee to the addressee of an individual decision, together with that decision. It shall make the opinion public together with the individual decision, having regard to the legitimate interest in the protection of professional secrecy.

Article 51 Amendment to Directive (EU) 2019/1937

In Point J of Part I of the Annex to Directive (EU) 2019/1937, the following point is added:

'(iv) Regulation (EU) 2022/1925 of the European Parliament and of the Council of 14 September 2022 on contestable and fair markets in the digital sector and amending Directives (EU) 2019/1937 and (EU) 2020/1828 (Digital Markets Act) (OJ L 265, 21.9.2022, p. 1).'

Article 52 Amendment to Directive (EU) 2020/1828

In Annex I to Directive (EU) 2020/1828, the following point is added:

'(67) Regulation (EU) 2022/1925 of the European Parliament and of the Council of 14 September 2022 on contestable and fair markets in the digital sector and amending Directives (EU) 2019/1937 and (EU) 2020/1828 (Digital Markets Act) (OJ L 265, 21.9.2022, p. 1).'

Article 53 Review

1. By 3 May 2026, and subsequently every 3 years, the Commission shall evaluate this Regulation and report to the European Parliament, the Council and the European Economic and Social Committee.
2. The evaluations shall assess whether the aims of this Regulation of ensuring contestable and fair markets have been achieved and assess the impact of this Regulation on business users, especially SMEs, and end users. Moreover, the Commission shall evaluate if the scope of Article 7 may be extended to online social networking services.
3. The evaluations shall establish whether it is required to modify rules, including regarding the list of core platform services laid down in Article 2, point (2), the obligations laid down in Articles 5, 6 and 7 and their enforcement, to ensure that digital markets across the Union are contestable and fair. Following the evaluations, the Commission shall take appropriate measures, which may include legislative proposals.
4. The competent authorities of Member States shall provide any relevant information they have that the Commission may require for the purposes of drawing up the report referred to in paragraph 1.

Article 52 Amendment to Directive (EU) 2020/1828

In Annex I to Directive (EU) 2020/1828, the following point is added:

'(67) Regulation (EU) 2022/1925 of the European Parliament and of the Council of 14 September 2022 on contestable and fair markets in the digital sector and amending Directives (EU) 2019/1937 and (EU) 2020/1828 (Digital Markets Act) (OJ L 265, 21.9.2022, p. 1).'

Article 53 Review

1. By 3 May 2026, and subsequently every 3 years, the Commission shall evaluate this Regulation and report to the European Parliament, the Council and the European Economic and Social Committee.
2. The evaluations shall assess whether the aims of this Regulation of ensuring contestable and fair markets have been achieved and assess the impact of this Regulation on business users, especially SMEs, and end users. Moreover, the Commission shall evaluate if the scope of Article 7 may be extended to online social networking services.
3. The evaluations shall establish whether it is required to modify rules, including regarding the list of core platform services laid down in Article 2, point (2), the obligations laid down in Articles 5, 6 and 7 and their enforcement, to ensure that digital markets across the Union are contestable and fair. Following the evaluations, the Commission shall take appropriate measures, which may include legislative proposals.
4. The competent authorities of Member States shall provide any relevant information they have that the Commission may require for the purposes of drawing up the report referred to in paragraph 1.

Article 54 Entry into force and application

This Regulation shall enter into force on the twentieth day following that of its publication in the *Official Journal of the European Union.*

It shall apply from 2 May 2023.

However, Article 3(6) and (7) and Articles 40, 46, 47, 48, 49 and 50 shall apply from 1 November 2022 and Article 42 and Article 43 shall apply from 25 June 2023.

Nevertheless, if the date of 25 June 2023 precedes the date of application referred to in the second paragraph of this Article, the application of Article 42 and Article 43 shall be postponed until the date of application referred to in the second paragraph of this Article.

This Regulation shall be binding in its entirety and directly applicable in all Member States.

ANNEX

A. 'General'

1. This Annex aims at specifying the methodology for identifying and calculating the 'active end users' and the 'active business users' for each core platform service listed in Article 2, point (2). It provides a reference to enable an undertaking to assess whether its core platform services meet the quantitative thresholds set out in Article 3(2), point (b) and would therefore be presumed to meet the requirement in Article 3(1), point (b). Such reference will therefore equally be of relevance to any broader assessment under Article 3(8). It is the responsibility of the undertaking to come to the best approximation possible in line with the common principles and specific methodology set out in this Annex. Nothing in this Annex precludes the Commission, within the time limits laid down in the relevant provisions of this Regulation, from requiring the undertaking providing core platform services to provide any information necessary to identify and calculate the 'active end users' and the 'active business users'. Nothing in this Annex should constitute a legal basis for tracking users. The methodology contained in this Annex is also without prejudice to any of the obligations laid down in this Regulation, notably in Article 3(3) and (8) and Article 13(3). In particular, the required compliance with Article 13(3) also means identifying and calculating 'active end users' and 'active business users' based either on a precise measurement or on the best approximation available, in line with the actual identification and calculation capacities that the undertaking providing core platform services possesses at the relevant point in time. Those measurements or the best approximation available shall be consistent with, and include, those reported under Article 15.
2. Article 2, points (20) and (21) set out the definitions of 'end user' and 'business user', which are common to all core platform services.
3. In order to identify and calculate the number of 'active end users' and 'active business users', this Annex refers to the concept of 'unique users'. The concept of 'unique users' encompasses 'active end users' and 'active business users' counted only once, for the relevant core platform service, over the course of a specified time period (i.e. month in case of 'active end users' and year in case of 'active business users'), no matter how many times they engaged with the relevant core platform service over that period. This is without prejudice to the fact that the same natural or legal person can simultaneously constitute an 'active end user' or an 'active business user' for different core platform services.

B. 'Active end users'

1. The number of 'unique users' as regards 'active end users' shall be identified according to the most accurate metric reported by the undertaking providing any of the core platform services, specifically:
   a. It is considered that collecting data about the use of core platform services from signed-in or logged-in environments would *prima facie* present the lowest risk of duplication, for example in relation to user behaviour across devices or platforms. Hence, the undertaking shall submit aggregate anonymized data on the number of unique end users per respective core platform service based on signed-in or logged-in environments, if such data exists.
   b. In the case of core platform services which are also accessed by end users outside signed-in or logged-in environments, the undertaking shall additionally submit aggregate anonymized data

on the number of unique end users of the respective core platform service based on an alternate metric capturing also end users outside signed-in or logged-in environments, such as internet protocol addresses, cookie identifiers or other identifiers such as radio frequency identification tags, provided that those addresses or identifiers are objectively necessary for the provision of the core platform services.

2. The number of 'monthly active end users' is based on the average number of monthly active end users throughout the largest part of the financial year. The notion 'the largest part of the financial year' is intended to allow an undertaking providing core platform services to discount outlier figures in a given year. Outlier figures inherently mean figures that fall significantly outside the normal and foreseeable figures. An unforeseen peak or drop in user engagement that occurred during a single month of the financial year is an example of what could constitute such outlier figures. Figures related to annually recurring occurrences, such as annual sales promotions, are not outlier figures.

C. 'Active business users'

The number of 'unique users' as regards 'active business users' is to be determined, where applicable, at the account level with each distinct business account associated with the use of a core platform service provided by the undertaking constituting one unique business user of that respective core platform service. If the notion of 'business account' does not apply to a given core platform service, the relevant undertaking providing core platform services shall determine the number of unique business users by referring to the relevant undertaking.

D. 'Submission of information'

1. The undertaking submitting to the Commission pursuant to Article 3(3) information concerning the number of active end users and active business users per core platform service shall be responsible for ensuring the completeness and accuracy of that information. In that regard:
   a. The undertaking shall be responsible for submitting data for a respective core platform service that avoids under-counting and over-counting the number of active end users and active business users (for example, where users access the core platform services across different platforms or devices).
   b. The undertaking shall be responsible for providing precise and succinct explanations about the methodology used to arrive at the information and for any risk of under-counting or over-counting of the number of active end users and active business users for a respective core platform service and for the solutions adopted to address that risk.
   c. The undertaking shall provide data that is based on an alternative metric when the Commission has concerns about the accuracy of data provided by the undertaking providing core platform services.
2. For the purpose of calculating the number of 'active end users' and 'active business users':
   a. The undertaking providing core platform service(s) shall not identify core platform services that belong to the same category of core platform services pursuant to Article 2, point (2) as distinct mainly on the basis that they are provided using different domain names, whether country code top-level domains (ccTLDs) or generic top-level domains (gTLDs), or any geographic attributes.
   b. The undertaking providing core platform service(s) shall consider as distinct core platform services those core platform services, which are used for different purposes by either their end users or their business users, or both, even if their end users or business users may be the same and even if they belong to the same category of core platform services pursuant to Article 2, point (2).
   c. The undertaking providing core platform service(s) shall consider as distinct core platform services those services which the relevant undertaking offers in an integrated way, but which:
      (i) do not belong to the same category of core platform services pursuant to Article 2, point (2); or
      (ii) are used for different purposes by either their end users or their business users, or both, even if their end users and business users may be the same and even if they belong to the same category of core platform services pursuant to Article 2, point (2).

E. 'Specific definitions'

The table below sets out specific definitions of 'active end users' and 'active business users' for each core platform service.

Core platform services	Active end users	Active business users
Online intermediation services	Number of unique end users who engaged with the online intermediation service at least once in the month for example through actively logging-in, making a query, clicking or scrolling or concluded a transaction through the online intermediation service at least once in the month.	Number of unique business users who had at least one item listed in the online intermediation service during the whole year or concluded a transaction enabled by the online intermediation service during the year.
Online search engines	Number of unique end users who engaged with the online search engine at least once in the month, for example through making a query.	Number of unique business users with business websites (i.e. website used in commercial or professional capacity) indexed by or part of the index of the online search engine during the year.
Online social networking services	Number of unique end users who engaged with the online social networking service at least once in the month, for example through actively logging-in, opening a page, scrolling, clicking, liking, making a query, posting or commenting.	Number of unique business users who have a business listing or business account in the online social networking service and have engaged in any way with the service at least once during the year, for example through actively logging-in, opening a page, scrolling, clicking, liking, making a query, posting, commenting or using its tools for businesses.
Video-sharing platform services	Number of unique end users who engaged with the video-sharing platform service at least once in the month, for example through playing a segment of audiovisual content, making a query or uploading a piece of audiovisual content, notably including user-generated videos.	Number of unique business users who provided at least one piece of audiovisual content uploaded or played on the video-sharing platform service during the year.
Number-independent interpersonal communication services	Number of unique end users who initiated or participated in any way in a communication through the number-independent interpersonal communication service at least once in the month.	Number of unique business users who used a business account or otherwise initiated or participated in any way in a communication through the number-independent interpersonal communication service to communicate directly with an end user at least once during the year.
Operating systems	Number of unique end users who utilised a device with the operating system, which has been activated, updated or used at least once in the month.	Number of unique developers who published, updated or offered at least one software application or software program using the programming language or any software development tools of, or running in any way on, the operating system during the year.
Virtual assistant	Number of unique end users who engaged with the virtual assistant in any way at least once in the month, such as for example through activating it, asking a question, accessing a service through a command or controlling a smart home device.	Number of unique developers who offered at least one virtual assistant software application or a functionality to make an existing software application accessible through the virtual assistant during the year.
Web browsers	Number of unique end users who engaged with the web browser at least once in the month, for example through inserting a query or website address in the URL line of the web browser.	Number of unique business users whose business websites (i.e. website used in commercial or professional capacity) have been accessed via the web browser at least once during the year or who offered a plug-in, extension or add-ons used on the web browser during the year.

Core platform services	Active end users	Active business users
Cloud computing services	Number of unique end users who engaged with any cloud computing services from the relevant provider of cloud computing services at least once in the month, in return for any type of remuneration, regardless of whether this remuneration occurs in the same month.	Number of unique business users who provided any cloud computing services hosted in the cloud infrastructure of the relevant provider of cloud computing services during the year.
Online advertising services	For proprietary sales of advertising space: Number of unique end users who were exposed to an advertisement impression at least once in the month. For advertising intermediation services (including advertising networks, advertising exchanges and any other advertising intermediation services): Number of unique end users who were exposed to an advertisement impression which triggered the advertising intermediation service at least once in the month.	For proprietary sales of advertising space: Number of unique advertisers who had at least one advertisement impression displayed during the year. For advertising intermediation services (including advertising networks, advertising exchanges and any other advertising intermediation services): Number of unique business users (including advertisers, publishers or other intermediators) who interacted via or were served by the advertising intermediation service during the year.

TABLE OF CONTENTS

BULGARIA

CROATIA

CZECH REPUBLIC

DENMARK

ESTONIA

FRANCE

GERMANY

GREECE

IRELAND

PORTUGAL

ROMANIA

SLOVAKIA

SPAIN

SWEDEN

Concurrences
Competition Laws Review

Concurrences Review

Concurrences is a print and online quarterly peer reviewed journal dedicated to EU and national competitions laws. It has been launched in 2004 as the flagship of the Institute of Competition Law in order to provide a forum for academics, practitioners and enforcers. Concurrences' influence and expertise has garnered contributions or interviews with such figures as Christine Lagarde, Bill Kovacic, Emmanuel Macron, Antonin Scalia and Magrethe Vestager.

Contents

More than 15,000 articles, print and/or online. Quarterly issues provide current coverage with contributions from the EU or national or foreign countries thanks to more than 2,500 authors in Europe and abroad.

Format

In order to balance academic contributions with opinions or legal practice notes, Concurrences provides its insight and analysis in a number of formats:

- Forewords: Opinions by leading academics or enforcers
- Interviews: Interviews of antitrust experts
- On-Topics: 4 to 6 short papers on hot issues
- Law & Economics: Short papers written by economists for a legal audience
- Articles: Long academic papers
- Case Summaries: Case commentary on EU and French case law
- Legal Practice: Short papers for in-house counsels
- International: Medium size papers on international policies
- Books Review: Summaries of recent antitrust books
- Articles Review: Summaries of leading articles published in 45 antitrust journals

Boards

The Scientific Committee is headed by Laurence Idot, Professor at Panthéon Assas University. The International Committee is headed by Frederic Jenny, OECD Competition Comitteee Chairman. Boards members include Douglas Ginsburg, Benoît Cœuré, Howard Shelanski, Richard Whish, Wouter Wils, Joshua Wright, etc.

Online version

Concurrences website provides all articles published since its inception, in addition to selected articles published online only in the electronic supplement.

Write for Concurrences

Concurrences welcome spontaneous contributions. Except in rare circumstances, the journal accepts only unpublished articles, whatever the form and nature of the contribution. The Editorial Board checks the form of the proposals, and then submits these to the Scientific Committee. Selection of the papers is conditional to a peer review by at least two members of the Committee. Within a month, the Committee assesses whether the draft article can be published and notifies the author.

www.ingramcontent.com/pod-product-compliance
Lightning Source LLC
La Vergne TN
LVHW020630300926
849161LV00004B/656